B & T
$14.95
DEC 19 '77

W9-BCG-750

News from Molokai

News from Molokai

Letters between Peter Kaeo

& Queen Emma 1873–1876

Edited with Introduction and Notes

by Alfons L. Korn

The University Press of Hawaii · Honolulu

Wingate College Library

The photographs of Peter Kaeo and Queen Emma, and
Emma's letter to Peter of May 10, 1876, are reproduced
herein by permission of the Bernice P. Bishop Museum.
Peter's letter to Emma of July 7, 1874, is reproduced
herein by courtesy of the Archives of the State of Hawaii.
The pen-and-ink drawing, *Honolulu Harbor, 1871*, by
Alfred Clint is reproduced on the endsheets by courtesy
of The Hawaiian Historical Society.

Copyright © 1976 by The University Press of Hawaii

All rights reserved. No part of this work may be
reproduced or transmitted in any form or by any means,
electronic or mechanical, including photocopying and
recording, or by any information storage or retrieval
system, without permission in writing from the publisher.

Manufactured in the United States of America
Composition by Asco Trade Typesetting Limited, Hong Kong

Book and jacket design by Steve Reoutt

Library of Congress Cataloging in Publication Data
Kaeo, Peter, 1836–1880.
    News from Molokai, letters between Peter Kaeo and
Queen Emma, 1873–1876.

    Includes bibliographical references and index.
    1. Kaeo, Peter, 1836–1880. 2. Emma, consort of
Kamehameha IV, King of the Hawaiian Islands, 1836–
1885. I. Emma, consort of Kamehameha IV, King of
the Hawaiian Islands, 1836–1885, joint author. II. Korn,
Alfons L. III. Title.
DU627.17.K28A44   996.9′02′0922   76–16823
ISBN 0–8248–0399–X

To Laura

072524

Contents

Preface   ix

Introduction   xi

THE CORRESPONDENCE

Part One. *A Long Farewell, 1873*   5

Part Two. *Torches in a Cloud, 1874*   161

Part Three. *The Release, 1875–1876*   275

Epilogue   321

Appendix   325

Indexes   333

Preface

This is not a history book, but it is nevertheless about Hawaiian history: the three critical years, from 1873 to 1876, that marked the end of the reign of King Lunalilo and saw the beginning—the uncertain beginning—of the reign of King Kalākaua.

As the title indicates, the volume is made up of a bundle of old letters exchanged between Peter Kaeo, a leprosy victim of Molokai, and his cousin Kaleleonālani, Queen Emma. If one is seeking a label, the book might be described as a biographical study. The correspondence that resulted from Peter's anxious exile to Kalaupapa, and from Emma's devotion to his welfare and hoped-for recovery, constitutes a compellingly authentic record of their personal lives during this three-year period. In addition, as an account of the affairs of the Hawaiian Kingdom during the same interim, as viewed through the writers' Hawaiian eyes and as expressed in their own words—a reflection of island politics, dynastic intrigues, interethnic rivalries and animosities, American-Hawaiian diplomatic strains and frustrations during a time of grave national crisis—the 122 letters surely have no close counterpart elsewhere in Hawaiian historical archives.

I have described in the Appendix how a visitor from New York City, back in the 1930s, while rummaging in a Honolulu pawnshop in search of old sheet music, discovered a mass of Queen Emma's private correspondence and family papers. I have likewise relegated to the Appendix the complicated story of how this hoard of manuscript materials, including the Peter Kaeo–Queen Emma letters, after being lost sight of, came finally into the possession of the Archives of Hawaii. Here I must thank a number of persons as well as several institutions for their assistance in making this book possible.

My chief indebtedness is to the State Archives and its staff, as acknowledged further in the Appendix. I am very grateful also to the Bernice Pauahi Bishop Museum for allowing me access to several indispensable manuscript collections at an early stage of my study; also for permission to publish Queen Emma's important letter to Peter Kaeo of May 10, 1876, the final letter of the Molokai correspondence. My thanks go also to Mr. and Mrs. W. Thomas Davis, of Beverly Hills, California, for their kind permission to publish nine letters from Peter Kaeo to Queen Emma now deposited at the Hawaiian Mission Children's Society Library. For help especially in connection with newspaper sources and other references, I am greatly indebted to the past and present staff of the Hawaii and Pacific Collection, Gregg M. Sinclair Library, University of Hawaii.

Acknowledgments and special thanks are also due the following for their help of various sorts and at important stages, from first to last: Janet Azama, Dorothy B. Barrère, Janyce Blair, Agnes Conrad, Gavan Daws, John Paul Engelcke, L. L. Langness, Elizabeth Larsen, Mary Kawena Pukui, Jane Silverman, Nancy Sutterfield, Margaret Titcomb.

August 1975   Alfons L. Korn
Honolulu

Introduction

When Isabella Bird, the Victorian lady-traveler, was strolling along the beach at Lahaina, Maui, one blazing day in late March of 1873, she happened to glance across the water to where the mountainous island of Molokai "floated like a great blue morning-glory on the yet bluer sea." Her sudden vision, Isabella Bird instantly realized, was an illusion, enchanting only at a distance: "for its blue petals enfold 400 lepers doomed to endless isolation, and 300 more are shortly to be weeded out and sent thither."

Among that desolate company of new arrivals at the Kalaupapa settlement was one Hawaiian of whose existence Miss Bird at that time probably had not yet heard. He was Peter Kaeo, a descendant of ancient kings of Kauai and a great-grandson of Keli'imaika'i, a younger half-brother of Kamehameha I (175?–1819), the founder of a united Hawaiian Kingdom. He arrived at Kalaupapa in late June of 1873, at the age of thirty-seven, in the same year though not in the same month as Father Damien. In the newspapers of Sydney and San Francisco, Molokai in the 1870s had already achieved geographical distinction as the "Leper Island of the Pacific." Meanwhile, in the weekly press of Honolulu, in English as well as Hawaiian, the Honorable Peter Young Kaeo (1836–1880) won a modest local fame. People sometimes spoke of him as the alii, the high chief or prince, among the inmates of the settlement.

It is characteristic of Peter Kaeo, especially during his stay on Molokai, that he preferred to think of himself by the name of an aristocratic ancestor, Kekuaokalani, a sacerdotal chief who had been chosen by Kamehameha I to be one of his two heirs to the Kingdom. Not long before his death, Kamehameha had assigned to his nephew, Kekuaokalani, the guardianship of the war-god, Kūkā'ilimoku. The old conqueror wanted Kekuaokalani, in a priestly and military capacity, to rule jointly over the islands with his son, Liholiho, who would bear the dynastic title of Kamehameha II. However, because of a dispute with Liholiho over an ancient tabu—the 'ai kapu, regulating the eating customs of the sexes—Kekuaokalani became a rebel. He fiercely opposed the revolutionary innovations embraced by his cousin, and especially by their sacrilegious female relations, that women should be allowed to eat freely of the same food and at the same tables as the men. In 1819, on the Kona Coast of the island of Hawaii, the conservative of the old order who was Peter's granduncle died bravely in battle for the sake of the traditional Hawaiian religion.

Peter was allied also by differing and in some instances tenuous degrees of family relationship with most of the other high chiefs and chiefesses of his own generation: King Lunalilo, David Kalākaua, Bernice Pauahi Bishop, and Liliʻu Kamakaʻeha Paki Dominis, better known as Liliʻuokalani. Queen Liliʻuokalani's short tormented reign, which ended in her overthrow in 1893, marked the final decline and fall of the century-old Hawaiian monarchy. But perhaps Peter's prime claim to historical notice is that since their earliest days together in Honolulu, when they had been neighbors and schoolmates, Peter was ever after a favorite companion and protégé of his cousin, Queen Emma, the consort of Kamehameha IV.

Social oblivion followed by a harrowing form of death, sooner or later, was the common lot of Molokai lepers during the later nineteenth century. The fate of Peter Kaeo, however, turned out to be an exception to the rule. The Hawaiian Board of Health, reconsidering earlier and more pessimistic conclusions, suddenly decided in 1876 that Peter Kaeo's case had been successfully arrested: just how or why, none of the records today actually reveal. At any rate, the board straightway granted Peter a release and he was permitted, under certain tolerant restrictions, to return to his home in Honolulu. After his astonishing release from the settlement, he lived very quietly for four more years in the capital city of the Kingdom, near Queen Emma. He died on November 26, 1880, after only a few days of unspecified illness, not necessarily the consequence of his leprosy, and was buried at the Royal Mausoleum in the company of various earlier kings, queens, chiefs, chiefesses, and other dignitaries of the nation.

During the term of his segregation on Molokai, Peter wrote numerous letters to his friends and relations, especially to those in Honolulu. Occasionally he wrote as many as three or four letters a week, whenever he felt in the mood, but the person he wrote to with true devotion and great punctuality was, of course, Queen Emma. Luckily, in order to keep track of Peter's well-being and to meet his constant need of supplies, Emma fell into the habit of saving many (unfortunately not all) of Peter's letters. She herself from time to time carefully preserved the scribbled memos and copious rough drafts of some of her own correspondence with her "Dearest Coz." Thanks largely to Emma, on

Peter's side alone more than one hundred of his letters from Molokai have survived. All of them describe in circumstantial detail, often with oddly vivid effect, though in irregular but expressive English interlaced with shreds and patches of his native Hawaiian, Peter's day-to-day experiences among his fellow lepers of Kalaupapa.

Emma's far fewer letters from Honolulu (at least those that have been discovered) make up in length, which is to say in a certain gift for gossip and digression, whatever they may lack in number. As might be expected, her letters derive historical as well as purely biographical significance from her anxious concern about important political issues in the Hawaii of that era: the abortive annexation movement of 1872–1873; the question of a reciprocity treaty with the United States; the dispute over the leasing or cession of Pearl Harbor; the dynastic rivalries of Hawaiian high chiefs and their ambitious families; and always and above all, the threatened hope of the protagonists to maintain the independence and political control of their Kingdom. The 122 letters here selected and published probably make up the most extensive private correspondence in existence conducted between Hawaiians of the nineteenth century.

Such a collection of letters is a rarity. That it should have come into being at all was the result of a most unusual and precarious set of personal and political circumstances. If Peter Kaeo had lived out his lifetime in Honolulu, if he had never undergone the ordeal of his malady, and if likewise he had not endured the added onus of his three-year Molokai exile, it seems most unlikely that he would ever have devoted so many hours to the writing of a mass of family letters to a relative living on another island scarcely forty miles away. However, Peter's correspondence with Queen Emma cannot be accounted for solely on the basis of his experience as a leper of Molokai: by the trauma, if one wishes to think of it so, of his physiological and geographical alienation. Not enough has been said so far about other exceptional features of Peter's family and background, his earlier biography in general, his schooling, and especially his aspirations.

❧

For good reasons I have emphasized the Hawaiian alii (noble) lineage Peter shared with his cousin Queen Emma. But he was also, like Emma, descended on his mother's side from an English grandfather of historical note who was one of the two earliest known white men to have settled in the Sandwich Islands. The English ancestor was a marooned sailor named John Young (1742–1835), known among Hawaiians as Olohana, who had made himself useful as a royal artillery officer during the 1790s when Kamehameha I was conducting his serial conquest of the islands. This one-time able seaman of solid and resourceful character took a Hawaiian chiefess as wife, and he was himself granted many of the privileges proper to a high chief. If Olohana had been a man of undistinguished achievement, his influence upon the lives of his Hawaiian children might have proved negligible. As it happened, Peter's membership in the Young family formed a part of his whole proud, complicated legacy, in which the descendants of a common sailor of dim British background became linked with the fortunes of the Kamehameha Dynasty. For someone like Peter, being an alii and having one's career depend largely on the Kamehameha connection doubtless carried great advantages; but the responsibilities were also great and the disadvantages serious.

John Young had four children by the High Chiefess Kaoana'eha, a son and three daughters. The son, John Young II, also known as Keoni Ana, became Peter's foster father. Keoni Ana held high offices under Kauikeaouli, Kamehameha III, at the time when that ruler, with the aid of American missionaries and other foreign advisers, was actively seeking to inaugurate in Hawaii a governmental system designed to be that of a monarchy, but still to function somehow along constitutional American lines. As a chief the *hapa-haole* (half-white) Keoni Ana seems to have been a useful servant of the Kingdom. His character, unlike his father's, was not without grave flaws, however, including that downfall of numerous Hawaiian leaders of his time, an immoderate appetite for liquor. One may well wonder about the example set by his guardian uncle during the boyhood of Peter.

More important than John Young II, for possible effects upon Peter's upbringing, were his mother and his two aunts, the three Young sisters: Grace Kamaikui, Fanny Kekela, and Jane Lahilahi. Grace, the wife of Dr. T. C. B. Rooke, was childless. Fanny, the wife and widow of George Naea, was the mother of Emma. Jane, the youngest of the sisters, was Peter's mother. Of her husband, Joshua Kaeo, descendant of kings of Kauai and a privy councillor of Kamehameha III, the record is slight. It does not look as if he could have played much part in the rearing of his boy. Jane Lahilahi seems to have been more of a personality and a force, how much for the good it is hard to estimate. There is reason to suppose that she had beauty, for her sisters and her brother were fine-looking people; she was probably clever as well as a little frivolous. An amusing poet, she was skilled in the old allusive figurative style of her mother's ancestors. In 1851 Jane Lahilahi Young Kaeo brought into the world a second boy, named Albert Kūnuiākea, a love-child whose father was King Kamehameha III. From early on, Albert (named after Queen Victoria's consort) proved himself averse to all discipline. In fact, the days of Albert's young manhood were made up of a steady succession of escapades and scandals, a consequence usually of his spendthrift ways, culminating on several occasions in such jail-able offenses as forgery. A running formula among Peter's stock of family salutations was his frequent query, when told of his half-brother's latest outrage, "What ever will become of poor Albert?" Peter's concern over Albert was not necessarily insincere. One suspects, however, that the scapegrace of the family was useful to Peter as a measure for assessing his own struggles, by no means uniformly en-couraging, to become virtuous and win Emma's approval.

⟨≈⟩

Official records and unofficial manuscripts and newspapers, with a few notable exceptions, reveal much less than all one would like to know about the lives of historic Hawaiians during the nineteenth century. Yet it is possible, through the family papers of Queen Emma, to catch glimpses of Peter Kaeo and form at least a hazy notion of his life as a boy. One gets the impression that from childhood, through the rest of Peter's days, he spent many of them—perhaps too many—in the company of women. As an adopted son in the household of his uncle John Young II, he had been surrounded by the bevy of aunts visiting back and forth, three or four of them at least, counting the wife of John Young and counting *her* sister. To be surrounded by the aunts meant to be surrounded also by numerous female friends and retainers. Emma's situation in this respect was like Peter's. Instead of living with her own mother and father on the island of Maui, Emma had been adopted from birth by her aunt and uncle, Grace Kamaikui and Dr. T. C. B. Rooke. The records suggest that Peter was a familiar visitor at Rooke House, as a playmate for Emma. Occasionally in writing from Kalaupapa, the thirty-seven-year-old chief closes with a phrase straight from the lips of babyhood: "Good Bye Queen Emma (By By to me)." When a tide of memory was running strong, Emma would sometimes recall episodes from her early life with Peter. In the summer of 1873, writing from Hanauma Bay on Oahu, looking directly across the water toward Molokai, Emma remembered how she and Peter, like Florence and Paul Dombey by the shore of the North Sea, used to wonder "What are the wild waves saying?" Late in Emma's life, after Peter's death in 1880, she spoke of him always as the cousin who had been like a brother to her. In his bleaker moments on Molokai, Peter sometimes broke away from his more formal and stereotyped salutations.

> "It has been a little over two Months since I left you, but Years cannot chill the love I cherish for You and Sweet Home." . . .

> "Sunday was the day that I left you and dear Home, and today is the day that I first set foot [a year ago] on Kalaupapa *ino ino* [shattered]." . . .

> "I send my first Flowers. Not the last Rose of Summer but the first Rose of my Winter here. Their are Eleven Buds in all on the Bush, but these are the ones to blossom first." . . .

One may surmise that on Peter's side his attachment to Emma was something other than brotherly, and more than the love of a child or a boy. In the end it expressed itself in a lasting servitude and dependence, speaking an old-fashioned language of devotion, a mixture of the naïve and the self-conscious and artificial, with notes of self-pity and subdued sexual overtones, lacking perhaps in full virility.

Peter's earliest letter[1] to Emma is one he wrote at the age of eighteen while on an excursion in 1854 to the island of Hawaii. He had just visited the snowline region of Mauna Kea and was sending Miss Emma Rooke, also eighteen, three bracelets (or anklets) of boars' tusks—three *kūpeʻe*. In substance and tone the sentiments of the youth are not greatly different from those of the sick man on Molokai nineteen years later. Whatever the wild waves may have been saying, their song never changed much for Peter.

Waimea, Hawaii
October, 1854

Dear Cousin,
    I have something to tell you now about our going up to Mauna Kea. . . . We started last Wednesday for Kalaieha, and on Sunday we

went up the Mountain. We have seen something that very fiew have seen, this is a large Pond called Waiau. This Pond is situated on one of the Most highest Summit of Mauna Kea.

I send by the bearer three little *Kupees*. I don't know whether you will like them or not, there are no better ones than those of what I know or else I should try all my best to get them for you.

There are not much things here for me to tell you about. We only pass our time here by going up to Mr. Kenway's [ranch] and from there back again. I find Waimea to be a very unplesant weather. It is constantly raining. I haven't any Water to send you for one reason. I will tell you when I get back.

Don't forget to write to me—to thy cousin far far from thee.

Yours

P. Y. Kekuaokalani

Except during Peter's absence on Molokai from 1873 to 1876, there was only one other period of importance when Peter and Emma had long been separated. That was after the death of King Kamehameha IV in 1863, when Queen Emma, not yet recovered from her grief over the earlier death of her first and only son, traveled abroad on a year-long visit to England, the Continent, and several American cities of the Atlantic seaboard. During her stay in three great nations (1865–1866), the young dowager queen of Hawaii was presented to their rulers and heads of state: on two occasions to Queen Victoria, at Windsor Castle, where Emma passed an agreeable weekend; to the Emperor Napoleon III and the Empress Eugénie, at an informal reception *en famille* in the Tuileries palace in Paris; and finally, on her homeward journey, to President Andrew Johnson in Washington, D.C. Otherwise, during the years of her marriage and motherhood, Emma's life and Peter's moved along close neighboring channels.

Born in 1836, they were almost exactly the same age. Together they had both imbibed some of their earliest education at that unique fount of learning in Honolulu, the select boarding school for chiefs' children (of which Emma, however, was only a day pupil) established in the 1840s by American Congregational missionaries. At the Chiefs' Children's School, Peter Kaeo learned to count in numerals and to form his first round building-block letters, under the tutelage of Mr. and Mrs. Amos Starr Cooke, formerly of Massachusetts. Later he read with enjoyment, sometimes merely in extract, standard works by Sir Walter

Scott, Lord Byron, and Charles Dickens. These alii pupils of Mr. and Mrs. Cooke, "Pita" and Emma being among the youngest, included Prince Alexander Liholiho, Lot Kamehameha, David Kalākaua, Lydia Paki, Bernice Pauahi (who married a young American customs official, Charles Reed Bishop, who became Hawaii's first banker), and William Charles Lunalilo. They were all of them being counted on to acquire the type of Christian instruction, bolstered by training in correct deportment, deemed suitable for leading a happy and useful life whether in Honolulu or Albany, N.Y., or Worcester, Mass. Five of the children, not including Emma, were later to become rulers of the Kingdom.

Emma's early schooling was to be furthered and much enlivened later by her year of foreign travel, as the dowager queen of Hawaii. Her knowledge, even before her European tour at the age of thirty, far surpassed in range and sophistication that of her cousin. Besides, she was simply more quick, if not necessarily brighter, and she had been fortunate in the circumstances of her childhood, in a way Peter was not, owing an immense debt to the attentive care of her foster father, a Londoner of respectable antecedents who had gained his early medical training at St. Bartholomew's Hospital, during the later years of the reign of George IV. Dr. Thomas Charles Byde Rooke, who had arrived in Hawaii in 1829, made a comfortable living by attending to men of the whalers and of the China trade. In addition to his practice as such, Dr. Rooke supplied drugs to the crews and medical equipment of all shapes and purposes, from tourniquets to catheters (he had them shipped out from England), to officers and sea-going surgeons of the numerous foreign vessels. Of course, he also treated regular residents of Hawaii, both foreign and native, especially those of the highest class.

Perhaps because the Rookes had no children of their own, Dr. Rooke grew very fond of his part-English niece. He regarded her from the start as if she were his own daughter—except, as he once playfully explained to his mother in England, the little daughter had turned out to be a dusky Polynesian princess. He also saw to it that Emma was provided Honolulu's equivalent to an English lady's education, so as to become a fit bride whether for some Polynesian prince or perhaps even an English gentleman. For several years during the 1840s, Dr. Rooke employed a genteel English neighbor from one of the southern counties, Mrs. Sarah Rhodes von Pfister, recently arrived in Hawaii, to give Emma lessons in reading aloud from the Book of Common Prayer. There was at that time no organized Anglican Chapel or

Episcopal Church in Hawaii. To supplement the lessons at the Chiefs' Children's School, Emma also studied under Mrs. von Pfister's guidance the beginnings of French and the fundamentals of geography and history, with emphasis on the British Isles.

It is easy to detect in Emma's letters to Peter the fruits of her Victorian Anglo-Hawaiian education, with its Yankee trimmings, its echoes of Longfellow in his *Excelsior* vein, the edifying set-pieces calculated to improve Cousin Peter's conduct and refine his character. Through loving encouragement, buttressed by much patient exhortation, Emma hoped to make Peter a leader of the Hawaiian people. Nor was this hope merely an expression of her haole—"foreign"—sense of duty. Emma's application of the Victorian ethic of work-plus-Christian ideals was amalgamated almost instinctively with a thorough awareness of the high lineage she shared with Peter, along with its privileges and responsibilities. No doubt she owed her Christian humility to her Anglo-American upbringing; but her pride in her name, her full acceptance of noble rank and honored reputation, she derived from the mighty pantheon of the ancestors.

> During these days of your probation there, dear Peter, be ambitious and bold to hold our ancestral renown ever in its place high. Let not inferiors step into our places. Speak and act with weight or authority where you are at present. [Speak] often—either to few or many—[so] that by frequent practice it grows to a habit. [Thus you] perfect yourself in public speaking besides accomplishing one end, which is bringing these people to look to and lean on you as the head mover in all things. . . . Have perseverence. Make a name to yourself and consequently add another laurel to the ancestral tree.[2]

So Peter's ordeal on his sad island was to be a test of his chieftainship, a latter-day substitute for some traditional rite de passage.

❦

In accord with Emma's counsel, Peter did his best to prove that "his stay on Molokai need not be waste time." In view of conditions at Kalaupapa in 1873, to say nothing of the nature of his disease or the state of medical knowledge generally in the 1870s, it is hardly surprising that no miracles occurred. Sound principles of hygiene were first on Peter's list: no physical contact with lepers; no entering their grass huts; no drinking of spirits; and plenty of outdoor exercise—Molokai weather permitting. On the intellectual side, Emma assigned systematic reading and a self-taught course in language arts. Peter was to study "the newspapers of the day, and compare them, finding out who is for [Hawaii's] independence and salvation of the race and who is against."[3] Foreign affairs should not be overlooked: "The unsettled state of Spain and the suspicion of Prussia against France are all interesting. The former is armed at a moment's pretext to war against France and keep her down." Finally, Peter must learn to speak up. He should make himself heard, among the Hawaiians first, but also in the foreign community and at large, by cultivating "the habit of debating and discussing." If he found himself frequently with nobody listening, he could follow Emma's example and try reading to himself aloud.

> To enter into an argument is sometimes instructing, as it sharpens one's thoughts on the subject. . . . Reading aloud to oneself is more improving than you think. Interesting subjects or passages I read slowly, and sometimes almost act them. I do so constantly think of your place at the legislative debate, and giving your oppinion in councils, that I grow tiresome to you by letter.[4]

As the alii of the settlement, Peter understood very well that he never should allow himself to appear timid, tongue-tied, or diffident. After all, he was still a member, even *in absentia*, of the House of Nobles, the Hawaiian version of a senatorial chamber. The descendant of Keli'imaika'i and Kekuaokalani had every reason to expect to play a leading role in the life of the Kalaupapa community. Indeed, two supervisors of the asylum, first Jonathan Napela and then later his far more efficient successor, William P. Ragsdale, consulted frequently with Peter Kaeo on matters concerning operations at Kalaupapa, and sometimes invited him to accompany them on horseback during their official rounds of inspection. In the course of time, Peter found himself inexorably drawn into the politics of the settlement. Already during its seven years of existence the colony had achieved a history of factionalism and backbiting, of internal troubles that erupted periodically in outright threats of sedition among the inmates. Unfortunately, during the winter of 1873–1874, a severe poi shortage arose throughout most of Hawaii, on Oahu as well as on Molokai, and the Board of Health found it necessary to place the Kalaupapa lepers on a curtailed diet, omitting their full ration of poi and substituting more salt beef or salt salmon, along with a fluctuating allowance of rice. Many lepers, grown too accustomed to the staple of the ancient Hawaiian diet, the first prepared food of their childhood, began to complain bitterly. Several of the most extreme cases of malnutrition and anemia died. Finally, a sizable number of patients, not less than two hundred, signed a petition circulated by a disgruntled petty official, Constable Kamaka, requesting the board to dismiss William P. Ragsdale as luna (supervisor) and appoint the Hon. Peter Young Kaeo in Ragsdale's place. Though Peter was naturally flattered by this display of confidence in his abilities, for good reason he refrained from seeking the post directly. Peter, who had sources of information, knew very well that the majority of the Board of Health warmly approved of the popular Bill Ragsdale, both as man and as official, and that they would support Ragsdale firmly in his strict enforcement of their unappetizing regulations. A *de facto* appointment as luna of Kalaupapa Peter would probably have accepted, as a matter of duty, proudly; but he was unprepared to campaign openly against Ragsdale, and not at all eager to engage in bureaucratic intrigue involving a full-scale battle of wits against both Ragsdale and the Board of Health.

> Kaawa has asked me whether I wished to be chosen as Luna, and that it was the wish of the Natives. I informed him that I did not care for it, not [because] it was a responsible [position] but that I if chosen as Luna did not wish to be under no obligations to anyone save that I performed my duty as Luna. He informed me that Kamaka's Petition was signed by over 200 names. I requested Kaawa to thank the Natives for me, but until then I would stand Neutral.[5]

It is all too conceivable that Peter's life on Molokai might have ended in idleness, repellent forms of emotional consolation and debauchery, depression, apathy, death. In the absence of adequate medical documentation, one can only guess at the causes that ultimately brought Peter home to Honolulu, shattered, but in some ambiguous manner healed. On the other hand, what is easily discerned in the Molokai correspondence, and can be at least partly accounted for, is the change that took place in Peter's character as he began to feel, think, and behave in ways resembling those of his pre-Christian ancestors. His great alii forebear, Kekuaokalani, was killed in battle in 1819. The first of the missionaries sent out from New England by the American Board of Commissioners for Foreign Missions arrived in 1820. The period between the coming of the *Thaddeus* with the First Company and the establishment in 1866 of the leper asylum at Kalaupapa was less than fifty years. It was by a natural enough process and through no paradox of transformation that the farther Peter journeyed from his old easy-going life in Honolulu the more he proved himself kinsman and name-sake of the priestly rebel, Kekuaokalani.

⌘

Anthropologists have frequently observed that in various preurban, preindustrial societies, when certain kinds of competition for power, status, and resources get too far out of hand, people are likely to turn to sorcerers for help and encouragement. Conflicts and tensions inaccessible to "reasonable" adjustment as provided in the law and the courts then tend to express themselves in the form of mystical beliefs and magical practices, including sorcery and witchcraft, which attribute the disturbances to the wickedness of individuals. That such beliefs are often quite irrational, and that they may even add to the underlying disturbances, does not mean that the beliefs or the rituals that accompany them are without valid purpose or effect, particularly at times of crisis and acute social change. Indeed, some authorities consider that such beliefs in the mystical operation of forces of good and evil, forces thought to be more or less amenable to the control of persons adept in the moral mysteries, may "enable a society to continue functioning although it is fraught with conflicts and contradictions which it is helpless to solve."[6]

The hypothesis-conclusion here set forth, however sketchily, appears to be borne out by some of the extraordinary experiences of Peter Kaeo among the kahunas, the sorcerers and mediums, of Molokai. Apparently the longer he stayed at Kalaupapa the more Peter began to discover magical powers at work in his world, and to interpret the operation of these powers in terms of the behavior of feared or envied individuals, especially King David Kalākaua, members of the Kalākaua family, and the followers of the king's "party," the contemptible "D. K.s." Peter's preoccupation with old Hawaiian ideas of the supernatural is not at all a prominent feature in his earliest letters from Molokai. It is true, however, that as early as his second month at Kalaupapa Peter had heard of the existence on Molokai of the female kahuna named Paniku Hua, a prophetess and healer who was herself a leper, and who was said to be in regular communication with the spirit of the great Queen Ka'ahumanu. Yet never for a moment when Peter first heard of the kahuna did he imagine that he might soon become one of Hua's Molokai friends, let alone count himself among even her sporadic disciples. It was in fact only after Hua's ministrations appeared to have almost instantaneously cured one of Peter's attacks of acute gastritis that he began to look upon Paniku Hua with respect, indeed with a touch of awe.

It was certain painful developments of 1874 that strengthened Peter's interest in Hua and her art intensely. Furthermore, whatever he learned from Hua caused him to be much on the alert for magical warnings and revelations of many kinds, foretelling the future course of Hawaiian history and the fates in store for the nation's prospective rulers. King Lunalilo, who had ascended to the throne only a few months before Peter was transported to Molokai, died on February 3, 1874. His successor to the throne, David Kalākaua, in the estimation of Peter and Emma, was a mere upstart of an alii, lacking the proper qualifications for the royal office. A schooled politician and demagogue of charm, surrounded by crooked, self-seeking, or stupid henchmen, Kalākaua could even stoop so low as to bribe the native electorate with handouts of jackets, liquor, and dollar bills. Worst of all, it was reported that Kalākaua patronized that most deplorable class of Hawaiian kahunas, the 'ana 'ana sorcerers, the specialists in "black magic" who could be hired to kill their victims by a variety of wicked practices. Their nefarious arts ranged from praying a person to death through the recital of the appropriate magic formulas to the disposal of him by poison: for example, by summoning into effect the noxious emanations of kālai-pāhoa, the "dagger-carved," the lord of all poisons.

Now, a disturbing structural flaw in the Hawaiian form of constitutional monarchic government was its inadequate or faltering provisions for ensuring the succession to the throne. Under the old pre-Christian system, the rivalry and competition of high chiefs for this or that chiefdom had been encouraged and regulated by a number of institutional arrangements.[7] These included awesome genealogical qualifications; privileges and sanctions as represented in the many tabu practices; the religious and quasi-judicial collaboration of certain orders of kahunas; and, not seldom but rather as a frequent matter of course, resort to combat on the field of battle. An enlightened bill of rights and a constitution, drafted and adopted under mission influence and with missionary help, rendered most of the old sanctions and practices obsolete, indeed in some cases, as it seemed, barbarously anachronistic.

Furthermore, too many of the highest and most capable alii were childless; the royal stock of the Kamehamehas, the stirp of the Conquerer, was dying on the vine. Biological proclivity (sometimes described as racial "decline" and degeneracy) found complex expression in the constitution and temperament of the individual chief. An innocent vulnerability to various new diseases or strains of disease could fatally shape personality, influence control over affairs of state, even threaten the existence of the monarchy, as when the gentle and modest but also tubercular and alcoholic King Lunalilo ("King Bill," the "people's king"), himself of eminently distinguished ancestry in the Kamehameha line, democratically insisted that he would rule only if authorized to do so by popular ballot. This was in 1872–1873, when Lunalilo's autocratic predecessor, King Kamehameha V, at the age of forty-two, had thrown the government into a crisis by dying without having been able to settle upon his heir and successor. Only a little more than one year later, when Lunalilo died likewise without having made up his mind about a successor, the decision again had to be referred to a plebiscite. This time the voting was confined to the forty-five members, Representatives and Nobles, making up the Hawaiian legislature. In the critical election of 1874, the resilient and resourceful David Kalākaua had no difficulty in winning the legislative victory by a handsome margin: thirty-nine voted in his favor and only six for his royal opponent, Queen Emma.

It is not surprising that during the succession crisis of 1874, Peter suffered another nervous attack, more emotionally exhausting than his earlier attack of gastritis. Normally, if Peter had been a well man in 1874 and not a Molokai leper, he would have taken up his seat in the House of Nobles. There he at least would have had the satisfaction of casting one more ballot for his cousin. As a member of His Majesty's loyal opposition, Peter could have continued to voice his disagreement with Kalākaua's legislative program by speaking up in the debates; he could have helped to plot his party's stratagems and parliamentary maneuvers. But now on Molokai with almost every regular outlet for his loyalties blocked, Peter's rancor toward the D. K.s could find release only in extralegal, if not illegal, channels. The result was that Peter tended increasingly to interpret political events in moralistic and imaginative terms, to dramatize the Hawaiian fable by means of insights and formulas taken over from the old religious system—or, rather, from its tattered remnants and guises. Whether he was poring over the weekly newspapers from Honolulu, or consorting with Molokai kahunas (for a while he supported a private kahuna of his own), Peter came to envision Hawaiian history as if it were some "shadowy spirit world and drama"[8] hovering over the life of the Hawaiian people and reflecting their destiny as a race and nation.

By late autumn of 1874, it was no longer only Hua's prophecies that repeated over and over again the same ghostly legend. All signs and portents, the sinister crumbling away of a point on the cliff, the coffin-shaped figure of some cloud on the sunset horizon, apparently foretold the impending death of the false king, Kalākaua, and the accession to the throne of Hawaii's rightful sovereign, Emma Kaleleonālani. Peter's last recorded meeting with Paniku Hua did not lessen his respect for the kahuna's uncanny power.

> After she had spoken, I informed her of [the coffin] I had seen in the Clouds on Satuarday Evening. She replied that this was shown in order to confirm me of what she had predicted heretofore. When we were leaving, she bade me *Hoomanao* [to continue to pray] to which I replied "Ae." After I reached home I could not help thinking of what she told me. Her looks and the manner she spoke, slow and clear, and so sidate that I could not help ponder over it long after I had retired for the night.[9]

The old Hawaiians made much of their dreaming and their dreams.[10] From their memories of night dreams (*moe 'uhane*) and their experience of certain "waking" visions, Hawaiians logically inferred the existence of a complementary world, another source of knowledge, that somehow replicates, darkly reflects, or synchronizes with, events and forms in "the world of light"—that is, the world of ordinary life. Because later experiences and events seemed often to prove that these forewarnings were truly prophetic, traditional beliefs in such a secondary and "shadowy spirit world and drama" were sustained and reinforced. Undoubtedly, Hawaiian dream lore and dreaming behavior of pre-Christian times survived down through the nineteenth century, and such a social setting as that of Kalaupapa may well have fostered the survival.

In any event, when Peter Kaeo "on Satuarday Evening" beheld the coffin of King Kalākaua "in the clouds," he took care to report his vision to Paniku Hua. Hua's grave instructions that he should "continue to pray" may well have bolstered his political hopes and trust in Divine Providence. Yet it must be pointed out that Peter himself, in this same letter, tends to withhold explicit final judgment upon Hua and her reliability as a prophetess, though he highly approved of her air of professionalism and impressive style: "Her looks and the manner she spoke, slow and clear, and so sidate that I could not help ponder over it long after I had retired for the night." These nocturnal ponderings of Peter, which were apparently frequent, suggest that from time to time he may have experienced states of consciousness not wholly different or cut off from those "waking visions" (akakū, derived from aka, meaning reflection, shadow) known to the old Hawaiians: "clear flashes of imagery that seem so tangible, so real, across the threshold of sleep, generally just as waking consciousness dawns, particularly in the dim early hours of morning. They may come at the moment of dozing. Or akakū may be a sudden total shift of vision, displacing or overlaying physical sight, in full daylight when all the faculties are alert. ...."

Despite their hunger for political power and eminence, their cult of the ancestors, and their absorption in magic and divination—the last a very marked interest of Peter on Molokai, but temporary in Emma and contrary to her more considered judgment—neither Peter nor Emma deserted their Christian worship. Their shared Anglo-Catholic faith was one of the most enduring bonds of their lives; but it appears also, when examined, to have been the signature of an essential difference between the two cousins in temperament and personality. In another country at some other time, under certain conditions, Emma might have achieved sainthood. Especially after the successive deaths of her son and husband, the consolations of sacramental religion became above all else the groundwork of the queen's being. Nevertheless she did not think of her spiritual search as a quest for mere comfort. Kekuaokalani, on the other hand, was "satisfied" with his present pieties, as he once explained to Father Damien, who would have rejoiced to welcome his friend into the Roman Catholic fold. The soul's experience of torment, the burden and mystery of Divine Providence, as known to Emma, were as foreign to Peter's Christian aspirations as any form of penitential self-abasement would have been irrelevant in 1873 to Peter's transparent and humble needs.

Unto man much has been given [Emma once wrote to Peter in a moment of intense self-examination] in the way of position, influence, and oppertunity, and yet no convert have I made, nor benefited him in any way. Jesus has said to the unprofitable servant, "Get thee unto outer darkness where there is weeping and gnashing of teeth." How different is my reward to Alex's—awful—oh pray dear Coz for me that he may "make me love him more and more."[11]

As I have suggested, Emma discerned in Peter's exile to Molokai's wilderness a kind of test: a period of probation, if it were rightly used, for the career he hoped some day to resume as a member of the House of Nobles. Apart from the question of Emma's particular hopes for Peter, a reader of his letters today may well decide that simply by managing to survive Kalaupapa, the existential shock and suffering of that destructive scene, he passed his major tests well. It is possible to over-simplify the letters, especially at first sight, and to perceive in Peter merely a figure of endearing pathos; or perhaps, at a further level, to discover in him a 230-pound puppet, a sort of comic-grotesque Hawaiian Petrouchka, manipulated by more or less "blind" sociocultural circumstances, intricate psychogenetic forces and codes. Such summary descriptions, whether as rapid profiles or as drawn-out abstract paradigms, indeed may have their uses. Yet both formulas can fall short in biographical perspective and detail. To correct and amplify any special theory or approach, it is well to try again to retrace Peter's early experience and examine every tell-tale shard, so to speak, of his scattered story.

The record of his early life before Molokai (one hesitates to speak of it as a career) is chiefly composed of fragments and gaps; if a chronological focus can be established at all, it is dim and likely to be uninformative to an extreme. As "Pita," when he first appears during the 1840s as one of the younger ones among the dozen or so high-born pupils at the Chiefs' Children's School, he registers as scarcely more than a little boy's Hawaiianized name. It is safe to assume that his missionary instructors demanded less of him than of the other boys of more direct royal lineage. His seniors by several years, Alexander Liholiho (Kamehameha IV) and Alex's elder brother Lot Kamehameha (Kamehameha V), were being especially tutored, groomed, and on occasion rather sternly disciplined, so as to equip them for positions of highest leadership in the embryonic Western-style government. For purposes of studying Peter's life history, it would be interesting to know the facts—to have any details at all—about his earliest relations with David Kalākaua. What did these two small scholars, scions of the same branching set of warfaring eighteenth-century chiefs, make of one another at the tender age of nine or at eleven and sixteen? Despite a lack of anecdotal corroboration, there is nevertheless reason to believe that their rivalry, which on Peter's side became a deep and unabating jealousy of David Kalākaua, can be traced back at least as far as the mid-1850s and early 1860s. This was the period of Peter's formal advent into the life of the *aloali'i*, the royal court, and also into the larger arena of Hawaiian civic and political activity.

Alexander Liholiho, adoptive son of Kauikeaouli, Kamehameha III, succeeded the latter to the throne in 1854. In 1856 he married Miss Emma Rooke, and the appointment of the Hon. Peter Young Kaeo to a position as royal aide must have followed almost as a matter of course. Five years later, at any rate, Peter Kaeo and David Kalākaua were serving simultaneously as aides-de-camp at the palace, among that circle of convivial young men, both Hawaiian and haole, some of them notoriously dissolute, who surrounded the king and his personal staff. The spring and early summer of 1861 was a relatively eventful season in Honolulu, where a common cry of writers of editorials, when not engaged in the week's political disputations, was that "nothing ever happens." The great occasion of the year, an event that directly assisted the establishment of an Anglo-Catholic mission in Hawaii, was the visit to the Sandwich Islands of a famous world-traveler and honored widow, Jane Franklin. Lady Franklin was the relict of Sir John Franklin, the Arctic explorer, who in 1847 had perished among his men on an ill-fated expedition to discover a Northwest Passage. During her two-months' stay in Hawaii, she was accompanied by Sophia Cracroft, a a niece of Sir John, and a systematic writer of travel journals, who mailed them regularly in installments (often by British diplomatic pouch) to her close-knit family in Lincolnshire. In her letters from the Sandwich Islands, Sophia Cracroft includes three separate references to Peter Kaeo, which, taken in context, strongly suggest that Peter had good reason to feel jealous of Kalākaua, and especially to be wary of him as a competitor for royal favor.

On the day of the ladies' arrival in Hawaii, April 21, 1861, King Alexander Liholiho and Queen Emma were not in Honolulu. The English visitors were welcomed to the Kingdom by the minister of foreign relations, Robert Crichton Wyllie, a courtly and rather eccentric Scotsman in his sixties, who brought them by carriage to his summery upland house in Nuuanu Valley, high above the harbor and the plain. On Sunday afternoon, on Rosebank's tree-shaded verandah, Mr. Wyllie presented to his guests Mr. David Kalākaua, the king's emissary, and both Lady Franklin and her spinster niece were at once impressed, almost enraptured, by this specimen of young Hawaiian manhood.

> He was a pure Hawaiian [Miss Cracroft effused to her relatives], but of most gentlemanlike manners and appearance, dressed exactly after the morning fashion of Englishmen in light grey. He is *very* dark-brown (not black) with acquiline nose and thick lips—whiskers and moustache and hair much more woolly in its crisp curliness than is usually seen among this people. Queen Victoria's Aide-de-Camp could not have acquitted himself better. He had been commanded by the King to present his respects to my Aunt: to express his great pleasure and that of the Queen at her visit to the Kingdom and to make it as agreeable as possible, and say that the Queen desired to place her carriage at my Aunt's disposal during her stay in Honolulu.
>
> This was given in excellent English and with the accent and intonation of a perfect gentleman, which he evidently is. He would not sit down, but made his farewell bow after receiving my Aunt's reply and message of thanks. We certainly received a most favourable impression of the style of court manners in the Sandwich Islands from this visit—he is styled "Colonel." The Honble. David Kalakaua is a member of one of the highest families on his mother's side, his father being a Chief of somewhat less degree. The King has six A. D. C.'s.[12]

On the very next day, April 21, quite early in the morning, Lady Franklin and Miss Cracroft accompanied Mr. Wyllie down into town and to the palace. The reception room was their destination, and there they were soon presented first to Queen Emma and then, a few moments later, to the slender, athletically handsome King Alexander Liholiho, "who came in alone, *looking* the perfect gentleman, his manner very cordial and unaffected." At the close of his brief word of welcome, Kamehameha spoke warmly of his admiration for England and of his interest in British institutions in general, dating from his visit to London at the age of sixteen. Last of all, he invited Lady Franklin and Miss Cracroft to consider themselves as his personal guests during their projected tour of the island of Hawaii. In fact, he would assign to them one of his aides, Mr. Peter Young Kaeo, reported Miss Cracroft, to serve as attendant and guide during their ambitious journey by sea and by land.

> The King spoke of his love for England and the obligation he felt for the kindness and attention he and his brother received there: he

wished he could go again, the more so as he wished his son to be educated at Eton or Rugby. We were thoroughly surprised by this announcement. He mentioned our visit to Hawaii, where, he said, were the only two things worth visiting in the Kingdom—the spot of Captain Cook's death and the volcano—and that in order to secure for us every facility, he was going to send one of his A. D. C.'s with us, whom he presented as our attendant—Mr. Peter Young [*sic*], a grandson of old John Young and cousin to the Queen—who would accompany us everywhere and provide all we required.[13]

Miss Cracroft's omission of as much as a single phrase describing Peter's appearance at this first meeting is possibly significant. Perhaps because she could find nothing to say even grudgingly in his favor, she chose politely to pass over the question of his person in ladylike silence. In any event, for reasons never specified in Miss Cracroft's letters, Kamehameha IV promptly changed his mind. He decided that David Kalākaua, not Peter Kaeo, should do the honors during the expedition to Kilauea's molten wonders and Kealakekua's celebrated tragic shore. Sophia Cracroft's mention of this abrupt switch of plan is again significantly laconic.

> We drove back to Mr. Wyllie's house, dined and went aboard the steamer *Kilauea.* . . . We had just gone down into the cabins when to our surprise the King followed us and explained that he had come to introduce another A. D. C. to us in place of Mr. Young, and he accordingly presented our old acquaintance Mr. Kalakaua, to whose charge we were committed. The King also explained that he had put his own boat and its crew on board the steamer, so that whenever we stopped we might land—that it was, in fact, at my Aunt's disposal. Was not this very kind and handsome?[14]

Miss Cracroft's third and final reference to Peter Kaeo, under the date of Friday, June 21, confirms one's guess that the visitors did not care for what they had seen of Peter. On this occasion, after their return to Honolulu from a side trip to the island of "perennial spring," Kauai, the plan for the morning was "an excursion to the *pali* [cliff] at the head of Nuuanu Valley," and both Colonel Kalākaua and the Hon. Peter Young Kaeo were to accompany the party and watch over their safety and comfort. One gathers that the outing, while scenically and historically rewarding, was not managed very smoothly, and there is more than a hint that Peter Kaeo was somehow individually to blame.

Col. Kalakaua was to be our escort, and the Queen wished to go also but sent word this morning that the unfavourable weather prevented her—there were frequent and very heavy showers rushing down the valley. The road was exceedingly rough, and the King sent his break with four horses, which took us safely over some very bad places, until we came to an unsafe bridge, when my Aunt got into the litter and I mounted a horse. We had also with us another of the King's A. D. C.'s, a cousin of the Queen, partly descended like herself from old John Young, and who goes only by his European name, Mr. Peter Young (I forget his native name). We did not particularly admire him and were very glad to have had Col. Kalakaua with us in Hawaii, who was at first fixed on by the King and introduced to us as our future escort.[15]

Of course, insights and inferences are risky when based on such scanty and dismissive allusions as Miss Cracroft's. Though she was factual-minded, and when she cared to do so could report meticulously exactly what she saw, she was also capable of being a tremendous snob, and on many political, religious, and social matters anything but an unbiased judge. She comments fairly frequently on the Hawaiian male, both young and old, and appears to have admired him most when he combined youth and an attractive physical presence, including a dark-coppery Polynesian coloring, with the "unaffected" and easy good manners of a highly idealized mid-Victorian gentleman. Here, for example, is her account of Isaac Davis, no product of the strenuous Chiefs' Children's School, but the country-bred cowboy "grandson of the Isaac Davis who with John Young was the first white man who settled on the Islands."

He is an exceedingly handsome, gentlemanlike-looking man of thirty-four (or thirty-six) he says—6 feet 2 inches in height, with well-cut features, wavy hair, and dark complexion, very becomingly dressed in a buff-coloured shirt with a pretty pattern on it. He speaks English, but no raillery or encouragement from Kalakaua would induce him to keep up any conversation in English. . . . Now and then he was betrayed into answering us in English, and he was mightily ashamed of his undress costume. . . . His manners are shy but gentlemanlike, and my Aunt was so pleased with him that she begged he would return with us and dine at Mr. Allen's, overruling all his scruples on the score of undress.[16]

It is evident that in 1861, on the score of manners and looks, in the judgment at least of Sophia Cracroft, the most attractive, courtly, and affable members of their race and sex were Alexander Liholiho and David Kalākaua, in that order. As for Isaac Davis the Younger, however lacking in conversational ease, he was obviously delightful to the eye. It is fair, I think, without straining the limited proof, to conclude that Peter Kaeo ("we did not particularly admire him") was not only unprepossessing in appearance; he may also have been, like numerous other natives of modest scholastic and social attainments, uncomfortably aware of his deficiencies in grammar and pronunciation, and consequently ashamed to display his faulty speech in public. The fact that English and not Hawaiian was his primary language made it all the more imperative, as Emma was later to admonish him, to learn to speak up and speak well.

That Peter may have been sadly handicapped by what, in today's parlance, is sometimes referred to as a "poor self-image" is easy to imagine. Yet I am not at all sure that our contemporary epithet is in the end an appropriate one for describing his character, in the old-fashioned sense of that useful word. Whatever that quality in Peter's nature may have been, there was something in him that permitted him to offset his suffering and humiliation as a miserable leper with a balancing measure of self-acceptance, a sense of his own worth, dignity, and pride. Emma clearly helped him on Molokai to preserve this saving element of his ego. Fostered both by his rank and his famous name ("The-[sacred]-back-of-the-chief"), that personal and collective heritage of pride may even have become more forthright and assertive during his "probation," when he was publicly identified as the alii of the settlement. Moreover, his sense of self-worth was being nourished constantly by his capacity to hope, a basic attitude perhaps deeply grounded in the biological stamina of his race and of his own hybrid constitution, as well as in the theological teachings of his Christian creed. In any event, his innate hopefulness almost inevitably took a political direction at Kalaupapa in 1874, impelled and made urgent by the death of Lunalilo and, above all, by his cousin's aroused, if at first hesitant, ambition to achieve the Kamehameha throne.

Thus the national crisis threatening the continuity of the monarchy coincided with Peter's private struggle to outlive the fluctuating ravages of his disease. To what extent Peter's traffic with kahunas may have contributed to his therapy—that hygienic program devised by Queen Emma, the more professional but still dubious treatments of

Dr. Trousseau and Dr. Akana, supplemented by assorted patent- and folk-medicines—is impossible to determine today. Perhaps all that can be said is that Peter's hope for his future, like his hope for the Kingdom, became for a time closely intertwined with his experience of the potency and meaning of the Hawaiian past. Eventually, that past found expression for Peter in a set of odd and rather makeshift rituals: in the revelations of the *haka* (spirit-medium) Paniku Hua; in the seances in the little hut of the conjurer Kukeliaiau; in the messages signaled in the configurations and colorings of the clouds; and perhaps in Peter's mentioned, but never verbally spelled out, prayers of petition "in the plain." For Peter it was as if these portentous acts and objects and others like them—the gaunt cliffs, the brackish pool amid the breadfruit trees of Kauhako Hill, Kahōāli'i's cave, indeed the whole ecological setting— provided the bracing solace he needed to endure his own wretched existence and to envision, in spectral imagination, the enigmatic future confronting the Hawaiian people and their islands.

Nevertheless, despite their grip upon his feelings, these same rituals and their symbolism were in many respects not only foreign to most of Peter's training, they were also alien to his own particular temperament as an alii. This normally gravitated to the mundane and to the practical; he was primarily a faithful plodder, a man of average common sense. Certainly, Peter was not himself a charismatic type: not at all one of those persons who appear to others to embody sacredness in themselves, like Paniku Hua who was said to commune with the great Queen Ka'ahumanu, nor like those Christians of primitive times who possessed the miraculous gift of grace, and could heal the sick and speak in tongues. Despite the precedent of his brave martyred ancestor, Peter's role in life was never that of the priest, certainly never the priest by vocation. It was a wholly secular role, but quite dignified: that of senator, law- maker, civil magistrate, and even sometimes (except where Kalākaua was concerned), the moderator.

"Civility is the virtue of the citizen, not the virtue of the hero or private man,"[17] writes Edward Shils, and the distinction, although taken from a late twentieth-century essay on "The Theory of Mass Society," can be profitably applied to the Peter Kaeo of the 1870s. In fact, Shils' more extended definition should be carefully considered as a possible corrective. Because of the sensationalism of some of the subject matter, it is tempting for a reader of Peter's letters during the 1970s to make too much of his preoccupation with magic and divination.

By doing so, however, one may overlook or distort other even more significant qualities of his character. One of these is his sturdy, though often wavering and unreliable, reasonableness. Yet if civility involves "the tasks of the management of public affairs in collaboration with others and with regard to the interests, individual, sectional, and collective of the entire society,"[18] then it is a virtue that characterized Peter's behavior more often than not.

Take, for example, that tense public gathering described in a letter of 1874 when Peter addressed an assembly of dissident and very angry lepers. He was speaking not as a hero, not primarily as an absentee member of the House of Nobles, but simply as a citizen concerned about the health and well-being of his country. Because Kalākaua had not promptly granted them their freedom after his accession, Peter's audience of his leper-peers were hoping that Queen Emma would soon do so: that she would close down the settlement and transport them all home again, bag and baggage, to their loved ones on their respective islands. Here, then, are the words of Peter, as he recalled and wrote them down for Emma, speaking in his role as moderator.

> I have frequently spoken to the Natives in regard to Hua's Predictions as to your ascending the Throne, informing them that should you be our Ruler, you are to abide and not to go or act against the Constitution. I also told them that I was one of the Lawmakers, and that this Law was made in order to check the Progress of this horrible disease, and should Queen Emma allow all of us to return to our Homes, thus allowing this disease to spread, why, it would be the ruination of the Hawaiian Nation and perhaps the whole world.
>
> It would immediately stop our Commerce, no Foreign Vessels will touch our ports for fear of this disease. All the Foreign Powers who we are in Treaty with will not Sanction this Act of Queen Emma's, and what would be the Consiquence—why, we lay ourselves liable to be seized at any moment, for favouring a few hundreds—Queen Emma will be the cause of the death of Thousands. I for my part would be willing to remain here, for says I [by] remaining here I have saved some 10's and *oukou* [all of you] some Hundreds. . . .[19]

I have identified hope and pride and civility as central strengths of Peter's character and conduct, as reflected in his Molokai letters. This trinity of abstractions does not begin to suggest the full range of his traits, certainly not their shadings, interrelations, and frequent contradictions, as these find idiosyncratic written expression through his self-evolved scenic-narrative-dramatic mode of utterance. The three attributes are at the same time universal, with deep roots in human nature. Everyone who lives discovers in himself and in others certain distinguishing marks and stigmata, certain "personal dispositions," to borrow again a term from Edward Shils, and each of these find their counterpart and reflection in Peter's Molokai correspondence:

> Qualities of rationality and impulsiveness, amiability and surliness, kindliness and harshness, lovingness and hatefulness are the constitution of the individual. Felt by himself, acknowledged by himself, coped with by himself, they are formed into his individuality. The perception and appreciation of individuality in others moves in unison with its development in the self.[20]

Peter Kaeo's letters often provide clues suggesting how such "development in the self" could occur in a leper of Molokai during the 1870s.

⟨꣠⟩

I have described the cousinly boy-and-girl bond, the quasi-elder sister and "baby" brother relationship, that conjoined Peter and Emma throughout his lifetime. I have noted also a distinction between Peter and Emma in their two characters, in their individuality, especially in their shared Anglicanism as members of the Hawaiian Reformed Catholic Church. If to live one's religion means to follow ordered and exacting religious rules, then Emma did so with far more energy and constancy than, in general, Peter Kaeo ever did. "Unto man much has been given in the way of position, influence, and oppertunity, and yet no convert have I made, nor benefited [Jesus] in any way," wrote Emma in that letter of 1873 of astounding self-admonishment and humility. If one hopes to understand Emma's experience of either Christian suffering or of Christian joy, her remorse deserves to be taken at full value. To study her life for biographical and historical purposes, it is necessary to consider again both her genealogical rank and her public role during the later 1860s and in the 1870s as dowager queen.

Emma's affectionate relationship with Peter, based on their kinship, was not simply an aspect of their interaction as two persons. Their attachment to one another was one of those intimate, and clearly for some persons ultimate, relationships that can be defined as primordial. The term broadly refers to the bond that arises from the "givens" of man's social existence, among which membership in this or that race, for example, is likely to be one of the strongest of human ties. In general, the term covers especially such immediate personal bonds as those of kinship and geographical contiguity, that identifying "we-conscious-ness" shared by families living in a particular region, for instance, as on an island or an island chain. Other circumstances that contribute directly to primary group identity, and thus to the ethnic makeup of individuals, are such additional "givens" as being born into a particular religious community or sect; speaking a particular language or dialect (a pidgin would be a pertinent example); or, in some settings, attending the same school system or school. Clifford Geertz has described how such affinities, such "congruities of blood, speech, custom, and so on," may even come to have

> ineffable, and at times overpowering coerciveness of themselves. One is bound to one's own kinsmen, one's neighbor, one's fellow believer, *ipso facto*, as a result not merely of one's personal affection, practical necessity, common interest, or incurred obligation, but at least a great part by *the virtue of some absolute import attributed to the very tie itself.*[21] (italics added)

The fact that affection may or may not pervade the primordial tie should here be emphasized. It is the tie itself that binds the individuals together, producing a heightened sense of "we-consciousness," but not necessarily any significant degree of personal liking or love. In fact, wherever love exists, there is always, it seems, the possibility that its opposite may intervene. Primordial groups within their own ranks, as in their communal behavior as close neighbors, obviously can display those same polarities of disposition and temperament characteristic of the individual self, as described by Edward Shils: in other words, they may swing between rationality and impulsiveness, benevolence and ill-will, love and hate, and so forth. Hence the prevalence in history of "ethnic" conflict between otherwise closely connected or very similar peoples, such as Flemings and Walloons, Great Russians and Little Russians, Hindus and Moslems at the time of the partition of India, and French and English Canadians. "It is not those who are tremendously different from us that we slay or hate; it is rather those similar to us," observes Andrew Greeley in a recent study of ethnicity in the modern world.[22] Peter Kaeo's Molokai correspondence provides minute documentation of this truism, particularly in those letters concerning sour, staling genealogical disputes in Hawaii during the later nineteenth century, and the rival claims as to which could claim the higher lineage, Queen Emma or David Kalākaua.

Nevertheless, even where affection is not particularly strong, the presence and immediacy of the primordial tie, its very tangibility, can acquire commanding value. When deep and spontaneous love is added to the bond, its symbolic function and force can prove all the more ineluctable. This seems an appropriate point to call attention to the various salutations, the ranging language of personal address and sentiment, employed by the cousins in their letters. For Emma, Peter (her "obedient servant") remained simply and always her "dearest Coz." For Peter, Emma was invariably "Queen Emma," the barest and most direct acknowledgment both of her royal status and of the girl he had known since their earliest childhood. As I mentioned earlier, Peter chose during this period of his life to complement and echo Emma's Hawaiian name (Kaleleonālani), signing himself almost always by the name of his martyred namesake. (The warrior-priest Kekuaokalani had been a half-brother of Peter's and Emma's grandmother, Kaoana'eha, whose own name—"The-spear-thrust"—was a reference to Kekuaokalani's death on the field of battle.) Thus the allusive and sometimes nostalgic greetings and terms of address appear to have accommodated themselves alike and gracefully to the claims of personal sentiment and to the whole hierarchical ranking system, resting on the remembered and still palpable glory of the ancestors.

Indeed, it was that system operating in a dynastic context that had led, in 1856, to the marriage of Alexander Liholiho, Kamehameha IV, to Miss Emma Rooke. Of course, in addition to being a descendant of Keli'imaika'i, Emma possessed other highly desirable personal attributes, including an attractive appearance, superior intelligence, and a marked charm of manner. Yet these assets alone, without the genealogical foundation, would never have qualified her simultaneously as acceptable bride and as charismatic dynastic symbol. Likewise, in 1866, when Emma's cousin, Peter Young Kaeo, became by royal appointment a member of the House of Nobles, the kinship system expedited the official honor and helped to make his political career as a legislator look somewhat feasible.

It is interesting to observe, however, that the constitutional procedure in Hawaii for the appointment of Nobles contained its own intended ambivalences concerning inherited status. Under the recent constitution of 1864, as under that of 1852, Nobles were to be appointed by the king—twenty of them—and they were to hold office for the rest of their lives. Significantly, this autocratic provision was then modified by a merit principle, personal and individual. The king could single out for the honor able white males, haoles—that is, foreigners even, if they were naturalized—as well as talented native Hawaiians. Preserving hierarchy, but rejecting rigid racial and genealogical criteria, the system possibly encouraged consensual flexibility and necessary innovation. In the legislature of 1874, which sat for eighty-four days, a total of eighteen Nobles were registered in official rosters as present most of the time. Among those eighteen, nine apparently were Hawaiians or of racially mixed Hawaiian background, the other nine being haole. The numerical balance, of course, had not the slightest relation to the demographic pattern of the Kingdom's population. Henry M. Whitney's *Hawaiian Guide Book for Travelers* (1875) contains a very informative table[23] showing the proportion of Hawaiians in the islands to the rest of the population, along with other instructive vital statistics. (Readers may want to skip this table at the moment, but they will profit from occasionally referring to it later.)

Total number of Natives, December 1872 49,044
Total number of Half-castes, December 1872 2,487
Total number of Chinese, December 1872 1,938
Total number of Americans, December 1872. 899
Total number of Hawaiian born, foreign parentage 849
Total number of Britons, foreign parentage. 619
Total number of Portuguese, foreign parentage 395
Total number of Germans, foreign parentage 224
Total number of French, foreign parentage. 88
Total number of other Foreigners. 364
    Total population, December 1872. 56,897

Total number of Natives and Half-castes in 1866. 58,765
Total number of Natives and Half-castes in 1872. 51,531
    Total decrease of Natives and Half-castes 1866–1872. . .7,234

Total number of Foreigners in 1872. 5,366
Total number of Foreigners in 1866. 4,194
    Total increase of Foreigners 1866–1872. 1,172

Decrease of Natives and Half-castes 1866–1872 7,234
Increase of Foreigners 1866–1872 1,172
Total decrease of population 1866–1872 6,062

It would be misleading, though by no means impossible, to try to divorce Queen Emma's political identity in the 1870s from her merely ceremonial role as dowager queen. In Mr. Whitney's *Guide*, she is listed under "The Court" as third in rank directly following "His Majesty the King" and "Her Majesty Kapiolani, Queen Consort." In other words, for special purposes and on certain court occasions, Emma's royal rank exceeded that of "His Royal Highness, the Heir Apparent," Prince Leleiohoku, Kalākaua's younger brother, just as it was superior to that of other lesser members of Kalākaua's immediate family. The chief reason for focusing on this fact is to remind one that monarchy in Hawaii, as elsewhere in the world, always by its very nature tended to invest the ruler with charisma, an aura of sacred significance. Hence the system was not only maintained in Hawaii but increasingly encouraged, of surrounding the monarch physically with an array of charismatic symbols, whether in the European form of a crown and a throne, or in the more indigenous shape of gorgeous feathery capes, feathery wreaths, feathery kahilis—ceremonial standards or wands—in the traditional Polynesian manner. Such symbolism became a spectacular feature of Kalākaua's dynastic pageantry, a calculated synthesis of Western and Polynesian materials and motifs, especially in evidence at the time of Kalākaua's coronation in 1883.

Although Kalākaua and Queen Emma at that time still did not care for one another, there is every reason to believe that they agreed well enough about how the court-and-kinship system had to operate. By lending her symbolic presence at the palace on certain occasions of state, Emma herself pragmatically helped to demonstrate that Kalākaua's rule, like that of the Kamehamehas, possessed its own quotient of "the magic of monarchy." Likewise, Kalākaua was well aware that Queen Emma's occasional attendance at his court, however grudgingly granted, gave a mystical fragrance to his reign. Indeed, her mere visible presence helped to dramatize, to render epiphanic and real to the popular imagination and to the world, the vigor and self-renewing power of the Hawaiian throne as a sacred institution.

Queen Emma is remembered today in Hawaii mainly because of the institutions founded through her efforts, or because of her perhaps indispensable example. The Queen's Hospital, the first public hospital in Hawaii, was established in the late 1850s largely through the preparatory planning of her adoptive father, Dr. T. C. B. Rooke, vigorously supported and only brought to fruition in 1860 by the young king and queen. Originally intended to provide medical services for needy Hawaiians, the Queen's Hospital, as it was known from its start, has for many years been the largest in the Hawaiian Islands, with the exception of a military hospital built and first operated during World War II by the United States government.

The introduction into Hawaii of an Anglican mission, followed by the establishment during the 1860s of an Episcopalian church, was likewise the consequence of the religious dedication of Kamehameha IV and Queen Emma. Urged by Emma, who hoped to have their four-year-old son baptized by an Anglican clergyman, Kamehameha IV in 1859 initiated correspondence with the British Foreign Office that led to the establishment in Hawaii of an Anglican bishopric in 1862. Because the Hawaiian constitution prohibited any state-supported religion, the new denomination was designated the "Hawaiian Reformed Catholic Church." Queen Emma gave a handsome piece of property to serve as the new church's site, virtually adjacent at that time to the old palace grounds of the Kamehamehas. St. Andrew's Cathedral derives its name from St. Andrew's Day, the date of the death in 1863 of Kamehameha IV. During the 1870s and 1880s, Emma concentrated her interest on episcopal schools, notably St. Andrew's Priory, established as a concrete result of her visit to England in 1865–1866.

Indeed, an important facet of her career, of her continuing influence upon the development of twentieth-century Hawaii, was her role as "the Englishwoman," as some of her people called her, not always admiringly. In this respect she resembled her foster father, Dr. Rooke, trained in London at St. Bartholomew's Hospital, and also her grandfather the British seaman, the original John Young ("Olohana"), both representatives not merely of Western civilization in the islands, but also of distinctively British values, attitudes, and prejudices. It is no great wonder that some of Emma's native supporters, during her perfervid contest for the throne in 1874, composed chants in her honor comparing her favorably with another royal widow.

> There are two great women in the world,
> Victoria of London
> and Queen Emma of Hawaii,
> worthy of wearing crowns.
> This concludes my praise
> of Kaleleonālani.[24]

Two experiences, two profoundly internalized encounters with death, greatly affected Queen Emma's character. These two events, the death of the Prince of Hawaii on August 27, 1862, followed by the death of his father on November 30, 1863, help us finally to place in biographical perspective the woman and the mother, the widowed queen who called herself Kaleleonālani, the reluctant yet scheming seeker after the throne, and the writer of the Molokai letters to her "Ever dear Coz." When one reads the correspondence, it is impossible not to be reminded now and again of Emma's own ordeal, the sudden deaths in succession of the prince and the king. For Queen Emma, too, as it was for Peter Kaeo, the period of her deepest anguish was followed by a reprieve, by at least the token of recovery.

A notion of flight, like a descent or ascent from ordinary mundane experience, seems to underlie the two significant names assumed by Queen Emma after the deaths of her child and his father. In 1862, when the boy died, Alexander Liholiho bestowed upon Emma the name Kaleleokalani: "The flight of the heavenly chief." After the king's death in 1863, Emma altered the formula to its plural number: Kaleleonālani, "The flight of the heavenly chiefs." Henceforth the queen would herself embody the two vanished chieftains. The thought of flight, followed by a return and transformation, appears also to have been in the mind of Manley Hopkins, who knew Queen Emma well, when he described in his history of the Hawaiian Kingdom Emma's grief over her loss.[25] Manley Hopkins spoke of the queen's "deep instinctive anguish" after the death of the boy; of how "for four days and nights she never stirred from the little grave beneath the tamarind tree"; and of how, finally, when the king died only fifteen months later, her first response was one of stupor: a "dull disbelief," followed eventually by a "certain knowledge," though as yet the queen "remained unconscious of the whole outer world."

> The only sound which reached her, and which soon by its continuance became unobserved, was the wail of men and women, which during two months went up incessantly by night and day round the walls of the palace. Yet there was one influence which made itself a way to the Queen in the very flood of her distress—it was that of the Bishop, as he came at the Queen's desire to administer to her at 7 o'clock the morning after her bereavement, the sacramental bread and wine, the instrument to which she looked for consolation if not for comfort.

Though far removed in her trance of sorrow, as Manley Hopkins reminded his Victorian readers, Kaleleonālani never let go the ligament linking her to the source of the mystery: her Lord's presence and person as manifest in the Holy Communion. Robert Crichton Wyllie, minister of foreign relations of the Kingdom, in a private message to a friend in London, corroborated Manley Hopkins' thoughts on the Resurrection and the Life; but Wyllie chose also to expose fragments of old Hawaiian custom (dissociated members, one supposes, of some archaic ritual for the dead) surviving on down through the 1860s in Emma's graveside behavior.

> The remains of Queen Emma's only child [reported Wyllie to Lady Franklin in Kensington Gore] now lie with those of her husband in a new mausoleum of stone and lime, in Gothic style. . . . You will be distressed to learn that the tender-hearted and unconsolable Queen Emma sleeps in the vault along with the bodies of her husband and child, although it is quite damp and unventilated.[26]

Robert Crichton Wyllie further remarked to Lady Franklin that Emma had shown only a slight interest when he had invited her to spend at least her nights at his delightful house, "Rosebank," in Nuuanu Valley, from where she might return to the nearby royal cemetery for vigil as often as she liked: "She has not positively declined, but says she must remain night and day near the tomb at least for a fortnight."

One of the urgent reasons, other than the religious and political considerations, why her friends and advisers had persuaded Queen Emma in 1865 to travel abroad was to awaken and rescue her from what Wyllie described as a "dejection deep and dangerous." It was hoped by everyone that novel scenes and exotic customs of England, France,

Italy, and Germany might arouse Queen Emma's normal cheerfulness and restore her to her eager and still youthful self. And, indeed, this is precisely what happened. Readers of the letters of Kaleleonālani and Kekuaokalani should recall her own dark journey and return: from an island of desolation back to the land of the living.

1. Hitherto unpublished (Queen Emma Collection, Archives of Hawaii [hereafter cited as AH]).

2. Letter 63.

3. Letter 16.

4. Letter 16.

5. Letter 61.

6. M. G. Marwick, *Sorcery in Its Social Setting: A Study of the Northern Rhodesia Cêwa* (Manchester: University of Manchester Press, 1965), p. 286.

7. Ethnographers and experts in the unwritten literature of Hawaii have pointed out that genealogical rank or primogeniture were not alone sufficient claim to kingship. In addition, the king had to have "the personal qualifications to make him a leader or ruler over the rest." (E. S. Craighill Handy, in *Ancient Hawaiian Civilization, a Series of Lectures Delivered at the Kamehameha Schools* [Honolulu, 1933], p. 32; see also Samuel H. Elbert, "The Chief in Hawaiian Mythology," *Journal of American Folklore*, 69 [Oct.–Dec. 1956]: 310.) In other words, the old hierarchic system was sufficiently ambiguous to permit exceptionally successful, and in that sense meritorious, individuals to attain high chiefdoms apart from genealogical status. Despite such flexibility in historical practice, Queen Emma's and Peter Kaeo's conceptions and attitudes concerning the royal power appear to have been deeply conventional and in accord with what has been defined as the essential character of the old society *as a whole*: "a world based upon the fundamental conception of social rank. The family tie and the inherent rights and titles derived from it determine a man's place in the community. The families of chiefs claim their rights and titles from the gods who are their ancestors." (Martha Warren Beckwith, *The Hawaiian Romance of Laieikawai by S. N. Haleole, 1862*, Bureau of American Ethnology, Washington, D.C., 23 [1919]: 308.) Despite their almost automatic claim to supreme status, it is not likely that either Emma or Peter as Christians would have claimed to have been descended "from the gods." Excisions and revisions in Emma's hand in her rough drafts suggest that she sometimes (as in Letter 63) avoided references "to the ancient royal blood" and substituted a more ambiguous metaphor: e.g., "to the ancestral tree." In other words, she tended for practical purposes to emphasize the historical achievements, good deeds, and fame of the ancestors rather than blood lines as such. In short, her ideas and feelings in the matter were ambivalent.

8. E. S. Craighill Handy, Mary Kawena Pukui, Elizabeth Green Handy, *The Polynesian Family System in Ka'u, Hawaii* (Wellington, N. Z.: The Polynesian Society, 1958), p. 127.

9. Letter 109.

10. For the following comment on dreaming and related experiences in old Hawaiian culture, I am much indebted to E. S. Craighill Handy and Mary Kawena Pukui, *The Family System in Ka'u*, especially chapter six, "The Psychic Phase of Relationship," pp. 126–135.

11. Letter 37.

12. Alfons L. Korn, *The Victorian Visitors: An Account of the Hawaiian Kingdom, 1861–1866* (Honolulu: University of Hawaii Press, 1958), p. 32.

13. Ibid., p. 34. Kamehameha IV (1834–1863) was a grandson of Kamehameha I through his mother, the high chiefess Kina'u. Educated at the Chiefs' Children's School; traveled in England, France, the United States, 1849–1850. As heir apparent and successor of Kauikeaouli, Kamehameha III, he ruled over Hawaii for nine years, 1854–1863. He married Emma Rooke, descendant of a half-brother of Kamehameha I, on June 19, 1856, in a ceremony conducted by a Congregational missionary, but according to the marriage service of the English Book of Common Prayer. The birth of a son, Albert Edward Kauikeaouli Leiopapa o Kamehameha (1858–1862) augured at first a happy reign. Although the young king and queen were genuinely fond of one another, Alexander Liholiho in 1859 became involved in a scandal that he subsequently called "the great false act of my life." After several days of hard drinking, while on an excursion to Maui accompanied by a party of young people, he shot and severely wounded his American secretary and close friend, Henry A. Neilson. Contemporary witnesses are generally agreed that the act was motivated by an irrational and groundless suspicion of Emma's fidelity. While the king debated whether to abdicate, Emma's devotion to him remained unshaken. His immediate remorse and his rededication, with Emma's constant support, to religious and humanitarian aims are described elsewhere in this book.

14. Korn, *The Victorian Visitors*, p. 35.

15. Ibid., pp. 165–166.

16. Ibid., p. 77.

17. Edward Shils, "The Theory of Mass Society," *Diogenes*, No. 39 (1962), reprinted in *Selected Essays by Edward Shils* (Chicago: Center for Social Organization Studies, Department of Sociology, University of Chicago, 1970), p. 26.

18. Ibid., p. 26.

19. Letter 95.

20. Shils, "The Theory of Mass Society," p. 27.

21. "The Integrated Revolution," in *Old Societies and New Societies*, edited by Clifford Geertz (Glencoe, Ill.: The Free Press, 1963), p. 109.

22. Andrew Greeley, *Ethnicity in the United States: A Preliminary Reconnaissance* (New York: John Wiley and Sons, 1974), p. 11.

23. Rutland, Vt., C. E. Tuttle, 1970, p. 120.

24. From a collection of Queen Emma chants, Bernice P. Bishop Museum (hereafter cited as BM).

25. *Hawaii: The Past, Present, and Future of Its Island Kingdom*, 2nd ed. (London: Longman's, Green, and Co., 1866), pp. 425, 426, 427, 447, 449.

26. Robert Crichton Wyllie to Lady Franklin, Honolulu, Feb. 6, 1864 (Lady Franklin Collection, Gregg M. Sinclair Library, University of Hawaii, Honolulu).

The
Correspondence

As the Vessel sailed on its course to Westward, I followed by land watching as she was ploughing the Sea. I could not see Sweet Home, so following the Vessel with my Eyes, I thought of Home, and of those so dear to me, And you especially, Surrounded by so many Wicked People, till the Coming night bade me seek my Cottage on the cliff, So on looking again for the Vessel, I saw it but a Speck on the Ocean, so waving my Hat in the direction where she is seen, And reciting the words Adieu, Adieu, my Native Land, I rode back as it was then after Sunset, and the Evening being nice, and cool, I walked my Horse all the way, thinking still of you, and of Home,—

PETER TO EMMA
Letter 83

Jack Smith was not discreet enough, & course this rheumor reached the Palace, & there was where I feared for you in case the powers that be should have step the mark & take the law into their own hands, but yet Mr Preston said through out that once you landed here every one would be in defence of your rights & probably that would bring things to a climax he said a stir is wanted now to check the present unscrupulous managment of the Govt. So that when Kalawaia nui walked into my mauka bedroom silently I could not guess what the issue had been so left him to break the subject & felt both relieved & disappointed, he told me all as you had written & says he now knows the coast of that part of Molokai, & can very well land at night walk up to your house & come down together with you & pull off to ship, his destination is Punaluu Koolau & says he can well stand off on at Kalaupapa for you, but I must write more about this when I hear more. In order to carry on the pretence that I knew nothing of the plans for your rescue (should you have come) that I sent as usual every article of food save the sheep or

EMMA TO PETER
Letter 122

PART ONE / *A Long Farewell*

July 1, 1873–December 17, 1873

Peter Kaeo became a victim of leprosy during the 1860s. By 1868 his case was so serious that King Kamehameha V, Queen Emma's brother-in-law, wrote to her saying he wanted to intervene: "Peter Kaeo ought to be put in Kalihi Hospital.[1] . . . It would be an act of humanity to have him removed there, because he would get the proper restraint on his appetite and person. Shall I see that he is put in? He will come out a well man."[2]

What was done, if anything, about the king's urgent proposal is uncertain. But five years later, under King Lunalilo, when the Hawaiian government was making a vigorous effort to bring the disease under control, Peter Kaeo was among the first Hawaiians to be sent to Molokai under the new regulations. Isabella Bird, whose six-months' visit to Hawaii in 1873 coincided with the accelerated drive to round up the lepers, reported that there had been as many as 400 scattered up and down the various islands, still living among families and friends: "The healthy associated with them in complete apathy or fatalism." But now, because of vigilant law enforcement, lepers were being "informed against," neighbor reported on neighbor, so that

> it became the painful duty of the sheriffs of the islands on the statement of a doctor that any individual was truly a leper, to commit him for life to Molokai. . . . There were no individual distinctions among the sufferers. Queen Emma's cousin, a man of property, and Mr. Ragsdale, the most influential lawyer among the half-whites, shared the same doom as poor Upa, the volcano guide, and stricken Chinamen and labourers from the plantations.[3]

On June 28, 1873, the schooner *Kinau* left Honolulu carrying a company of lepers, including Peter Kaeo and Bill Ragsdale, their personal belongings, and a cargo of freight and miscellaneous supplies, bound for Molokai. As a man of property Peter moved at once into his own private cottage, one of a scattering of small frame dwellings not far from the hospital but well separated from the cluster of grass-thatched huts that constituted Kalawao, the main village of the settlement.

Peter's cottage stood on the lower reaches of a treeless slope extending down to some abandoned sweet potato patches. Beyond the potato patches stretched a narrow rock-strewn beach along Molokai's northernmost shore. Behind Peter's place, but of no very great height, rose Kauhako Hill, the broken-down remnant cone of the least of three volcanoes out of which aeons ago the island had been formed. On

Peter's eastern side loomed the austere headlands and palisades that shut off the Kalaupapa peninsula, that "almost-island" scarcely four miles square in area, from the rest of Molokai. Peter's cottage faced directly into the winds and waves of the Pacific. When he looked out his window he could sometimes glimpse the shadowy coast of Oahu. Makapuu Point, a mirage on the marine horizon, was only about twenty miles away.

1. The Board of Health established a new fifty-bed hospital, in 1865–1866, in the Kalihi district of Honolulu near the waterfront. After the establishment of the Kalaupapa settlement in 1866, Kalihi Hospital served as a way-station for lepers en route to Molokai.

2. King Kamehameha V ("Ali'iolani") to Queen Emma ("Dear Madame"), Honolulu, Jan. 18, 1868 (AH). The allusion to "appetite" probably refers to overindulgence in general, not simply to Peter's interest in food.

3. Isabella L. Bird, *The Hawaiian Archipelago: Six Months among the Palm Groves, Coral Reefs, and Volcanoes of the Sandwich Islands*, 5th ed. (London: John Murray, 1882), p. 294.

Letter 1
Peter to Emma

Kalaupapa
July 1, 1873

Queen Emma

I have arrived safe. The next morning at Sunrise we were just off Makapuu and so near that a person could have Swam on Shore with ease. It was then that I wished I could come to you once more and repeat the sad word "Good Bye"—but no. Since it has been my lot—now as I am torn away from the Kindest of Aunt,[1] from the dearest of Cousin, dearer itself then the World to me—I must humbly bow my head to the maker of all things and say, Thy Will be done.

Every evening I could see the setting Sun set on dear Oahu Knowing thou art so near yet cannot hear thy Gentle Voice. It makes me so sad that I cannot rest with ease for some time, till the evening shades hide from me the dusky form I so dearly love. "Home"—I will not dwell on this sad subject for It might be tiresome to you, but to me it is comfort to think of the past and the future and while the weary hours away till fatigued by freting I bow to the direction that holds my all—then retire.

On my arrival one of my little birds died so I've only one left. My stove is minus of Teapot and cooking Knife, my Lamp I cannot find, my looking glass also—the frame I've put up but no glass—the top pieces to the bed, my Basket for clothes, no saddle and bridal. I am going to write to Wilder[2] to allow a man to stop with me. He is a Kamaaina.[3]

I wish you would send me up a pair of rideing Gloves—and the shooues please.

A long Good Evening
Your Obedient Servant
KEKUAOKALANI

My Aloha to Kekelaokalani

1. Fanny Kekelaokalani Young Naea (1804–1880), Emma's mother, widow of George Naea. She was a daughter of John Young, an English mariner, and the High Chiefess Kaoana'eha, a daughter of Keli'imaika'i, a younger brother of Kamehameha I.

2. Samuel G. Wilder (b. Leominster, Mass., 1831; d. Honolulu, 1888);

owner of business firm Wilder and Co., member of the Privy Council and Board of Health, managing agent of the government-owned steamer *Kilauea*. Authorized in 1873 by the Board of Health to act as its commissioner to supply the Kalaupapa settlement with foodstuffs, merchandise, and building materials. Member of the House of Nobles 1874–1888; Minister of Interior under Kalākaua 1878–1880. Wilder's later commercial enterprises, in steam navigation and island railways, kept pace with the development of the sugar industry.

3. A regular resident of Molokai; an old-timer and not a leper.

Letter 2
Memorandum
Emma to Peter

[Honolulu]
July 2, 1873

Ever dear Coz

Oh I am so happy to receive your first letter of yesterday. It is a sad happiness though, but still happiness nevertheless. I got it at 12 o'clock this noon and fancy you reading my unfinished notes about the same time. We all cried very much over it.

[KALELEONĀLANI]

Things sent to Peter per *Kinau* July 7th, 1873.
5 lvs bread
35 potatoes
onions
25 ct beef
4 [bales of] hay
Newspaper *Advertiser* July 5th
2 pumbkins
2 poke ahi[1]
a bundle of squash seeds

1. Slices of tuna fish.

Letter 3
Peter to Emma

Kalaupapa
July 4, 1873

Queen Emma

I have received yours of the 30 of June and July 1 with pleasure Knowing it comes from my Queen I so much respect and the relation so dear to me. Words cannot express the feeling I had when I read the contents, but Life is like the shades of Evening whare it gradually decreases in light till enveloped in darkness, it fades from vew.

I have received all the articles you sent but the meat which was thrown overboard—it was spoiled. The Teapot to the Stove I have not got, and the end piece to the chimney which goes into the Stove and the top piece which takes the smoke out of the House. The Beef I have not tasted for I dare not, until alterations are made in the Killing and delivering—"Disgusting."[1] My share of Poi I dare not touch so it goes to my fowl. My Poi is about out so I am haveing my bag of tarrow cooked.[2] I wish you would send me up another bag of Tarrow to make Poi.

So far I am geting on very well as I have two Kamaainas to wait on me. [One of these is] an old man servant to old Kaleikoa, Kaeo's father,[3] but they are to leave as they are sent away by the Board of Health. Until then, comes the tug of War.[4]

Send me up a couple of Wheel Borrows to cart the stones away. I am completely surrounded with stones. I thought of puting a stone wall up but was told not to as the rats and mice get into it and from there into the House. If you can get a man to come up to stop with me on pay I wish you would, as I feel the need of it, and when all the Kamaainas are gone I will need it more—so long as he is clean. The natives here are all on the make charging rather heavyly.

This morning I lost my other little companion the Dove for it pined right away for want of a mate and died. The Carpenters are puting up my Cook House and the Bath.

I must now finish my letter. Remember me to Fanny and Grace[5] and all your domesticks. Your Majesty a long *Aloha*.

I remain
Truely Yours
KEKUAOKALANI

1. A reference to beef from local bullocks slaughtered at Kalaupapa, after being brought over the pali trails from ranches on Molokai.

2. The inedible poi was Peter's official ration, as supplied by the Board of Health and its agents. Numerous letters refer to poi, the starchy Hawaiian food made from taro corms cooked, pounded to a paste, and fermented. His references to *kalo* (*Colocasia esculenta*) usually refer to the plant in general, including the root, stalk, and leaves, all of which could be eaten in various forms. In certain letters, especially those describing the unloading of supplies at the landing, he distinguishes between prepared poi and *pa'i 'ai*, hard pounded but undiluted *kalo* tied up in a bundle (*pa'i*). In still other letters, such as this one, where he mentions "another bag of Tarrow," he may be thinking either of entire plants or merely the roots.

3. Peter's grandfather; a genealogy in one of Emma's guest books lists Kaleikoa as the father of Kaeo-ehu, husband of Jane Lahilahi Young. See "Guest Book—Rooke House," BM.

4. "Meanwhile, the local residents resist being forced to leave Kalaupapa."

5. Grace Kamaikui Wahinekaili Kahōāli'i (1854–1916), a young high chiefess and cousin of Queen Emma, descended from a half-brother (Kahōāli'i II) of Emma's maternal grandmother, Kaoana'eha.

Letter 4
Peter to Emma

Kalaupapa
July 7, 1873

Her Majesty Queen Emma

I received yours of the 2d and 4th with the things you sent up, with the exception of the Beef—that was spoilt. Do not send anything up any more in the shape of beef and Hay. My Horse I am going to turn out it is so poor. I have bought another one to fetch water and wood and to send my little boy on little errends. The girl, Napaepae's dauther, who washes my clothes, has not got it. They are all to return to Maui when the Schooner *Waiola* returns here to take away another lot of Kamaainas, who are not effected with the diseas. Her Nephew is my Horse boy. He has got only two of his fingers effected, but his body and everything else is all right.

Do not send my dog yet till I send for it. I killed my little Ship Mate yesterday—the "Pigey"—I would not have done it could I have got anything else freash. As soon as my fence comes up I will begin to put it up and Keep the troublesome Hogs away. When the carts are not buisy I will engage it to cart away the big stones. Do not send up any of the Trees as their are no water. I think that the plants will not grow, the soil is so bad. Whare my House stands it is completely surrounded with stones. Everything is finished with the exception of the articles I am sending for—the picket [fence] and Trogh for the Water Cask. It is [explained] in another letter wrote preveious to this.

If you can find out in bills stuck on fences for Sale of Sardines and Halibut at Auction, I wish you would send me up some—it will take the place of fresh meat or fish. My fowl is so poor I cannot eat them, and eating too much salt meat I know is not good. But I can't help it so far. I have just bought some corn, but the Fowls do not eat it. My share of the Poi I get I give to my little Pig—it is not worth eating. The Schooner is quite ready to sail, so I must bid you Farewell, but whenever

> Thou welcome the hour
> That awakens the night Song
> Of mirth in your bower,
> Then think of the one
> That once welcomed it too
> And forgot his own griefs
> To be happy with you.
> His grief may return,
> Not a hope may remain
> Of the few that have brighten
> His pathway of pain,
> But he will ne'er forget
> The short vision that threw
> Its enchantment around him,
> Whilst lingering with you.[1]

Give my Aloha to Grace and your Folks.

I remain Yours etc.

KEKUAOKALANI

P. S. Do not send up any more Poi in Barrels, but send me up some Tarrow in a Bag. I will send the Barrel of Poi down by the next return of the Schooner. A man has just volenteered to stop with me. He is about Sixty and over. I am going to write to Hall[2] about him and get his permission to let him stop with me.

Good Bye
P. Y. K.

Wingate College Library

1. The verses, quoted as Peter probably would have recited them, are from Tom Moore's "Irish Melodies": "Farewell!—But whenever you welcome the hour."

2. Edwin O. Hall (b. Walpole, New Hampshire, 1810; d. Falmouth, Maine, 1883; buried Honolulu); Minister of Interior and chairman of Board of Health, 1873–1874. Arrived in Hawaii 1835; served in secular capacity as overseer of Protestant mission printing press 1835–1850. On resignation from mission became director of government press and editor of government-owned newspaper, *Polynesian*, holding post for about five years. In 1855, he founded the mercantile and hardware firm of E. O. Hall and Son, which continued into the twentieth century.

Letter 5
Emma to Peter

Mosoleum[1]
July 7, 1873
3 o'clock in the morning

Ever dear Coz

You will see from the top of this letter where I am writing from. Poor old Nahalau,[2] one of dear Alex's nurses, breathed his last at 1 o'clock this morning. Mother, Hanaoile, Kamai, Hiram and I are here.[3] This afternoon he's to be buried by the side of his wife near Hinau's[4] grave. He sent for me yesterday feeling his end was near. Mother and I came up and remained since. Pamalo[5] saw him and pronounced his disease to be aneurism. He suffered great pain the last 3 months. Joe Keaoa,[6] his half-brother, whom you may remember was cockswain of *Kehukai*, one of our boats, lives with him. Numerous events of one's past life are cast up by blessed memory and dear faces live with me again as of yore.

Mother told me last night that Albert[7] has been in town since Friday. He ran after Miss Nohea for bad intentions at her place back of Mrs Colburn's, much to their terror. An old man named Waiahole, who is recently from Molokai, told Mother he saw Napela[8] and W. Ragsdale[9] land drunk from your schooner *Kinau*, and that you poured some spirit into a glass and offered it to him at the house of the person who entertained you with a dinner. Naturally, connecting this with Albert's story of your departure pains me very very much. Dear Peter, recovery depends solely on yourself—prey do nothing to retard its progress, if you have any consideration for acting out God's purpose of filling our fathers' places, as well as love for me.

2 o'clock noon

Dear Peter

The latest news is the Ministers are wickedly desperate to almost force the King[10] to sign his name to the treaty for ceding Puuloa[11] to U.S.A. The people of town, natives and haoles, save the Americans, are strong against it, and I am so heavy of heart about this that I can scarse write. The King has been asked two days ago to do so but refused, at the same time explaining his reason for not consenting— that as the people chose him their ruler, he could do nothing in the way of giving away any territory without their knowledge and acquiesence. . . . He came in for a very short while at noon and is going out again to Waikiki. It is this new attitude he has taken that makes the Cabinet force him to consent. Your prayers for strength to our King's resolution can do much towards saving our Kingdom from utter anihilation.[12]

Your servant Kahele is firmly resolved to come up and live for ever with you till you return. I shall do my all towards helping her noble self-sacrifice.

[KALELEONĀLANI]

1. The royal burial ground and earliest crypt in Nuuanu Valley, Honolulu, where the remains of various Hawaiian kings, queens, high chiefs, and chiefesses have been deposited since 1864.

2. He had been an honored attendant (*kahu*) of Prince Alexander Liholiho, later Kamehameha IV, Emma's husband, during the king's childhood. For main note on Kamehameha IV, see Introduction, note 13.

3. Hanaoile was one of Emma's female retainers. Kamai was probably the young High Chiefess Grace Kamaikui; see Letter 3, note 2. Hiram Kahanawai (d. 1874) was a relative of Queen Emma by a junior line of descent; also a relative of David Kalākaua. Hiram had been chief steward in the royal household under Kamehameha IV and continued to serve Emma in that capacity during her widowhood. In 1874, after the election of Kalākaua to the throne, Hiram married Kapo'oloku, a younger sister of Mrs. David Kalākaua (Queen Kapi'olani), and received official appointment under the new dynasty.

4. A high chief; husband of Emma's attendant Kamakaaiau, and father of Stella Keomailani; see Letter 16, note 8.

5. Dr. Robert McKibbin, Jr. (d. 1901), a native of Ireland; for many years physician-in-residence at the Queen's Hospital, Honolulu. Arrived in Hawaii 1856; a close friend as well as personal physician of Kamehameha IV. His

Hawaiian nickname, "Pamalo," meaning "dry," "without expression," probably referred to his brusque speech and manner.

6. Coxswain of the royal canoe *Kehukai* ("Seaspray"), when Lady Franklin and Sophia Cracroft traveled by outrigger canoe along the Kona Coast in 1861. Appointed keeper of the Royal Mausoleum, July 1873.

7. Albert Kūnuiākea (1851–1903), Peter's half-brother and a cousin of Queen Emma; a natural son of Kauikeaouli, King Kamehameha III (1813–1854), by Jane Lahilahi Young Kaeo, a younger sister of Fanny Naea, Emma's mother. As a boy and young man, Albert had lived in the household of the Dowager Queen Kalama, widow of Kamehameha III, and was a perennial worry to his family, teachers, and successive guardians. Member of the House of Representatives 1880; delegate to the constitutional convention under the Provisional Government 1894.

8. Jonathan ("Jonatana") H. Napela (?1813–1888), Mormon elder and assistant supervisor of the Kalaupapa settlement at the time of Peter's arrival; of chiefly rank, educated at Lahainaluna Seminary by Congregationalist teachers; formerly a Maui magistrate. One of the first three natives converted to the Mormon church; assisted in earliest translation of Book of Mormon into Hawaiian. Moved to Kalaupapa in 1873 to take care of his wife, the Chiefess Kiti Richardson Napela. At that time J. H. Napela was not a leper, but he finally became one; died at Kalaupapa.

9. William P. Ragsdale (183?–1877), a part-Hawaiian of American descent who became a popular hero by volunteering to go to Molokai, when no one suspected that he was a leper. Formerly an interpreter in Hawaiian legislature; also practicing attorney. Later, in 1873, he succeeded J. H. Napela as assistant supervisor of the settlement. Mark Twain, who visited a session of the Hawaiian legislature in 1866, was fascinated by Ragsdale's talents as an interpreter: "Bill Ragsdale stands up in front of the Speaker's pulpit, with his back against it, and fastens his quick black eye upon any member who rises, lets him say half a dozen sentences and then interrupts him, and repeats his speech in a loud, rapid voice, turning every Kanaka speech into English and every English speech into Kanaka, with a readiness and felicity of language that are remarkable. . . . There is a spice of deviltry in the fellow's nature, and it crops out every now and then when he is translating the speeches of slow old Kanakas who do not understand English. Without departing from the spirit of a member's remarks, he will, with apparent unconsciousness, drop in a little voluntary contribution occasionally in the way of a word or two that will make the gravest speech utterly ridiculous." (*Mark Twain's Letters from Hawaii*, ed. A. Grove Day [New York: Appleton-Century, 1966], pp. 110–111.) In June 1877, Ragsdale's condition was very bad: "The disease has made progress on him, his right hand was a mass of ulceration and writing is of considerable effort to him." (R. W. Meyer to C. T. Gulick, Kalaupapa, June 14, 1877; Correspondence, Board of Health [AH]). His death on Nov. 29 was reported in the *Hawaiian Gazette*, Dec. 12, 1877.

10. William Charles Lunalilo (1833–1874), king of Hawaii Jan. 1, 1873,

to Feb. 3, 1874; a grandson of a half-brother of Kamehameha I; traced his high rank through his mother, Kekauluohi, who served as premier (*kuhina nui*) of the Kingdom. A Congregationalist, educated at Chiefs' Children's School; well liked by haoles and Americans, who considered him democratic. When Kamehameha V (1830–1872) died without appointing a successor, Lunalilo and David Kalākaua became rival candidates for the throne. Lunalilo asked all male citizens to go to polls on Jan. 1, 1873, and "peaceably and orderly express their free choice for a King of the Hawaiian Islands." After winning the election, Lunalilo was confirmed as ruler by vote of the Hawaiian legislature, although he had little experience in public affairs. His brief reign was disturbed by two handicaps, his chronic alcoholism and the inroads of pulmonary tuberculosis. He never married; and like Kamehameha V he died without naming a successor.

11. Region of the Pearl River estuary and lochs; Pearl Harbor. An ancient Hawaiian mele celebrated the "labyrinth harbor of Puuloa" ("*ke awa lauke'e o Puuloa*"). On May 3, 1873, the *Pacific Commercial Advertiser* carried a brief descriptive article pointing out the exquisite beauty of the region, of which the hilly north side (*pu'uloa*: "long hills") was especially memorable for its "rich bits of Arcadian attractiveness and fertility"; furthermore the spot had "capacities in a commercial point of view, furnishing as it might anchorage ground and wharf-room for the largest fleet that could be concentrated at any point in this ocean."

12. In 1872–1873, the depressed condition of agriculture and the sugar industry in Hawaii stimulated renewed agitation in favor of a treaty of reciprocity with the United States. "The transition from reciprocity to territorial cession, and thence to annexation," wrote Theophilus H. Davies, acting British commissioner, to Lord Granville, "appears so easy that the advocates of the first of a week ago, are today boldly urging the last, and there is a great feeling of insecurity, lest the King himself in a moment of weakness should be persuaded to sell his throne." (Davies to Granville, Feb. 11, 1873 [confidential] [Public Record Office, London, Foreign Office 58/136].)

Letter 6
Peter to Emma

Kalaupapa
July 9, 1873

A distant Good Morning to your Majesty

I will now write to you about our situation. My House stands on a rise at the foot of Kauhako Hill.[1] I am about half way from Kalawao to Kalaupapa, a distance of about Two miles. On my Left is a long line of Mountain quite perpendicular runing westward into the Sea. To my right the ground is rough, Hilly and volcanic in character. To my front the land is flat and rocky, studed with Potatoe patches of old. To my rear is a little incline plain till you get to the settlement, the Kalawao Valley. The Hospital stands right on the road, which we have to pass going to bathe at Waikolu, a distance of about Two miles more. That is the only river. The lepers do not go their much it is so rough, and at some places we have to face the fury of the Sea.

The Kamaainas say in Winter that place is so bad and dangerous that nobody ever ventures to pass. The width from the Sea to the Pali[2] is about 35 or 40 ft. wide so you can judge how bad it must be. I have sat on my Horse watching the wild waves comeing with all its fury and dashing itself against the Pali, which towers Majesticly up quite perpendicular, and I have immagened this Mountain looking down and mocking its efforts.

I went up yesterday to look at the inside of Kauhako Hill. It is about 80 or 90 ft. high and about the size of Punch Bowl.[3] Inside is hollow— Breadfrute, Ohia, Lehua, Kukui, and other trees grow in it. On the Mauka or Windward side whare the trees grows most thickest Napela holds his Meeting on Sundays with the Mormons. In the Center of this hole is another hole quite circular in form and about 30 or 40 ft. deep. Their are three collors to the Sea in this little Lake. First is a kind of Redish. Then it turns into a light brown. When in this collor the Shrimps all die and nothing Alive is seen moving inside of the Sea. Thence from that collor to a lighter one. The breadfrute and Ohia the Kamaaina says were planted by "Akuas."[4]

We just have had a good Shower and if my Casks were up I would have commenced to plant a little. Do not Send up any plants as the rocks have not been taken away yet. After that is done I will commence to make the beds for them. With the help of Water and the Fence to keep away the Hogs I hope to have a garden.

Good Bye. My Aloha to Lucy,[5] Grace, Aunt and your Folks.

I remain

Kekuaokalani

1. A volcanic hill and extinct crater about 500 feet above sea level at its highest point, approximately one mile distant from the shoreline. Its most unusual feature, which still exists, is the lake or pool within the hill's crater, whose changing colors fascinated Peter Kaeo. Filled with semibrackish water, the lake is fed by interior springs, the degree of saltiness being determined by rainfall and the high or low tides.

2. Cliff. The 1,600-foot ridge of East Molokai Mountain; also called "Kalae" ("The Point" or "The Promontory").

3. A prominent volcanic hill formed by an extinct crater overlooking central Honolulu; now the site of the National Memorial Cemetery of the Pacific. According to Hawaiian oral tradition, the crater once contained a fire oven for the sacrificial burning of persons who had violated a privilege of a divine kapu-chief.

4. The gods.

5. Lucy Kaopauli Kalanikiekie Peabody (1840–1928), a part-Hawaiian high chiefess, one of Queen Emma's maids-of-honor. Her father was an American physician, Dr. Parker Peabody (1805–1849), originally from the state of New York. Her mother, Elizabeth K. Davis, was a granddaughter of Isaac Davis (?1757–1810), Welsh mariner who with John Young, Queen Emma's grandfather, was an adviser and companion-in-arms of Kamehameha I.

Letter 7
Peter to Emma

Kalaupapa
July 10, 1873

Queen Emma

I have just received yours of the 9th per *Warwick* with the things you sent up by her. The Wheel Borrows has come. I will now commence to cart the little stones away from around my House. The big stones I will hire a cart Ox to carry. My Health is good. My right Hand is a little better then it was, it moves easier. My face is the same, but my foot is a little swolen, and the sores that were once healed have broken out again.

I have just engaged a man to cook my Tarrow at 25 cts a day and to get me water at 50 cts a day. So do not send up any more of any things with the exceptions of Tarrow Bag until I send for them. The rainy season is setting in so when my Casks are put up I will have enough for my own use and also for my plants when they come up. The wind has commenced to blow, and the Kamaainas say that this is nothing compared to what it will Blow when the Winter sets in. Rain and Wind comes together tearing down Houses, blowing the Roof off some of them. Their is the frame of what was once a Church but the roof was blown off last year but I hope this [year] will not be so bad.

The different religions are going Fast.[1] The Mormons on Sunday comeing 13th, the Calvanists on Tuesday 15th and the Catholics on Friday 16th. Napela has spoken to me to join the Calvanists, but I pointed to my Prayer Book which was lying on the table in front of me.

One man died this morning and was burried. I heard this and told it to Mrs Napela. She said it was nothing new as they die almost every day. I employ myself by reading Scott's works [which] I got from Ragsdale. The poor fellow is so poor in health that he is confined the greater part of the time to his bed. I see him accadantly when Napela and I ride to the beach when their is any arrivals.

I must now close. My Aloha to Aunt Fanny and All your Domestics.

Farewell

KEKUAOKALANI

1. After establishment of the settlement in 1866, the Reverend Anderson O. Forbes, the American Protestant clergyman for Molokai, occasionally visited Kalaupapa by coming over the pali trail from the mission station at Kaluaha on the south side of the island. Before the end of 1866, about thirty-five inmates organized themselves with Forbes' help into a church body with names inscribed in a register. Funds were raised, a site was selected, and Siloama Church (Church of the "Healing Spring") was completed between July and October 1871. Meanwhile Roman Catholic priests also occasionally visited Kalaupapa. Brother Bertrand in 1872 built a wooden chapel in Honolulu and transported it to Kalawao, where it was set up on a hillside not far from Siloama. Father Damien took up his permanent station on Molokai on May 10, 1873. Later, a stone church, built and almost completed by Damien, replaced Brother Bertrand's wooden chapel of Saint Philomena. J. H. Napela, assistant supervisor of the settlement and a Mormon elder, held meetings outdoors, frequently among the trees in the crater of Kauhako Hill. On May 3, 1873, John Moanauli, member of the Privy Council, published in the Hawaiian newspaper *Kuokoa* an optimistic report on Kalaupapa, including its religious facilities: "They have two fine churches, one for Catholics and the other for Protestants. They are filled every Sunday. Their members serve as preachers." (Translated.) No white Protestant minister went to live at Kalaupapa until after the death of Father Damien in 1889.

Letter 8
Peter to Emma

Kalaupapa
July 11, 1873

Queen Emma

I was reading over the *Hawaii Ponoi* when I came across Hiram's Article.[1] Oh how it made me feel so sad. Recollections of the past was like a Panorama to me.

In some of my former Letters to you I wrote to you to send me up some Sardines etc. If this letter is not too late, do not send it up as the Store at Kalawao is opend today and Eatebels can be got as well as clothing. But shoes—their are none fit to wear and no cloth shoes of white, which is the esyest for my foot. The discription I believe I gave to you in my letter of Yesterday the 10th. A pair which will fit Hiram will fit me, as my foot is swolen and he wears a large shoe.

I have not been to the Store yet for I know it will be full of Sick people. But what came up for the Store I learned from Mr Rose,[2] Wilder's Book Keeper. He flattered me very much when he came into my House and saw how it looked inside. [He] said it was Clean, Neat and Airy enough for any King to live in [and] that nobody ought to be afraid to stop in it although it's in Kalawao. The men are begining to carry away the stones on the little Wheel Borrows which is very handy.

I have received a letter from Mr Hall saying as the Schooner *Warwick* was to sail so soon he could not hold a meeting of the Board, but as Trousseau[3] is comeing by the *Kilauea* he could do what he thought propper with orders from the Board of Health.

I can now expect my dog if you will send it up as I have got a Milking Cow. Thank Lucy if you please for me for takeing care of my little Dogy that I left in her charge. I wrote to Aikoe in my letter to her to send me up a little calabash of Poi as the one I have here is too large for the use of one person. I think it must have been left behind.

I must say Good Bye as Mr Rose is going over the Pali and am in a hurry.

Aloha
KEKUAOKALANI

1. I have been unable to trace an article by Hiram Kahanawai, Emma's steward, in *Hawaii Ponoi*. Perhaps the article was unsigned; or perhaps it was published in some other newspaper.

2. S. B. Rose, an employee of Samuel G. Wilder, member of the Board of Health. Rose was bookkeeper for Wilder's merchandising firm, but he also assisted Wilder in matters related to the Board of Health and the operation of the steamer *Kilauea*.

3. Dr. George Trousseau (1833–1894), port physician of Honolulu and member of the Board of Health; son of Armand Trousseau (1801–1867), noted Paris physician and authority on clinical medicine, author of three volumes in *Cliniques médicales de l'Hôtel-Dieu*, considered a masterpiece of French medical literature. Dr. George Trousseau studied at École de Médecine, Paris; practiced in Algiers and Italy while serving as a member of a French military battalion. Arrived in Hawaii by way of Australia and New Zealand in 1872; appointed almost immediately to King Lunalilo's Board of Health.

Letter 9
Peter to Emma

Kalaupapa
July 16, 1873

Her Majesty Queen Emma

I was taken all aback when I read your letter of 7th from the Mausoleum and also of the death of poor Faithful Nahalau who died performing his duty as Keeper of the Royal Mausileum—may he rest in peace.

You also say of a man by the name of Waiahole told Fanny that Napela and Ragsdale landed from the Schooner drunk, all of which is a falsehood. Napela came on board as Luna,[1] a white man also came off by the name Beers[2] who had a case of Whiskey. They, Napela, Beers, the Captain and Halulu[3] drank one Bottle of his Whiskey. When all was ready we went ashore and was entertained by Kupihea.[4] It was on shore that Ragsdale came to see me, and it was at Kupihea's that Ragsdale pointed out this man to me and he Waiahole began to cry. At table another Bottle was opened. I asked Kupihea to take a glass and he refused, so I made the remark, ʌ "We are two missionaries.",ʌ [5] All the rest took a glass and Waiahole too. After breakfast this man began to *Hula*[6] which was quite evedant the Liquor was taken effect. All the rest were quite sober. Two Bottles could not have made Seven men drunk. So I hope, dear Emma, you will cancele this off your mind.

I am still takeing my medecine regular. My Foot has broken out again. I think it must be the work of the medicine, as I do not walk much. I am at home all the time till the Schooners arrive. Then I saddle up and go down to the landing with Napela, he as Luna, and I to look out for my things, for a person cannot be too careful here. Send me up a Pair of White Shoe with India rubber on the sides, No. 11, such as Hiram use to wear. Also send me up a small Bottle of Camphire, as that is used to put on the kerchief to smell when passing the Hospital on our way to Bathe.

> Let fate do her worst
> Their are relix of Joy
> Bright dreams of the past
> Which She can ne'er destroy
> Which comes in the night time
> Of Sorrow and care
> To bring back the features
> That joy used to wear.
> —Moore—

Now Your Majesty let me bid you another long Farewell.

Your Humble Servant unto Death
KEKUAOKALANI

1. Supervisor.

2. Probably Henry A. Beers, who in 1872 applied for a license to operate a store at Kalaupapa but was refused.

3. Constable and inmate of the settlement.

4. S. K. Kupihea, a kamaaina of Molokai, magistrate, and later member of the Hawaiian House of Representatives.

5. This passage and all passages hereafter enclosed in carets are translated.

6. The word may refer to dancing or to singing and chanting or to both. Molokai was famous for its sportive dances (*hula ku'i Moloka'i*), but this performance was probably untraditional. Which particular member of the party began the revelry is not clear.

Letter 10
Peter to Emma

Kalaupapa
July 16, 1873
5 o'clock Evening

Queen Emma

My last letter was writen in such a hurry I did not have time to say about Our affairs up here. As I write this the rain is just seting in and I have just had a Shower Bath. It has just cost me $3 for water for Cooking, my Horses and myself. Until I get my Casks up when the Trough for the Verandah comes, I will then probably send for the Plants, but shurely not before.

I have had a call from the Catholic Priest.[1] He has been Converting some Natives and a Woman by the name of Hila, Mrs Tallant once,[2] has become a member of that Church. He has not spoken a word about Religion to me. I think that Bill Ragsdale told him that I belong to the Reformed Church. He is a very nice man and he has told Napela for all the diferent Religions to set aside a day for Fasting.

Captain Ahuihala of the Schooner that took me up has just asked me who was to pay for the things he took up for me. I told him I did not know, unless it was you, but I could as I have some money left.

Napela has just told me that they tried a man for burying another one which was eat by the Hogs. It seams the now Prisoner was the son of the man he buryed and the decision is Six days in Prison, which we have one.[3]

I am going to get as much *Kokuas*[4] as I can get from Trousseau, as we need them a great deal. Their are some without fingers and some without foot, and those that are diseased will not take care or help them unless paid, but the Kokuas do have some sympathy for those inflicted with the disease.

The woman Fanny wrote to me about, *Lelekahanu*, I have spoken to, and she is wiling to wash my clothes. Her Husband died yesterday, and until I get permission from Trousseau for Napaepae's daughter to remain, I think I have got to send for her. Their are quite a number of persons not inflicted, Men and Women that are here hiding themselves in day time and till night, [when they] come out to their several relations. Their is a rumer here that the Board of Health is going to have all the Horses killed as they eat all the grass and [leave] none for the Cattle. The Natives say if so, ^ "There will be trouble," ^ as that is their only means of conveying their water from the watering place.

July 17.—The Natives has just heard that the Doctor is sick and have not come up. The Kokuas especially are scared of being all sent away, so some of them are hiding in caves, and some of them calling themselves Kokuas.[5]

I must now wind up as the *Warwick* is about to sail.

Good Bye

KEKUAOKALANI

1. Father Damien (1840–1889), member of the Congregation of the Sacred Hearts; son of Frans and Anne-Catherine De Veuster, Flemish farmers; born at Tremeloo, near Louvain, Belgium, and baptized Joseph De Veuster; died at Kalaupapa of nodular leprosy. He arrived on Molokai to "work among the lepers" on May 10, 1873, about two months before the arrival of Peter Kaeo. Gavan Daws has written a discerning biography, *Holy Man: Father Damien of Molokai* (New York: Harper and Row, 1973), which succeeds in making "historical and biographical sense out of the life of a man who may one day be the Congregation's first saint."

2. The wife of N. W. Tallant of Maui, who was granted a divorce in July 1873. Hawaiian laws facilitated divorce when one spouse contracted leprosy.

3. A description of the Kalaupapa jail written by an ironic observer was published in *Kuokoa*, Sept. 20, 1873:

> The lepers' prison is a beautiful building. . . . Here it stands on the south-west side of the Superintendent's house. . . . The house was built as place of confinement for any patient who creates a disturbance and for those who break the rules of the Board of Health. Therefore this is a Report to you who are stricken with leprosy, those who still live in various parts of the Kingdom, that here in Kalawao stands a majestic jail awaiting you. Honolulu is not the only place with a jail—here is one for you in Kalawao. It crouches like a cat about to pounce on a rat. When small creatures grow a little careless, Bonaparte catches a bird to eat—a little breakfast of a lazy morning!
>
> The son of the beautiful grove now goes home.
>
> [S/] W. N. P. Heleiokalani
[Translated]

4. Native "helpers," willing to serve the inmates, often relatives.

5. A reference, perhaps, to nominal *kōkua* who shirked their jobs.

Letter 11
Emma to Peter

[Honolulu]
July 18, 1873

... Piolani[1] has just written to Kapo[2] from town saying (I suppose
her authority is Taffy)[3] the Americans since Colonel Steinberger's[4]
arrival have changed the selection of spot to take away from us from
Puuloa to Hilo Bay where the Colonel has gone to be with Mr Henry
Peirce.[5]

I like the *excessive* impudance of that race. What people possessed
of any love of country, patriotism, identity and loyalty can calmly
and passively sit and allow foreigners to their soil arrogating to
themselves the right of proposing cession of the native borns' soil,
in spite of their unanimous protests? My blood boils with resentment
against this insult. The sentiment is so thorougerly and entirely a
wrong one on the part of the foreigners.

Do you keep your notebook or journal? If so you will find it will
give pleasure in after days to look back over them and see how time
has been spent, whether idled or some good to others. People,
incidents and facts forgotten will all be there fresh for you to laugh
or be vexed over. It keeps one in the habit of writing and you know
practice makes perfect.

When you speak of the differance of churches to the people there,
that is should you have occasion to do so, be particular to give the
Roman Church her proper distinction which is the Roman Catholic
Church whilst ours is the Anglican Catholic Church, the ancient name
of Great Briton. There are more branches than one of the Catholic
Church, just as each [of the] 12 apostles catered to different parts of
the old world to spread the new religion at our Savour's death,
according to his express orders, "Go ye into all the world and baptise
them in the name of the Trinity, preach the gospel to every creature."
You will find that command at the end of the four gospels and read
of their carrying it out in the "Acts of the Apostles."

Some of them went to Persia, others to Africa, to Russia, and
Saints Peter and Paul were portioned out to convert the great world
renown city of and country near Rome to the new religion which was
destined to permeate the whole world. Rome then was the seat of all

learning. Consequently their efforts took effect quicker than those who worked in other parts of the world. All worked with constant danger to their lives and did end at the cost of their lives. All the north of Europe when our Savour lived on earth was almost unknown and their inhabitants called savages. St Paul[6] landed in England and planted the Church there and when in after years, as the same Church of Christ had flourished splendidly in Rome and became large and strong, it also got somewhat sadly corropted.

She appointed a head over herself called a Pope, which none of the other branches of the Catholic Church did, and began to assert her authority over the other branches of the same religion, till she the Roman Church finally denied the works of the other apostles and declared there's was the only true Catholic Church (Catholic simply means universal or one, everywhere and always) and took those verses in the Gospels where Jesus after his reserection particularly repeated to St Peter, "If you love me feed my lambs and sheep," and again in another place, "Thou art Peter and on this rock I shall build my church and the gates of Hell shall not prevail against thee."...

[The Roman Catholic Church deteriorated] till she assumed that the Pope is God on earth and therefore can do no sin. He is Immaculate. There are numerous wicked things she teaches that are strongly opposed by the Greek, Anglican and the rest of the Catholic Churches, and it is just these wickednesses in her [that] caused the reformation 400 years ago by Martin Luther, who was a Roman Priest, and again the reformation of 1869 when Bishop Maigret[7] of Honolulu went to the meeting of Roman Bishops at Rome and was present when a very great many of them stood up and dared to face the Pope and hundreds of other Bishops, [denounced] the errors of their Roman branch and left it just as Luther did and for the same reasons, which has grown worse of late years. Those Bishops are now exposing the errors of the Roman Church and have formed themselves into a Church which they call the "Old Catholic Church."

If you were to tell a Roman priest that, they will deny such events occured. If I should find a small book called *A History of the English Church* which is somewhere among my books, I will post it to [you so] it may help you understand the diferance of the two branches of the Church Catholic.

When the casks are up you had better have the two water barrels you took with you put up also under one of the troughs. There is no harm to have all the water you can get. Whenever the ship captains ask about payment of freight refer them to me.

You have beaten me in the commiting of poetry to memory. . . .

[KALELEONĀLANI]

This letter was written from Kahala, July 17th.

[Memorandum]
bottle of Camphire
pair of white canvas shoes   } to be
sardines   sent
dog   this
small calabash   week

1. Mrs. David Kalākaua, later Queen Kapi'olani (1834–1899); grand-daughter of Kaumuali'i, last king of island of Kauai. Married twice, first to a Maui chief named Namakeha; then in 1863 to Kalākaua. She was crowned queen in 1883 at the time of Kalākaua's coronation; in 1887 she attended Queen Victoria's Golden Jubilee, where she received royal honors. Kapi'olani and Kalākaua had no children. After Kalākaua's death, her principal interest was the Kapiolani Hospital, Honolulu, still in existence, which she established and helped to support.

2. Familiar name of Kapo'oloku, a younger sister of Mrs. David Kalākaua; for main note, Letter 17, note 4.

3. Nickname of David Kalākaua, later King Kalākaua; for main note, see Letter 16, note 7.

4. Col. A. B. Steinberger, personal friend of President Grant and confidential agent of Hamilton Fish, U.S. secretary of state, charged with gathering information about the Samoan Islands. His stopover in Hawaii had nothing specifically to do with Pearl Harbor or Hawaiian affairs, although Fish had made to him an "oral suggestion" that he might be an "observer" while in Hawaii on his way to Samoa.

5. Henry Augustus Peirce (b. Dorchester, Mass., 1808; d. San Francisco, 1885); United States minister resident at Honolulu 1869–1877. Former Honolulu merchant 1831–1843; a founder of twentieth-century firm of Charles Brewer and Co., Ltd. In ministerial reports, Peirce stated that the majority of American missionaries, sugar planters, and merchants were in favor of annexation, that more than three-fourths of the natives were opposed. He recommended a policy of watchful waiting and prompt adoption of a reciprocity treaty with Hawaii, accepting in return cession of Pearl Harbor: "This measure would bind the island to the United States with hoops of steel";

the Hawaiian nation was "destined to pass through the throes of a new national birth before it is prepared to adopt the proper measure to give security and prosperity to the people"; the death of King Lunalilo or the economic breakdown and bankruptcy of the government might "precipitate the desired event." (Henry A. Peirce to Hamilton Fish, no. 206, May 26, 1873 [U. S. Dept. of State Dispatches, Hawaii, Vol. XV].)

6. It was St. Augustine of Canterbury (d. 604) who brought Christianity to England from Rome.

7. Louis Désiré Maigret (1804–1882), vicar apostolic to the Sandwich Islands, under the title of bishop of Arathia, from 1848 for more than thirty years. He had attended the Vatican Council convoked by Pope Pius IX, which sat December 1869–October 1870, and eventually issued the definition of Papal Infallibility.

Letter 12
Peter to Emma

Kalaupapa
July 20, 1873

Queen Emma

I hope this will reach you in good health—Oh would that I were in its place. I am going to kill my little Pig tomorrow the 21st—Aunt's birthday—"Fanny." Yesterday I told my man to go and fish for some fish for tomorrow. It has commenced to blow very strong and is blowing still as I write. A Schooner hove in sight yesterday and when near the landing I saddled my little Pony and rode down but was disappointed, as it sailed away to the windward as though mocking me.

My horse J. Puni[1] I have hired a man to look out for, to take him from place to place inside the place fenced in for cultivation. He is rather poor. The poor natives are begining to die almost dayly. I went to Waikolu last week to bath and heard that Lelekahanu's husband was dead, so send for her. I asked her to stop with me, but she said she had another Kane.[2] On my way back, I met the natives carting a dead man to be buried roled up in a blanket.

I have used the last of my Poi you sent up in the bags—*Tarrow*—and am now eating my allowance as a Leper of Pai.[3] It is so stormy that the boats cannot come close in shore, but throw it on the rocks. . . .

The Catholic Priest called on me last Friday the 18th. He had been calling on the Sick. We got to talking on diferent matters till we got to Religion. He asked me whether I was ever Babtized. I told him I was. He asked me whether I had any Catholic Papers. I told him I had not but pointed to my Prayer Books. He then opened one and asked me whether I belonged to the Church of England. I told him I did. Then he said their was very little diferance between the English and Catholic Church, that they the Catholics acknowledge the Pope as their head and the Queen as the head of the Church of England. I told him I believed and was satisfied in the Church I am now in and that alone. So we dropet the subject but I do really believe he wanted to get me in theirs.

The ox carts have been so buisy that they have not had time to cart the big stones away from before my House, [none] but the little stones. The Wheel Borrow has done its duty, till my fence and Trough for water comes up. Then I will commence to clean my little Garden.

July 22d.—I had my little dinner yesterday the 21, and my little House was very near set fire by a match thrown after lighting the pipe, but [that] was put out and nothing *Pilikia*.[4] Today has been the best day here, quite calm and not so much wind. I watch daily the Horizon to see if I can see a Sail—but no, so I must wait.

Good Bye

I remain

KEKUAOKALANI

1. Named after a friend of Peter who had given him the horse as a going-away present. During the 1860s, John Puni operated a Honolulu cooperage business, a portion of which housed a bookshop and circulating library patronized by Queen Emma.

2. Husband or lover.

3. A reference to *pa'i 'ai*: pounded undiluted taro forming hard cakes.

4. No damage done.

Letter 13
Emma to Peter

[Oahu]
July 21, 1873

Ever dear Coz

My Mother is this day 70 years old. Is not that a good ripe age to live out on this miserable melancholy earth of ours? Yet she is erect, strong, active, full of work, fun and scolding. What would not 70 years doing good to our fellow being be to us? Would it not be grand to have done something of like nature to God's when He lived on Earth?—

No more of this, or I may scare you with anticipations of another dry religious sermon. I was so carried away with my subject of the right title to give the differant Catholic Churches that I forgot myself last time.

That is a good description of your house, situation, and distances. Just as you have watched the fury of the sea near the bath place, so has your Coz at the Hanauma Bay[1] points, looking towards Molokai, [been] enjoying the grandure of nature's display in the dashing waves which

so limp and no hurt when lying amidst

but death itself in its extreme motion then the words of the duet we used to sing by C. Dickens, "What are the wild waves saying"[2]

and seemed full of voices as if threatened to snatch
me off the narrow ledges of rock along the cliff into
its murderous bosom
at those times terror would only seize me

[KALELEONĀLANI]

---

1. A picturesque rocky cove on the windward coast of Oahu, facing Molokai and Lanai, about ten miles from central Honolulu. Emma probably was visiting a favorite country place and fishing ground formerly owned by her brother-in-law, Kamehameha V, sometimes described as his "marine villa," at Koko Head, near Hanauma Bay.

2. Title of a popular Victorian set of verses and song, in ballad form, by Joseph Edwards Carpenter, based on little Paul Dombey's "conversation" about the North Sea in Dickens' *Dombey and Son* (1847–1848). In performing the duet, Emma sang the verses of Florence Dombey, Peter those of little Paul.

Letter 14
Peter to Emma

Kalaupapa
July 23, 1873

Queen Emma

Oh how happy I was when I received your letters. I have been watching so, daily, for a Schooner to come up from Honolulu and bring me news from Home Sweet Home, and likewise to hear from you. Never did that word *Home* sound so sweet and dear to me as it does now. I was so sorry to hear that your little Black Horse is dead, and to hear that his poor mate is left alone.

I wish people would mind their own business and let mine alone.[1] Ragsdale is down to the beach and I do not see him till I go down to deliver my letters. In order to get out of the Sun[2] I have to go to his House and set by the mauka[3] window till I come home. It is when riding to Waikolu that he comes up going into Kalawao, that we go together, as he hardly ever dismounts. His foot is so swolen I gave him my white shoes, as they were too small for my swolen sore foot, and he has given me his Rubber shoes he use to wear outside of his Boots.

My health is good. I rest coumfortabley and I hope with time and patience I may with the Allmighty's care recover.

My little cottage is very neat, the neatest and most airy (although I have to say it myself) here. My house stands on a rise faceing the Sea on a flat between the Pali and Kauhako Hill. On the right side of my house in the corner is my Beurow. Back of that on the sides hangs my Hats, near the windows hang my Coats, under the window is my old Koa trunk,[4] in the mauka north corner is my bed, between the front and back door hangs the curtain seperating my dresing and bedroom from the seting room and Palour. On the left or East corner is my Sofa, by the window my Rocker, makai[5] or South corner my little table. Nearest the corner on the Table is my Atlas, Journal, Dairy and Prayer Books. Next to that are my American Papers I got from Crabbe[6] through Wilder, and Portfolio. Next to that is my English and American Papers I got from you, and also the Honolulu papers. Above the table hangs the clock. A little in front of the Atlas is my writing materials. Takeing it all through, it looks quite respectable.

On the right side and little to the rear of the House is my Cook house with two rooms, one to cook and another for to pound Poi and Keep my Potatoes, etc. My two back rooms, one is a store room kept lock, the other a dining room. So here I am, quite well in health but not in mind.

I am glad to here Joe[7] has got the place left vacant by poor Nahalau's death, as I think he is a good man. I am so glad to hear the King will not consent to giving Puuloa. I hope he will keep his word. I have just herd that no Schooner will touch here but *Warwick*. . . .

I commenced to hire men to work yesterday the 22d, Four men to dig the stones up and throw them in the Ox cart at .50 cts a day, and two Ox cart drivers at the same price, amounting to $3 a day, which will last all this week I think. I stop at home to overseer them, but the ground is so hard that I had to borrow the Pic Ax and Crowbar, which belongs to the Board of Health, for them to work with. I wish when I send for the plants for you to give a discription of them and what kind of Trees, whether I have seen them at Home, so that I will know whare to plant them, [like] the Trees that are growing at the Hospital.[8] I should like to plant them in a row behind my House to shelter my House from the wind, and the others on the Sides and in front of my House, but I will not send until the rainy season sets in.

We the people of Molokai sent here by the Board as Lepers are under Allowance of food. A House whare it holds two or more patients [is allowed] one [share of] Pai and 3 pounds of rice, half of Pai and half of Rice everywhare. The natives began to grumble on account of their having rice all the week round and very little Poi. Napela has begun to have Beef killed at the Beach so as not to let those poor men without fingers handle the meat for those at the Beach. Our meat is so poor that we do not see any fat or signs of any hardly after it is dressed and delivered.

I was just reading a article in the *Advertiser* and a Letter writen by Ragsdale to Severance, and stating the condition and affairs of the poor.[9] Some have no cooking utensils to cook with, so they ask for Salmon in place of Beef—but no Salmon. Some ask for rice in place of Pai, as the Pai is bad and sower, but Rice is scarce and only for those in the Hospital. And it has actually been so [bad] that it is just as much as I could do for me to hear them ask for something and to not get it. I came very near giving some of what little I got, but I did not know when my turn would come so I kept mine and am going to keep it too. Thank God I have a kind Queen to take care of poor me. I have alwais thought what heart Napela have to refuse these poor people, but he cannot give what he cannot and has not got. It is now just a fortneight since the last Schooner touched here to bring up some more rice, and I cannot see how Ragsdale [could] say in his letter that the people here are better provided for then at their own home—he might [be] but not all.

July 24 at 5 in the afternoon.—I have just got back from Waikolu, the only River here whare a person can have a good Bath—Mrs Napela, Hila, Ragsdale, and four or five more. Knowing it quite safe to go with them in Open Air and bathing in runing water, I was not afraid.

I have heard my Picket fence is come but have not seen it, as I cannot go just now, but got to write to you at Home as the Schooner is in a hury to sail. I think you have forgoten the Shoes I wrote to you [about]. I hope you are enjoying yourself at Hanauma.

I cannot come to see you so you must excuse me till a more convenient time. Good Bye.

In haste
Your Humble Cousin
KEKUAOKALANI

1. Peter resented gossip about the drinking party; see Letter 9.

2. Lepers were advised to avoid sunburn and skin injuries of any kind.

3. Side facing mountains.

4. Made of native wood, *koa*, from tree of same name, *Acacia koa*.

5. Side facing ocean.

6. Horace G. Crabbe (b. Philadelphia, Penn., 1837; d. Honolulu, 1903), King Lunalilo's chamberlain. Son of H. N. Crabbe, one-time U.S. naval agent, who arrived in Hawaii with his family in 1847.

7. Joe Keaoa had recently been appointed keeper of the Royal Mausoleum.

8. Eucalyptus trees (*Eucalyptus globulus*), at that time a novelty in Hawaii, growing in front of the Queen's Hospital, Honolulu. Their aromatic oil, according to an item in the *Pacific Commercial Advertiser*, Apr. 25, 1873, was "an effective remedy against malarious diseases of all types," and the trees when "cultivated in gardens, will contribute to sanifying the atmosphere from those emanations which give rise to epidemic diseases."

9. Dr. George Trousseau, physician and member of Board of Health, published a letter on leprosy in the *Pacific Commercial Advertiser*, July 12, 1873. Peter may well have read this letter, but articles and correspondence on the subject were frequent in all newspapers in 1873. Ragsdale's personal letter to Luther Severance, sheriff of the island of Hawaii and agent of the Board of Health, was published in Hawaiian in the native newspaper, *Hawaii Ponoi*, July 9: "I have been meaning to write you a few short lines from this place, where my responsibilities are so heavy, and show that I have not forgotten you. ... I have found that the lepers living here have been very well fed and clothed, better cared for than they were in their own homes. ..." In a later letter to Severance, *Pacific Commercial Advertiser*, Oct. 18, 1873, Ragsdale gives an equally complacent account of conditions, with fuller details.

Letter 15
Peter to Emma

Kalaupapa
July 27, 1873

Queen Emma

Last evening a Schooner was in Sight, so I had my Pony ready to go down this morning, but on riseing she was no whare to be Seen. I felt so sad that I sat watching from my Verandah the Island you are on—*Home*. I had a dream last night that I was at Home and was dressing to go out, but on looking at the Glass I saw my Eye Brow was gone so I felt so shame that I came back to Molokai.

Then I climbed a Pali with several other natives, and they called out to me not to go up any more for fear I would fall, but I kept climbing till I reached the top. Then I looked down and saw my perilous position and was so frighten of falling, and in my fright woke.

I told this to Napela, and he said if this was a true Dream, that I am not going to remain here long but that I am comeing home. Oh happy hour if ever it does come.

Last Friday I paid the men off for working—Ten Dollars, and not one Quarter of the work through, as the [stone walls for] beds of the Once Potatoe Patches are so well imbedded in the ground that It is quite dificult to get them up unless dug out. But tomorrow the men are going to commence again, with some more men that are not bad with the disease that I think I ought to get through by this Week. Kumalae also is going to commence to finish the Cook House and also put the fence up.

My health is good. My Hand is improveing. I wear the Gauntlets on every night, and three pieces of flat sticks that I put inside the Gloves on the back of my Hand between the fingers and the glove, repeating the process every night. Now they are quite straight. My foot is still Sore, but blood comes from it when I walk much on it, instead of matter. The Swelling also still remain. The pain is not much but enough to be disagreeable. I do not walk much, only in and about the House, and around the yard to see whare the fence is to be put up.

All the remaining "Kamaainas" have chosen Ragsdale to be their Lawyer to plead their case to Wilder when he comes up, as they wish to remain here and die. . . .

As I pen these lines to you, I can distinctly see Oahu, the Nuuanu Pali, and that large Gap at Kalihi—"Oh Home sweet Home.". . .

Monday 28th. . . . The Kamaainas and Sick men at the beach have joined together and want one of themselves to be their Luna, instead of one appointed by Napela. Ragsdale is at the head of all this.

July 30. This morning Ragsdale came up with his men to help my men to work, when the mail man made his appearance from Kaunakakai, who informed Napela that Meyer[1] was on his way here. So Ragsdale told all his men to go home to the beach to hear him Plead their case, and the Kamaainas to go home also their place, till they heard again from him—"Ragsdale."

So not a Kamaaina is to be seen, as they are strickly prohibited by the Board of Health not to go prowling from House to House and assosiating with the Lepers.

Mr Meyer called on me as soon as he came from the Pali, my house being the nearest to the road, and right on the way to Napela's. I spoke to him about my Man and Girl, and their being old Kamaainas. He spoke very kindly and said it was not the wish of the Board of Health to deprive any person of help from Kamaainas so long as they "Kamaainas" wished to remain here and die, and not to go away from the Places set apart for the Lepers. But it was to keep persons away from comeing and mixing with those that have got the Leper. He said he had got orders from the Board of Health to assist those that have not got a Permit from the Board. But as he is alone, and [the problem is] not his business, so he has notified Smith, the Sheriff of Lahaina, [whom] he "Meyer" expects next week, [along with] Wilder and Trousseau [who] will be up by next Tuesday. So they will all come up and over the Mountain together. Ragsdale says he is ready to plead for the remaining Kamaainas. Some of them are quite *desparate.* . . .

A man just said to me after Meyer left, in presence of Kaawa, that they were only waiting for orders from me—that they were willing to do anything I said in the way of disturbance, as they were sent here to die by the Government, and as they were willing to die now as any other time. But I checked him and told him to tell the rest to have patience till we hear from Wilder or from the Board.

I must rest now till I hear more from Meyer when he returns from Kalawao. . . .

5 P.M. Mr Meyer has consented to let the Kamaainas remain till Mr Wilder comes up. I think I have got a good chance to speak for them myself and not Ragsdale.

July 31. 10 A.M. The Schooner *Warwick* has just arrived and is to Sail as soon as the Freight is discharged. . . . So I will write and send over to Kaunakakai and let you know whether I have received everything safe. The Dog is all right.

Good Bye
KEKUAOKALANI

1. Rudolph W. Meyer (1826–1897), rancher of Molokai and chief supervisor of the Kalaupapa settlement from its origin in 1865–1866 until 1897. Born in Hamburg, Germany; arrived in Hawaii in 1848; married the Chiefess Kalama, who owned land at Kalae, Molokai. He also became manager of an extensive cattle and sheep ranch on Molokai owned by the Princess Ruth Keʻelikōlani, half-sister of Kamehameha IV and Kamehameha V. The ranch, covering a total of about 150,000 acres, stretched from the vicinity of Kaunakakai to the western end of the island, and from the seashore to the *pali* back of the settlement. After the princess' death in 1883, Meyer continued as manager for her principal heir, the High Chiefess Bernice Pauahi Bishop.

Letter 16
Emma to Peter

[Honolulu]
July 29 [1873]

Ever dear Coz

The *Warwick* takes up a few things as per list. Jane Jasper[1] was here yesterday and told Hipa[2] that Kanaina[3] has got the Leprosy and is taken to Waikiki. The truth of this I cannot vouch for. Wait till you hear further. Mr Charles Judd[4] met Lucy on the Square[5] Saturday afternoon [when she] took Grace out for the music and sight, and asked if I had heard from you. She replied in the affirmative, so he said, "Tell him not to have any communication with Bill Ragsdale, for we hear Bill has been much with him."

People have all heard of the feast you gave on Hipa's birthday, when many unfortunate lepers gathered round the house and it [so narrowly] escaped fire. I know it is (as you say) very anoying to have everything noticed and reported concerning oneself. I think you should know [the lepers], but realize that although out of Honolulu [you are] yet observed with interest.

So you see you cannot be too careful of yourself. Ultimate recovery is worth years of patient, happy working to hasten that, and our country will need [and] does need your services. Prepare yourself for her by reading the newsapapers of the day, and compare them, finding out who is for independance and salvation of her race and who against. And keep also the run of the names of the principle leaders of American and European Governments—they all are public characters. The unsettled state of Spain and very moveable foundation of the temporary Republic of Paris and the suspicion of Prussia against France are all interesting, for the former is armed at a moment's pretext to war upon [France] and keep her again down. The Dutch in Achten India[6] is watched by the world with interest.

To enter into an argument is sometimes instructing, as it sharpens one's thoughts on the subject, besides getting into the habit of debating and discussing. If you can be with Ragsdale (in the air not the house) and converse without personal contact, do so—for he is a superior mind, and [while] you are away improve yourself without his suspecting you, using him for your means. Reading aloud to oneself is more improving than you think. Interesting subjects or passages I read slowly, and sometimes almost act them. I so constantly think of you taking your place at the legislative debate, and giving your oppinion in councils, that I grow tiresome to you by letter.

But never despond or slacken—"Excelcior" be our motto. Then we will take our ancestors' places with worth. Taffy[7] is constantly meeting and filling the natives' minds with public sentiments of the day—on cession of territory—and tells them to suggest at the coming Legislature displacing or dethroneing the King for ignorance, drunkeness, utter incompetancy, for by [these failings] he jeopredizes the country's fate. He tells them the King has agreed [to] cession and really some foolish men have imbibed the sentiment, but I believe it can be quickly dispelled. He held a drill last night I believe at the Armory—I do not know what troops. This is all for public display and [to] play on the people's credulity and ignorance.

Save and file your papers so as you can refer to them. I am up to my ears with work, geting Grace and Stella[8] ready for school on the 4th [of] next month. Aikoe[9] took down the name "Camphire" on a slip of paper to the white person who is treating you,[10] and she has returned with two bottles of camphor, which he says is the thing he advised you to smell whilst passing the leper establishment, or when near any leper. So here they [call it] "Camphor" instead of "Camphire." . . .

I am in a hurry so end with Aloha nui loa[11] from your ever dear Coz.

KALELEONALANI

The old man Waiahole comes up by this trip and has your little dog. He never said you *were* drunk, but that he saw others drinking in your company, which corresponds with what you wrote me. He has heard of his wife's death—that is why he goes up.

1. Jane Loeau Jasper (1828–1873), a descendant of high chiefs of Kauai; divorced wife of John Jasper, American lawyer. Attended Chiefs' Children's School when Emma was also a pupil.

2. "Sheep"; affectionate name of Fanny Kekelaokalani, Emma's mother.

3. Charles Kana'ina (1801–1877), father of King Lunalilo, husband of High Chiefess Miriam Auhea Kekauluohi (d. 1845), Lunalilo's mother; for many years member of the House of Nobles and Privy Council. Gossip among Hawaiians that various well-known persons were lepers was common. Peter

later reported that Samuel G. Wilder, a member of the Board of Health, had become afflicted; in 1874 Emma noted a Honolulu rumor that Kalākaua had leprosy.

4. Charles Hastings Judd (1836–1890), Lunalilo's adjutant general; grazier and landowner on Oahu. A son of Dr. Gerrit P. Judd (1803–1872), former American medical missionary to Hawaii who became a cabinet minister and key figure in the government of Kamehameha III.

5. Queen Emma Square, in central Honolulu near present St. Andrew's Cathedral on the side toward mountains. With occasional irregularities in schedule, band concerts were held there weekly every Sunday afternoon. *Nuhou*, April 11, 1873, noted that Emma Square was "the only pretty green spot that belongs to this town as a public ground, and considering that real estate in Honolulu is not so enormously costly, and that shrubbery grows all the year round, and that we have plenty of water—it is a shame that we have no other umbrageous spot to show to strangers but this little patch of Emma Square." *Nuhou* earlier published a tribute to "The Band," Feb. 25, 1873: "This is an institution of more immediate interest and satisfaction to our townspeople than even a reciprocity treaty.... Our talented bandmaster and his smart kanakas who 'toot the horns' are of more consequence in promoting good spirits and good digestion than all the politicians and doctors in town."

6. Atchin, in Sumatra, whose troubled affairs were regularly reported in the newspapers. The Dutch had recently demanded authority over all Atchin and the Atchinese were calling on Turkey for aid.

7. Familiar name of David Kalākaua (1836–1891), later King Kalākaua; son of Caesar Kapaʻakea and Ane Keohokālole and direct descendant of Keawe-a-Heulu, a first cousin of Kamehameha I. Educated at Chiefs' Children's School; aide-de-camp on staff of Kamehameha IV; postmaster general under Kamehameha V and occasional attorney. A candidate for throne in 1873, he was defeated in a popular election by William Charles Lunalilo. After Lunalilo's death, Kalākaua announced himself as a candidate for the kingship, his rival being the Dowager Queen Emma. In a ballot of the Hawaiian legislature, thirty-nine voted for Kalākaua, only six for Emma. Kalākaua assumed office Feb. 3, 1874; he immediately proclaimed as his successor his younger brother, William Pitt Leleiohoku (1855–1877). During a royal progress after his election, Kalākaua set forth his aims: "Let us thoroughly renovate ourselves, to the end that causes of decay being removed, the nation may grow again with new life and vigor and our government may be firmly established.... The increase of the people; the advancement of agriculture and commerce; these are the objects which my Government will mainly strive to accomplish." (Quoted in Ralph S. Kuykendall, *The Hawaiian Kingdom: 1874–1893: The Kalakaua Dynasty* [Honolulu: University of Hawaii Press, 1967], p. 13.) Kalākaua had two close allies in his ambitious program: Walter Murray Gibson, who became premier in 1882, and Claus Spreckels, the California "sugar baron," who with Kalākaua formed the triumvirate that "controlled the government for the next few years." (Ibid., p. 88.) From 1883 onward, Kalākaua's reign was marked by mounting

political tension and conflict. A large part of his revenue was poured into the pageantry of the royal office, in order to bolster the national pride of the Hawaiians and impress foreign powers; he was injudicious in selecting advisers and ministers; he moved in the direction of absolute monarchy and met prompt resistance, especially on the part of Americans, from groups who would tolerate only limited monarchy. The last years of his reign were troubled by party struggles and civil disorders when the several interests—the king and his supporters, successive cabinets and legislatures, and various factions in the community—attempted to maintain or seize from one another control of the government. The king was on vacation in California at the time of his sudden death of Bright's disease, Jan. 20, 1891. The U.S.S. *Charleston*, bearing his casket back to the islands, sighted Diamond Head at seven o'clock in the morning on Jan. 29. Early in the afternoon of the same day his sister, Queen Lili'uokalani, signed and executed the oath of office pledging to uphold the Hawaiian constitution.

8. Stella Keomailani (later Mrs. Edwin K. Kea) (d. 1927), a high chiefess and granddaughter of an uncle of Emma named Namakehaokalani. She was a daughter of Emma's attendant, Kamakaaiau, and the deceased High Chief Hinau. Grace and Stella were pupils at St. Andrew's Priory, an Anglican school established in Honolulu in 1867 by the Reverend Mother Priscilla Lydia Sellon, founder of the Society of the Holy Trinity, at Devonport, England. The school buildings stood on a portion of the land given by Kamehameha IV for the cathedral (not yet constructed) of the Hawaiian Reformed Catholic church.

9. One of Emma's retainers, regularly assigned to looking after Peter's needs.

10. Jack Smith, a very close friend of Peter Kaeo, about whom not much is known. Among various letters Emma received in 1873 is a barely literate message from one "J Smith," swearing his loyalty to her cause. If this was Peter's friend, he may have been employed in a menial capacity in some general store in central Honolulu.

11. Everlasting love.

Letter 17
Peter to Emma

Kalaupapa
July 31, 1873

Queen Emma

Napela has just stopet the Schooner till the Tide comes down from Kalawao. So I can finish this better then I did the other one. . . .

I have been trying to find out from Ragsdale some secretes which I know he is possessed, as he gets private letters from Parke[1] and Wilder concerning Anexation, but he always answers my question in a off handed way, and for fear he may "Detect" and suspect me, I drop the subject to commence again at some more convenient time, always giving it a wide birth before opening the subject to him. This is generally done on Horseback going or coming from Bath.

I was so delighted reading Gibson's little *Nuhou*[2] giving it so to Bishop and Hall and the little questions and answers in Native that I read it to Napela and he also coinsided with me. He has been telling me to write to the King to marry you, but I told him that he had better write himself, so he said to me that he was going to write to you concerning Government and Private affairs, which will be in his estimation good for the King and Nation. The subject of his letter to you he has as yet not told me, so I think you will know it before I will, or perhaps I may never know about it.

I told my men to go and catch some fish for me, but when they returned with a very fiew, I asked the reason and they said the Lepers are everywhare in the water whare the "Kuunas"[3] are [so] that they cannot get much.

I hope Grace will have a good little companion and Schoolmate in Stella. Remember me to Aunt, Grace, Lucy, Kapo[4] and others. Good Bye.

Your Humble Cousin
KEKUAOKALANI

1. William C. Parke (1821–1889), marshal of the Hawaiian Islands from 1850 to 1884; born Portsmouth, N. H.; arrived in Hawaii 1843.

2. Gibson, editor of the scurrilously diverting newspaper called *Nuhou* ("News"), was Walter Murray Gibson, b. (?) 1822; d. San Francisco, 1888. Youthful adventurer in Central America and Sumatra; one-time Mormon

elder, excommunicated from church in Hawaii; editor of several Hawaiian newspapers during 1870s and 1880s; next to the king himself the leading personality in the government of Kalākaua. *Nuhou*, 1873–1874, was a mixture of political manifesto, folksy town topics, personal lampoon. Articles in Hawaiian as well as in English were devised, under policy of "Hawaii for the Hawaiians," to arouse the national consciousness of natives, frequently to the point of stirring interracial animosities among all groups. Article referred to by Kaeo is probably Gibson's editorial, July 22, 1873, entitled "The Ministers Have No Policy"; the attack was wholesale, Charles R. Bishop and E. O. Hall, banker and merchant, not being individually named. Same issue contains "the little questions and answers" mentioned by Peter; here probably a reference to article by Gibson headed "The Subsidized Native Organ of All Saints," in which Gibson attacks the Hawaiian-language newspaper *Kuokoa*.

3. Place where nets are set in the sea.

4. Short form for Kapoʻoloku (1841–1895), a younger sister of Mrs. David Kalākaua (later Queen Kapiʻolani); a descendant of ancient high chiefs of Kauai. Served several years in Emma's household as honored attendant. In 1874, after election of Kalākaua to the throne, Kapoʻoloku left Emma's service, married Hiram Kahanawai, Emma's steward and a cousin of Kalākaua, and both husband and wife transferred their allegiance to the new dynasty. Named Princess Poʻomaikelani by Kalākaua in 1883; at Kalākaua's coronation, a spectacular composite of Europeo-Christian and Polynesian symbolism, Poʻomaikelani presented Kalākaua with the *pūloʻuloʻo* (tabu stick), *palaoa* (necklace with whale's tooth), and the familiar feather standard emblematic of royalty, the kahili. Appointed governor of island of Hawaii in 1884. Served as first president of Kalākaua's secret genealogical-"anthropological" society, Hale Nauwa, established to study the ancient Hawaiian religion and way of life.

Letter 18
Peter to Emma

Kalaupapa
August 6, 1873

Queen Emma

I received yours of the 2d instant this morning with the greatest of pleasure. I was right glad to hear about Whitney's and Green's being put out by the Natives.[1] Serves them right. I see in the Papers [an item about] "Loeau's" death[2] which you did not mention. I hope the affair about Albert[3] will end as easy as the one when I was their, but the crazy fellow had better look out.

I took my ride last evening after my men got through their day's work to the Beach. I remained longer then usual, enjoying the Stillness of the Evening, inhailing the Sea breeze, casting a glance every now and then at *Oahu* to see if it was still visable, being glad to be alone and no one to intrude on my meditations. It was then that I felt one of those mystic attractions for "Home" which can only be explained by a person in my predicament. I was so taken with these thoughts that when I looked at Sweet Home it was lost to view, and I, benighted. So I returned Home by a very bad way over rocks and climpers[4] in order to be home for my Medicine before Supper. . . .

August 7. 9 P.M.—The Schooner is in sight and she only remains here long enough to discharge her Cargo, then goes right on, so I have to write and take my letter down as I go to the Beach and deliver them so as to make shure that they are on Board. Then if I have any letters from you, I ride back and read them and reread them to my Heart's content. Then I answer them and send them over land Via Kaunakakai, the Mail man going and comeing every Wednesday. My health is good, no change whatever. Napela says I am geting quite corpulent, although I eat very little, but my Appetite is also good.

My Aloha to Aunt, Grace, Lucy and Wikani.[5] I remain

Your Humble Servant

KEKUAOKALANI

1. Henry M. Whitney, editor of the *Hawaiian Gazette*, and J. Porter Green, Honolulu attorney, attended numerous public meetings in 1873, but there seems to be no record of their expulsion by Hawaiians. Probably Peter had in mind one or another of several important meetings held in late June and July 1873. An "Observer," writing in the *Hawaiian Gazette*, July 30, 1873, reported on a "Mass Meeting at Wailuku," July 24, on the reciprocity question, where there appeared "a slightly ferocious expression in the meeting, evidently induced by a much more pronounced expression of the same sort at Waihee on the evening before, at which the sentiment was said to be, 'Let the plantations go down if they will, they have been a curse to the country'—a reflection it will be seen from other quarters. This culminated at length when Mr. William Hoapili Kaauwai . . . brought in a series of resolutions . . . to the effect that as the ministers had shown their incompetence for anything better to save the government and nation than to cede away part of their territory, they be dismissed." An editorial in the *Hawaiian Gazette*, Dec. 17, 1873, later reported that "the attempt to put down Mr. Green at Kaumakapili Church certainly showed antagonism toward the speaker if not to foreigners generally. . . . At Wailuku, also, the animosity of a few natives towards foreigners was clearly shown, and came near terminating in open rupture." For main note on Henry M. Whitney, see Letter 55, note 2.

2. The sudden death of Loeau (Jane Jasper), July 30, "a descendent in the female line of the ancient chiefs of Kauai, and a reputed granddaughter of

Kamehameha I," was announced in the *Pacific Commercial Advertiser*, Aug. 2, 1873. Known for her good looks and lively ways, Loeau had been a continual source of Honolulu gossip after her divorce from John Jasper, a lawyer from Virginia. *Nuhou* carried a tasteless obituary: "Jane Loeau, daughter of Liliha, daughter of Kalani and son of Kamehameha Nui, being the sixth from Keawe, the seventy-sixth from Wakea, and the one hundred and fifth from Kane and Kanaloa. And now oh God, let her rest in peace. Amen."

3. Albert's spendthrift habits regularly landed him in difficulties; here perhaps the forgery charge mentioned in Letter 21.

4. Peter's usual spelling for "clinkers."

5. An elderly female relative of Emma and her mother, sometimes referred to as "Aunt Wikani."

Letter 19
Peter to Emma

Kalaupapa
August 8, 1873

My dear Queen

You must excuse me for my very short letter that I wrote yesterday the 7th, but I could not help it as the Schooner saild shortly after her arrival, and not wishing to let a chance pass without pening a fiew lines to you, I took the opportunity in haste to do so.

Hua,[1] the woman that once stoped with the late King, has prophesied that unless their is change in the Ministry, the King Lunalilo will be dethroned, as she has conversed in her dreams with Kaahumanu,[2] and that the Spirits of the departed Chiefs are hovering over and guarding over us. When she is relating these stories to the natives, she is dressed in Silk with a yellow "Lei Hulu"[3] on her Head, and a Lei Palaoa[4] around her neck, and she wears a "Pau"[5] of native Kapa around her middle, such as were worn by native Chieftesses of yore, in order to make herself look *Kohu*.[6] Thus showing what influence Superstition has over her, and what fools the listeners are to believe her, but all these little things quite pleases me.

When I am listening to Napela as he relates this Story to me, I put on a Sober face, in order to make him believe that I appretiate him, so all passes off O.K. I pen these lines to you thinking it might interest you, and also [to let you know] what is going on here. I am shure you do not believe that I believe in such nonsense, so on this I must rest.

August 10th.—Yesterday I rode to the Beach and had a Sea Bathe and was pointed out the spot whare Lonoikamakahiki[7] was on the beach konane-ing with his wife when a woman cried out to his wife. "The particulars you can get better from Aunt Fanny, better then I can describe it."[8]

My foot is as usual—no swelling but still Sore. I am putting some Tar soap on it, as the man at the Store whome I bought it from says it is good for all sores and this I apply on the Sore in place of Poultice, till I see any change.

I came very nearly looseing my little Dog, it had the distemper and would not eat but kept laying down and showed symptoms of fits, but now it has quite recovered and is quite lively and active.

It is very dry, no rain but alwais windy.

I must now bid your Majesty a long Good Bye. . . .

KEKUAOKALANI

1. Paniku Hua, a female leper recently arrived on Molokai; formerly a kahuna, an expert in native medicine and a prophetess, in the entourage of King Kamehameha V. Peter was correct when he identified Hua as a woman known to "the late King." In 1859, before Lot Kamehameha ascended to the throne, he first learned of Paniku Hua from the Dowager Queen Kalama, the widow of Kamehameha III. A great believer in kahuna medicine, Kalama was convinced that Hua possessed uncommon skill:

> Here is news from Honolulu. There is a woman kahuna by the name of Hua who was the kahuna who prescribed for Moehonua. Many men and women of Honolulu are seeking her help. She usually says to the sick person, "What do you want?" When the patient says, "I am sick," she asks, "What is your illness?" "I am in pain all the time—kahunas have worked on me and so far have failed to cure me." Then she says, "Have you a lizard god?" If the patient says, "Yes, I have a lizard," the questions and answers go back and forth until finally she says, "Go home and if you are better tonight, then come back tomorrow and I will talk to you again."
>
> I have heard that some persons who have visited Hua have really been cured. She is not entered by any spirit, nor does she pray to any images—only to the one God in Heaven. One cannot keep her from ferreting out one's inmost thoughts. I believe, however, that the Spirit of God has entered her body and that is why she is so successful in her practice. That is the news here. (H. K. Kapakuhaili [Dowager Queen Kalama] to Lot Kamehameha, Honolulu, June 1, 1859 [AH], translated.)

2. Queen Ka'ahumanu (1777–1832), favorite wife of Kamehameha I. Ruled as regent (kuhina nui) 1823–1832; according to one witness governed Hawaii "with a rod of iron." Her conversion to Christianity was considered a great triumph by the American missionaries. Peter's description of Hua's behavior differs somewhat from that of Kalama, who stated that Hua was not "entered by any spirit." Hua's relationship to Queen Ka'ahumanu seems to have been that of a haka: "a chosen person, who is a medium (haka) for a particular spirit." For an account of Hawaiian beliefs in "Spirits Speaking

through Mediums," see E. S. Craighill Handy, Mary Kawena Pukui, Elizabeth Green Handy, *The Polynesian Family System in Ka'u, Hawaii*, p. 132: "The characterization of the person [as a *haka*] implies the conception that the spirit *perches upon* the medium rather than entering by way of the mouth into the stomach.... Nevertheless, the spirit is heard speaking through the mouth of its *haka*."

3. Feather lei.

4. Lei with a walrus tusk or whale's tooth.

5. Skirt of tapa cloth.

6. Appropriate; striking.

7. Legendary ruler of Ka'u and Puna, island of Hawaii, famous for his hot temper and jealousy of his beautiful wife, Kaikilani. *Kōnane*, an ancient board-game resembling draughts or checkers, figures in at least two distinct episodes involving Lono and his wife. The incident mentioned by Peter occurred not on Molokai but at Kealakekua, Kona, Hawaii, according to a version preserved in Samuel M. Kamakau, *Ruling Chiefs of Hawaii* (Honolulu: The Kamehameha Schools, 1961), pp. 47–48. For a late prose version in English in which the same episode is assigned to Molokai, see "Lono and Kaikilani," in *The Legends and Myths of Hawaii*, ed. by R. M. Daggett (New York: Charles L. Webster and Co., 1888), pp. 325–326.

For remarks of Queen Emma on the episode, see Letter 24.

8. The quotation marks are Peter's. They perhaps imply that Emma's mother, Fanny Kekela, just as everyone always says, is the family authority on historical matters. Undoubtedly Fanny Kekela must have owed much of her knowledge of old Hawaii to her mother, Kaoana'eha (1768–1850), daughter of Keli'imaika'i. Kaoana'eha passed her last years in the household of Dr. T. C. B. Rooke, and so both Peter and Emma as children came into contact with a grandmother who was over fifty years old at the time of the breaking of the eating-tabu and the arrival of the first Protestant missionaries.

Letter 20
Peter to Emma

Kalaupapa
August 11, 1873

Queen Emma

This morning Napela called to me to come over to his House, and said he had good News for me. I went over and after I was seated, he said that his Wife had had a Dream that night, and after he had got through relating the Dream to me, I asked him to interprete it to me,

and what good News he had for me, as I was all attention. He said
that it would not be long before I and we would hear of the
Engagement for Mariege between your Majestys, to end with
Marage,[1] but unless he resigned the Throne and give it to you to sit
as Queen and he as one of the Ministers then he will retain the
Government but otherwise he will shurely loose the Kingdom, as
their are Traitors in his Kingdom that are brooding a plan to dithrone
him or to have the Kingdom annexed to some other power, ‸"*America
probably.*"‸ So your Majesty perceive that we are all alive with
superstitious noncences.

Deaths occur quite frequently here, almost dayly. Napela last week
rode around the Beach to inspek the Lepers and came on to one that
had no Pai for a Week but manage to live on what he could find in
his Hut, anything Chewable. His Legs were so bad that he cannot
walk, and few traverse the spot whare His Hut stands, but fortunate
enough for him that he had sufficient enough water to last him till aid
came and that not too late, or else brobably he must have died.

Last night I was looking at Oahu and the Sky over it was burning
with the Setting Sun, and meditating on the Features that joy use to
wear when in your Company, when on looking again I discovered
that Oahu had faded from vew. Then I strained my poor eyes to
catch again a glympse of Sweet Home but I strained in vain, for it
was completely lost in the dark. So I sung the Air "The dearest spot
on Earth to me"[2] when a man passed on Horseback and he too struck
up a native song, and I could not help laughing at the impudent
chap's mocking me. He too, probably, was endeavouring to avoid
the anxietyes that his poor acheing heart was crying for, *Home*, like
myself, so riseing from my Seat I entered the House and ordered Tea.

Tomorrow, as Wilder, Trousseau and Nordhoff[3] is expected with
Meyer, Napela as Luna has ordered all the Lepers that are able to ride
and walk to congregate at the Hospital at Kalawao for examination
by Trousseau, and then when that shall have taken place, I will tell
you about the Meeting and its results.

August 12th. 5 P.M.—This morning the Parties from Honolulu
arrived, and I had the pleasure of being introduced to Mr. Nordhoff.
He said that he called on you Yesterday but did not see you. On our
way to the Hospital and on to Waikolu we had quite a chat on
diferent subjects. I found him out to be a nice man, but I assure you
I was quite uneasy when in his Company knowing him to be a

writer for a Paper, but I kept on my guard, for fear I might let out some words and he might detect my ignorance, but I would not allow him.

When we returned we called at the Store and from thence Home. I was reading your kind letter when Wilder sent a man to me for some Poi. I let him have some and told the man that took it to tell Wilder that the Poi was from Honolulu and not the [local] Pai and that it was mixed by clean hands, and the People I have around me were clean and not effected with the disease.

Trousseau told me this morning that he would come down and dress my foot this evening and also give me the directions for taking medicine which is on the *Warwick*. She is in sight but yet some distance from shore. I will write again tomorrow by the *Warwick*.

A long Aloha. Remember me to Aunt, Wikani, and Lucy.

Your Humble Cousin

KEKUAOKALANI

1. At various times during her widowhood there were rumors that Emma would remarry. Governor Nahaolelua in a letter to Emma reported that Peter Kaeo had informed him that she did not deny the possibility of her marrying Lunalilo. (Nahaolelua to Kaleleonalani, February [?], 1873 [AH].) In a letter of Emma to Peter, Sept. 2, 1873, there is a suggestion that she had considered the possibility of marrying Lunalilo, but had rejected the thought on various grounds, chiefly theological. On Oct. 20, 1873, Emma reported to Peter that Kalākaua and his relatives were interested in arranging a match with Leleiohoku, the heir apparent.

2. W. T. Wrighton's "The Dearest Spot on Earth" has been republished in George Goodwin, *Song Dex Treasury of Humorous and Nostalgic Songs* (New York: Song Dex, 1956).

3. Charles Nordhoff (1830–1901), writer and journalist, for many years editor of the New York *Evening Post*; he traveled in all parts of Hawaii in 1873 and found the natives everywhere "very strongly opposed to annexation." In 1878, Nordhoff published a widely read book called *Northern California, Oregon, and the Sandwich Islands*, in part a compilation and revision of articles on Hawaii published earlier in *Harper's Monthly Magazine*. In 1893, as a writer for the New York *Herald*, he reappeared on the Hawaiian scene as an ardent defender of the deposed Queen Lili'uokalani. Organizers of the Provisional Government found him, along with British Commissioner Wodehouse, a member of the "Royalist Gang," and Dr. J. S. McGrew, sometimes called the "Father of Annexation," wanted to have Nordhoff tarred and feathered, for conspiring with other royalists to oust the *de facto* Provisional Government from power. (Kuykendall, *The Hawaiian Kingdom: 1874–1893*, pp. 626–627.)

Letter 21
Emma to Peter

[Honolulu]
August 11, 1873
Monday

Dear dear Coz

Yours of August 6th and 7th I only got this morning, though "I hear" the *Warwick* came in Saturday night. Kuhina[1] is so constantly with Nahaolelua[2] when he is in town that I get behind time in reports from the wharf. . . .

When the lawyers left on Saturday, Nahaolelua intimated to Albert, Hipa, and myself his intention to resign as guardian of your brother's property. One reason he gave was that Albert may have instigators who urge him on to these wrong deeds. . . . If [he resigns] then it is the worst thing that could happen, for [my] mother [would become] his administrative guardian. But Albert asked him not to do so, but to overlook the past and watch the future. We all warned him [of] the consequences in future should he practise another forgery or other bad things, for then nothing but arrest [could be expected to follow] without hesitation. He appeared more searious than I have ever seen him before, and we were favourably impressed thinking (as he seemed) he had really felt his danger. But alas, no, it seem that seariousness was assumed to get some money from the Governor, which he ought not to get till the end of the month. The consequence is he will have to wait for the next monthly allowance, till the regular time of delivery, which is the end of every month. Instead of asking the Governor when here, he went home and wrote for it by Makanahoa, his nurse. Hipa asked him to come back and live here, be economical, share what we have in common, but no response was given. I am so jealous of his father Kamehameha III's[3] name—so very jealous to see it fall to the ground so.

With my love till this afternoon,

I remain
KALELEONALANI

1. One of Emma's young manservants.

2. Paul Nahaolelua (1806–1875), a relative of Queen Emma and Peter Kaeo, for many years governor of Maui. As a member of the Privy Council and the House of Nobles, he spent much time in Honolulu. Kalākaua, who made him an issue in his campaigns advocating the appointment of native Hawaiians to highest offices, selected Nahaolelua as minister of finance in his first cabinet, hoping probably to placate some of Emma's zealous followers.

3. Kauikeaouli, Kamehameha III (1813–1854), a son of Kamehameha I by Keōpūolani, and brother of Kamehameha II (1796–1824); reigned from 1825 to 1854, longest rule of any of the native monarchs. On Feb. 14, 1837, married Hakaleleponi Kapakuhaili, Queen Kalama (1817–1870); two children died in infancy. The king adopted as heir apparent Prince Alexander Liholiho (Kamehameha IV) at an early age; later acknowledged Albert Kūnuiākea as his son (by Jane Lahilahi Young Kaeo), but made no provision for Albert in his will. In 1839, Kamehameha III signed a bill of rights; 1840 conferred upon the nation a constitution framed by missionaries, chiefs, and native scholars in consultation; took into service numerous foreigners, British as well as American; encouraged marriage between natives and "foreigners of good character"; approved the *Māhele* (division), the allotment of lands between the kings and the chiefs. Under the guidance of two American advisers of missionary background, William R. Richards and Dr. G. P. Judd, and later during the long tenure of a Scottish foreign minister, Robert Crichton Wyllie (1798–1865), Kamehameha III followed an ambitious foreign policy. Its object, never entirely fulfilled, was to secure treaties with the great powers, particularly the United States, Great Britain, and France, by which these nations—preferably by means of a joint treaty—would guarantee the independence of the Hawaiian Kingdom.

Letter 22
Emma to Peter

[Honolulu]
August 11, 1873
Monday afternoon

Ever dear Coz

Two bags out of the 3 of your tarrows by the *Warwick* this afternoon (she has postponed sailing till 4) are filled by Aikoe from Kahananui's patches[1] under Punchbowl. The salve for your foot is in charge of the Captain of *Warwick*. Pamalo wants you to report how the sores get on. The two brass taps for water casks were packed amongst your things when you left. They must be inserted into the hole proposed for emptying the bad water. Can't you make use of that bad water for watering plants?—it is a pity to waist it.

When the *Kinau* returns I shall venture to send a bourgomvillia plant before it is ordered—the same as that on Polihale.[2] It is a climber bearing most gorgeous purple blossoms. It needs plenty of water (don't of course rott it by too much) and must be planted against the house so as to look like the one on Polihale. Dig the hole wide and deep. Then fill in the earth again. Keep the bottom of box in ground [and] do not move it—it will rott and become soil soon.

I am so happy to hear of those two kind faithful men who remain by you. It were well if you can give them money besides their food— say $4 or $5 apiece per month. If they refuse then keep it back for a time and commence to pay after a while. Do they sleep at your place? Get the doctor to examine them to arrange for their remaining with you, and if agreed see what they want in the way of clothes, kihei,[3] blanket, etc., without consulting them and write [it] down, for things can be got cheeper here than at the Molokai store. Be very economical of your money. Be sure they have not got the leprosy, [and that they] do not have contact with any. Pray smoke your own pipe and no other. Mind those men do not use it, and be a little authoritative and firm to them—they will respect you by seeing a slight distance exists between superior and inferior—thus far shalt thou come and no farther.

Manuia, Kaawa's brother, came to Hipa with a message from Kaawa to ask us to do something to prevent Napela and others who often get drunk up there from coming to you, because he fears you may be tempted by constant seeing to take also some strong drink. I have not received Napela's letter. Yet we all laughed over the proposed proposition of marrage to me very much. . . .

[KALELEONĀLANI]

1. Two persons of this name were well known in Honolulu. Moses Kahananui was a member of the House of Representatives in 1873; Bennet Kahananui was lst lieutenant in the Rifle Company during the same year. Probably one or the other, if not both, provided Aikoe with the taro roots sent to Peter. Pauoa Valley on the inland side of Punchbowl was famous for its choice taro patches.

2. Polihale was a grass or adobe house in Honolulu where Emma's mother, Fanny Kekela (Mrs. George Naea) lived during the 1830s and 1840s; also at various times later. It was situated on Beretania Street between Fort and

Nuuanu streets, only a few minutes walk from Rooke House, near a stretch of plain originally called Kaukeano. The old Dominis house (Washington Place) directly faced Kaukeano.

3. Probably a shawl; the term originally referred to the togalike garment of tapa worn by old-time Hawaiians over one shoulder.

Letter 23
Peter to Emma

Kalaupapa
August 13, 1873
7 A.M.

Queen Emma

I have again received yours of the 11 per *Warwick*, with the articles, Tarrow and Salve, safe. This morning Dr Trousseau called on me and examined my foot and told me to apply the Salve till the *Warwick* again arrived bringing up some Pai for the Settlement. Then he Trousseau will send up the Medicine for my foot and also my Medicine to take inwardly. In the meantime I am to take Pills which he has with him. I told him that I was taking and had been taken Kenedy's Discovery but he said that they—Doctors—did not believe in Patent Medicines. I asked him what food I am to take letting him know that I am eating Salt meat and fish every week. He said that I could eat anything, and fish occationly. I showed him how my Hands has improved. He said that he noticed it, so on that I feel quite well.

In your letter this morning you refered about Albert. The poor fellow will get in Prison yet if he do not turn a new Leaf. Just so soon as Nahaolelua resigns Guardianship over him, I will not at all wonder if I was to hear that he is Imprisoned for a Crime, which I hope may never occur.

You also mentioned about Napela's not writing to you. He has been teasing me to write to you about it, but I have always told him it would be better for himself to write, as he by writing to you could convey his own Ideas better then it would be for me, but he has promised to write. I have also put him up to write knowing it would interest you, and I have also told him that delaying was lost to time and time was prescious. He came over to me last night and gave me a long lesson saying, just so shure as their was a Almighty Being, unless he got married to you and resign the Throne to you and you sit as Queen—"which I hope you will"—and the young Chiefs hold the Ministerys, then our Kingdom will flourish. Then he Quoted from the Bible in Jeremiah 30. 21,[1] whare the Kingdom is ruled by their own Lords and Governed from their midst.

Wilder was asking me if deaths occur frequent here. I told him it did, and their was one now geting burried at the beach and their was another—I pointing to a Coffin being made. The Settlement is short of Poi as no more Tarrow can be got from Pelekunu, the usual place whare we are supplied from. But thanks to your "*Ahonui*"[2] I am safe from that.

Today the Dr Trousseau is going to examine those that are Curable of the Leper, and those that think that they were sent up here wrongly, at the Hospital at 10 A.M., so I must rest till after the meeting.

1 P.M.—I have just come back from the Store and also from seeing the natives examined. Some of them said that they are going to pour the Medicine out and keep the Bottle for Tobacco. The natives said that this Medicine killed Humphreys.[3] I inclose $2.50 and I wish you would tell Aikoe to take it to Jack Smith,[4] the man that fixed my Medicine for me, and tell him to go to McLean's Store and buy me some Salt Rheuim Ointment. It costs .50 cts a bottle so their will be five bottles, and Aikoe take it up to you, so that I may receive it safe.

Ragsdale has writen a Agreement between the Board and the Kamaainas, the Board allowing them privalidge to rimain and cultivate Waikolu on Halfs, for the term of 3 years.[5] I had to leave sooner then I wanted to but it was so warm and I had this letter to finish so I hastened Home in order to be alone.

Ragsdale, Halulu, Kamaka and One or Two more are all trying to get Napela's place.[6] The Story that Manuia told Fanny about Napela's drinking and comeing to my House is all falsehood. Their has been no Spirits or Intoxicating Liquor drunk since the day of my Arrival. Whare this story originated from I cannot say, but believe me if you [believe] anybody it is all false.

Another long Aloha. . . .

Your Humble Cousin
KEKUAOKALANI

1. "And their nobles shall be of themselves, and their governor shall be from the midst of them; and I will cause him to draw near, and he shall approach unto me: for who is this that engaged his heart to approach unto me? saith the Lord."

2. "Kind patience."

3. William Humphreys, a former inmate and assistant supervisor of the settlement.

4. See Letter 16, note 10.

5. On August 15, Ragsdale was charged by the Board of Health "to carry out a contract ... with 42 residents of Kalawao, Kokuas, and others, to cultivate taro." (Minutes, Board of Health [AH].)

6. Napela's dismissal and Ragsdale's appointment as luna did not take place until Oct. 17; see Letter 53, note 1. Immediately on arrival at Kalaupapa, Ragsdale had assured the Board of Health that he would keep them informed about conditions at the settlement: "I will do everything that lays in my power to prevent the cultivation of all feelings of enmity towards the members of the Board of Health, or any of its officers. . . . I will carefully report upon everything that occurs here, either to yourself or through Mr Meyer. . . . There ought to be some dicipline in the place, carried out to the very letter, but with kindness and mercy. But if every leper is allowed to do as he please in everything irrespective of the rights and comforts of others, confusion and lawlessness must be inevitable results. There seems to be no head and tail to the institution just now, because the Luna does not preserve his dignity, or at least the dignities of his office, and make all those who are under his charge respect him. He can be kind and keep his dignity at the same time; there *must* be some *system*, or else the Institution can *never* be carried on with *economy*." (William Ragsdale to E. O. Hall, Molokai, July 2, 1873 [Correspondence, Board of Health, AH].)

Letter 24
Emma to Peter

[Honolulu]
August 14, 1873

Dearest Coz

The *Warwick* came in before 5 o'clock this morning. I was watering my flowers at the time, when Lucy's old man Waiahole appeared. My letters did not arrive until J. Dominis sent Niagara[1] up with them at 9, although stupid Laanui was despatched to the post office long before for same. They are dated 8th, 11th, and 13th August.

It is not only stupid of Hua, to say the least, dealing out such false nonsense, but positively wicked, because telling untruths leads the minds and thoughts of those around, who are under the same severe punishment like herself, astray from that God who has their existance in His pleasure. Why not rather use her influence to be kind and help others, who you say are dying every day? She certainly is not so bad that she might [not] help a greater sufferer than herself. If she has nothing to spare, certainly she can bodily go take care of [a] certain number every day, visiting from one to the other, thus useing her time in releaving the sick and poor, and seek to know her God better by going to the Roman Priest.[2]

I mention him next best to priests in our Church because there are none there, and as I wrote the other day they[3] are from the diciples direct, as ours and the Greek Church are. But she is not so pure as the latter two—she has gone astray—nevertheless is a branch of the same lily. . . .

Get [Hua] often to do certain attentions to another unfortunate, and see she does it by asking her to perform them with you, [and] you thus accustom her till she grows unawares into the habit of kind acts. Give your comparisons of her good deeds from our savour's and diciples' sayings and wishes carelessly, but in a jockular manner—then it will be less like a dry religious sermon. Praise and encourage her for them—indeed encourage all who deserve praise, [but] take care to stand firm against the Roman Catholic Priest.

The story of Lonoikamakahiki and his wife Kaikilani—alii-o-Puna at a game of Konane is very poetical, and the poetical portions are very pretty—the call to her, for instance, of the woman from the overhanging pali above—the message from her love wafted gently but distinctly not only to her ears, [but] unfortunately [to] those of her liege lord too, who upsett the Konane board on her—

> ˄"O Ka-iki-lani, chiefess of Puna,
> Your lover of the shadowy hills
> Sends you his greeting of love."˄

I wish you would write the story down carefully, noting names of people, places, when and where things happened, what time of day or night. Some say it happened outside of house and others just inside the ˄doorway.˄ [4] The place must abound with ledgends and tales, as [do] all our Islands, so please take them down in both languages—first the native.

I suspect the Napela dream is but the father to the thought.[5] The King's conduct sometimes certainly gives us great anxiety for the future of these Islands. He does not seem to feel the the weight of his responsibility, and who knows what may happen when he is not sober. Did I ask you in [my] last letter to tell Kaawa I am satisfied with his explanation? Give him my aloha. Waiahole says you are ∧in fine shape∧—he found you carpentering on the fence with the men. . . .

Kaliko today told me she intends accepting an offer of marriage from Kapolini. The confession has been brought to a climax from my finding her sound asleep in his arms at 12 o'clock the other night when Kapo[6] and I went to Wikani's long house to rouse the people for Alalaua[7] fishing. Hipa objects to the young man because he is a servant of [the] Kahoalii family. Nahaolelua has gone to his house on Queen Street to sleep, but spends the rest of the time here. He does not go home till Monday after next. Kia, wife and child came down with him.[8] Deborah[9] poor girl has made a sad step and is likely to become a mother in 5 months—I cannot dwell upon it—prey for her that her sin may be forgiven for our Jesus' sake. . . .

I do not like Mr Nordhoff, as he impudently writes for anexation of our Islands to the U.S., for fear European powers may take us if they do not now.[10] He is a beast—a "nasty critter," as Alex would say, but is pleasent in company.

John Kamakini[11] has addressed the people, and contrary to the newspaper notices he agreeably disappointed the audience, which was entirely a native one, with the exception of [a] few haoles and reporters, spys of missionary sons and sons-in-laws. He distinctly opposed cession and annexation, which touched a sympathetic chord in his hearers, and produced cheers of approval.

Mr Henry Parker[12] of the Kawaiahao Meeting House[13] left before the close. The lecturer proposed a favourable consideration regarding distillation of spirits from waist materials, now thrown away at [the] sugar mills, and which would add to the revinew of the Kingdom. At the close he charged them to be true to their Independance and never yield a foot of soil to the coviter. In the address he took one of the opposition arguments strengthening their reason for Reciprocity— that everything will come in cheep and we all grow rich—∧"Our would-be usurpers lie to us very cleverly."∧ It will most likely be printed in Saturday's paper and come out tomorrow morning.[14] Johny Dimond[15] proposed 3 cheers for Kamakini but Mr Porter Green[16] objected because it was the house of God. Said the former,

"This meeting has not exactly been for the worship of God," but however in the end they did cheer, and lustily too.

Hiram, who favours Taffy's family, came back to tell me, in the midst of meeting, that a disterbance was breaking out. Taffy left and told him there were many prepared to increase it, but it was all a show—only Panee[17] was drunk and noisy. He was ordered to be quiet. Taffy came over and supped here when it was over, and from his tone of conversation I perceived he and Kamakini was not on the most confidential terms now. He answered me that he could not get a sight of the address before its delivery to the public, and that it is well known [that Kamakini] was speaking the King's sentiment favouring reciprocity, but which the people will never consent to.[18] Now that is sheer nonsense, because Kamakini spoke strongly against cession and if he was giving the King's idea then they are exactly one with the people's. He criticized or pretended to be a judge of the way Judge Kamakini collected his information before framing his address. The fact is it was sour grapes, because [the address was] not against the King.

He told us (which is quite true) that His Majesty was tipsy last Monday on the *Kilauea* when he went to see Dr Trousseau and Mr Wilder off, and intruded on the ladies, insisting upon shaking hands with them—Taffy himself exhibiting the King to the public in as ridiculous [and] mortifying a light as possible by repeated bows to Mrs and Miss Smithies,[19] this done to spite Cleghorn[20] at the King's expense, because they live out at Waikiki and exchange visits with the King.[21] His Majesty they say has wonderfully improved his place out there.

The natives are all awake now to the American intention of taking possession of these Islands for themselves, and they oppose them to their faces. Mr Henry Parker spoke from the pulpit of his meeting house last Sunday morning advising his congregation to favour reciprocity. Moehonua left directly the meeting house, [and] Mr and Mrs Dominis followed. In the afternoon Porter Green preached there on the same topic to a congregation of less than 10. It has taken the Hawaiian Nation nearly 20 years to learn their Dissenting Missionarys' true character, which Alex knew from the begining and tried to open their eyes to see the fact, but bitter experience it seems could be their only way of enlightenment.

Oh! do read in the *Advertiser* of August 9th a splendidly patriotic article signed "Waialua,"[22] which has the additional charm of being written by a son of old Emerson, one of those very dissenting Missionarys, opposing in toto their sentiment. I have [read it] over and over again. If it were in my power to shew him public appreciation of his perception [of] what the native heart is for—their own possession—I would do it, for he has a right honorable heart and principles, and I say God reward his true Christian sentiments.

The writer he speaks of and quotes is Mr Castle,[23] whose letter written in the U.S. was reprinted in other papers, and also his reply to Mr Rhodes's speech[24] a month ago at Kaumakapili. Look them over—then you will understand his disection—oh, it is good.[25]

[KALELEONĀLANI]

1. Niagara Kekoa, employed by John Dominis as clerk and errand boy. In *Nuhou*, Sept. 19, 1873, he was described as a "well-educated Hawaiian [who] has been long known as assistant in a medical office, and is now the Secretary of His Exc. the Governor of the Island." The medical post was possibly the pharmacy of Dr. Edward Hoffman. Niagara was also an employee at one time of the government dispensary operated under the Board of Health.

2. Father Damien.

3. The Roman Catholic priesthood.

4. *Puka pākākā*: side doorway of a grass house.

5. Napela's hope that Emma would again reign as queen.

6. Kapoʻoloku.

7. Young of the red *ʻāweoweo* fish. The *Pacific Commercial Advertiser*, July 14, 1873, found the arrival of the fish a noteworthy event: "Alalaua.—This is the Hawaiian name of a small fish that occasionally visits the shores of this group, coming in shoals. Its visits are capricious, for they are not to be foretold. In some years these fish are extremely abundant in the harbor, and are taken in great numbers about the wharves, with hook and line or with nets. When they abound the natives prophesy some portending event to their race. Just now they are being caught off the Esplanade, but not so numerously as in some years past."

8. Kia Nahaolelua, adopted son of Governor Nahaolelua, along with his wife and child accompanied the governor on his trip to Oahu from Maui.

9. Deborah Kanoa, daughter of Paul Kanoa (1802–1885), governor of Kauai for many years. In April 1873, her husband, Solomon Kamahalo, who had sued her for a divorce, was granted a final decree.

10. Emma's distrust of Nordhoff continued, though she later conceded that his printed statements on annexation were greatly qualified. In his book

published within a year after his visit, Nordhoff opposed annexation of Hawaii on various grounds. The offshore position of the islands rendered them difficult to defend; their economic resources were not attractive to American farmers and artisans; the mixture of races and nationalities posed difficult social and political problems. However, "justice, kindly feeling, and due regard for our future interests in the Pacific Ocean ought to induce us to establish at once a reciprocity treaty with the Hawaiian Government." As for Pearl Harbor: "It would answer admirably for a naval station in the Pacific Ocean. In our present condition, when no single power dares to make way with us, and when, unless we become shamelessly aggressive, no alliance of European powers against us for the purpose of war is possible, the chief use of distant naval stations appears to me to be as convenient out-of-the-way places for wasting money." (Nordhoff, pp. 95–96; see also Jean Ingram Brookes, *International Rivalry in the Pacific Islands*, pp. 350–351.)

11. John M. Kapena (Kamakini) (1843–1887), judge of First Circuit Court 1873–1874, Hawaiian orator and politician; educated at Royal School and Oahu College (Punahou School) 1858–1861. For a short period before entering politics, he was the editor of the government-owned Hawaiian language newspaper, *Ka Nupepa Kuokoa* [The Independent]. Kalākaua, who held control of the legislature by his additions to the House of Nobles, appointed Kapena to the upper chamber along with Prince Leleiohoku, Simon Kaai, and several haoles believed to be friendly to his campaign views. In Kalākaua's second cabinet, Kapena was appointed minister of finance, but the king abruptly dismissed the cabinet on July 1–2, 1878, in what William DeWitt Alexander described as an "Arbitrary and despotic act . . . without precedent in Hawaiian history." (*History of the Later Years of the Hawaiian Monarchy and Revolution of 1893* [Honolulu, 1896], p. 4.) In the succeeding cabinet, less under American influences and less conservative, Kapena held the post of minister of foreign affairs, a sign of Kalākaua's continuing trust in him.

12. The Rev. Henry Hodges Parker (b. Nuku Hiva, Marquesas Islands, 1834; d. Honolulu, 1927), pastor of Kawaiahao Church (Congregational) 1863–1917. Son of Rev. Benjamin W. Parker (b. Massachusetts, 1803; d. Honolulu, 1877) and Mary Elizabeth Barker Parker (b. Connecticut, 1805; d. Honolulu, 1907), missionaries who arrived in Hawaii in early 1830s after first being stationed in the Marquesas.

13. In early days often called the "Stone Church," because it was built of coral blocks from the harbor, thus being distinguished from four grass-thatched predecessors (earliest erected 1822). Designed by Hiram Bingham, pastor, and built by royal authority, the new *hale pule* (house of prayer) was dedicated on July 21, 1842. Before construction of the courthouse (Queen Street, 1851), Kawaiahao Church was used regularly as the meeting place for the "Hawaiian Parliament," so that its use in 1870s for secular purposes was hardly an innovation.

14. *The Pacific Commercial Advertiser* did not print the address but noted in a lead editorial on Aug. 16 that Kapena's oration had some sound features but unfortunately pandered to "ignorant prejudices, already sufficiently aroused."

Kapena did not understand "the great importance of the planting interest to the welfare of the whole country." Also he failed to remind his fellow natives that "'they are all in one boat' and must sink or swim together. . . . Nor if they were disposed to do so, can the natives go back to the *malo* [loin-cloth]."

15. His name "Johnny" is perhaps a nickname; probably a relative and descendant of Henry Dimond (1808–1895), a native of Fairfield, Conn., who came with his family to Hawaii as assistant missionary and bookbinder in 1830s. Henry Dimond had two sons, with whom he was later associated in a mercantile business.

16. J. Porter Green (1831–1886), a leading Honolulu attorney; son of early missionary Jonathan S. Green, pastor of the Hawaiian church at Makawao, island of Maui.

17. Disturbance was a fake ("show"); the irrepressible Panee was probably a member of the firm of Kealoha and Panee, house, ship and sign painters.

18. Emma was apparently unable to distinguish between Lunalilo's attitude toward reciprocity *per se* and his far more reluctant acceptance of the proposal to cede Pearl Harbor. At a meeting of the cabinet in May, according to Ralph S. Kuykendall, "The King listened patiently like a judge or arbiter, and at the end agreed, somewhat reluctantly it would seem, that Minister Bishop should negotiate with Peirce for a treaty of reciprocity on the basis of the cession of Pearl Harbor to the United States; the treaty, of course, would have to be approved by the legislature." (*The Hawaiian Kingdom: 1854–1874*, p. 254.) It is possible, of course, that in private conversation King Lunalilo expressed different views at different times. Isabella Bird, after a private conversation with Lunalilo in Hilo, wrote in her unpublished journal on February 26, 1873, that "King Lunalilo told me that he was willing to cede a harbour in Oahu for a Pacific naval station in return for a reciprocity treaty—but nothing more."

19. Wife and daughter of J. S. Smithies, Scottish clerk of the Interior Department.

20. Archibald Scott Cleghorn (b. Edinburgh, 1835; d. Waikiki, Honolulu, 1910), general retail merchant and political official. Accompanied his father from New Zealand to Hawaii 1851. Married High Chiefess Miriam Likelike 1870, younger sister of Kalākaua and Mrs. John O. Dominis (Lili'uokalani). Member of the Privy Council 1873–1891; House of Nobles 1873–1886; collector general of customs 1887–1893. Shortly after her accession in 1891, Lili'uokalani designated Cleghorn's daughter, Princess Ka'iulani (1875–1899) her successor to throne.

21. According to Emma, Kalākaua's effusive courtesies to the two Smithies were intended to snub the Cleghorns, calling attention at the same time to Lunalilo's insobriety. The Cleghorns were neighbors of Lunalilo in Waikiki.

22. Emma was mistaken about the identity of ".Waialua," as she noted in a following letter. The writer was not a son of early missionary John S. Emerson

(1800–1878). He was Theophilus H. Davies, acting British commissioner; for main note on Davies, see Letter 28, note 4.

23. Samuel Northrup Castle (b. Cazenovia, N.Y., 1808; d. Honolulu, 1894); arrived in Hawaii 1837 to serve as fiscal agent and assistant supervisor of secular affairs of the Protestant mission. In 1851, he established (with Amos S. Cooke, former teacher at the Chiefs' Children's School) the mercantile firm and later sugar factors Castle and Cooke, still in existence; 1865 severed connection with mission. Member of Privy Council 1863–February 1874, when Kalākaua became king. Castle's article, "Sandwich or Hawaiian Islands," *New York Evangelist*, June 7, 1873, caused considerable controversy because of its blunt statement of "the missionary attitude" toward reciprocity and the prospect of the extinction of the Hawaiian race: "The certainty of the extinction of the Hawaiian race at an early date has become a fixed fact, and to no other country do they desire a union, but to the United States, the land they most love. . . . The increased stimulus to industry under the new order of things would do more to arrest the depopulation (if it can be done) than anything else would do. With the assent of the people to the measure, there can be no doubt but that the consummation of the union to the United States would meet the cordial, hearty approval of every American."

24. Godfrey Rhodes (1815–1897), coffee planter, dealer in wholesale wines and liquors, long-time member of the House of Representatives and very active member of the Chamber of Commerce. In 1873, a member of the Privy Council; after 1876, the House of Nobles. A native of England, Rhodes arrived in Hawaii in mid-1840s. He opposed the reciprocity treaty and American influence in general in the Kingdom. Though Kalākaua appointed him to the House of Nobles to win his support, Rhodes broke with the Gibson administration on fiscal matters and after 1882 became an important figure in the opposition Independent party. In 1873, his views on reciprocity were made public in a much-discussed address given on June 30 at Kaumakapili Church. They were reported in the *Pacific Commerical Advertiser*, July 5: "Reciprocity would benefit three parties, viz.: the owners of sugar plantations numbering from fifty to a hundred individuals; the proprietors of large tracts of land who would make fabulous sums from the enhanced value of real estate; and the United States Government, which, if it once got a footing here, would most assuredly in a short time become the sovereign power of the land, however honest its pretensions might be."

25. T. H. Davies ("Waialua") largely agreed with Rhodes' views, but injected appeals to religious feeling in an impassioned argument. He especially deplored Castle's pronouncement that improved commercial conditions would tend to strengthen the nation as a whole and in this way defer the probable extinction of the Hawaiian race: "If men say to me on this subject, 'Why do you oppose what would make you richer and improve your prospects?' I feel disposed to answer as Paul did to Demetrius, 'Thy money perish with thee.' It is enough for me that the instincts God gave me He also gave to the Hawaiians, and that chiefs and people tremble as they listen to those who would teach them to 'eat and drink, for tomorrow they die.' "

Letter 25
Peter to Emma

Kalaupapa
August 15, 1873

Queen Emma

I write to you "Raped up around my neck with my Comforter and my Shawl over me."[1] I was taken with Dizzyness yesterday and Headache. I feel like a person on board a Vessel careing not whether she sank or sailed, and thinking it for want of exercice, I had my little Pony saddled and rode to the Landing. From thence I traversed the coast inhailing the Sea breeze, till I got to my old bathing place, so I dismounted and sat on a rock, with my back to the Sea facing the Pali, admiring the wild grandure of the Scenery, the long range of Mountain, the dull Bluff at Waikolu, as Mr Nordhoff terms it, "An Immense Cinder," which overhangs the Sea as you pass beneath it.

In the interior meditating as usual in order to enable myself to be of some use for the future, I was arrested in my fond meditations by the approach of a Horse, and, comeing nearer, I saw it was mounted by Kamaka the soldier paying his visits to the poor Sufferers. Kamaka has been appointed by Wilder Luna, in place of Halulu, [who was removed] for misconduct, to serve out Pai and Beef, Rice and Bread to the Lepers. I asked him how state of affairs were going on, and he said that some had no Pai for a Week and wanted some. As they—3 in number—had only a fiew Biscuits and salt Beef, and as that was not enough to satisfy them, but as the Board had no more Pai, they had to make the best in Rice, till the Pai came from Honolulu. So their we parted, he to go on to hunt up some more who have and had nothing to eat and I to my Home on the rocks.

When I got home I ordered Tea in order to bring on prespiration, and in so doing I was relieved considerable but I still feel drowsy as though in want of Sleep. But I think by keeping quiet in the House, which I am going to do, I may soon recover.

I forgot to tell you that when Wilder and his party were here Father Damien asked us to his House to partake of his Luncheon which he had served out on the table for the Party. We all sat to the table and a Bottle of Clarate was opened and served, some in glasses and the rest in bowls, as Damien had only three glasses. Mr Wilder offered me a glass, which I declined to take, leting him know that I was under the Doctor's Hands, and Liquer was strictly prohibited. On our way the party stoped at the Store to get out of the Sun, and likewise rest a while before returning Home.

5 P.M.—I feel quite well, with the exception of a little pain back of my neck. I think it is from laying so long on my back on a high pillow this afternoon. . . .

August 15th. 9 A.M.—I rose this morning quite refreshed and free from pain and other disagreeable little things. The first sound I herd this morning was that welcome word—"Sail Ho." O how delighted I felt, knowing I had a fiew welcome lines from you. Nothing new, deaths as usual quite frequent, the poor Sufferers complaining of no Pai, but Napela has relieved them by telling them that Pai is at hand by the *Warwick*. So dearest of Queen Good Bye for the present.

> Your Humble Servant
> KEKUAOKALANI

1. Peter is perhaps quoting instructions for the care of a cold.

Letter 26
Peter to Emma

> Kalaupapa
> August 16, 1873
> 2 P.M.

Queen Emma

I have just come back from the Beach with my letters. In reading over your letter, you referred about Taffy's saying to you that the King was Tipsy. Wilder told me of it. I was so sorry.

You also mentioned about Kamakini's Lecture against Anexation. I am so delighted. I think the *Traitor* Taffy finds Cleghorn a diferent man then his other Kaikoeke.[1] I should think the Missionaries ought to be disgusted by this time—Preaching Anexation from the Pulpit, and not Gosple as our little Church does, about Spiritual affairs and that Alone. And also of not allowing cheering in Kawaiahao, as it is the House of God. Why was Concerts allowed? They had better give up their wild Goose chase on Anexation.[2]

I am quite Sorry to hear poor faithful Kahele complain of not having received a few lines from me, which is very true, but I shall write to her and also endeavour to cheer her so far as lays in my power to do. The only reason that I must accuse myself for the negligence of not writing to her is I am holely taken up in thinking of you and Aunt and of that Brother of mine. He ought about this time realize the bad ways he has been doing and only saved by being your Cousin, but I hope he will perceive his errors and resist temptations, which is as yet not too late.

When I was at the beach this Noon, the poor natives were greatly complaining of no Pai comeing by the *Warwick*. The greater part were served last Friday, and those that had none were to have a double allowance. But no Pai, so they are laying the blame on Napela. I am safe on that point, my Poi will last me till about Thursday or probably Friday.

I am going to have my Casks filled with water from Kalawao, so as to take the bad taste from the wood in order to be ready for the rainy season. It will cost me about a couple of Dollars [but I will] be ready to receive the Seeds to plant in my Yard. In the meantime I will dig holes, and when I shall have finished that, all will be ready. When I have planted the Seeds I will draw out a sketch of my garden and send it to you,[3] but if you are going to send any plants up send a boy down to the Schooner to accertain if you please if she is too full or not. . . . I remain

Your ever Humble Servant
KEKUAOKALANI

1. Brother-in-law; a reference to John Dominis and again an allusion to Kalākaua's supposedly strained relations with Cleghorn.

2. The offer by the Hawaiian government to cede Pearl Harbor was officially withdrawn in mid-November. This reversal of government policy was caused by "the mounting tide of opposition to the idea of cession of territory" and the prevalent fear in many quarters that cession would be the stepping-stone toward annexation (Kuykendall, *The Hawaiian Kingdom: 1854–1874*, pp. 255–257).

3. Perhaps Peter never made the sketch; in any event it is missing.

Letter 27
Peter to Emma

Kalaupapa
August 18, 1873

Queen Emma

Your Majesty cannot form any Idea of how many diferent stories are Circulated in this little Settlement of ours. It is reported that Nahaolelua has got the Leper. I told Napela that you told me in your last letter that the Governor had gone to his Residence on Queen Street and you never mentioned about his having the Leper—but let them speak about it, so long as the Governor or any of our Family do not get it—"God Forbid." . . .

I am in good health, my foot is improveing greatly. Thanks for the Salve. The day following the visit . . . paid us by Dr Trousseau and Wilder, the natives which were supplied by the Dr. smashed the Bottles of Medecine on the rocks. . . . [They also] poured the Medecine out, and Kept the Bottles for Tobacco for other purposes [and] strewed the Pills on the ground, like planting Corn, and laughing over it. I do not believe that their is one that has any Faith in the Dr or his Medecine, which is quite evident by the Yell they utter. Another laughter [that] they give, ₍ "Medecine that can't heal,"₎ is the one and unanimous word they Say. Ragsdale told the Dr. that he knew the Medecine could not cure him or any that was inflicted with the Leper, but that the Dr. was administering the Medecine in order to check the disease from progressing, and Ragsdale was aware of the fact. But as he was to die sooner or later, he would not take it. Trousseau promised to send me up my Medecine by the *Warwick*, but I have not received it, so I will continue taking Kenedy's. . . .

Aug. 19. 8 P.M. . . . I Omitted to tell you that when Wilder was here the last time he appointed Ragsdale to Superintend the water works and have the Pipes laid, which is to lead from Kalawao Valley to the Hospital, a distance of about ½ a mile. Yesterday Ragsdale, Napela and some of the Lunas chosen by them (R. and N.) with the Kamaainas, Kokuas, and those inflicted which were able to work, went to Kalawao to dig the Ditch. On calling the names, Ragsdale saw that [the] greater portion of Lepers able to work had not come, so Ragsdale told Napela to have the names of the men that did not come to me to work writen down, and when the Pai came from Honolulu, that those men were not to have any.

One man got up and said to Napela that when he got on the Schooner he was told by Wilder that the Government would take the best of care of them, but he was not told to come up to work. He for his part did not want to work on the water works as he could get all the water he wanted. In the meantime Ragsdale agrivated the natives by calling them diferent names, swearing to them and abusing them. Ragsdale picked a stone and told the men if they did not work that he would break their heads with the stone. One man got up and told Ragsdale that if he threw that stone he must expect another in return. Consiquently [he] picked up a good size one, rather too large for Ragsdale, so Ragsdale dismissed them and told them to come again tomorrow.

This morning when Ragsdale came back, going to the Beach I told him what I had heard from the natives [about] what took place inland. He said that if I was to come tomorrow to look at the men work, ... my presence would help a great deal. I told him to encourage the men and not to to provoke them, or use any threatening language to them, for they might get dispirited, for some are saying,ᴧ "We're dead people."ᴧ So it might end with something that you Ragsdale might not anticipate....

After I broke my fast this morning a man came down from the other side, notifying Napela that 10 Head of Cattle were comeing down the Pali for the Lepers. Knowing that I wanted Exersice I had my little Pony saddled, mounted [and] away I rode over rocks towards the Pali. My Cottage stands about half a mile from the Pali, on a Slope from the foot, and as I was advancing the Natives cried out,ᴧ "The bullock is falling down the cliff,"ᴧ so I looked up and Oh, a Bullock was rolling in the air, which had probably sliped or made a false step. So I reined in my Pony and sat looking at the Beast comeing down, or rather falling, from the height of about 400 to 450 ft, before it got to the foot. It struck a Point projecting out, the striking made it bound further out from the side of the Pali, looking like an immense foot Ball, till it struck with a dull sound "Firma Tierra." Then all was silent save the clattering of the loose stones that was rolling down the Pali.

I wanted to get up and have a look at the poor beast, but Napela stoped me. We were talking about the cattle when another one fell off too, but lower down, probably about 100 or more ft, and he too met the same fate Smashed into a Jelly. When the cattle and their drivers were come to the main Land, one man (their Luna) reported to Napela that they drove 10 head of Cattle for the Settlement. One had fallen off the Pali on the other side, two on this, so their were but Seven remaining. Napela asked the reason for the Cattle's falling off, and the man replied, it was the narrowness of the path—and, I may say, the miscalculation on the part of the Dumb Beast's that they fell off. . . .

The rainy season, I think, now is setting in. My Casks are very nearly full, but the water does not taste good. I blame it to the new Cask and [?wood], the Colour is redish and the Smell not good. . . .

I have named this place of mine Kilohana,[1] for a time, but if you will be so kind as to give me a name for it, it will be far more dearer then if I named it myself.

Good Bye. . . . And remember me to be your Majesty's ever Humble Servant and Cousin

KEKUAOKALANI

1. Months passed before Peter and Emma could settle upon a special name for Peter's cottage. Beginning with Letter 57, November 1, 1873, Peter uniformly used the name "Honolulu" as his address in his remaining Molokai correspondence with Queen Emma. To avoid confusing readers of this book, the private address used after Nov. 1, 1873, has been silently eliminated and "Kalaupapa" within brackets has been supplied in its place.

Letter 28
Emma to Peter

Honolulu
August 20, 1873

Dearest Coz

Two more letters dated 15th and 16th from you this morning by the *Warwick*. She leaves tomorrow afternoon, which is preferable to the outlandish hour of 6 and 7 in the morning. No matter how much time ahead you have [commenced] your letters, still they are never closed till the vessel is ready to sail, and there is "ahoys" [and] hurry-scurry at that hour to get [things] on board in time—[the ship is] delayed often purposely to the last so as provisions may reach fresh and last bits of news gathered. There has been no chanse for that Island since she left a week ago. . . .

The King is very ill from a kind of feaver. John Kamakini told me of it over the fense yesterday morning on his way to the Court House, and at noon he stopped in to repeat Dr Hoffman's[1] good word of "better today." Nahaolelua was at the King's [at] Waikiki on Sunday [and] found him recovering from a drunken spell. He drank a few glasses during this call whilst he was there, and complained of a stiff back. Monday he was downright ill. When Kamakini called on Tuesday he found His Majesty looking very ill indeed and weak, but the last report is however "better today." I heartily trust it is so—likewise, speedy recovery with [a] long reign. His repeated intoxication the past month has hurt the sore on his breast again, which the doctors do not like. The King's conduct sometimes certainly gives us great anxiety for our future of these Islands. He does not seem to feel the weight of his responsibility, and who knows what may happen when he is not sober.

Whilst I was at Hanauma, Ii the King's boy accosted Hanaiole, [asking] if there was anything the matter with the Queen. "No," she replied. "Isn't there any trouble in her *opu*?"[2] "No," said she, but he persisted gently [and] repeated the inquiry. So she asked what he meant, and if he was insinuating or supposing me with child. He answered, "Yes," for that was the report at the *Alo Alii*.[3] "Who is the father?" asked Hanaoile. "No doubt you suspect the King's visits to the Queen are attended with evil communication." He said they did [suspect this]. She most indignantly said, "No, never anything of the kind." . . .

Take some Algeroba and monkey pod seeds to plant amongst the rocks at the beach, where you indulge in evening revery and bath. If some were scattered at regular intervals along the road to and from the settlement to the beach, it might in time grow and be named to [future] generations as Kekuaokalani's Aveneau, and many a poor cast-off sufferer whilst resting under their grateful shade will bless the hands that planted them. And is not that enough in itself to repay for care and watching them now? Plant them close. Grow some inland near the foot of Pali road. Aikoe is always here to pack and help send your things off every ship. I forward the Bourgonvillea plant by this ship. Have it planted by the front verandah. Plenty of water will not hurt it—let it go with [the direction of] the wind. . . .

How sad I felt when reading the mention of your illness—giddyness, headache, wollen comforter round the neck, thick shawl, medicinal cup of tea effecting a prespiration—all this alone far away, and yet not so far, but strangers must needs take our places to attend—tears were in our eyes. "So mote it be," for a time—do nothing to retard recovery and progress. You said Dr Trousseau has prescribed medercines, and disapprove of Kennedy's cure. Do you intend following his advise? . . .

Oh! I am sorry to undo the pleasent illusion of Mr Emerson's patriotism. The entire article supposed to be his, with "Waialua" [for] signature, is not so. But now you must not tell—it was from the pen of Theo Davies, the Acting English Consul General.[4] He does not wish it known because of that public capacity. I am disappointed the other is not the author. It was pleasent to think there is one redeaming person out of the lot of missionaries. Alas, no—not one now.

My next letters will probably be by *Waiola's* overland mail of Kalae. Hipa, Wikani, Lucy, Kapo, Kamakaaiau and all our people send their loves to you, and my great one must always be with you. Never allow a day to pass without talking to our friend Jesus—even only an "Our Father who art in Heaven," etc.—at your quiet sea bath where there is no intrusion. Say it aloud if you like.

Aloha pau ole[5]
from your Coz
KALELEONALANI

1. Dr. Edward Hoffman (b. Germany, 1813; d. Honolulu, 1884), physician and pharmacist; arrived in Honolulu 1847. Served at Kalihi Hospital, the receiving station for leprosy cases; a member of the Board of Health. He was considered a fine pianist and performed frequently on social and charitable occasions.

2. Belly.

3. The royal court.

4. Theophilus Harris Davies (b. England, 1833; d. Southport, England, 1898), head of British import firm; arrived in Hawaii 1857, first as employee and later as member of firm of Janion, Green and Co. From 1865–1867 in charge of company's Liverpool headquarters; returned to Honolulu 1867 as head of firm, under style of Theo. F. Davies and Co., predecessor of later Theo. H. Davies Co., Ltd. Remained in Hawaii until about 1882, when he returned permanently to Southport, near Liverpool, leaving the Honolulu establishment in charge of a younger partner, Thomas Rain Walker. Son of a Wesleyan minister, Davies in Honolulu became a member of the Hawaiian Reformed Catholic church, but retained some of his dissenting views.

5. Endless love.

Letter 29
Peter to Emma

> Kalaupapa
> August 20, 1873
> 8 A.M.

Queen Emma

. . . Kamaka was up here a half hour ago and told Napela that he was going to serve the men out with Beef at the usual allowance, and not as Napela proposed, for he was afraid of the Natives, as some of them are geting to be quite desparate threatening to Kamaka that they will have their allowance in full, or pilikia[1] will follow.

4 P.M. Nothing of any importance during the day, only grumbling for the Leanness of the beef. . . .

August 21st. 10 A.M. Yesterday the Natives were all alive as two Boates with Pai arrived from Wailau. I rode up to Kalawao for a ride and met Men and Women Large and small on their march to Kalawao for their Pai. What a [p]ityful sight I did see, some just as much as they could do to troddle along and eager to lay hold of their native food Pai, for fear that they might get cheated by some rascal, which is done here by these bad fellows.

When I got to Kalawao, their the people were, thick on the beach— "Rocks"—waiting for the names to be called. . . .

P. S. August 23. . . . Ragsdale gave me a letter from you dated the 9th with the Local Papers and amongst them the *Advertiser* of the 9th which I have just received. So according to your desire, I rode home and read the Article signed Waialua. Let me assure you it did please me very much, and I cannot form any idea how a missionary's son can write such an article, so diferent from the generality of their stamp— whare he says, "It shall never be said that I had any hand in tearing from the Hawaiian brow one leaf of the reath I love to see there."

That is so very benevolent in the writer, although a foreigner. . . .

> Ever dear Queen
> Good Bye
> KEKUAOKALANI

1. "Trouble."

Letter 30
Emma to Peter

[Honolulu]
August 25, 1873
Monday

Dearest Coz

Yours of August 18 [and] 20 arrived yesterday and that of 24th this morning. Napela's letter has also come to hand. I am so sorry the Bourgomvillia plant is injured, for it is one that requires care and plenty of watering. . . .

Notwithstanding the mishap to the climber, still I venture sending two trees [of the] Poinciana Regia in two boxes. They have a bright vermillion blossom which covers the tree when in flower. Keep them in their boxes till the holes are deep as a man's height or 6 ft. and a fathom wide. Fill with manure, bones from the butcher shop, or [use] anything, even the dead bullocks you saw roll down the mountainside —slops from kitchen. If there is any space for a square of Public garden about the Hospital and Government buildings at settlement, you can have as many more Poincianas as you wish for there, a double row of them forming an Aveneau will be nice. Three or four years from now they will flower. Sketch me the position of Government buildings and where the water works are to be laid. Write me exactly how the firewoods land. . . .

Nahaolelua and party leaves today for Maui. He went out to see the King yesterday and says he is not free of feaver, but is much better. With this ill turn he has had another slight attack of plurisy again. When you are at your quiet beach retreat, never omit to ask God's gracious Mercy on our King. If you forget others in your devotions never do his name. Always present him with all his faults to Jesus, and He will carry that precious freight to the presence of his Father and ours, too, because Jesus himself has said to his deciples somewheres in the Gospel of St John, chapter two, before the account of his death, that "Whatsoever ye ask of my father in *my name* it shall be granted." So whatever you prey for, recollect that no preying to the Virgin Mary was ever recommended by our Savour.

Taffy is forming a military company[1] of young Hawaiians, hoping to get 3 or 4 hundred. The ultimate object is to secure their tickets at next election for members opposing cession or annexation. The object given out thus is good if only that, but I cannot help thinking more is at the bottom. Perhaps such are erroneous suspicions on my part. . . .

With all our loves to you I remain with the greatest,

From your affectionate Coz
KALELEONALANI

1. For further accounts of Kalākaua's military activities, see Letters 16 and 40; also Kuykendall, "Mutiny of Household Troops," *The Hawaiian Kingdom: 1854–1874*, pp. 25–26; and Richard Greer, "Mutiny in the Royal Barracks," *Pacific Historical Review* 21 (1962): 349–358.

Letter 31
Peter to Emma

Kalaupapa
August 25, 1873
9 A.M.

Queen Emma

After I rose I went to look at my Plant, and to my sorrow I saw that the leaves were faded, but I poured some water on it and after breakfast I went again to look at it and I was quite delighted to see that the leaves were again its natural colour and quite healthy. . . .

I am going up to Kalawao and look at the men work on the ditch to lay the water Pipe, from thence on to Waikolu for a Bath. Ragsdale has told the men that he is going to give a Party to those that help dig the ditch, and also give them money as he has got orders from the Board to do so, useing the word "Papa Ola"[1] emphaticly in order to give weight to what he say. He says my appearance will help his work a great deal, so I am going to call their on my way to Waikolu. Being in the open air and likewise mounted, I shall have no fear of mixing with them, but might as he thinks help. . . .

3 P.M.—I have come back from Bathe. On my way up I called to see the men work and saw them hoisting stones and haveing them removed. It put me in mind of your Husband, my beloved King, when if your Majesty remembers at Kona, hoisting the old Canons and shiping them on the Schooner, and the Captain who use to say,

ˆ"Pull with all your might."ˆ[2] Oh you cannot form any Idea how I felt then. Remembrance of the past made me feel quite sad, I could see the Canons geting hoisted on the Schooner, Hiram geting put in the Canoe after he got his ancle sprained, and several other little things which were done when we were together, the little Prince runing to meet his King—"Papa." But let that pass, it unmans me.

August 26. 4 P.M.—I was roused this morning with a very severe pain in the Stomache, and not knowing [what to do] as my House was dark I laied [in bed] although suffering intense pain, not wishing to intrude on Napela's sleep as his Wife also is not well. I had to wait for daylight. When it came, I got some Salts from Napela. It worked me but did not relieve the pain, so I have kept still indors all day, till about half an hour ago I felt a little better. So I got up, and not wishing to allow a chance of sending a fiew lines to you to escape, as the Mail man goes over tomorrow morning early, I am pening these lines. . . .

My servant Girl is cooking me a Fowl and rice. When ready it will be my first and last meal of today, as it is nearly sunset and I feel quite week. I must bid you a long Good Bye. . . .

Your Humble Servant and Cousin
KEKUAOKALANI

1. "Board of Health."

2. The incident occurred during the autumn of 1861 when King Kamehameha IV, Queen Emma, the prince of Hawaii and a small staff spent several months at Kailua, Kona, island of Hawaii. The king, an asthmatic, was concerned about his health. His chief interest at the moment was his cotton and coffee plantation at Waiaha, on the mountainside above Kailua. Meanwhile, Lot Kamehameha, minister of the interior, and John Dominis, governor of Oahu, for purposes of retrenchment decided to sell all obsolete military equipment as scrap iron. The king supervised the loading of the junk onto the vessel: "By the good Schooner *Kaluna* I send you down all the big guns [cannons] that were laying on the beach, some 7 or 8 in number. We were one day and a half at them. . . . Besides the guns I send a whole lot of old iron in the shape of old musket barrels, the stocks I had taken off, old bayonets, old ramrods, boxes of grape and canisters of anything else I could pick up in the way of old iron." (Kamehameha IV to John Dominis, Kailua, Hawaii, October [?], 1861 [AH].)

Letter 32
Emma to Peter

[Honolulu]
August 26, [1873]
5:30 in the morning

Dearest Coz

It seems the *Warwick* did not leave last night as intended, so [I] send
a few more lines. Rooke House[1] escaped total destruction by fire last
night. The lamp in [the] aipuupuu room[2] burst and the flames
instantly spread where oil ran, licking it up and burning the sides of
the room. There was no one in save Laweoki, a little boy 7 years old.
Lucy and I were sewing in the room above when I heard him utter
a subdued, surprised exclamation, "Auwe,"[3] and call for Mamaina.[4]
I detected at the moment also strong smell of lamp smoke. We both
ran down and found the room in flames, dark with smoke. Lucy
shouted for help. Hiram ran in and smothered it with a towel, as well
[as] he could. By that time a crowd was outside and Laanui's bed
quilt extinguished the fire, so no harm was done, but it was quite an
escape. Everyone was terribly excited and noisy after the accident.

There is not time for more as the vessel leaves directly. So "The top
of the morning to ye," as Alex used to love to say from an Irish novel.

From your loving Coz
KALELEONALANI

1. Erected in the 1830s by Dr. T. C. B. Rooke; its lower floor served Rooke
as a dispensary. It stood on a piece of land called Kaopuana ("Raincloud"), on
the road leading up Nuuanu Valley, approximately at the present (1975)
intersection of Beretania and Fort streets. The setting and atmosphere of
Rooke House were described by Isabella Bird, who visited Queen Emma in
1873: "Indeed, it is the most English-looking house I have seen since I left
home, except Bishopscourt at Melbourne." (*Six Months in the Sandwich
Islands* [London, 1875], pp. 262–263.)

2. Steward's room.

3. "Oh!"

4. A servant of Emma, one of three who received $100 each in her will.

Letter 33
Peter to Emma

Kalaupapa
August 28, 1873

Queen Emma

Yours of the 25th has come to hand, but I am Sorry to say it has found me in poor health. I have been suffering ever since Tuesday with Pain in the Stomache.

Yesterday Mr Meyer came over to see how we are geting on with meat (Beef), and was told by Napela that he Napela had been expecting Cattle from Meyer, as our killing day was passed, which was on last Tuesday, and not a Bullock that belonged to the Board fit to kill, as Napela did not wish to have the Milking Cows killed. Napela told Mr Meyer that the natives will not have any more Salmon and want freash meat in place and also for a change, so Napela has ordered 12 cattle to be killed, 9 for Kalawao and 3 for Kalaupapa.

The sick persons are moveing to the Beach for fear of the comeing Winter, which blows and comes from off the Sea into the Valley, making it very cold for the poor sufferers, and being weak they generally die. I rode up inland yesterday with Meyer, thinking it would better me, which it did at the time. When we came back we stoped for a fiew minutes at my Man Keleau's House to read the Aggrement between the Board and the Natives who wishes to remain. When that was through I came Home.

The Pain then had decreased to a little Griping. After Tea, I retired not feeling well, and was woke by a very excruciating pain in my Stomache. It was so severe that I called to my Servant Girl Kamaio, who slept outside of the Paku,[1] to come and Lomi.[2] I sat up in the Bed [and] while she lighted the lamp [I saw] it was 3 o'clock. She came and pressed my back, while I had both of my Hands on my side, and I tossing on the Bed first in a siting position, then change, laying with my face down, till broad daylight, when I felt a little easier. I roled over and tried to sleep, but was woke by a voice, "*Sail Ho.*" I got up quite revived by the welcome name, knowing that I had a fiew lines from you, which came shortly [after] I was up. I see that your dear Rooke House very near came to grief, but excaped without damadge, which I am very very glad to hear. . . .

Mrs Napela has been unwell all this Week. She does not leave her room. I have not seen the articles you had sent up, as I am not well enough to ride. The Griping I have yet—I have taken Janes's Pills and Salts, but of no use. The only remedy that releaves me is Kenedy's Discovery. I have stoped taken Trousseau's medicine till I am releaved of this infernal pain.

Good Bye. My Aloha as usual to all and also Hiram. Allow me to remain

Your Humble Servant
KEKUAOKALANI

1. Curtain separating Peter's bedroom from sitting room.

2. Apply treatment by massage.

Letter 34
Peter to Emma

Kalaupapa
August 29, 1873
8 P.M.

Queen Emma

I have had a good ride today and feel quite well. Yesterday I was so weak and the pain so severe I had to remain at Home, but sent my man Keleau to go to the Beach and to look after the Articles you had sent up. He came up and informed me that the Tarrow and Wood were in a little Straw Hut. So I rode to the Beach and on inquiring for the Boxes, I was told that they were left at Honolulu as they were too large to go in the Hole.[1] So I engaged a Ox Cart to have them taken up to my House tomorrow and rode Home.

This morning the cart came with the Tarrow and Wood and on counting them, the pieces numbered 161 which ought to have been 202, as you stated in your letter that their were 82 pieces in one Box and 120 in the other. So I am minus of 41 pieces. After I had got through counting and paid the man 50 cts for haveing had them taken up and 25 cts more to fetch me all the Bullocks Head[2] that he could find, [and also] after I had broken my fast, Napela came over and

asked me how I felt. I informed him that I was still suffering from
pain, so he sudjested to ride to the Beach and let Hua look at me.
I consented to the sudjestion, but allow me to assure Your Majesty
that it was not for my belief but for the novelty of the matter that
I consented.

So when all was ready we started. On our way down he requested
me to avoid speaking and [being] spoken to, and if possible meeting
anyone. I immediately knew that he was not far from Superstitious,
if not in reality. He questioned me whether I had any belief in
"Aumakua,"[3] and likewise in Hua. I noded in the affirmative and thus
we proceeded until we reached Hua's newly thatched House, which
made it all the better on entering.[4] We found her asleep, and she was
woke by her Husband.

I broke the silence by saying to her that I had come expressly to see
her, as I had and was then troubled with Pain in the Stomache—
"Nahu."[5] She looked at me and said it was nothing. I replied by
saying ("puting on a sober face") that it was nothing, as she was gifted
with foresight which I did not know anything about. She looked
again at me and again replied that I was very near well, and by the
time that I had finished my ride, I would be entirely well.[6] Napela
turned the conversation by asking her how we the Lepers were geting
along. She answered by saying:

> ˄ The heavens are open to me and the darkness has vanished. It
> was the King, Kamehameha III, who brought our peril upon
> us—he committed the wrong for which his subjects have paid a
> severe price. The gods of his ancestors permitted small pox to
> enter his Kingdom. He did not recognize his wrong before he
> departed from this world, and neither did his successors. Neither
> Kamehameha IV nor Kamehameha V prayed to the gods of
> their ancestors, and because Kamehameha V did not do what
> was right the gods of his ancestors permitted leprosy to enter the
> Kingdom.[7] The people have suffered greatly and they follow
> him in death. We now have a new King. Let us see what will
> happen in October. He will be like a bar of soap that helps to
> wash away evil, so that we may return to our homes and proper
> places.˄

So after a fiew more words amounting to nothing we parted.
Napela proposed that we prolong our ride, so we rode inland and

when we got to the Hospital, he went in as he had some business and I went into the Store to looke at the goods, inquiring their diferent prices—very fiew articles for men. I weighed myself and I found that I weighed 237, gaining three pounds. When Napela came over for us to go Home I asked him to stand on the Scale and weigh himself. He did so and weighed 197. We left the Store and came Home. After I entered the House, I felt my Stomache and found that the pain had completely left me. Whether it was Hua's doings or not I cannot say, but however I am well.

I must now close this with a long Good Bye. . . . I remain Your ever

Humble Servant

KEKUAOKALANI

1. The hold. The wood had been removed from the boxes and the loose pieces were then carried either on deck or below.

2. For use as fertilizer.

3. Ancestral gods.

4. Peter had promised Emma to shun physical contact with inmates. He believed that because the hut was newly thatched it was relatively safe to enter.

5. A biting pain, as in acute stomachache or childbirth. Hawaiian medicine distinguished different types of pain by giving them special terms.

6. Hua's treatment here seems to be a form of "faith-healing," such as was involved in the Hawaiian art of ho'oponopono: a clearing of the mind of the sick person through discussion, suggestion, and prayer.

7. Hawaiians especially attached to traditional ways sometimes believed that the rulers who had encouraged the Christianization of Hawaii—Kamehameha III, who first appointed Congregational ex-missionaries as councillors, and Kamehameha IV and Kamehameha V, Anglican converts who inaugurated the Hawaiian Reformed Catholic Church—were responsible for various catastrophic diseases that afflicted nineteenth-century Hawaiians.

Letter 35
Peter to Emma

Kalaupapa
August 31, 1873

Queen Emma

I am well of all Pain. Yesterday morning Napela came over to my House and said that he was going to ride over to Kalaupapa and Kalawao to accertain for himself from the poor unfortunates [who] that have and have not got anything to eat. So I told him that I should like to go also, knowing it was all in the Open Air and not entering Houses. After all was ready we started. I looked at the clock and it lacked a fiew minutes of Ten. We went over climpers in order to get to the little Huts and Sheds whare the Sick were, commencing our route from the Eastward going Westward.

The first Party we came across were in a large cave, 7 in number, 3 Men and Woman[1] and a Boy of about 5 or 6 years old. Oh you cannot form any Idea how they looked. Some spoke in a dull Hoarse voice, others completely disfigured, the Mother never would not know her own Child. Some without any fingures—Oh it was Dreadful. Napela asked them whether they had anything to eat, and they answered that they had sufficient enough to last them till Wednesday, which is the day the Poi is served. Napela also asked them why they did not go to the Hospital, and they replied that their Cave was more preferable to the Hospital as the Hospital was "Anu Anu."[2]

Leaving them we went on and saw Five more by the side of a Stone Wall which they had build and covered over with mats. Napela asked them their pilikia and they replied that they had Pai and Salmon to last them till Wednesday but were *Anu Anu*. Going on we met a man and a woman. Napela spoke to them and I and my Horse boy Haalilio rode on to the Beach. I rode as far as was safe and sat and looked at the wild Waves of the Northern Sea[3] come dashing with all its fury against the rock on which I was [sitting]. Then another one would come and another one. I sat and watched them as they came in rotation to try their strength, but of no avail. So I sang the air "What are the wild Waves saying," "Love not," and other Songs.

When we neared my Bathing place the rain poured and wet us very nearly through, but as there are no Trees and nothing to shelter us we had to take it and go on, looking for them amongst the rocks, in

Caves and by stone walls, puting the same question and telling those that had nothing to eat to come along with us to Kalaupapa, whare they would get some to last them until Wednesday. We saw a Woman that recognized me, leaning against a stone wall. Napela asked her her pilikia, and she replied that she had got no Dress. I asked her how long had she been here and she answered 3 years. She said that she had worn all her clothes till she had to wear her Holoku without a Muumuu[4]—opening the front of her Dress and showing to us her bare skin. Napela told her that on Monday if she came up to the Store she would get some clothes, as clothes were going to be served to the neady on that day. She showed her Leg, and she had an awful sore foot, the Leg from the knee down inflamed. She said she can only crall and that's all.

We left her and rode on, inquiring and hunting for them till we got to Kalaupapa, whare the Men and Women were waiting for us. Kamaka the Soldier was called to serve out five pounds of Pai to each and every one. The Pai is in Barrels from Honolulu, quite hard, put on the Scale, weighed and served in Tin buckets. All this time it was Showering and blowing, so not wishing to catch cold, I asked Napela to come Home. When we got Home I looked at the Clock. It was 10 minutes past six. From yesterday morning till evening we did not see the sun at all. Cloudy, rainy and windy—it begins now to feel cold. I am wearing my warm clothes, both in and out doors.

I have quite a good supply of Water for my Plants, which I am in great fear will not thrive on account of the Wind's blowing so strong. The only Tree that seems to grow good here is Pu Hala.[5] As I write it is still blowing quite strong.

Good Bye. Aloha to Hipa and the others of your Place.

I remain etc.

KEKUAOKALANI

1. There were three men and three women and one boy.

2. Very cold.

3. Perhaps an allusion to the North Sea of *Dombey and Son*; see Letter 13.

4. She had no undergarment.

5. Pandanus tree.

Letter 36
Peter to Emma

Kalaupapa
September 2, 1873

Queen Emma

Yesterday morning I rode to Kalawao to look at our waterworks Superintended by Ragsdale. Whilst their Napela came up and at Noon We rode to Waikolu, Ragsdale going to distribute the Tarrow Patches amongst the Kokuas and Kamaainas which are allowed by the Board to remain and cultivate the Land at Waikolu under Contract. After the distribution we had a Bath, and when we had got through Ragsdale and I rode up a Hill to inspect the Land for cultivation. A man came after us and said that Meyer and a Haole Kane[1] and Wahine[2] were at the river. Ragsdale came back and I remained watching the Sea break over the rocks, reminding me of Makapuu when I saw it last on my trip up here.

When I retraced my steps back I saw that the Haoles and Meyer with Ragsdale were going home. I inquired of Napela who the Haoles were, and he replied it was the Doctor of the *Costa Rica*.[3] I having no inclination to form his aquaintance rode Home to write my letters and also to change my dress after Bath, so when my letters were addressed, I sat on my verandah and looked at Oahu, before sunset just visable, so I quoted from Byron

> Yon sun that follow us in our flight
> Farewell a while to him and thee
> My Native Land, good night.[4]

After saluting Sweet Home with a Song I entered the House for the remainder of the night. This morning it was raining a little but cleared off soon, so I told the men to commence to dig the Holes for the Plants. They have to use Crowbars in order to break the large flat stones that is deep in the ground. They work rather slow but it being right in front of my Cottage I can sit on the verandah and see that [they] do work.

I think that after everything is planted and growing my place will be the best and pretiest spot in Kalaupapa. As soon as all the holes are all dug and filled with manure and bones, I will sketch a picture of it and let you know whare and how I have planted my trees and flowers.

But I should like to have a fiew Mangoe seeds if not Plants from Rooke House yard, if such can be procured, and likewise it agree to Your Majesty, a Name for my Place[5]—it will forever be remembered by me and buried in the deepest recess of my Heart, knowing it is from the only friend which I have, as I linger on alone far from relations and Home.

My health is Maikai,[6] my foot healing nicely. My hands lately have had shooting pains, and I can feel the Fleash creeping. I hope it will be for the better. I must close as the Overland mail goes tomorrow and I have to deliver my letter at the Kalawao Store. Tomorrow Mr Meyer is going to come, so when that shall have taken place I will write.

Good Bye. Aloha to Hipa and others.

> I remain
> KEKUAOKALANI

1. White man.

2. Woman. The reference in the next paragraph to "Haoles" indicates that the woman was also white.

3. Dr. Adams, physician of the *Costa Rica*, instead of returning to San Francisco on his vessel, was stopping in Hawaii to tour the Kingdom, including a visit to Kilauea Crater on the island of Hawaii.

4. A free echoing of Childe Harold's "last 'Good Night'" on leaving "Albion's Isle," in Byron's *Childe Harold's Pilgrimage*, Canto the First:

> "Adieu, adieu! my native shore
>   Fades o'er the waters blue;
> The Night-winds sigh, the breakers roar,
>   And shrieks the wild sea-mew.
> Yon Sun that sets upon the sea
>   We follow in his flight;
> Farewell awhile to him and thee,
>   My native Land—Good Night!"

5. See Letter 57, note 1.

6. Good.

Letter 37
Emma to Peter

[Honolulu]
September 2, 1873
Tuesday

Ever dear Coz

I got your letter of August 28th with the plan of the lay and situation of houses and land at Molokai on Sunday morning.[1] I read it to Hipa and tears were our silent response to your voice relating your illness. That we should not be by you at such times made our hearts ache, but thank God your trouble was only slight and temporary. Look to the end wished for, which is recovery and return—do all in your power to accomplish that end. I think myself the Doctor's medercin[2] is best for you, as he has seen and understands the case, but still all rests with you. Have nothing to do with Lepers—it is said they are about you and fraternize daily. . . .

Peter, the one important event now is the King's health. Seariously, we have escaped narrowly just by mear chanse another but a worse repetition of our Kingdome's experience last December.[3] Without a head, strife [and] bloodshed inevidable would have followed. As you know from Mr Wilder, the King's state the day he and Doctor left for Molokai—in fact before that—he had been drinking for a week or more, and ever since then has kept so till little over a week ago, when we heard he was ill, but supposed it was the consequense of it. One night he slept out on the grass in front of his house [at] Waikiki where he is now and took cold in his injured lungs. [This] brought on another attack of plurisy, for which the Doctor put on a blister to the shoulder blade and below his ribs. Then an intermittent feaver came on every day in the afternoon. His people about him stopped his drinks. He lost appetite and with the other two troubles on him and a constant cough grew weak rapidly, till last Saturday August 30.

Dr Trousseau told him, after sounding [and] feeling and examining him thorougerly all over, that he could not tell why he continued to grow weaker, everything internally did not give any cause for it, and asked his permission to call in another doctor, naming over several. [The] King chose Dr McKibbin Jr, who went out that morning and found him to his horror on the point of death—pulseless, no circulation over the man, and all but breathing his last. You see how near distress, agony and trouble we have been. They instantly forced him to take brandy eggnog and gave strengthening and narcotic draughts. By evening he was slightly better and slept all that night for the first time for several nights past.

I went Sunday noon [for] the first time since his illness. He talked with me incessently for 2 hours or more and did not wish me to leave so soon. When I returned to his bed and wished him goodby, he said, "Oh, that is too long—as if you will not come again—say good day instead." Poor man, he was very weak, the lips and nose drawn, as a very ill person's does look sometimes, and appeared extremely ill. He attempted to get out of bed Saturday and fell on a chair—hurt his head and neck badly. He is forbidden to leave the bed now. I go out this afternoon to see him. . . .

[Last week] Col. Prendergast[4] kindly drove [into town] to tell me of the King's danger, and urged going out that Saturday evening, but my hilahila[5] overpowered my loyalty—feeling people will be uncharitable and say I wished to get appointed successor, and try my last chans of marriage. Wikani and I actually started in one of Ward's carriages, but ordered it up the valley and down by Fort Street to the house again. [I] could not resolve to go out, but it seems Mrs Bishop[6] instantly jumped into Col. Prendergast's waggon and drove out, when he told her of [the] King's illness that evening.

Taffy was ready with Ka,[7] Kahananui,[8] Moehonua[9] and others to assume authority, should worse have happened to our King. Taffy sent Mr Meyer to Nahaolelua that night with a message he would be at Government House to consult him regarding the impending crisis, but he did not come, probably hearing [of] the King's improvement. Mr Meyer however saw Lua[10] and told him the plan of chieves was that all should meet the following day (Sunday) in His Majesty's presence, and one [was] to ask him [to] appoint a successor, and whoever he may choose must be accepted. So the old man advised my going and [I] did, with heart full of hilahila.

Mrs Cleghorn was there but none of the others. About 2 o'clock Kalahoolewa[11] came out, [and] then I left. Taffy never appeared, for Mrs Dominis[12] [had] met him going out and she reported improvement. They both came back [together] to town. Mr Bishop and J. Dominis was at Waialua and Kahuku during this time. Their wives sent for their immediate return and they reached here Sunday evening.

Pamalo[13] tells me (private) [that] the King's life is worthless—his lung and liver etc. are not sound and his constitution [is] broken—cannot stand drinking and illness as formally, and another drinking bout such as this carries him off without doubt. Pamalo has advised me strongly not to allow my private feelings to rise above my duty to be appointed successor to Throne, which he feels sure will be given me. The choise rests between Mrs Bishop and me, as the King does not like David, and, says he, Mrs Bishop does not sit idly back and do nothing—no, she is seeing that all influence be made in her favour. But he feels sure I would be named without any trouble, as the King prefers me to any other—he urges my frequent visits there. So I suppose my scruples must be pocketed—oh dear me—and be ambitious. Dreadful—....

The doctors still see him twice a day, till he is well out of anxiety. He is very much better, there is no danger now. Pamalo is going to talk to him earnestly soon about the succession and his own state. Hiram brings a report of some influential American citizens holding a consultation with the Captain and officers of [the] U.S.S. *Portsmouth*[14] [on] Saturday, and [it was] decided should anything happen to the King the latter was to take possession of Palace, Punch Bowl, Government offices, etc., in their Nation's name, hoisting the American flag.

Mikauahoa, Ka's woman, told Aikoe that David with others—Ka included—have had private consultations at Abigail Maikai's house when they found the King growing weaker. Ka asked and got the promise of living in Ihikapu,[15] Kahananui takes Kanaina's house near it at Pohukaina,[16] if David should become King. Mrs Dominis was to have Kinau Hale.[17] Thus you can judge how high disloyal speculations were going on, and the man not dead. He is very kind to me and sent Mr Selfe[18] yesterday to offer horses, carriages, and anything I wish from his stables at all times.

Another of Hiram's reports is that the Cabinet Ministers have done and said their uttermost to [the] King, not to marry me—one objection being my church—dear little church sought for, transplanted, laboured over, tended [and] watered by my beloved Alex, Hawaii's noblest gem. Knowing her true genuine origin, and of course consequently believing in her Lord's wishes, power, commands and promises, he gave this boon of salvation to his people, [but] they are not yet fit to appreciate it. He dearest mate of my life's journey improved the tallents given him to bring forth fruit while on earth, and our good rewarding God will repay him tenfold in the Relm of the Achme of Happiness, to be and enjoy to his fullest God's face. Can your imagination ascend to such prospect of vast perpetual bliss, enjoyment and rest? Fancy all that actually in store for my dearest darling husband. With all his faults he is my husband and I love him still, he is ever with me I know, for my prayer book and bible says so, and as I believe in ministering spirits and Guardian Angles, why should not one naturally think that their loved ones are given a charge or work in the world? They live over those [left] behind in this place of trial, and you do not know what comfort I take in the knowledge that Alex and Baby are being used by our Heavenly Jesus as his workers like as the Bishop and priests are his visible workers or agents here to guard me from harm and sin. Although I cannot see them, because being mortal, still they see me for all that—rejoice and grieve with that Jesus and God, according as I do every day. I am told this in many places—one is the Apostles' Creed, [the] morning prayer, where we say, "I believe in the Communion of saints," and again in the Communion Service, "Therefore with Angles and Archangles and with all the company of heaven we laud and magnify thy glorious name," etc.

So we three are together always at church, especially at the Holy Eucarist feast, it is such a happy knowledge, and I go on feeling their angle voices near and about me. Yet notwithstanding, lazyness will overcome me, and anger, envy, untruthfulness—all sorts of the devil's atributes succeed. How hurt and sore their dear hearts must be when such [occurs]—Oh what must my God's be then? Have I any fruit to yield as return for what is given me to do?

Alas no, his Church has not succeeded fast [to free herself] from the Godlessness of her members—and I one of the worst. Unto man much has been given in the way of position, influence, and oppertunity, and yet no convert have I made nor benefited him [in] any way. Jesus has said to the unprofitable servant, "Get thee unto outer darkness where there is weeping and gnashing of teeth." How different [is] my reward to Alex's—awful—oh prey dear Coz for me that he may "make me love him more and more."

I see Bill Ragsdale and others from [the] leper settlement has writen to the native newspapers of August 27th. . . .

Some Molokai folks by yesterday's *Warwick*, whilst giving an account of you, say that Napaepae's daughter is being kept as your Mistress, and gets quite cross with you when other women are in your company, and it is from her love potions that you have suffered those pains in stomach. . . .

We have had a showery week with bright moonlight nights. The cause of Mr and Mrs Pratt's[19] quarrel was John Reeve's inviting some American officers of *Portsmouth* to stay at his house [at] Waialua, which is not *his* house but Mr Pratt's, and he had no right to ask anyone there. . . .

Mrs Dominis has a new love, a native boy of Waikiki. She gives a birthday ahaaina[20] today at Hamohamo.[21] David has one at Kahananui's place (Punchbowl) and Mrs Bishop also has a large ladies' lunch party to [honor] Mrs Nordhoff at her house, in spite of King's illness. Keaoa and Kalama were married in Church Sunday morning.[22] I sent for Albert Sunday but [he] has not yet made his appearance.

Mrs Cleghorn shamefully cut off Waihoikaea's hair to the skin in some parts, and long locks left in some—and inch or two long in spots—on the girl's head. She is Makue's granddaughter by Kamuela her son. He complained at Police Station of Mrs Cleghorn's treatment of his child's hair, and both Mr and Mrs C. were brought before Court and cautioned not [to] repeat such again. The original offence is Waihoikaea's—[she] never returned after delivering a message from Mrs C. . . .

I send this old letter as it is, with much love from your loving

KALELEONALANI

1. A very rough but interesting sketch map exists in the Archives of Hawaii.

2. Trousseau's medicine.

3. The succession crisis at the time of the death of Kamehameha V, 1872–1873.

4. Henry Prendergast (?1815–1875), court chamberlain under Kamehameha V; member of the household staff of King Lunalilo. A Tipperaryman, he arrived in Hawaii in 1854.

5. Shyness or embarrassment.

6. The High Chiefess Bernice Pauahi Bishop (Mrs. Charles R. Bishop); for main note see Letter 55, note 4.

7. Probably William Ka, 1st lieutenant in the Rifle Company, later captain (1874); a supporter of Kalākaua.

8. Probably Bennet Kahananui, 1st lieutenant in the Rifle Company.

9. William Luther Moehonua (1824–1878), court official, poet, politician; uncle of Kalākaua, being a natural son of Aikanaka, Kalākaua's grandfather on his mother's side.

10. Paul Nahaolelua, governor of Maui.

11. William Pitt Leleiohoku (1855–1877), younger brother of David Kalākaua, Mrs. John Dominis (Queen Liliʻuokalani), and Mrs. A. S. Cleghorn (Miriam Likelike). He was an adopted son of Princess Ruth Keʻelikōlani, a half-sister of Kamehameha IV and Kamehameha V. Educated at St. Alban's School (Iolani School), established by the Anglican mission; a talented musician and actor. On his accession, Kalākaua named Leleiohoku heir apparent, thus strengthening the dynasty through ensuring support of Princess Ruth. Emma often refers to him by an alternative chiefly name, Kalāhoʻolewa, or more condescendingly by a malicious nickname, "Master Willie," "Buff," "Ke Koʻi" ("Young Red Snapper"), "the Moʻo" ("Lizard" or "Lizard God").

12. Mrs. John O. Dominis (Liliʻu Kamakaʻeha Paki), later Queen Liliʻuokalani (1838–1917), last ruler of the Hawaiian Kingdom. A sister of David Kalākaua, she was adopted at birth by Abner Paki and Konia, parents of Bernice Pauahi (Bishop), and was closer to Pauahi than to most of her brothers and sisters. After the death of Leleiohoku in 1877, Kalākaua appointed Liliʻuokalani as his heir apparent; she succeeded him to the throne after Kalākaua's death on Jan. 20, 1891. During her brief reign, lasting barely two years, Liliʻuokalani sought to restore the power of the Crown, weakened by the "Bayonet Constitution" forced upon Kalākaua in 1887. When, in January 1893, Liliʻuokalani tried to proclaim a new constitution by royal fiat, she met strong opposition within her own government as well as on the part of dominant elements in the community. The republican movement in Hawaii, led by Americans, most of them Hawaiian citizens, gained ground under both Kalākaua and his sister. Describing themselves as the "Committee of Public Safety," the leaders of the movement decided to dethrone the queen, set up a provisional government, and apply for annexation. Acting in concert with the United States minister, John L. Stevens, and supported by the presence of troops he called ashore from a U.S. Navy cruiser, the committee took possession of government buildings in Honolulu. On Jan. 17, Liliʻuokalani was reluctantly persuaded to surrender to "the superior force of the United States . . . until such time as the Government of the United States shall . . . reinstate me in the authority I claim as the Constitutional Sovereign of the Hawaiian Islands." From January to September 1895, she was held prisoner in her former palace by the Provisional Government.

After her full release in February 1896, she journeyed to Washington to urge her cause. President Cleveland had consistently resisted pressures from annexationists both in Hawaii and the United States. However, upon the outbreak of the Spanish-American War, the Republic of Hawaii, instead of remaining neutral, offered to the United States the use of harbors and other facilities. A joint resolution for annexation passed Congress in mid-June and was signed by President McKinley on July 7, 1898. Though she visited the United States on later occasions, and continued to petition Congress to compensate her for loss of income from Crown lands, Lili'uokalani came to realize after 1898 that the Hawaiian Kingdom had faded into history.

13. Dr. Robert McKibbin, Jr.

14. There was basis for Hiram's report. Anxious American residents had asked Henry A. Peirce, American Minister, to persuade Commander J. S. Skerritt, U.S.S. *Portsmouth*, to remain in harbor until Sept. 15, to meet any emergency. The mutiny of barrack troops on Sept. 7 gave Peirce added cause to use his influence upon Skerritt. Meanwhile, when news of the king's illness reached San Francisco, Admiral Pennock's flagship, *Saranac*, was dispatched to Hawaii for an indefinite stay, to serve virtually as a naval guard. For detailed account of U.S. and British policy in Hawaii especially in regard to naval and military security, see Merze Tate, *The United States and the Hawaiian Kingdom* (New Haven: Yale University Press, 1965), pp. 27–38.

15. House near King and Beretania streets within the royal enclosure, built by Kamehameha IV for Queen Emma, near the Old Palace and approximately on the site of the great banyan tree near the present (1975) Archives of Hawaii.

16. House of Lunalilo's mother, Kekauluohi, on ocean side of Old Palace.

17. House formerly owned by Emma's uncle, John Young II (Keoni Ana), who obtained a grant for the house after the death of Kina'u, mother of Kamehameha IV and Kamehameha V; situated on Richards Street side of the palace.

18. Robert Selfe, an English settler who served as royal coachman under Kamehameha IV, Kamehameha V, and King Lunalilo.

19. Mr. and Mrs. Franklyn S. Pratt were close friends of Queen Emma. Mrs. Pratt, the High Chiefess Kekaaniau (1834–1928), educated at Chiefs' Children's School, and bridesmaid at Queen Emma's wedding in 1856, frequently attended Queen Emma as lady-in-waiting. She was the daughter of High Chief Laanui and High Chiefess Owana, one of twin daughters of Jean Rives, a French adventurer from Gascony and court favorite of Kamehameha II. In 1864, Kekaaniau married Franklyn Seaver Pratt (1829–1894), formerly of Boston. For many years Pratt served in Honolulu as registrar of public accounts; later as Hawaiian consul general in San Francisco. John Reeves, Mrs. Pratt's uncle, was the part-Hawaiian son of Jean Rives. John Reeves later contracted leprosy and moved to Kalaupapa.

20. Feast.

21. Beach property and cottage at Waikiki of Mr. and Mrs. John Dominis.

22. This sentence and that immediately following have been transposed from an earlier portion of the letter.

Letter 38
Emma to Peter

[Honolulu]
September 3, 1873

Ever dear Coz

When my letter to you written from Waikiki Tuesday was closed, Mr Crabbe, not having any stamps, detained it till he received some from town by the boy he despatched, but not coming soon, Lucy made Laanui take into town and post. I remained out there till 6 in the evening, when the Doctor's last visit was made.

The King talked cheerfully but was weak and quite unconscious how near death he was. When I went into his room he asked, "Do you ever get letters from your Cousin Peter?" "Yes, by every mail," said I. Then he expressed wonderment at not receiving a line from you. He says Horace Crabbe sends the foreign papers regularly up to you but they never have been acknowledged. Do write and thank His Majesty's kindness.

Eliza,[1] Waiaha[2] and Beke[3] amused me very much by keeping a strict watch over me that day when we entered the grounds. They were out on the verandah [and] that instant the two first went back into the sick room. Eliza never left it whilst I was there during the day. The King sent her with various messages to get rid of her presence, but not a bit of it—she knew better than to leave us alone together, so called someone else to do it.

I was exceedingly low at heart about him that day, silently praying for recovery and an altered good Life hereafter by becoming a member of God's own church. The Doctor told him plainly all depended now on his eating well. If not he will die, for mortification will set in [and] nothing can bring up strength then.

The above three women, Horace Crabbe, Honokaupu's wife, a grey-headed old woman, Kapahu and Keeaumoku,[4] with one of Victoria Mahiole's boys named Kawika, are the sole attendants—no others. They all said (likewise the Doctor) he becomes cross and stubborn when they urge him to eat, but each day I have been there he takes food—the arrowroot and milk and his brandy punch with egg, milk, sugar and nutmeg—not from me but at the Doctor's and Mr Crabbe's hands.

Once when I persuaded him to eat his arrowroot he asked me to have some with him. When we are all away he won't take it from his folks and they are afraid of him. Once after a doze I cut up 4 or 5 mouthfuls of water mellon and made Eliza give [it] to him to moisten his lips. He could not see me for I was back of his head. He would not take it [and] finally asked who gave it him to eat and she said the Queen, so he took them quietly, but of course it was all forced. When we left in the evening he held out his hot hand and wished me good evening. Horace asked me to go again the next day which I did, remaining till night, and the doctors said he was a great deal better from the quantity of food he took the day before. Actually the inflammation of lungs and setting in of pneumonia had been arrested by strength gaining the ascendancy, so death was escaped from but danger is still not free. Great care and nursing is required now to bring him round.

Yesterday Mother and I drove out after 5 in Evening [and] found John Dominis driving away. Charles Judd was with him. He was sitting up in bed looking stronger. He had to be lifted to a sitting posture before. Dr McKibbin has just gone from here and says His Majesty is about the same this morning, not much better than the last two days. There is great difficulty in getting him to eat. I have so much writting to do for the foreign mail by *Costa Rica* tomorrow that I shall not go out again till Sunday noon.

He is a very good quiet patient [and] gives no trouble whatever. [The] doctors say another such drunken bout will carry King off without doubt.

Monday, Tuesday and Wednesday no visitors called save Mr Mackintosh,[5] Moanauli,[6] Mr Wilder, Mr and Mrs Pratt. . . .

Various and many are the rhumors and speculations about town connected with the King's expected death. Some officers of U.S.S. *Portsmouth* say we must have a Queen next and Mrs Dominis must be it. I think myself Mrs Bishop will be the one whome the Ministers will ask the King's acceptance to appoint as successor to Throne for the great objection to me is my American antipathy and the dear dear church which I *never* will resign or place to one side for public favour. My God sees me from his Throne—what I do openly or not. Frank Judd, Mr Hall, Bishop, Allen[7]—all will be against me unless the King is firm for me.

Kalakaua is playing a deep game for himself to let no chanse slip for the family. Mrs Dominis has written for Keelikolani[8] to come down, hoping she may persuade the King to have herself appointed. Then naturally it will fall on Kalahoolewa and all of their family of course will rise to the first place now. Mrs Bishop on Tuesday said to several ladies she only regretted not accepting the late King's offer of throne.[9] Of course she will not let oppertunity slip now to gain it. Of course the Missionarys all will go for her on account of her American sympathy and upholding Calvanistic religion.

Makalena[10] told Nahaolelua at Government office yesterday, when John Dominis [and] Mr Cleghorn called David out into one of Mr Stirling's departments,[11] that they were severely taking him to task about a report they heard by this steamer that Taffy has ordered several hundred firearms to supply his volenteer company with, which is direct treason and violation of the law, subjecting him to disgrace and public punishment. You would know the law better than I.

The King tells me he is firmly resolved, whenever this illness of his passes over, to give up drinking altogether and perhaps join one of the Temperance societies—that named after me. It is not [a] very dignified course to take, still perhaps better so than fall again. I advised him to make a resolve to himself and keep it. [It] would be the best way of breaking this fatal habit. Mrs Weed[12] repeats to me this evening from Charles Polapola,[13] Taffy's friend, that [the] King is going to die in about three weeks and David becomes King, as Kanaina has advised the King to choose David [as] his "Keiki,"[14] which His Majesty quite agrees to, saying he had thought first of Kalahoolewa, but he is too young. Nahaolelua gave His Majesty a searious talk on Monday about appointing his successor to the Throne. It is best for all it should be made. He pointed out the error of [the] late King in not providing beforehand, thereby bringing on all the late anxieities and troubles. So preparing does not mean he will die soon but is in accord with civilized usages and rules. He told him of the numerous speculations and rheumors afloat regarding his health and anticipated death, [also] of David's message by Moehonua to all meet at [the] King's last Sunday for that purpose, but they did not come, and also of the proposed anexation or seizure of [the] Islands by Americans. He spoke as one of the people and on behalf of them for a successor. The chieves have property and means and can leave the country, go where they like should the place be seized by [a] foreign power, but they the commoners have to bow and bear the foreign yoke, without any other alternative. The King listened without a reply. Isn't that sound, deep, good advice of the old Governor's? So there you have had all the many-sided gossips pertaining to this anxious subject.

September 6th.—Now for a scant gathering of local news. Your friend Mr Nordhoff and family leaves today for California—good riddance. They had the band at the Hotel last night to a farewell reception by her to all her friends. I did not go. He has changed on paper for the time [being] his sentiments regarding annexation of us to U.S.A., because the people are at present against it. Another reason is because the Island soil can only give employment and wealth to a few capitalists and employees, making it not worth the while of his great country to take. Sour grapes. . . .

In the *Gazette* is an editorial "concerning Reciprocity"[15] which says as plain as anything can do [that] the King favours cession of Puuloa [and] treaty and he wishes his subjects not to Petition or set their faces against it. Did you ever see anything so disheartening? . . .

Hua certainly has wonderful curative power judging from her prophetic trial upon your stomach pain. I have no faith in any one like her and believe not her prophesies.

The young mangoes you wish from our trees at Rooke House are ready for you when ever sent for—and [also] other trees. We have been so absorbed about the King's illness that giving a name for your garden has quite escaped me till now. Forgive my negligence but will do so in next letter. I was so happy to see your hands are recovering sensation. That is indeed good news.

Ruth sent for Mrs Cleghorn, Mrs Dominis and Taffy as soon as he arrived and held a private consultation. Ruth says she is going to take the King to Hawaii to cure him.

[KALELEONĀLANI]

1. Eliza Meek (1832–1888), sister-in-law of Horace Crabbe, the king's chamberlain; a part-Hawaiian daughter of John Meek (1792–1875), New England sea captain (b. Marblehead, Mass.) who first arrived in Hawaii about 1809 and who served for many years as harbor master.

2. An elderly attendant; one of several old women who, according to Emma in an earlier unpublished letter (to Peter, Jan. 25, 1873), had supplied Lunalilo with a "piece of banannah stalk pressed to drink, medicated with love potions, to produce intense affections for Eliza Meek."

3. Perhaps Elizabeth or Betty ("Beke") Meek Crabbe (Mrs. Horace Crabbe), sister of Eliza Meek.

4. William Charles Crowningburg, a descendant of high chiefs and namesake of Lunalilo; for main note see Letter 89, note 1.

5. The Reverend Alexander Mackintosh (d. England, 1903), principal of the Royal School, Honolulu; originally sent to Hawaii by Society for the Propagation of the Gospel to assist Bishop Thomas N. Staley, first Anglican Bishop of Honolulu.

6. John Moanauli (d. 1883), member of Lunalilo's Privy Council 1873; House of Nobles 1874–1882.

7. Elisha H. Allen (1804–1883), legislator, jurist, diplomat; former member of Congress from Maine; appointed U.S. consul in Hawaii 1849; arrived in Hawaii 1850. Minister of finance under Kamehameha III, 1849; chief justice of supreme court, 1857. Sent to Washington, D.C., on several occasions to negotiate a treaty of reciprocity. After the treaty was achieved in 1876, he was appointed resident minister to the United States and lived in Washington until his death in office.

8. Ruth Ke'euolani Kauanahoahoa Ke'elikōlani (1826–1883), daughter of Pauahi (granddaughter of Kamehameha I) and Mataio Kekuanao'a (1791–1868), for many years governor of Oahu; a half-sister of Kamehameha IV and Kamehameha V. She was appointed governor ("governess") of the island of Hawaii in 1855 and held the position until 1876. One of the wealthiest of alii, she owned extensive lands on several islands which on her death were inherited by her principal heir, Bernice Pauahi Bishop. These lands, leased to plantation companies and private individuals, have formed in the twentieth century the major portion of the Bishop Estate's holdings.

9. The deathbed offer of Kamehameha V, Dec. 11, 1872, to name Pauahi his successor to the throne; see Kuykendall, *The Hawaiian Kingdom: 1854–1874*, pp. 239–242.

10. J. W. Makalena (d. 1877), government surveyor and member of the Privy Council under both Lunalilo and Kalākaua 1873–1877.

11. Robert Stirling (d. Ashford, Kent, England, 1889), Scottish settler and minister of finance during last months of reign of Kamehameha V; served in same post under Lunalilo; member of House of Nobles 1872–1874. Opposed cession of Pearl Harbor to the United States in exchange for reciprocity treaty.

12. Mrs. Sarah K. (Chapman) Weed, part-English and part-Tahitian wife of Frederick Maltby Weed (b. New York City, [?]; d. Honolulu, 1898). During mid-1860s F. M. Weed and a relative operated a Honolulu photographic studio. Mrs. Weed was a granddaughter of a native Tahitian missionary, Mr. Cook ("Kuke"), a namesake of Captain James Cook (b. Huahine, Society Islands, 1781; d. Honolulu, 1858).

13. Charles Burnette Wilson (1850–1926), referred to also as "Bolabola" (Borabora) because of his Tahitian origin and ancestry; one-time blacksmith; member of Hawaiian Rifles 1866–1884; marshal of the Hawaiian Kingdom, 1891–1893, at time of overthrow of the monarchy. He was the part-Tahitian descendant of Rev. Charles Wilson (b. 1770), Scottish missionary to Tahiti. C. B. Wilson and his second wife, Mary Beckley Ahea Wilson, were close friends of Queen Liliʻuokalani before and after her reign. He was father of John B. Wilson (1871–1956), educated at Stanford University, territorial official, and for many years mayor of Honolulu.

14. Child; son.

15. Emma oversimplified the qualified statements in the article, *Hawaiian Gazette*, Sept. 3, 1873, "Concerning Reciprocity." The writer pointed out that Lunalilo had authorized his minister of foreign affairs, Charles R. Bishop, to approach the United States government with an offer to enter into negotiations on a treaty of reciprocity, and to include in the discussions the Pearl Harbor question. The offer had been forwarded to Washington by U.S. Minister Peirce, July 17. Emma was disappointed because of the king's readiness to negotiate and his advice that judgment be withheld: "His Majesty has expressed the wish that his subjects suspend their judgment until a reply shall be received from the American Government, as to whether it is willing to treat with him on this basis. Should it decline to do so there will be nothing for us to do but drop the subject; should it consent to treat we shall then have to wait and see if any basis mutually acceptable to both parties can be adopted."

Letter 39
Peter to Emma

Kalaupapa
September 4, 1873

Queen Emma

As I pen these lines the Schooner is in Sight and I can also see Oahu and Makapuu quite plane, the red Pali on this side of Kawaihoa[1] and the rough Valleys of Home Sweet Home, bringing back the features that joy use to wear when at Home with you. . . .

I have just returned from the Beach and I see in yours of the 2nd from Waikiki also [about] the state of the King. I will on my bended knees beseach the Almighty to spare our young King from danger and all harm. Your being near him will I know releav him, for your presence and kind words to the poor Invalids is a Consolation as well as help. The news of the King's being sick is in almost everyone's letter here, but not the particulars. I hope I may yet be happy to hear that in case of Vacancy to the Throne of Hawaii [I may] call you my "Queen and Soverign."

What F. Judd[2] says about Taffy is true. Better a republic than that Bastard of Blossom's[3] to disgrace the Throne earned and won by our Fore Fathers, which I hope will never occur. I will leave it to you—if the King gets better to give my Aloha to him. I will ask the Almighty fervently in my Prayers to spare the King and restore him to his usual good health to become a Good King to his subjects and a true Christian to his God.

The Schooner sails directly so I must close, but [will] write [again] by the Overland Mail. Hopeing to hear of the King's spedy recovery, I remain Yours

Humble etc.
KEKUAOKALANI

1. Pointed outer edge of Koko Head on the windward coast of Oahu in the vicinity of Portlock Road east of Honolulu. Koko is a small canoe landing where red earth on side of Koko Head is visible in clear weather from Molokai.

2. Albert Francis Judd (b. Honolulu, 1838; d. Honolulu, 1900), member of the Privy Council and associate justice of the supreme court; appointed chief justice by Kalākaua in 1881. A son of Dr. Gerrit P. Judd, former medical missionary and cabinet minister in government of Kamehameha III; brother of Charles H. Judd, Lunalilo's adjutant general.

3. Peter apparently believed an old and persistent piece of Honolulu gossip that Kalākaua was not a son of the High Chief Kapaʻakea but that of a certain John Blossom, early Negro settler on Oahu. Henry A. Peirce, American minister to Hawaii, reported to Hamilton Fish, secretary of state, that Kalākaua was "the natural son of an American mulatto and pugilist by the name of Blossom, who resided here about forty years ago." (Peirce to Fish, Dec. 18, 1873, no. 231, [U.S. Department of State Dispatches, Hawaii, 15].)

Letter 40
Emma to Peter

> [Honolulu]
> Rooke House
> September 10, 1873
> Wednesday

Dearest Coz

The King I am happy to say is on the highroad of recovery. The great excitement and event of the week is the disobedience of [the] household troops and assumption of Authority over their superior officers.[1] It has been a most mortifying, rediculous and altogether disgraceful affair, with a Russian man-of-war[2] and Europeans in town looking on and chuckling.

The whole thing commenced on Sunday noon.[3] Eight of the men had been locked up in confinement room[4] for various misdemeanour by the Hungarian Captain[5] who told the guard not to open the door till he returned from [church]. To his surprise on return he found the prisoners had forced their way out by battering the door open with their handcuffs and were sitting outside the grounds. He drew his sword and struck one of them on shoulder and lifted the wepon to repeat the blow when the man chocked [him] and knocked him down, keeping his hold on him. Others helped their injured messmate whilst Daniel and one or two got between to seperate them. Some ran for Charles Judd and John Dominis.[6] When they reached the spot the soldiers would not obey Charles Judd. He assumed as much authority as he could, ordered them into the room and took one by the back of his neck to enforce his words, when the insubordinate fellow struck him on the nose and floored him. Nothing could be done. Mr John then made his appearence but the soldiers told him to take no steps against them or they will treat him in the same way. They told these three commanders all they wished was to have Charles Judd and the Captain removed from office,[7] nothing more. They had no wish or intention to be mutinous but demanded that only. When the three gentlemen tried to get into Barracks these soldiers would not let them in.

During the King's illness Taffy never went near him, instead of which he has studiously circulated the report of King's approaching end as a fact accompli. Last Sunday however he rode out, [when] I had been all day at King's with Ruth. John Kamakini[8] came out also for the first time with him. Taffy was not an hour there when Keeaumoku, who had occasion to go into town, rode out with the news of the mutiny. John Kamakini came round to the back verandah where we (Taffy also) were dining and told us the news. Taffy exhibited no surprise. I concluded he knew of it before coming out, and told His Majesty it looks suspicious, the men's rising against their new officers and instead listened to John Dominis. He rather differed from me and thought more leniently of Dominis, Buff and Taffy clique. "Oh when we hear more of this I think it will not turn out to be so bad." So I said no more on it.

Monday however proved otherwise. Charles Judd's cowardice and ignorance made matters worse. The Captain was turned away and also him, who said threatening them without intending to do so but only to frighten them into subjection, that if they don't mind they will see he shall go and bring the Bible Core[9] to make them mind. He [was] no sooner gone than they went into the Palace and took the field artiliry, ammunition etc. over into Barracks and when Mr Judd went over again loaded arms were charged to him. Then and only till then did matters change aspect and then commenced a series of fufu,[10] conciliatory knuckling down parley between the whole authority from King and Ministers down to these men. All the troop by this time sided to one party against authority. Finally 14 were brought round and they were lodged in Kawa[11] because there was no accomodation for them anywhere as well as to keep them away from the rest.

The band was brought out on Tuesday and now there only remains 24 men. They have the Barrack and nearly all the ammunitions belonging to Government and will not surrender. Yet every and any body [among] their friend, men and women from outside, is admitted and they get drink, but [when] the authorit[ies] go and try to talk over and [reason with them] and ask [them to cooperate]—no, they only say we want to see Charles Judd and John Dominis and Buff reinstated.[12]

The universal strong belief is that Taffy with these two are at the bottom of all.[13] They three all go in and out but yet cannot make these men subject. The King sent orders not to hurt the soldiers. The water supply was cut off. Yesterday the Volenteers[14] were called out to attack the Barracks, but when [they] arrived in front John issued contrary orders that no blood was to be spilt and no offensive movement taken, only to keep guard and see they do not get out. The streets were thronged with people and Richard Street cramed, so also Punchbowl Street.

John Dominis left the sene at 6 last night and did not return till 9. During that time the mutineers walked out boldly, took their poi ration of a couple of barrels in and filled their water butes and buckets, in face of this company who could not touch them. Charles Gulick[15] as Captain biting his lips with rage and impatient to get orders to charge and make them surrender to authority. When Dominis came back and heard what had been done he cooly asked Gulick why he did not fire. "Because your orders were not to fire."

Today Charles Judd and the Captain are dismissed from their recent commands. The orders and plans now is that they are to be starved.[16] The Europeans laugh heartily that 24 men should balk the whole authorities. Do you suppose that such a thing could have happened in Alex's time? Certainly no. When the artilery company was ordered out only 7 appeared. Hiram laughs heartily over all this like the Traitor that he is, and sides with Taffy. Dr Trousseau cannot bear Dominis. He calls him a mean coward and a cur. All that the volenteers and outsiders want is a brave man to lead them—that is all.

Goodbye—God bless you.

KALELEONALANI

1. For a day-to-day reconstruction of the episode, see especially Richard A. Greer, "Mutiny in the Royal Barracks," *Pacific Historical Review* 21 (1962): 349–358; also Kuykendall, *The Hawaiian Kingdom: 1854–1874*, pp. 259–261.

2. His Imperial Majesty's corvette *Askold*, Capt. Tyrtoff, arrived at Honolulu Aug. 10, forty-one days from Valparaiso, en route for the Sea of Amoor via Japan. A new vessel of 2,150 tons, carrying a crew of twenty-two men and twelve guns, the *Askold* remained in harbor forty-nine days for painting and repairs.

3. Sept. 7.

4. In the Royal Barracks, then located on Palace Walk (later Hotel Street) on site of present (1975) State Capitol. In 1965–1966, the old barracks of coral block was moved to its present location on the Iolani Palace grounds to be preserved as a historic monument.

5. Joseph Jaczay, a Hungarian who had been trained in the Austrian army, employed in Hawaii on a five-year contract as drill master and military instructor. The blank space following is Emma's. She omits mentioning that the imprisoned soldiers claimed they broke out of their confinement because of toilet needs, during Jaczay's absence at church.

6. Charles Judd was adjutant general; John O. Dominis was governor of Oahu and secretary of war.

7. The mutineers strongly objected to Jaczay's strict standards of discipline. Complaints about Charles Judd, building up over a period of a month, concerned alleged unfairness in issuance of clothing and food.

8. John M. Kapena.

9. Perhaps a volunteer group of Protestant clergy or laymen organized to provide charitable help or perform various spiritual offices for prisoners.

10. Feeble confrontations and defeats. For a similar use of the term, see Letter 113, note 7.

11. The Oahu prison in Iwilei, Honolulu.

12. They insisted that certain parties be restored to office, including Leleiohoku (Buff) and Major Moehonua, Kalākaua's uncle; this proviso lent color to the theory that Kalākaua was the moving spirit behind the mutiny.

13. There is general agreement that Kalākaua's role was suspicious. Though hardly an impartial reporter, Emma noted that Kalākaua took part in numerous parleys with the mutineers. H. A. Peirce, American minister, in a report to Washington, referred to Kalākaua's "secret machinations," aided by foreign demagogues. Peirce was undoubtedly thinking of Walter Murray Gibson, editor of *Nuhou*. Theophilus H. Davies, acting British commissioner, emphasized the antiforeign, especially anti-American, sentiments generated by the reciprocity-Pearl Harbor controversy. Davies gave Kalākaua credit for persuading the mutineers finally to accept Lunalilo's offer.

14. The volunteers were the combined forces of the Honolulu Rifles and the Hawaiian Cavalry, about forty men. It is likely that Dominis' commands ordering restraint and no bloodshed helped to prevent general rioting.

15. Charles T. Gulick (1841–1897), military officer, government official, royalist; son of an American schoolteacher and nephew of Rev. Peter J.

Gulick, but deviated from the political and religious views of his missionary relations. Arrived in Hawaii 1850. In a political lampoon of 1885, *Vacuum: A Farce in Three Acts*, by Sanford Ballard Dole, Gibson appeared as Palaver, John Kapena as Calabash, Gulick as Cockade.

16. On Thursday a delegation representing the hold-out soldiers were permitted to visit King Lunalilo, who promised a message to the troops in writing. On Friday the mutineers received the king's statement (to "my loving people") ordering the men to relinquish government property and go to their respective homes. After further negotiation, the soldiers carried out these orders and Lunalilo issued a decree abolishing the Household Troops. This left the Kingdom with no regular military forces, until the later systematic reorganization of a Hawaiian army and national constabulary under Kalākaua.

Letter 41
Emma to Peter

[Honolulu]
September 17, 1873[1]
Wednesday

My dearest Coz

Your three letters of the 9, 11, and 13th arrived this morning with the enclosure for His Majesty and its copy for me. Thanks—I have delivered your letter[2] this evening to the King when I called at 5:30. The Doctor was seeing that he took something to eat. He asked me to Share some of his dinner with him and laughed because I refused if it was to be only milk. However I sat up to center table with him and cut up some salt beef for him and prepared his cooked crabbs. He eat several pieces of beef, great many spoonsful of poi, then drank a cup of tea with half a slice of sponge cake, which was doing wonders. That was the first time he has eaten solid [food] for a month, save thin arrowroot and egg and sherry punch till a week ago he gave up all that and only lived on milk, so this meal was doing splendidly. He finished first and wanted me to eat for him as well as myself. He was in late Queen Dowager's drawingroom.[3]

During this time he talked and joked of Horace's family jars with his wife.[4] She is a terrible growler and when her husband's patience is exhausted he quietly adds to her, "Oh be quiet, you lioness," which of course was fuel to the fire and redoubles the strength of her growl, and more such amusing chat. The King kept up in a cheerful tone till

I left him at 7:30. They brought him into town last Monday 15th and [he] has improved since then.

On Thursday last (11th) Moanauli rode out to the King's and halted at Pawaa turning,[5] to speak to a man. This man's dog the meanwhile senting something in midst of road 6 ft. from makai stone wall scratched till he discovered a string in hole and pulled out a bundle which attracted Moanauli's attention. He told the man to see to it— lo and behold, it was an ana ana bundle done up in Ape[6] leaf and containing Kumini,[7] crabbs, and other stuffs—some burnt to ashes— stupid Hawaiians use for preying one to death. It is supposed to have been placed by Taffy's party for the King's death, two or three days before that when it was known his Majesty was to have come to town that day. I think that is only supposition on people's part. I drove over the very spot later that evening to see the King.[8]

Taffy's Polapola friend[9] told Mrs Weed that David originated and instructed the soldiers throughout the late disorderly Barracks mutiny by using his hands in the native negative or vice versa. The men were to understand they must obey or do contrary to his address to them (for Mr Parke got him to speak to soldiers to be subordinate). Buff and Kamakini were [leagued] with him. They knew all about it and *allowed* soldiers to take away amunition from Palace as they liked.

Here is another story about David which also is a fact. On the Sunday [on] which the meeting happened, September 7th, Simon Kaai went very early down to Reverend Pilipo's (the preacher of Smith's meeting house at Kua Makela)[10] to see Judge Hoapili[11] of Kona, Hawaii. Pilipo gave him a letter to read, which was from David to Pilipo asking him to notify his congregation that morning of a political meeting the following Tuesday there [at] Kaumakapili for the purpose of choosing a successor to Throne. The Reverend Gentleman did not give the notice and before night Taffy personally called and urged he should do it that evening, which he did, feeling at the time mortified with such [a] proposal, because the King only has the right to appoint who he likes. The people has no voice about it. When the meeting took place Tuesday, September 9th, a man (schoolmaster of Kawaiahao school, Kalauli I think is his name) addressed the meeting and proposed resolutions which were prepared by Taffy, naming himself candidate to the throne, and to have these proceedings sent first to the King's father. The resolutions were strongly objected to by everyone save Taffy's adherents who purposely were scattered in the house to support the resolution. Lewi, Mahoe, and other lawyers strongly opposed it, and Porter Green spoke opposing, and pointing to Taffy [stated] that this thought originated with the serpent who opposed our King at election last January. The proceeding are in the papers, but what I now tell you is the correct tale. Hiram came home and told us a contrary report—that all wished for David.

Poor Hiram is again ill. He suffers frightful pain underneath the curves of ribbs, shooting through to the small of his back. He can now only sleep in a sitting posture in a chair. I asked Dr Trousseau what is his disease and he said he fears Anurism, but it is just commencing and he must have longer time to watch before pronouncing decidedly. ₍I feel tender love for my subject and loyal servant.₎ [12] For Alex and Baby's sake I hope he will get over it.

Upon the King's asking Doctor at that point if he ate poi at his meals, Doctor replied, "Seldome unless he could get nothing else, as was the case on Molokai." [The King] told us both he had received a letter from you reporting yourself much better, and sending a message for His Majesty's speedy recovery. He told me he had already answered your letter. I thanked him warmly for so kindly answering your gossipy note. Mr Crabbe has an awful aversion to Charles Judd.

Sister Bertha[13] refused to take back the money paid in advance for Albert's house,[14] which they never occupied last July, and wishes me to spend it upon some wants of poor lepers, so if there is any leper you wish to care for, write down what they will require and I will get it from this money. . . .

I read your relation of Hila's cloud vision of the kneeling, praying female. It must have been striking to see. I am so glad you did not give in to first impulses of anxiety for the King and consult superstitious Kahunas. That *most* decidedly would have been wrong and offensive to our God, for he said, "Thou shalt have none other Gods but me." It was such good resolution on your part to resist that temptation and certainly was that good God's kind response to your prayers, because he always helps those who trys to ask him for aid. Then and then only can he come to our rescue. . . .

September 18
Thursday

Oh my dearest dear Coz—I am so grieved that my letter yesterday was too late for the *Warwick*. I know so well your disappointment will be great, with no explanation why or wherefore. I pictured you riding home surmising all manner of suppositions to account for the omission, [as when] entering the house [you] lye down with clasped hands over head, silently resigned to the disappointment. It was owing to two reasons—Kakuhina having been drunk since Monday was somewhat stupid and did not take a boat to go for her when [the ship] was even near the wharf, and the other was my writing to the last moment.[15] . . .

Pamalo says King is much better this morning. The lung is clearer. The last news is that Eliza had a quarel with Kaheiheimalie last night soon after we left and [she] has left [also]—King did not turn her away. David went early this morning to King's and whilst the Doctors were there at 8:00 King asked Crabbe who let David in and told him not to let him come again. Do not tell this to David's friends up there or they may try to injure King.[16]

Hipa has not been well and there is a great deal of low feaver and colds from this long continuance of hot southerly windy weather, but the last two days regular trades have returned, which has greatly helped all the sick of town from King down. I am obliged to leave my seacrets pertaining to the succession till next mail for Molokai for want of time. The Band plays tonight for a short time before going to the hotel for His Majesty's pleasure.[17] Goodbye for the present.

Your Coz with much love
KALELEONALANI

1. Memorandum of Emma for same date contains some of same information as letter. I have transferred without comment a few sentences of interest from the memorandum to the letter.

2. The first indication that Peter perhaps wrote to Lunalilo thanking him for the supply of newspapers.

3. The late Dowager Queen Kalama (Hakaleleponi), widow of Kamehameha III. Her house, Haimoeipo ("Lovers' Rendezvous"), stood on land now (1975) occupied by the new State Capitol.

4. The family of Horace Crabbe, the king's chamberlain, including especially his wife, Elizabeth (Meek), sister of the king's mistress, Eliza Meek.

5. On the road to Waikiki, in the vicinity of the present intersection of King and Kalakaua streets, in the general region of what is still called Pawaa. The bundle for working black magic ('ana 'ana sorcery) was buried in the corner of a stone wall on the ocean (makai) side.

6. Leaf of large tarolike plant (*Alocasia Macrorrhiza, Xanthosoma roseum*). Various beliefs concerning its properties have been recorded, including the notion that it should never be planted near the house lest the inhabitants be made ill. It was also believed that *ape* planted near a gate or fence would ward off evil spirits because of its irritating sap.

7. Cummin seed. The standard Hawaiian spelling is *kumino*.

8. Emma suspected that the evil bundle might have been intended to injure herself.

9. Probably Charles B. Wilson; for main note see Letter 38, note 13.

10. Kaumakapili (Congregational) Church, situated originally on Beretania Street near Maunakea Street; built in 1838 under pastorate of Rev. Lowell Smith, who continued in charge until 1868.

11. J. G. Hoapili (d. 1896), magistrate of Maui and relative of Kalākaua; former member of House of Representatives 1866–1867. Kalākaua appointed him to the Privy Council June 28, 1886; briefly a member of the House of Nobles 1891–1892 under Liliʻuokalani.

12. Hiram had been a devoted attendant of the late king and the prince of Hawaii. For this reason Emma would pray for Hiram's recovery, though she resented his growing attachment to Kalākaua.

13. Sister Bertha (Elizabeth Bertha Turnbull), Society of the Most Holy Trinity, an Anglican order also known as the Devonport Sisters of Mercy, in Honolulu simply "the English sisters." Of Scottish descent (b. 1823; d. Ascot Priory, Berkshire, England, 1890); professed Jan. 13, 1851. She was first Sister Superior of St. Andrew's Priory, a school for girls, Queen Emma's Square, Honolulu (1867–1877); first Sister Superior, St. Cross School, Lahaina, Maui (1864–1867), earliest foundation of Anglican nuns to serve in Hawaii. Recalled to England as successor to Mother Lydia (Priscilla Lydia Sellon), the order's founder and—together with Queen Emma—founder of the Priory School.

14. The house, probably in the vicinity of the square, may have been intended for school purposes, possibly to provide quarters for boarding pupils.

15. The preceding paragraph has been transposed from a separate memorandum of September 18.

16. Through evil sorcery.

17. Perhaps Lunalilo was well enough to attend the concert at the Hawaiian Hotel. As the hotel was situated on land close to Haimoeipo, one of the royal residences, the king would in any event have been able to listen to the music.

Letter 42
Peter to Emma

Kalaupapa
September 18, 1873

Queen Emma

It has been a little over two Months since I left, but Years cannot chill the love I cherish for You and Sweet Home. As Byron says, Time at last sets all things equal.

Sunday and Satuarday has been the Calmest Days and Yesterday the hottest. It put me in mind of the Days when we were at Kona,[1] with the Sea Breeze fanning to cool us from the Schorching Sun, and nothing to disturb the monotony of the Night save the low Hum of the distant Wave. Oh how the happy past came to me like a dream— Your Angel Son, Lord of Hawaii—your Husband, Sovreign of the Isles, my Honored Master. As I think of these things that I saw and knew and compare it to this hubbub rumer at your Town—Would that he were in our midst—So Stern in Council, Strict in orders, and yet so kind and generous to All—"Alexander, Farewell."

Our Settlement is yet pilikia[2] for want of Poi. The poor Invalids are all longing for their Poi which have been promised them, but the last three weeks past they have been under allowance of from 2½ to 5 pounds per Week, the balance consisting of a fiew pounds of Rice and Buiskets. It is as much as Napela can do to keep them from breaking into the Store House, although they have threatened to do so, if Poi did not come. So the expectation is that Poi will be supplied us from Wailau, Pelekunu, and Halawa.[3] The Board has made a contract with these places to supply us weekly with Poi, and Napela has got a letter from Wilder to that effect. It is called *Pai*, but I called [it] Tarrow scarcely pounded put in La'i.[4]

Napela and Kaawa has got a native Medicine for this disease, pronounced [a] Cure, and the experiment is being tried on Hila. The roots and Barks of diferent shrubs are pounded with Noni,[5] then put in a cloth and applied like a Poultice to the place or places effected, till a Blister is raised. Then a cloth wet with Water is next applied, which draws the water from the place effected, the process to be followed up dayly, until five days shall have expired. Then the Patient shall take a opening medicine, such as *Kowali*,[6] etc., the result being—Cured. During all these five days trial, the Patient is to remain indores all the time, the windows and doors shut, to allow prespiration to run freely, the more the better—Coffee and Tea allowed, no salt meat nor fish. Kaawa is acting as doctor until the five days shall have expired. Then I will let you know more about it.

I am going inland to look at the waterworks, then on to Waikolu for a Bath. When I return I will finish this letter, as the Mailman goes over this afternoon.

3 P.M.—I have returned from my Bath and feel quite refreshed from it. Our waterworks is improving slowly but we will not be able to drink from it for some weeks to come, as the Iron of the Pipes are rusty and old. . . .

The story you heard concerning Kamaio, Napaepae's Daughter, geting angry to women comeing to my place is all falshood, as no woman comes to my place, with the exception of my old man's Wife who both stay in the Cook House, and my man Keleau's Wife comes down occationally to peal the Tarrow on my cooking day. My old man has commenced to make a new Net out of the Twine you so kindly sent me.

My health is good, but the Anxiety for Home is the only dificulty. Farewell a while to you. . . .

Yours Humble and Truely

KEKUAOKALANI

1. Probably the summer and autumn of 1861, when Alexander Liholiho, Emma, and their young son spent several months at the king's ranch at Kailua, island of Hawaii.

2. Disturbed.

3. Valleys on Molokai where taro was grown.

4. Ti leaf.

5. The Indian mulberry (*Morinda citrifolia*), from which Hawaiians obtained dyes and medicines.

6. A variety of morning glory. Hawaiians used various kinds of morning glory for medicinal purposes. One was *koali-'awa* (*Ipomoea congesta*), native to Pacific islands, whose bitter-tasting roots and stems when pounded were used externally for broken bones and bruises. Peter does not indicate exactly what type of morning glory was used by Kaawa.

Letter 43
Emma to Peter

[Honolulu]
September 20, [1873]
Saturday

Dearest Coz

So glad the schooner *Juanita* Capt. Charles Dudoit sails for Kaunakakai this afternoon and you will get my letter of Wednesday 17th, which ought to have gone by the *Warwick*, and one written Thursday. I send today 3 newspapers. This morning Lucy and I resumed our sea-bathing again at Waikiki, now that the King is not there, but whenever he goes back we will take the baths from Kewalo or Kalia beach.[1]

The change at King's place is that of his calling in Dr McGrew[2] to attend him Thursday noon, September 18th. This change is unaccountable to his Doctors Trousseau and McKibbin, for he was most amiable when they saw him that morning, joking and laughing —asked the last thing when to take his next dose of medercin. Dr Trousseau answered he would come up himself at 12 to give it him, so when he saw the King at noon for that purpose, to his surprise he found him obstinate [and] cross. The King told Trousseau he was not going to take any more of his medercin (he has taken them the past month) for they did him no good, but instead he was growing worse (which is quite untrue, as I told you in my letter of Wednesday). At the same time he told Trousseau he had sent for McGrew and was already taking his medercins. "All right," answered the Doctor. Then the King charged him [with] giving out about town that he was going to die—"If you know I am dangerously ill why didn't you tell me?" After some words together, [the] King asked if he thought Dr McKibbin would come again to see him. Trousseau told him no he thought not. . . .

The reason of this change in the King is still unknown as yet. I and Dr McKibbin [think] it is political—that Americans and aspiring chieves for Throne—[Mr.] Bishop, the Dominises, Taffy, etc.—have suspected them of influencing the King's mind against them and the Americans in favour of me, so have used means and people to go to the King and told stories prejudicial to these two gentlemen, in order to produce a revulsion of feeling against them, and put an American in their place who strongly favours Mrs Bishop as a successor to King, because through her America will soon be possessed of our poor Isles. All these chieves and Americans find me a great obsticle in their way.

Perhaps the rupture between Eliza and Kaheiheimalie[3] may have helped it a little. Not much, Kaheiheimalie told Governess Ruth. Eliza complains to her[4] of [Kaheiheimalie's] taking the entire management of the King's person and wardrobe. She took the keys of all beaureaus, trunks, etc., into her keeping, and waits on the King without reference to Eliza, which she has no right to do. The other[5] said, "You have only right to be conserned with his Person when he wished you for that purpose."

After my visits to His Majesty, Miss Eliza growls and scolds on my account. He tells Kaheiheimalie of it—she carrys everything to Ruth who told me—she was here last night till nearly 10 o'clock. The general report downtown for the week past has been the supposition that [the] King intends appointing me his successor—not from anything he has said, but his evident pleasure when I visit him, and from things he has from time to time said of me since his accession.

People have now put together and concluded from his obstinacy to the Ministers, when proposing the names which I mentioned in [my] letter of Thursday,[6] that [the King] has surely made up his mind in my favour. Charles Judd the other day during the meeting said to Nahaolelua,ᴧ "That body of chiefs [?cabinet ministers] was strongly in favor of a candidate of their own choosing as successor to the Throne. Now this is a matter of most serious concern to the Queen, for she is very desirous herself of becoming the next ruler, according to Lunalilo's own wish."ᴧ

It is these reports which have depressed the parties mentioned and all have worked against me, one way of which has been the overthrow of the Doctors. I am very sorry for the King's sake they are not in favour [of me], for being gentlemen their influence will be good.

Yesterday a Russian funeral went by up the Valley. The priest[7] of the Greek [Orthodox] Church walked in front of the hearse, wearing a long black velvet robe exactly the shape of [a] Royal Ahuula,[8] nearly touching the ground, bordered all round with a 3 inch silver ribband and dimond shaped pieces of same scatered over the robe. He wore underneath this a purple cassock (the long dress a priest usually wears every day) and both hands held an oil painting[9] 8 by 8 inches to his breast. The hat was for all the world like the Sha of Persia's, and only tucked into the [?headpiece] in front over the face.

Hiram has been very much frightened about himself.[10] So too have we all. He has been going to Dr Trousseau till yesterday. He asked if Pamalo would not see him again. I got Pamalo to do so. He said first that he will only do it because I have asked him to. He examined him thoroughly and said he detected no symptoms of Anurism. If there is, it must be in its infancy and cannot be perceived till more developed, but he thinks it is only some offensive stuff in stomach which when relieved of it, will be all right again. [He] warned Hiram never to drink fermented drinks of any description nor intoxicating spirits.

Thanks for your brief note of yesterday by *Kilauea*. This evening I have by same mail a letter from George Davis (Kewiki)[11] at Kiilae, saying Taffy had sent up a notice to their part of Hawaii in the name of Government (as I suspect he has put "By Authority" to this document to give it additional weight) to choose a new Sovereign. It must have been written during the first days of King's danger, for Kewiki's letter is dated 7th September. Kewiki wishes me to allow people to vote for me as new Soverign. They want me to occupy [the] Throne—people there are of one mind unanimous on that point.

> September 24
> Wednesday

After 9 o'clock on Sunday the 21st Wikani drove with me to His Majesty's. One of his coughing fits was on at the time and lasted ten minutes or more. He is stronger and walks about the house. He repeatedly hinted that since I made him eat so heartily Wednesday week, he has gone back to arrowroot and punch daily. He supposes it was my company made him do wonders that day, and said if he only had that company he would probably eat more, but I would not respond to the hint, as I saw he was doing very well and growing better, in spite of all he says about not eating without me.

I went to Kanaina's cottage and found Kuihelani[12] there. He told me of his paddling near to the Kalaupapa landing, but not allowed to land, and saw you afar off on horseback. I thought of your disappointment, sitting low-spirited looking on. Poor old Joe is very low and perhaps may not last long, but is still strong with it all, considering his age. Hiram is well again, quite out of danger.

September 26
Friday

I have answered Kewiki that the subject of appointing a successor does not belong to the makaainana[13] to dable with, but rests solely with the choise of Reigning King or Queen to choose whome they like or think fit for that responsibility. The last bit of news yesterday morning is the King's anger against Eliza Wednesday (yesterday) night for being impudent to him. He threw a chair at her head and a spitoon also, which made a great cut on the side of her head. The nearest Doctor was sent for [and] both McGrew and McKibbin arrived. It seems the King told her to come to bed—she replied what right has a dog or a bitch there, which instantly gave vent to his ill temper that he had been brooding some days, and used a word of four letters belonging only to Waterclosets. She retorted, "Oh, I suppose that is what you eat to exist on." This brought the King's rage to an instant climax and [he] threw the articles at her head.

I had intended to call yesterday to see how he continues to improve, but this domestic fracas of the Royal household puts it out of the question, till a few days more when the King will be settled and not so upsett. He has taken daily drives this week and begins to pick up strength as well as health slowly. . . .

The Russian Captain Tyrtoff presented his duty to me yesterday. He wore several orders, one of which was a plain aggot cross with a small gold rim round—St. Vladimir—which belongs to one of the highest orders of his country, and if confered upon a plebean the recipient would rank as a noble, but being one by birth it gives him an admitance to the Emperor's presence. He is an agreeable gentleman [and] speaks English nicely.

Keano[14] was here last evening and appeared to be looking thick round the waist. She reports Kiliwehi[15] recovering under Dr Hutchison's treatment. . . .

Take care how much you confide to Napela—Hoapili is his nephew. All the Wailuku party[16] are living in town at Taffy's— Hoapili and Keano, Kumaka and Namahana, Keohokalole and Kapukini, besides many others. . . .

[KALELEONĀLANI]

1. Beaches connected by country roads and trails joining central Honolulu and Waikiki.

2. Dr. John S. McGrew (1825–1911), graduate of Ohio Medical College, Cincinnati, 1847; began practice in Hawaii 1866. For many years he was in charge of the Marine Hospital supported by the U.S. government for its nationals on vessels in the Pacific. Strongly in favor of annexation, he was very active in the annexationist movement during the reign of Lili'uokalani.

3. An elderly high chiefess (d. 1877), perhaps named after Lunalilo's grandmother; a relative of Bernice Pauahi Bishop. The original Kaheiheimalie was a younger sister of Queen Ka'ahumanu.

4. The Princess Ruth Ke'elikōlani.

5. Kaheiheimalie.

6. Letter has been lost or destroyed.

7. Father Arkady, who arrived in Hawaii on Aug. 10, 1873, in the Russian man-of-war *Askold*; see Letter 40, note 2. The funeral was for a Russian seaman accidentally killed by diving into shallow water from a dredge moored in Honolulu harbor.

8. Feather cloak.

9. An icon.

10. The "sudden death" of Hiram Kahanawai of heart disease was noted in the *Hawaiian Gazette*, Aug. 12, 1874: "On Friday last [Aug. 7], Captain Hiram Kahanawai died very suddenly, as is supposed from aneurysm. He had just entered the King's preserve, and bowed to His Majesty, when he dropped on the floor, and was carried out dead. He was a true and faithful servant, of a quiet and reserved disposition, and made a favorable impression upon all who knew him."

11. Grandson of Isaac Davis, British mariner marooned in Hawaii in 1792. The original Davis and John Young, Emma's grandfather, were the two first white men known to have settled in Hawaii. The two families became closely linked by intermarriages in the second and third generations.

12. The Hon. Huaka Kuihelani (?1806–1892), a high chief and member of the House of Nobles 1873–1886; member of Kalākaua's Privy Council 1883. Probably a son, nephew, or namesake of High Chief Kuihelani, councillor of Kamehameha I and overseer of Kamehameha's lands on Oahu. A relative of Mrs. Napela, Huaka Kuihelani adopted the Napelas' daughter, Harriet Panana, who in 1871 married Samuel Parker, prominent rancher of Waimea, island of Hawaii.

13. The common citizens; people in general.

14. The mistress of William Hoapili Kaauwai, kinsman of Kalākaua and former chaplain of Queen Emma; see Letter 69, note 3. Earlier in her letter of Sept. 20, 1873, Emma had included an item of scandal: "Hoapili and Keano are at David's Hamohamo. It is said she is with child by him again."

15. Mary Ann Kaauwai (1840–1873), divorced wife of William Hoapili Kaauwai, a sister of the late Jane Loeau Jasper. The report of Kiliwehi's recovery from pulmonary tuberculosis was an error; see Letter 51, note 6.

16. Supporters of Kalākaua from the island of Maui, some of them Kalākaua's relatives or namesakes of relatives.

Letter 44
Peter to Emma

Kalaupapa
September 23, 1873

Queen Emma

   Since my last letter to you my man has found three Bags of Tarrow with my name marked on them, but no letter. On Last Satuarday afternoon as Napela and I were riding to the Beach, we met a Woman comeing up, and her features struck me of haveing seen her before, so I bid her the time of the day and asked her whare I had seen her, so she informed [me] that I had seen her in Honolulu in company with Hannah, Kahai's Wife, and that she was Hannah's Sister, Makanui[1] by name.

   By the arrival of the *Warwick* last Satuarday, Kaawa received a letter from Kalakaua accusing me of being a desendant of *Kipis*, as Kekuaokalani[2] was a *Kipi*, and so all of *Us* are *Kipis*. Kalakaua haveing no cause to accuse me of such a name, I inquired into the matter and found out that when Kaimimoku arrived, he was asked the News at Honolulu. He replied that he was in the Hospital at Kalihi, but had heard the natives mention Kalakaua's name as *Kipi*, and this News had passed from mouth to mouth till it was reported that they, the natives, had heard it from me, as I was the only one that had letters from the *Alo Alii*.[3]

   Kaawa on hearing this wrote to Kalakaua informing him that I was sirculating the News here among the Natives that he Kalakaua was a Kipi and also his Fore Fathers before him. I asked Kaawa if he had wrote to Kalakaua to that effect, and he answered that he had done so. I then told him that David was a dissendant of Traitors and Rebels, and as Keaweaheulu was a little petty Chief, and would not be followed by the *Makaainanas*, Kekuaokalani was such a far superior Chief to Keaweaheulu that he Keaweaheulu got Kekuaokalani to Rebel against Liholiho.

Napela put in a few words which coroborated with what I was telling Kaawa. I also told Kaawa that Kepookalani's Grandchildrens[4] were not ashamed to what their Fore Fathers had done, as they were high in rank, and their Deeds were Noble and generous [and] worth [being] talked about and listened to—so shall their Grand Children follow in their footsteps. I then alluded to you, [and how] when we came out of School you was courted by a Prince and they by Book Keepers.[5] The result was that you was finally married to a King and you sat on the Hawaiian Throne as Queen of the Hawaiian Islands, and that Title you still bear and will always bear, but Keaweaheulu's desendants have been trying and are still trying to get that Position, and they may try until Kilauea freezes, [but in] this they will never succeed.

He got so angry (Kaawa) that he left us and went Home. Napela asked me whare I had learned so much about "*Kuauhau*."[6] I told him that I had heard the Natives speak of it. So ended that.

The Five days have expired since Kaawa's experimental trial on Hila, and the consiquence is that Hila is not cured, but has to undergo another trial for Five days more.

I wish you would send me up some more Ducks, some Female. I have been eating some of them with the Fowls, as we did not have any Beef all last Week and what I have left I wish to reserve for Winter.

We have had no rain since the last Fortneight and our Waihanau stream is all dried up. I think it best for you, if you please, to have my Plants sent up, as the Sea is quite calm and the Landing safe for the Boat.

A Long Farewell. . . .

> Your Humble Servant and Cousin
> KEKUAOKALANI

David has wrote to Kaawa telling him to have patience as he D. will yet be a King. (Yes, when Captain Cooke comes back.)

1. A sister-in-law of John Kahai, member of the House of Representatives; for gossip about his death, see Letter 82, note 3.

2. A cousin of Liholiho, Kamehameha II (1796–1824), and a half-brother of Peter's and Emma's grandmother, Kaoana'eha. Kaouwa Kekuaokalani (d. 1819) became a rebel (*kipi*) when, in 1819, he refused to join Kamehameha II and female relatives of the young king in breaking the eating tabu ('*ai kapu*) and to allow "free eating" between women and men. Ancestors of David Kalākaua were involved in the same rebellion against forces of innovation. In fact they had even fought on the same side as that of Kekuaokalani. But, according to Peter, Keawe-a-Heulu, the forebear of Kalākaua, was only "a little petty chief, and would not be followed by the Makaainanas [common people]." In his ambition to overthrow the Kamehameha tyranny and destroy the new "free" ways, Keawe-a-Heulu had been obliged to join forces with the rebel cousin of the king, Kekuaokalani, because the latter was "such a far superior chief."

In a discussion of "Cultural Fatigue: Taboo in Hawaii," A. H. Kroeber described the dispute between Kekuaokalani and the High Priest Hewahewa, his sacerdotal rival who urged the breaking of the tabu, as a conflict between forces of cultural and social innovation and conditions of sterility: "There can be little doubt that we have here, in fact, a culture change due to new contacts. It is also evident that at least some of the reformers were activated by motives of personal advantage or convenience.... But the main factor seems to have been a kind of social staleness; the Hawaiians had become disillusioned, and tired of their religion." (*Anthropology* [New York: Harcourt, Brace and Co., 1948], p. 404.)

3. Royal Court.

4. Descendants of Kepookalani Keli'imaika'i, Peter's great-grandfather, a younger half-brother of Kamehameha I.

5. Kalākaua served as postmaster general during the later reign of Kamehameha V; in 1873 he was employed as a clerk in the office of Robert Stirling, minister of finance. Leleiohoku was working in 1873 as a clerk and copyist in the Foreign Office. John O. Dominis acted as business agent and accountant for Kamehameha IV and still served Emma in that capacity. Archibald S. Cleghorn, husband of Kalākaua's younger sister, owned a shop selling general merchandise, especially dry goods and clothing.

6. Historical knowledge, particularly genealogical lore.

Letter 45
Emma to Peter

[Honolulu]
September 26, [1873]
Friday

Ever dear Coz

Thanks very very much for the three letters of September 16th, 20th and 23rd. Dear Coz, indeed no—not from negligence was the reason for non-arrival of letters—forgetfulness of you can never find habitation within me. It was very kind of Kiti to send you cake [and] poi, etc.

In reading the account of Kaawa's antagonism against you, and bickerings back [and forth] to Honolulu, [and] false gossips regarding his wife's hanais,[1] I understood exactly your heart's yearning for our sympathy and help, and preyed for you—your defending the family honour alone without my Mother to refer [to] for accurate facts against their ancestors, who have been subordinates [to ours] for generations back. Only when Kapaakea's absence[2] happened did they begin to claim to almost a connection, but [they are] not nearly our equals by many degrees. All these oppositions are good for us. It should make you and I think and search our ancestral [claims] as well as those of opposing chieves' geneology, and whilst so doing become acquainted with ancient songs, their origin, object, composer, effects— also the history of different events and ceremonies—why one should be and others not—for that is the way our Island history has been preserved—entirely oral.

Both of us must listen to these accusations and think over them, search if they be true, answer accurately, for we must march on now and fight against opposition reasonably. I say you and I because your brother is not fit for these reflections and contentions. Yet some more years of waywardness must be passed through before experience is purchased. We must prey God it be not worthlessly. My Mother according to the course of human law must pass away before us, and it rests solely with your constant never forgetting exertions whether to get well. I must work alone here for you to return, and fight for our ancient rights together.

You must make the duration of Molokai a school for the graduation [from] which learning is to be exhibited in altered manly desires and aspirations—a leaving off of low companions, and selecting the company of gentlemen—[joining] with me, if you feel at first awkward [alone] with them. Your voice must be heard in the law-making of our country, giving deep thought and sound reflection. Your stay in Molokai need not be waist time, but the very fact of "being so near and yet so far" ought to be a strong stimulation to read up books on law, or lives of great men connected with governments, and exersise your memory by committing to memory poetry [and] prayers, and declaim aloud alone when out riding and on various occasions—you know best. To hear yourself repeat things makes you detect the utter deficiency in pronounciation and then know how to go on modulating the voice and gestures, as the subject indicates.

To me I see your days and evenings perfectly over-crowded with occupation, besides the comforting interest which your growing plants will call [to] your gentle attentions every day. . . . Besides by doing these things the uneducated around you are taught unawares that a love of Nature and animals shows an elevated [mind] that appreciates beauty in everything God has made—the dashing waves, rosy pink clouds, black majestic mountains and rocks—all inspire us with the immensity of power that is possessed by the one God who has made all of them—even the little troublesome flea, giving it laws to live by, the flea that has such [a] wonderfully sharp sence of smell—and so on through all the minute attoms of life and lifeless things that make up this world of ours.

Did it ever occur to you with feelings of sorrow—it has to me often—that these beautiful Islands, valleys, high mountains, fragrent ferns, wild flowers, spots where far calm lovely views lye before the eye, as at [?Pu'u-ka-'Ilio[3]], Kona,[4] Kalaieha,[5] Maunakea,[6] glittering stary gems at night in the firmament above, with the lustrous full moon, numbers of places and things—will all curl up like paper on fire, for as Holy Writ tells us, a new Earth and new Heaven will be given—

This southerly wind often wafts my thoughts and imagination to weaving and traveling lands of my own, making and peopling many of them—strange and pleasent—

But dear me, how I have rambled quite away from my original subject, David and Kaawa—each a ball ricocheting over the water. I kiss my hand—please forgive the diversion.

With Taffy's faults we must give him credit for a great ambition. He has worked and exerted himself both lawfully, and to be sure unlawfully, as well as right and wrong, to obtain his desire. But there is the fact—he has exerted himself, tried ways and means to secure his covited object, the Throne. All these efforts too are made against strong dislike from the whole country, who are unanimous against him. Still he has not faltered, but keeps on trying for the end. This is a good point in him which we must copy. He is not idle. He has stumbled and blundered before the public till actually he really has gained courage amongst them, and can both speak out and write boldly. Now practice makes perfect. He has done the practicing and it is to be infered [that he] will be perfect consequent on it.

He strives for his ruling passion, which we ought to do, but in an honorable straightforward way—not like him have recourse to base wickedness. Wickedness is abhorent to our Blessed Triune God, so it must not be practiced by either of us to arrive at the same covited high elevation. But we should work in every way to make our occupation there now secure. Be cautious how you bragg or it may end the contrary—as you [bragged] once to them, [when they were in] poverty and degradation. [It] looks at present as if these words have returned upon us instead of them. The reason of it is that you did not determine that what you predicted then should be carried out by yourself—[to rise] from your old surroundings, watch to keep on a par with them, surpass them in all things, regard their movements and outrun them always—

But this is past now. Perhaps we may be able to pull up after all. It is for this end—of coming home victorious over their unkindnesses, and actually using that unkindness as a means of gaining a victory over them, by returning a different man in every respect, refined, gentlemanly, superior in mental acquirements.

[That is the reason] why I have so strongly cautioned and urged a total separation of intercourse with Lepers. Do not eat what they give or use their articles—so as we may overcome the enemy who are many, and shew that our Dear Jesus has indeed listened to our prayers. And we on our parts must not forget to shew his loving kindness in all ways. In the *Advertiser* of September 20th on second page is a long editorial that ends at top of 3rd column, where it says "All successful leaders in the world's history have been agressive rather than passive.

Passive inactivity is not virtue." It keeps people nobodies, neither felt nor missed in the community. Therefore, we should see that our characters do not becom quiet stagnent ponds by constant retirement and inactivity, mistaking such for proper reserve.

Enough of this. Aikoe's box of young monkey pods are left over till next *Warwick*, so as to recover transferance to the box.

> [September] 29, [1873]
> Monday
> St Michael and All Angles Day

The Gospel and Epistle for this day is very nice—Matthew XVIII and Revelations XII. The Psalms for 29th day is applicable to us, as a prayer next Sunday will be, the 17th Sunday after Trinity. If at 9:30 you will read over the morning prayer, etc., I shall go over it together with you on the day in our dear little Church. I was to have gone with the Bishop[7] at 2 o'clock today to translate for him to Lanaila[8] at Hospital, who has asked to be confirmed. The Bishop prepares him for that Rite today, but having so many letters and packages to send you and others, I have substituted Hiram in my stead. Lanaila thinks he will not recover from this illness.

Hipa and I went to see the King after 9 o'clock service yesterday. [We] found he is looking well. . . . The Doctors have left off attending him, pronouncing him well. His own medical man of course sees him daily. Makalena gave Hipa different reason why King hurt Eliza. She got slightly intoxicated and teased to get into bed with him, which led to words and resulted in the way it did. . . .

Hoapili drove round Rooke House with Keano to see Hiram—it was done purposely I think as an impudent slight to me, thinking it would hurt. What a mistake. . . .

My dear Coz, I have bored you tremendously, and as my paper is at an end I will say adieu, and close this rigmarole with the last message of,

> God bless you with my never-ceasing love
> KALELEONALANI

1. Foster relations.

2. The High Chief Caesar Kapaʻakea, father of David Kalākaua. According

to Emma, the family had made no great claims of royal ancestry while Kapa'akea was alive.

3. Mountain peak and view at Kolekole Pass, Waianae range, on Oahu.

4. Probably a reference to the Kona Coast of the island of Hawaii, although the term (literally, "leeward") referred to coastal portions of other islands as well. Poetic associations with the island of Hawaii suggested clouds over a calm sea; a streaked sea with whispering waves.

5. An arid upland plain (6,738 ft.) in the North Hilo District, island of Hawaii, lying between Mauna Loa and Mauna Kea and affording a magnificent view of both mountains. The area abounded in certain wild fauna, especially boars and wild dogs, and was frequented in the 1850s and 1860s by hunters in search of the native Hawaiian goose, the nene.

6. Highest mountain (13,792 ft.) in the islands, Hamakua District, island of Hawaii.

7. The Right Reverend Alfred Willis (b. Lincolnshire, England, 1836; d. London, 1920), Episcopal bishop of Honolulu 1872–1902; M.A., St. John's College, Oxford, 1864; consecrated at Lambeth Palace, London, 1872. Spent last eighteen years of his life, after Hawaii became a U.S. Territory, as head of the Anglican church in Tonga.

8. For reference to Lanaila's illness and death, see Letter 49.

Letter 46
Peter to Emma

Kalaupapa
September 30, 1873

Queen Emma

It has been now two long, long weeks since I last heard from you. Oh how I have watched dayly, yes hourly, the Ocean which seperates us. I have strained my poor Eyes scaning the horizon to catch a glympse for a welcome Sail comeing towards us, which I know would bring me a kind letter from you, but as yet none has come to releave me from the anxiety for which my poor heart is crying—"A Letter." . . .

The greater part of this and last week I have been on the Plains with my men hunting wild Pigs and we have succeeded in catching two, [which] when salted will come in play for Winter. So I am quite ready in the Meat line. The Poi is my only draw back.

Napela and his Lunas seem to be watching one another and write letters to Wilder informing Wilder of every little things done among themselves, in order to be in favour with him—"Pekapeka."[1] As soon as the first rain falls I will commence to plant my plants you sent me. I will then christen them after yours and Fanny's native names, Kaleleonalani and Kekelaokalani. The Monkey Pods I will plant in rows, and some young Mangoes, plants which I got from Waihanau Valley. When I shall have planted them all, I will send you a sketch of my Yard and garden. It has been very dry all this and last week.

My Eye being week I cannot write well at night so I must close by bidding you a long good Evening. . . . I remain ever

Your Obedient Servant
KEKUAOKALANI

1. Informers; stool pigeons.

Letter 47
Peter to Emma

> Kalaupapa
> October 1, 1873

Queen Emma

Thanks, a Thousand Thanks for your kind letters of the 17th, 18th, 20th and 29th of September last, which has duely come to hand. Also with all the articles you have so kindly sent for me. The little *Warwick* was sighted on Tuesday Evening, and on Wednesday yesterday she arrived, but as the Landing was so rough for the Boat to come ashore at Kalaupapa the *Warwick* sailed on to Waikolu, a distance of about 3 Miles to the Windward. I rode to Waikolu with my Men but when the Boat came ashore with her Freight, I saw amongst them that some were for me, until Kaimimoku came up to me with my letters, and the first one I opened was the one containing the list of things. So I told Keleau my Man to hire some men to help him carry the articles, as the road they had to traverse was rocky and slipery by the Sea breaking near, and the spray weting the stones, which made it slipery. . . .

You mentioned about the $30 which you wish to dispose for the poor Lepers who are in need of clothes. Allow me to inform you that there are Fifty at the very least cases of that sort. About half of the number of Lepers here are more or less in want of clothing. Last Week Napela sent Kaawa to go and ask the poor Lepers whether they had received their share of Pai or Beef. They replied that they had something to eat at the time [but] at times they were hungry, and that they were in dread of the comeing "Hooilo" (Winter),[1] showing at the same time their Blankets, the Wool all worn away and hardly anything left but the thread, others no pantaloons, women without a Muumuu but a Holoku only, children with rags, their elbow and knees exposed to view.

I have not entered any of their Houses to see, but I will send somebody that I can trust, and I will find out in that way. Blankets are greatly wanted, but of course other clothing besides. I gave my two men, Maloi and Keleau his son, their Pea Coats. Keleau was delighted, but Maloi my Fisherman looked at the coat for a long while and then answered, ^ "The descendants will be provided for." ^ So he told his son Keleau to remain with me as long as he lived.

5 P.M.—I have just come back from inland. I have inquired at the Store for those who are really in need of clothing, and a Boy said to me, "This is the only pair of Trouses that I own, and when I go to wash I have to wait until it is dried to wear again." Several more complained of haveing no Blankets, Holoku, etc. The poor Lepers have been promised by the Board of Health that they are to have some clothing, but as yet none have come up save only for the Store, and those that have not the means to buy have to go without it.

Today when I was at the Hospital I told Williamson, who has charge of the Premises, if he would have Holes dug in the yard that I would have some Monkey Pods brought and planted, as I have some young trees in Boxes from the seeds you sent up.

Ragsdale and others have been and are takeing Awa root, instead of the medicine that Trousseau have left for them to take, and they have improved wonderfully. Ragsdale now is a well man from what I saw of him first, with the exception of his Hands.

Mrs Napela has been quite unwell these last three days past, and has improved a very little. I am quite well. I hope Aunt Fanny has recovered and [is] in good Health. I have sent 18 Bags by the *Warwick*, but this letter goes overland with a letter to you from Napela. . . .

Your Humble Servant and Cousin
KEKUAOKALANI

1. Peter's translation. The word also implies the rainy season.

Letter 48
Peter to Emma

Kalaupapa
October 3, 1873

Queen Emma

Reading over your letters this morning, as I generally do when alone, I found to my astonishment that I had [misunderstood] the one dated September 17th refering to the $30 which Sister Bertha have so kindly given at your disposal for the poor Lepers. Their are indeed some which I should like very much to assist, and since you have so very kindly asked me, I will avail myself the oportunity.

I think the best plan will be for you to give Money to Wilder and let him give me an order on the Store, so when I receive the Order, I can ascertain from the Parties who I wish to assist their wants, and by buying myself, I can either give or send the articles wanted, which I think will save a great deal of time and expense and also trouble.

I was so buisy reading your letters, and also in seeing that the Plants were properly handeled, that after I had finished reading, I had got it into my Head that you [personally] wished to supply the poor Lepers with clothing. Not wishing a chance to escape to write to you, and that subject being in my mind, I wrote in a hurry and delivered it by the overland mail. It was not until this morning when I was all alone [that] I got all my last letters from you to read, which I always do when alone, and read them over and over again, that I found my mistake. So if this is not yet too late all yet will be right. . . .

7 P.M.—I was at Kalawao this morning and Ragsdale read a letter from Wilder informing him that the Board intends giveing clothes to the Sick, a promise which the Lepers have had these two Mounths past.

I am going to pay a man One Dollar to take this over to Kaunakakai tomorrow, so as to catch the *Warwick* when she comes from Lahaina, touching their on her way to Honolulu.

Good Evening till next.

Truely yours
KEKUAOKALANI

Letter 49
Emma to Peter

[Honolulu]
October 6, [1873]

Ever dear Coz

Thanks, thanks for the letters of September 30, October 1st, and 3rd, and so glad to hear your hands and feet are well. The poi you say is your only drawback. Tell me if these 4 bags full are enough for the week.

The small young tamarind is a hardy tree and struggles on in the most barren dry spots, but [it is] very very slow growing. Never mind that—you can set them out and leave [them] to grow up in their own time. They will never die when once farely started.

If the public road to the settlement passes by your fence perhaps it would do well to plant some of them along that end of your lot with monkey pod and algeroba—a bag of its seeds you have by this ship. If it is allowable that you may fence in roughly with stones another enclosure adjoining yours near that high road—I mention high road because they will be serviceable to the passersby—I would advise you to plant it closely with algeroba seeds now that the wet season is coming on. Just dig the earth a little and cover the seeds—one pod will fill many holes. The seeds can be planted now even before they are fenced in. Ride over the planes and beach some time and put seeds into the ground or wherever they will be most useful, ornamental and conspicuous.

Our Kula o Kahua[1] is quite studded with Algerobas now. Most of them are large trees. That is one of the ways I should like you to leave your mark behind. . . .

I am sorry Mrs Napela has been ill. Her husband wrote me a short note expressing his wish the King may choose me successor to Throne. Thank him from me for all his kind wishes and remember me to her. Mrs Weed tells me that Hua fortold 6 years ago when Ruth had that brain disease in 1867 [while] we were at Kona [that] Lunalilo would succeed Kamehameha V and after him a Queen should reign. Then would follow a republican form of Government and these Islands become the foreigners' soil. Nothing more is heard about King's successor, Annexation, etc.—all is kept quiet till near the election of representatives to Parliament.

I was on the point of going up today with Ruth to Hawaii and back by this trip of *Kilauea*, but hearing Mrs Dominis escorts her up in place of John, as an excuse I made the most of Hipa's bad sore on her head that caused one side of her face to swell up. Pamalo opened it yesterday. Ruth remains two weeks, then comes back and accompanies the King to Kona for his health.

His Majesty drives out every morning. He was out at his place [in] Waikiki whilst I was bathing. He has had a large and higher addition put on to the town end of his cottage, consisting of a large drawing room, splendid bedroom, with a large bow window looking towards town, and a dining room. . . .

The man Lanaila died yesterday at Hospital. He lived back of Ka's place. Last Tuesday as I told you we spent a pleasant day at Mr and Mrs William Pfluger's and one night this week we went to Sumner's house on the reef[2] and the boys and women went out fishing by moonlight. . . .

The U.S.S. *Portsmouth* is reported to leave on Thursday—good ridance.[3] Jim,[4] the man who shot at Dr Trousseau, is harboured by the crazy woman of Waianae named Koleka, at Mauna Ewa—his wife is there.

Prey don't tamper with your recovery by experimenting on other remedies than that advised by Dr Trousseau, for it may not end well.

Kaliko, Kahoe's wife, died of dropsy on Saturday.

[KALELEONĀLANI]

1. A reference to property in "the plain" (*kula-o-kahua*) owned by various members of the Young family and their heirs and descendants. Kulaokahua extended in the Beretania Street direction as far as lower Makiki.

2. John K. Sumner (b. Honolulu, 1820; d. Oahu, 1915), landowner and vessel owner, whose "house on the reef" was the scene of much entertainment during 1860s and 1870s. Second son of Capt. William Sumner (b. Northampton, England; d. Honolulu, 1847) and a Hawaiian woman named Hua. The elder Sumner arrived in the Pacific as a cabin boy, jumped ship in 1807, became the friend of King Kaumuali'i of Kauai, later friend and naval aide of Kamehameha I; employed in earliest government-operated shipping service between the islands. In lieu of wages, he was promised certain choice lands by high chiefs; these claims later involved him in complicated legal hearings before a land commission appointed to quit titles. The original Sumner was the owner of Kahololoa Reef ("Sumner's Reef") in Honolulu harbor; this feature of old harbor had entirely disappeared by 1909–1910 as a result of dredging. John K. Sumner, Emma's friend, married in 1850 a

Tahitian high chiefess of royal birth named Ninito; see Letter 51, note 14. An elder brother of John K. Sumner, William Sumner II (J. S. Keolaloa), one-time member of the Hawaiian legislature, became a leper and moved to Kalaupapa, where he served briefly as assistant supervisor in 1878.

3. Anxious American residents had successfully requested H. A. Peirce, U.S. minister to Hawaii, to persuade Commodore J. S. Skerrett of the *Portsmouth* to remain at Honolulu till Oct. 15, in order to be on hand in the event of another civil emergency such as that of the Barracks Mutiny. The unexpected arrival of Admiral Pennock's flagship, U.S.S. *Saranac*, Oct. 19, made the presence of the *Portsmouth* less imperative. Through long service in Hawaiian waters, the *Portsmouth* had become a symbol of American power in the Pacific, dating back to 1846 when the *Portsmouth* had cut short a Hawaiian cruise to take part in the conquest of California under Commodore Stockton. For Emma's views on the arrival of the *Saranac*, see Letter 52, note 1.

4. In the spring of 1873, Kimo ("Jim") Kamai, well-known boat boy and shipping agent, was being held for observation at the leper station at Kalihi Hospital, Honolulu. On Apr. 2, 1873, when Dr. George Trousseau arrived to conduct a medical examination, Kimo Kamai aimed a pistol at Trousseau, fired point blank, but missed. A half hour later he managed to reload the same weapon and fire at Marshal Parke, again missing his target. On Apr. 17, 1873, Kimo Kamai was given a jury trial at which he was acquitted of attempted murder on grounds of "emotional insanity." The verdict, first of its kind in Hawaii, was deplored by the *Pacific Commercial Advertiser* because of the likelihood that the decision would set a precedent for acquitting later offenders on the same excuse of "temporary insanity." Furthermore there was reaon to believe that Kimo Kamai's mental stability as well as his aim might have been affected by his drinking *awa*. Two days after acquittal, Kimo Kamai was returned to Kalihi for further observation, but managed to escape to his home in Nuuanu Valley. He was again arrested and brought back to Kalihi, although his wife had employed an attorney to obtain a writ of *habeus corpus* to prevent his detention. Kamai was examined by a commission of three physicians who declared him to be a leper. He was also placed behind lock and key. Then, for a second time, Kimo Kamai escaped and remained in hiding until November 1874. The *Pacific Commercial Advertiser*, Nov. 21, 1874, recorded the circumstances that led to Kamai's capture and successful removal to Molokai: "[S]ome eighteen months ago, he escaped from the prison and has been ever since at large, hidden in the recesses at the head of Manana Valley in Ewa District. Here he was well supplied with food, etc., by his friends, had the company of his family, and frequently made nocturnal visits to the sea-shore. The police of Ewa knew perfectly well of Jim's whereabouts, but the Deputy Sheriff was his friend and had no wish to arrest him. That official however having been superseded, one morning last week Jim was surrounded at his 'cottage by the sea,' and brought to town. Last Tuesday, November 17, 1874, he was dispatched to Molokai at last. He was quite resigned to going, being as he declared, quite tired of hiding from the vigilance of the Board of Health." Kimo Kamai's third and last attempt

to escape, so far as is known, was reported in the *Hawaiian Gazette*, July 28, 1875: "Runaways.—A whaleboat landed near Coco Head on Monday morning, containing three lepers—Jim Kamai, Anoho, and Naakaakai—who secretly left the settlement on Sunday evening. Kamai has been captured and lodged in the Station House.... His companions fled to the mountain, but will be taken, if they have not been already. Kamai says the reason he left was because he preferred to live on Oahu. He will probably be taken back and placed under some restraint." For further mention of Kimo Kamai at Kalaupapa, see Letter 120, note 1.

Letter 50
Peter to Emma

Kalaupapa
October 13, 1873

Queen Emma

In my last letter to your Majesty I omitted to inform you of a little News that I heard from Napela. Kaawa by the last Mail received a letter from David saying that Bernice Pauahi and Yourself went to the King's and asked the King to appoint Keelikolani as his successor.[1] This I cannot credit, but being on my guard and not wishing them to know that I did not believe it, as I still bear in mind the warning you gave me of Hoapili's Uncle,[2] I took it all in good part.

Deaths occur quite frequent. Two died yesterday at Kalawao, and one this morning. The one this morning was sleeping yesterday afternoon—Sunday—and woke from sleep crying, ʌ"Oh, I am dying." ʌ The men in the House "Lomi'd" him but of no avail. He gradually sank, till this morning [he] died. The name of the poor unfortunate man was Kaapuni. He was once Captain of a Coaster running to Kauai.

This afternoon we had quite a good shower from the Sea. I took advantage of it and got my Men and Boy to fill the Trough for the Ducks, pouring water on the Plants whare the water did not reach, washing my Verandah, Planting the Vergumbilia on the mauka side of my House, etc. Most of my Hens have got little chickens, but the weather do not seem to agree with them. . . .

October 14.—I rode inland this morning to see the Water Works and met a Funeral precession taking the Coffin to burry. When I got up to the Reservoir, Ragsdale was cursing at someone who through spite had put into the Pipes rubbish and other stuff to stop the water from running down. On my way Home I stoped to see the men put the joints of the Pipe together. Seeing that quite [a] number of men were collected together makai of whare I was standing, I asked the men working what was the Cause. They informed me that a Funeral Service was being held at the Catholic Church over a Woman that died that morning.

Both the Kokuas and Lepers have been drunk these past 3 or 4 days out of the Tea[3] root which they manifacture into Beer, raising disturbance, fighting, etc., and they are to be tried tomorrow.

Kaawa has been experimenting on Hila again, but instead of curing Hila his [own] Blotches have appeared about his face and body, and his face is swolen. I think he is ashamed of himself, as he keeps in the House all day and comes out in the nighttime. He has been expecting to go back, and has been saying that he has been rongfully sent up here, but I think that he thinks diferent of it since the swelling on his face has appeared.

October 15.—I rode into Waikolu this morning for a Bath, and on my way back I stoped at the Store to hear Napela Trying the men that were drunk and disorderly. Some being Policemen were discharged. Others, their allowance of Pai and Beef were stoped. From their Napela and I came to Ragsdale's and all three of us rode to the Beach. On our way down we sighted the *Warwick* at a distance, but becalmed. After we had strolled on the Beach looking at the Waves, we all rode home. The water is about 1/2 a mile from the Hospital, and those near the Church are quite delighted, the water being so near.

October 16.—Last night we had a very good shower, and on riseing this morning I saw that the ground was quite wet. All my Plants look healthy, but my two little Ohias are dead. We have had a rough Sea and Calm all this Week, the Wind blowing from the Westward, and no fish to be got.

The Schooner is just to be seen, but so far at Sea and in a Calm that she will not probably arrive until afternoon. I am going up inland and when I come back I will ride to the Beach. . . .

Yours until Again
KEKUAOKALANI

1. Emma later denied that she had spoken to Lunalilo about the Princess Ruth as a possible successor; see Letter 55.

2. Kaawa.

3. The ti (ki) plant (*Cordyline terminalis*), woody plant of lily family, common in tropical Asia eastward to the Hawaiian Islands.

Letter 51
Emma to Peter

[Honolulu]
October 13, [1873]
Saturday

Ever dear Coz

If I had only known the Steamer was to touch at your Port I would have gone up with Ruth purposly to see you, but alas we never suspected such an event, so instead of me seeing you it was Nahaolelua's and Mrs Dominis's fate to do so. Those on board who had touched there before pointed you out, also Napela's [and] Ragsdale's.[1] We hear Hila has become another of latter's mistresses.

Sister Bertha's $30 has been spent on clothing, as you wrote people were mostly in want of them. We have procured the articles here because cheaper than could be bought at Molokai, and send them up in two boxes. The things are tied in bundles with a slip of paper designating the men, women and children's parcles.[2] . . . In one of them are 3 bottles of mixed pickels and some sugar cane cut up. Your friend Jack Smith sends you 2 pigeons [and] the weekly papers. You will observe the *Nuhou* is enlarged and Gibson advocates the King seeking a bride from the Malayan Kingdom.[3] . . .

I am very glad the Bourgomvillia vine is still living. . . . The scarsity of water is a searious trouble to all agricultural persuits, especially where you are. Friday and Saturday the strange sound of rain pattering on the house tops was hailed with pleasure, but the ground has been so long baked and thirsty that an hour after the rain spells one could not tell from appearances of the ground [that] we had had such a thing—every drop absorbed, dust flying in clouds, since then no more rain.

Are the two water buts full? The air feels at present like rain, sun is vailed in clouds, dark banks of them threaten over the sea [and] Kaala and Ewa mountains. I wish it would come down to gladen earth, beast and man.

Poor Kiliwehi is at the Hospital[4] and bleeding dreadfully at her lungs. She arrived in the *Moi* Saturday morning from Kahului, sent down by foreigners of Wailuku. Koakanu[5] is there with his mistress to try the last remedies and comforts that could be obtained here. She drove straight up to Dr McKibbin and said to him she wanted to go into the Hospital. He asked if any other place could not be had outside amongst her friends. She said no, but soon after thought of Mrs Cleghorn's and refered him to her, but the Doctor declined, deciding it was a matter which only rests between friends and herself. She concluded finally to go to the Hospital. Dr McKibbin has quatered her in the most comfortable room at the Waikiki end of the women's wards upstairs looking out on the plains, cocoanut grove, Diamond Hill, and the blue sea.[6]

Taffy told me he was at the Wharf when she landed and blood was freely runing from her nose. He says a Captain West (I think that is the name he mentioned) expressed his rage and abhorance of Hoapili's conduct towards his wife by wishing him hanged.

Our folks in this yard have a strong suspicion Kamakaaiau is with child. They say all the symptoms of such a catastroph are hers now. I cannot tell the truth of such suspicions, but hope for herself, Stella and the child's sake within her (if any), [that it] be not true. The supposed fathers are Nahaolelua and Kaai. I do not think it is the first. . . .

Speaking of Mrs Dominis, the scandle is [that] he[7] is rather fonder of Miss Louisa Brickwood then public opinion thinks proper. His visits are three times a day. The parties upon first sight signalise each other through low whistles. Be careful not to repeat this till you hear it first from others, as it may return upon me and may be taken up for slander. It is perfectly true nevertheless.

Here is scandle No. 2 of the same stamp—both true. This you are at liberty to repeat. John Kamakini has, like the former person,[8] seen another woman whom "his fancy has painted all divine." Who do you suppose it is?—why Lydia Piikoi.[9] He absented himself with her a day and a night from home, so his wife sallied forth that night in search of him—first to Keawehunahala's[10] on Maunakea Street. He, suspecting her lord had gone astray, past [on to her the wrong advice by telling her that John] was most likely with the Major[11] at Kalia. From there [she went] to Mrs Colburn's, then to David Malo's[12] (her cousin). He was gone with her Husband. Thense [she went] to the Major's [but found him] not at home. [Then] on to Niagara's. It was then early morning and Taffy was there. She could get no information from them so wended her way home, breakfasted and learnt from a boat boy [that] he had been with John Kamakini that night at Lydia Piikoi's, [and the boy] left him there drinking. So in company with Deborah Kanoa she started for Lydia's place, but he had gone [by that time] to Naaoa's new house up the same Fort [Street] back of Napepe's.[13] Lydia received her with the cool impudent assertion that as she, the wife, had come in a mild manner seeking her husband, she (Lydia) would tell her honestly he had been there all night with her, pointing out the various spots he had lain. . . . "You are husbandless. But Emma," said she, "do not be sanguine of your possessing him long, for you are going to loose him anyway."

Emma left straightway and turned up to Naaoa's house, where she found her husband and cousin David Malo asleep. She went to her relative, woke him and scolded him, but did not go near her husband. Deborah woke John Kamakini. Finally Emma asked him to go home. This was then 9 o'clock and when once at home they shut themselves in a room and had a good quarrel. She screamed for assistance that he was choaking her. Someone went up to help her [and] the finale was [that] he turned her away, never to come back. But before the day closed, and when all her goods were collected ready for departure, he detained his wife. So there is a chaste pleasing constant pretty picture of matrimonial life.

October 14
Tuesday

Nahaolelua and Lucy went off in the *Kilauea* yesterday and Lucy through me arrived just too late. She had to pull off in a boat. The steamer waited for her and then went away.

Kamaipuupaa is as good as can be to me now. She always sends and gives us fruit, fish, etc., etc., when I am on my seabathing drives, which she never used to deign before. Reverses of fortune "makes us wondrous kind."

This morning the King sent me some splendid fishes—one is a beautiful Uhu.[14] I have not seen him except [for] an occasional meeting on our drives for 3 weeks. He is so far convalessent that our frequent visits are no more required, although he has waited and watched for me many days these weeks, and wonders why I do not go up now. . . .

Ninito[15] wrote to tell me that Queen Pomare[16] has lost another grandchild, making the fourth death in her own children, grandchildren and husband. She has now they say 2 sons very dangerously ill. The ship is nearly off. Hipa is almost well. All sends their aloha and my most attached goes with this

From your Coz
KALELEONALANI

1. Their several cottages were easily visible from the ship or landing.

2. The order of sentences in the manuscript is occasionally confused; some items and paragraphs have been rearranged.

3. A reference to Walter Murray Gibson's "enlarged issue" of *Nuhou*, Oct. 14, 1873, in which he announced with fanfare his program for arousing among the Hawaiians a more vigorous appreciation of their cultural kinship with other Pacific peoples, especially those of Malaysia: "We devote in this issue as we will hereafter the larger portion of our space to our native readers. . . ." Gibson's proposal that the Hawaiian monarch should seek a Malayan bride was only a part of a larger aim, to present to the Hawaiians "histories, traditions, stories, romances, and songs of the numerous and remarkable brown people like themselves who inhabit the great Malayan Polynesian family of nations . . . that they shall be inspired with hope for the preservation of their race . . . and so the world may behold the interesting spectacle of a race hitherto deemed moribund, arousing themselves . . . resolved to preserve their autonomy, and to keep their name forever alive in the land of their forefathers."

4. The Queen's Hospital, Honolulu, established by the Hawaiian legislature in 1859. The movement to organize and develop a public hospital in Hawaii was largely successful because of the dedicated leadership of King Kamehameha IV and Queen Emma.

5. Unidentified.

6. Kiliwehi was moved from her room at the hospital to Haleakala, the home of Mr. and Mrs. Charles Reed Bishop, where she died on Nov. 4, 1873, at the age of thirty-three.

7. John Dominis. The order of items in the manuscript is not clear, especially in the revelation of the two scandals.

8. Like John Dominis. For main note on John Kamakini Kapena, see Letter 24, note 11.

9. Lydia (Lilia) Piikoi Wond, a descendant of high chiefs of Kauai; in 1860 married William S. Wond, later clerk of the Police Court. She was a daughter of Jona Piikoi (d. 1859), member of House of Nobles under Kamehameha III and for many years clerk of the Honolulu Public Market.

10. Probably J. W. Keawehunahala, member of various sessions of the legislature.

11. Probably William Luther Moehonua, court functionary under the Kamehamehas; later a privy councillor of Kalākaua.

12. David Malo (b. ?1850), Hawaiian teacher, newspaper editor, politician; educated at Punahou School 1863–1867. Taught at Kawaiahao Day School 1869; assistant editor on staff of Walter Murray Gibson's *Nuhou* 1873–1874. In 1876 Emma spoke distrustfully of him as an advocate of the republican form of government. He was a nephew of David Malo (?1793–1853), educator and historian, graduate of Lahainaluna Seminary, adviser of Kamehameha III, and author of *Hawaiian Antiquities* (*Moolelo Hawaii*), trans. by Nathaniel B. Emerson (1898), Bishop Museum Publications No. 2 (Honolulu, 1951). Emma, wife of Kamakini (John M. Kapena), was a daughter of the original David Malo and cousin of David Malo II.

13. Nickname (Napepe'e: "Crooked-finger[s]") for Curtis P. Ward (d. 1882), native of New Orleans, owner of livery stable in vicinity of Fort and Merchant streets.

14. Kind of parrotfish, probably *Scarus perspicillatus*, marked by its abundance and size.

15. Tahitian wife of John Sumner, part-Hawaiian landowner of Honolulu, son of Captain William Sumner, British settler, who first arrived in Hawaii in 1807; see Letter 49, note 2. Ninito, whose full Tahitian name was Te-ra'i-a-po Ninitô (1838–1898), was a high chiefess of Papeari, but forfeited her title by living in the Hawaiian Islands. She originally arrived in Hawaii in mid-August, 1849, together with several other native Tahitians of title, in the entourage of Rear Admiral Legoarant de Tromelin, commander-in-chief of the French naval forces in the Pacific.

16. Queen Pomare IV (1812–1877), during whose reign Tahiti became a French protectorate (1843).

Letter 52
Emma to Peter

Honolulu
October 20, 1873
Monday evening

Ever dear Coz

I find the *Kilauea* does not go till midnight and that she touches at Molokai. If I were not ill I would most certainly have asked permission to land and see you, but the tyrant troublesome lumbagoe has made me its subject completely. I did not know the steamer was going there, so can only send a short note and your papers.

So the American Admiral Pennock is here again like a bad penny.[1] He arrived yesterday noon. Taffy told me over the fence this morning that he has come down with powers from the American Government to negotiate the reciprocity Treaty with out Government. Taffy also told me [that] he and Hoapili was up all last night concocting ways and means to frustrate this plan of Americans. One is for stirring [up] the natives (which Hoapili has done today) to call an indignation meeting this week to sensure the ministers for approving or favouring the treaty. They are to march through the Streets.[2]

I feel honestly indignant against the tribe of Americans or race, here and abroad. The Admiral's band (we do not know the ship's name) played our national anthem from the vessel. We heard it quite distinct from here, because the south wind was fresh from the sea. [It is] likely the King may have been on the esplanade then.

The Governess Ruth's house was burnt to the ground last Wednesday night.[3] Not a thing was saved from it. Next morning I went up and whilst viewing the ruins told Ahaula to get the people to search amongst the ashes for trinkets. [We] found several rings [but] most of the natives stood by [and] never offered to help or quench the fire.

Leleiohoku's house was only saved by the dead calm and giant bucketfulls of water. There was no water in the tanks. Many natives and foreigners expressed their minds upon the disaster as well deserved, because she or her pet relations had no right to late King's effects, and so the fates have decreed it as has turned out. The origin of [the] fire is not known exactly. Some say it is from without, but Leleiohoku maintains it is from within. Their people try to fasten it upon Kahoukua, Kamaipuupaa,[4] etc. I will tell you the particulars by *Warwick*.

Kamakaaiau has returned from Ewa. Last night another fire took place at Mr J. H. Wood's dwelling house near Dr Trousseau's. It commenced in the Kitchen and burnt the rear of house, but the abundant rains of Thursday and Friday has filled the Reservoir, so it was soon put out with only the rear rooms burnt in house. . . .

The *Murray* has not appeared yet. Our foreign mail arrives by the man-of-war. The Admiral was sent likewise to be here on account of King's reported dangerous illness, so as to take these Islands if necessary.

This is for you only. What do you think Keohokalole's children[5] have agreed upon with Ruth, amongst themselves? Why this great presumption to ambition—that Kalahoolewa should seek my hand in marriage, as there is none worthy for his alliance here. The Tahitian bride is given up, and our offsprings will be tremendous alii, and we ascend the Throne. If Taffy should succeed to the Throne he is going to discard his wife and—who knows?—perhaps he will presume for the same honor as his baby brother. They certainly are very impudent —their ambition knows no bounds.

My constant love follows you always.

From your Coz
KALELEONALANI

P.S. The *Warwick* has not come.

1. The U.S. flagship *Saranac*, Captain De Kraft, with Rear Admiral Pennock aboard, left San Francisco Oct. 7 and arrived at Honolulu Oct. 19, 1873. Arthur Moseley Pennock (b. Norfolk, Va., 1814; d. Portsmouth, Ma., 1876), in command of the North Pacific Squadron, had been ordered in 1872 to visit Hawaii on the flagship *California* on a mission of courtesy. He was to convey King Kamehameha V to Europe in the hope that the king's failing health would benefit from taking the waters at a German spa. When word reached San Francisco that Kamehameha V had already died, Pennock was given revised instructions to proceed to Hawaii with speed: ". . . and in concert with [Minister Peirce], use all your influence and all proper means to direct and maintain feeling in favor of the United States, and at least secure selection of successor favorable to our interests." One of Pennock's first actions was to place the *California* at King Lunalilo's disposal for a royal progress through the islands. Queen Emma's distaste for Admiral Pennock, whom she had met at official receptions, was probably intensified by his recent report to his superiors in Washington, D.C. According to dispatches

published in San Francisco newspapers as quoted in the *Pacific Commercial Advertiser*, July 5, 1873, Pennock had written that "danger exists of encroachments of foreign power in the Hawaiian territory, which will be prejudicial to our best interests. The danger lies in the approaching bankruptcy of the present government, and the consequent necessity of a foreign loan, through the influence of which our supremacy may be threatened unless sustenance and financial aid are granted by our people and government."

2. Kalākaua was in error as to the actual state of affairs at this date regarding U.S. policy on the reciprocity treaty and cession of Pearl Harbor. The primary mission of the *Saranac* in Honolulu harbor was to be on hand in case of a political or civil emergency, such as another succession crisis like that of 1872–1873, after the death of Kamehameha V. By Oct. 30, 1873, negotiations for a reciprocity treaty, with or without cession of Pearl Harbor, had broken down on both sides. The decision of Lunalilo's government to withdraw from negotiations delayed but did not end the movement for a reciprocity treaty. For full analysis of the policies of the two governments during these months, see Kuykendall, "Reciprocity—Pearl Harbor—Annexation," in *The Hawaiian Kingdom: 1854–1874*, pp. 247–257.

3. The fire at the Princess Ruth's house in Emma Street was discovered at 8 o'clock on the evening of Oct. 15, 1873. Fire engines arrived promptly but were unable to operate because "the water was shut off from the city," owing to dry weather and the shortage of supply. If there had been a strong breeze, reported the *Pacific Commercial Advertiser*, Oct. 18, 1873, "the most considerable conflagration seen in this city for some years past ... probably would have laid one third of our city in ashes."

4. According to Emma's informants, Leleiohoku and other members of the Kalākaua family believed that the fire was the work of kahunas and court favorites (Kahoukua and Kamaipuupaa) of Kamehameha V, who were disgruntled and jealous because the princess had inherited personal property from the late king. The fate of particular family treasures figured in Emma's correspondence with Lucy Peabody: "Ruth tells me that only a few native things are destroyed by fire, only late King's foreign furnature of bedroom and Palace grounds. Most of feather wreaths, Ahuulas [feather cloaks], large Kahilis [feather standards symbolic of royalty], wood calabashes, etc., were at Mrs Bishop's.... Our folks said that Ulii, Ihalau's daughter, told them nearly all the valuables were burnt, that Ruth and party only deny for shame." (Emma to Lucy Peabody, Honolulu, Nov. 1, 1873 [Peabody-Henriques Collection, BM].)

5. The Kalākaua family—specifically the children of the Chiefess Keohokālole, Kalākaua's mother.

Letter 53
Peter to Emma

Kalaupapa
October 23, 1873

Queen Emma

Yesterday was the Liveliest day here since my arrival. Mr Meyer and Rose came over. Napela received a letter from the Board of Health announcing his dismissal as Luna,[1] and Ragsdale as successor to the Lunaship. Poor Napela left the Store and rode Home. Ragsdale had received a letter from Meyer informing him to have all the Natives collect at the Hospital premises for Mr Rose to give them a check on the Store in Lieu of money for anything they might wish to purchase, the amount to be given in checks. Thus, those who have been here over Six Months $5.75, under Six Months $3, less then three months $1.50. When I left last afternoon Rose had given out 273 checks, and is to renew the giving today.

I rode Home and went over to Napela's. They were both crying over the letter which Napela had received from the Board of Health, notifying Napela to give to Ragsdale all what belongs to the Board of Health in his possession, and to leave the Leper Setelment for Home. Mrs Napela has been unwell lately and is now still weak, but if this seperation will really take place I think it will break her Heart. Napela I understand is going to write to the Board to allow him to remain with his Wife as Kokua.[2]

8 P.M.—The *Warwick* touched at Kalaupapa this morning, but the Captain would not discharge, and so beat up to Waikolu. My Pijones have come safe. It was a mistake in the Man saying that the Manuku[3] was dead, it was one of the Ducks. All my tarrows is [shriveled] so I will give it to my Pigs. The Plants are all dried up and all dead.

I am up every day at the Store to see Mr Rose pass the checks to the Poor unfortunates. Those that get a check for $5.75 are quite pleased, but since [there are some who get only] from $3.00 to $1.50 the Natives have began to grumble and say that it is not enough to get a Trouses and Shirt. I have never seen a melencholy sight compared to this, and I hope that the Allmighty may Spare you from ever beholding such a sight.

October 24.—Our nights are quite cold, so I have given up for the present my rides on the Beach. I feel quite Rich on looking at my Store which I have got for Winter. I have given my two men a pair of Trouses and Shirts and also my little Horse Boy, and some Sick which goes along with my Fisherman as *Kapeku*,[4] and also his Wife. When I go up to the Store to deliver this letter to Rose as he goes over to Kaunakakai for Honolulu, I will probably see some more [to whom] I wish to give Holoku, Mumuku and Blankets, and little Boys' clothing also.

The Story about Hila being one of Ragsdale's Mistresses is not true. It is Mahuna, wife of Kapeau, Okuu's son, which he has been keeping, and now as he is Luna he can have it all his own way.

I am well and hearty and nothing remain but to wait until my Hand is perfectly straight. . . .

Yours as ever
KEKUAOKALANI

1. On Oct. 17, 1873, the Board of Health voted unanimously to discharge J. H. Napela for "corruption" and appoint W. P. Ragsdale to the lunaship. The action was taken on the recommendation of Samuel G. Wilder who charged that Napela had been grossly negligent in allowing food rations to be issued to persons not on the official lists of lepers. (Minutes, Board of Health, Sept.–Oct. 1873 [AH].) Ragsdale informed "His Majesty's Board of Health," Oct. 23, 1873, that he would "try to the *best of my ability* to carry out the wishes of the Hon. Board in *every particular*."

2. J. H. Napela to E. O. Hall, Kalawao, Oct. 23, 1873; Correspondence, Board of Health, Sept.–Oct., 1873 (AH). His request to remain at Kalaupapa as his wife's *kōkua* was granted.

3. Dove.

4. A person who splashes water to scare fish and so drive them toward the fishnet.

Letter 54
Peter to Emma

> Kalaupapa
> October 27, 1873

Queen Emma

Since my last our little Settlement has been quite alive with the poor unfortunates going and comeing to and from the Store with their checks, some grumbling and others laughing at their checks, *Kala Pepa*,[1] and the Store has been very full all the time. Yesterday Napela rode in to Kalawao to deliver up to Ragsdale all of the Stock and all the articles in his hands. I accompanied him. After the Cattle were counted, I rode Home and passing the Store, I heard the Natives saying that ^ the Catholic priest was weeping. ^

On inquiring I learned that Father Damien, for that is the name of the Reverend Gentlemen, had lost some checks which belong to the Natives, and which he Damien had taken the responsibility to take from Mr Rose and give it to the poor Natives that belongs to his church, and are too weak to appear personally to Mr Rose. The poor Man was so confused that he was picking [up] strips of Paper that was scatrered on the floor, asking the Natives whether they had seen any checks, and whether he had given checks to the Natives by mistake, and all sorts of questions, and actually Crying. He Damien rushed over to the Hospital grounds whare the Luna's office stands and asked Ragsdale if their was not a mistake in the giveing of the Checks. Ragsdale informed him that all the Checks given to the owners, the names were crossed in the Book, and all the Checks that were given to responsible persons, the person responsible's name was set off of the name of the owner of the check as it is given to him.

The mail man is waiting for my letters so a hasty Good Bye.

> Yours
> KEKUAOKALANI

1. "Paper money"; in this instance, checks or vouchers issued by the Board of Health.

Letter 55
Emma to Peter

[Honolulu]
October 27, 1873

Ever dear Coz

Thanks much for the large budget of letters October 11, 13, 17, 23 and 25. I answer them in rotation.

Taffy has slightly confused his statements.[1] It is a mistake my having anything to do with influencing His Majesty's opinion in the least respecting his appointment of future Soverign, but Mrs Bishop has exerted herself on her own and Ruth's interest. Taffy never has been to see the King unless it may be lately, but I think not at all.

What I am about to tell you was given me in strict confidence. Therefore you must keep it as such. During the King's illness last month Mr H. M. Whitney[2] and Judge Hartwell[3] went to Dr Trousseau to ascertain the King's exact state of health. When they found out how he was, these gentlemen a day or two after returned to the Doctor with a message for him to put before Mrs Bishop, asking that she should accept the Throne.[4] The Doctor called and had a confidential interview with her, telling who requested him.

Her reply to him was to tell those gentlemen she could not accept the Throne even if offered by the King, on the grounds of affection for her husband, that she does not like to oppose her husband on the cession of Puuloa, which she would have to do. They have already now had several disagreements upon it, the first they have ever had. She opposes cession of territory whilst he favours. Then Mrs Bishop advised Dr Trousseau to use his influence on my behalf, as being the most capable person to fill the place.

Now comes another version of the story which is more natural and authentic. Ruth arrived from Hawaii on the 6th September, Saturday, and on the following Saturday the 13th Mrs Bishop hearing Ruth intended to return by Monday's (15th) *Kilauea* to Hawaii, went up and pressed her not [to go], urging the Governess to go out to Waikiki and speak to the King about the subject of succession, and strongly urged her to offer either herself or Mrs Bishop as candidates for his approbation, because said she (Mrs B.) if we leave this matter entirely to the King's choise, there isn't the least doubt he will appoint the Queen—"Everyone knows that. Therefore that is what we must guard against and prevent. It will never do for her to reign Queen over us, and the King must not be allowed to choose her. If she should become successor, then ‸ 'We will say to ourselves, the scepter of authority has been destroyed under her [misrule].' ",‸

This does not chime evenly with her advise to Dr Trousseau for having me on the Throne, [but] that speech to the Doctor was to produce a good impression upon him for her self-denial and hypocritical friendliness towards me.

When she left the Governess, the latter instantly sent for Simon Kaai—related word for word Mrs Bishop's coversation, and asked his advise upon it. He told her not to follow Mrs Bishop's advise. "What," said he, "would the King think of you, advocating your own chanse before him, and urging to be made Sovereign? Why that of itself would make him reject you. Besides, why doesn't Mrs B. go herself to the King? You know well that the objection to your incapacity for the Throne was [your] ignorance. Do you suppose you have gained wisdom and knowledge sufficient in these 9 months since the late King's death to fit you for governing this nation and settling these vexed questions of cession and annexation? Why the work would kill you sooner than if you remained as you are. I advise you not to entertain such ideas, but rather remain as you are and enjoy the immense wealth which has miraculously fallen to your lot, and if Mrs B. wishes to be Queen let her go for her [own] benefit, not you."

Upon these expressions of Simon, the foolish old woman readily gave an ear to and quite coincided with him—"But won't you go and speak for us, as Mrs Bishop wants it done?" He concented. That very evening he came to tell me all about it. Next day Sunday he rode out to see the King and got a chanse for private conversation, [and] repeated Mrs Bishop's mind word for word, saying that these two Women's object was to prevent him appointing me Queen. The King got very excited upon that and said to Simon, "Nothing can be said against the Queen. She is a good woman. Never mind, Simon, all will be right."

He never said another word about it. Simon returned to town and related his interview with the King, but kept back the King's remarks upon me. Mr Bishop told Mr Stirling at this time his wife would accept the Throne if people would press her strong enough.

I have been belated, so must finish this letter after the vessel has gone. My great love follows you always.

KALELEONALANI

1. Kalākaua's statements about the Princess Ruth Keʻelikōlani as possible successor; see Letter 50. According to Emma, Kalākaua had had no private interviews with the king and therefore could only speak at second hand; hence his "slightly confused . . . statements."

2. Henry M. Whitney (b. Waimea, Kauai, 1824; d. Honolulu, 1904); newspaper owner and editor, stationer, newsdealer and bookseller, politician. A son of the Reverend Samuel Whitney and Mrs. Mercy Partridge Whitney of New Haven, Conn., who arrived in Hawaii in 1820 with the first company of American missionaries. Educated in New England. After returning to Hawaii, served (1849–1850) as editor of the government-owned newspaper, the *Polynesian*. Established nongovernment newspaper, the *Pacific Commercial Advertiser* in 1856; followed editorial policy sympathetic to "missionary party." In 1870, Whitney sold the newsapaper to Capt. James Auld, who sold it to Walter Murray Gibson in 1880, who in turn sold it to Claus Spreckels, the California "sugar baron." During the rest of his life-long career in Hawaiian journalism, Whitney was connected in various capacities at different times, but on occasion simultaneously, with both the *Hawaiian Gazette* and the *Pacific Commercial Advertiser*.

3. Alfred Stedman Hartwell (b. Dedham, Mass., 1836; d. Honolulu, 1912); attorney and jurist. Attorney general under Lunalilo; held same post under Kalākaua but resigned in 1878 to take up private practice. B. A., Harvard, 1858; enlisted in Union Army, 1861, brevetted brigadier general, 1864; law degree, Harvard, 1866. Member of Massachusetts legislature, 1868, before coming to Hawaii. First associate justice of supreme court under Kamehameha V, 1868. In a brief memoir written late in life, Hartwell wrote that he called on King Lunalilo "a few days before he died and talked with him about appointing his successor, suggesting to him that it would save a great deal of trouble if he should make an appointment, whether Queen Emma or Kalakaua. At the mention of Kalakaua's name he ground his teeth in rage— could not bear him. I had learned from Mr. Charles R. Bishop that Mrs. Bishop, the Princess Pauahi, would under no circumstances accept the position of queen. I do not know why Lunalilo did not appoint Queen Emma, for he was very fond of her, and so were the natives. Possibly he thought that the vote should be made by the legislative assembly." ("Judge Alfred Stedman Hartwell," *Fifty-Fourth Annual Report of the Hawaiian Historical Society for the Year 1945* [Honolulu, 1947], p. 16.) Under Liliʻuokalani, Hartwell took no direct part in actions that caused the overthrow of the monarchy, but he was on confidential terms with leaders of the republican movement and annexationists. Though deeply sympathetic with their views, there is reason to believe he "weighed the seriousness of a permanent effacement of the Hawaiian monarchy"; but "once the new [provisional] government had become established, . . . Hartwell supported annexation as the only logical move." (Ethel M. Damon, *Sanford Ballard Dole and His Hawaii* [Palo Alto, Calif.: Pacific Books, 1957], p. 249.)

4. There is no proof that Lunalilo ever offered to name Mrs. Bishop as his successor. It is conceivable that had he done so, she might have been willing to accept the throne if Kalākaua had been a less enterprising candidate and if

she had been assured of support by a substantial majority of the legislature. Bernice Pauahi (Mrs. Charles R.) Bishop (1831–1884) was a daughter of the High Chief Abner Paki and the High Chiefess Konia; a descendant on her father's side of kings of Maui; on her mother's a great-granddaughter of Kamehameha I. Educated by American missionaries at the Chiefs' Children's School; a life-long Congregationalist. Her father, Paki, and Kekuanao'a, father of Lot Kamehameha (later Kamehameha V), originally intended her to marry Prince Lot, but after months of parental opposition she was permitted to marry the man of her choice, Charles R. Bishop, at that time collector general of customs. During the accession crisis of 1872–1873 she was offered the throne by Kamehameha V but refused it. Under Lunalilo both Mr. and Mrs. Bishop readily supported the new regime, Charles R. Bishop in the capacities of minister of foreign affairs and head of cabinet. There is evidence, however, that Bernice Pauahi did not share her husband's willingness to cede Hawaiian territory in return for a reciprocity treaty with the United States. After the election of Kalākaua, both Bishops disapproved of governmental extravagance; boycotted the coronation ceremony of King Kalākaua and Queen Kapiʻolani in 1883. The Bishops had no children. Before her death, of cancer, in 1884, Pauahi provided that her extensive estate should be used to establish and support the Kamehameha Schools for boys and girls, in which (according to a birthday address of Charles R. Bishop in 1887) Hawaiians should "have the preference ... in order that her people might have the opportunity for fitting themselves for such [modern] competition, and be able to hold their own in a manly way, without asking favors which they were not likely to receive." Under separate deeds of trust during the 1890s, Bishop established the Bernice Pauahi Bishop Museum, Honolulu. For biographical sidelights on Bernice Pauahi Bishop, see Harold W. Kent, *Charles Reed Bishop: Man of Hawaii* (Palo Alto, Calif.: Pacific Books, 1965).

Letter 56
Peter to Emma

Kalaupapa
October 30, 1873

Queen Emma

Your Majesty must pardon me for ending my last letter to you so abruptly, but as the mail man was in a great hurry to go, and had been waiting some time for my letter, I had to end in the way I did.

Yesterday, after I had delivered my letter, I went with my man and boy on Horseback into Kauhako after Breadfruit, and also to look for young Trees. The young Trees we did not Succeed in finding, but the fruit we helped ourselves [to], although young and not ripe, is very good eating. When cooked, the color is brown and not white as the color of the fruit generally are. We met some natives their who had come up from the Beach to gather fruit to take Home, as they had no Poi, as only 500 Pai had been distributed last Week between 792, which was not enough to go around.[1] Their were four in number of the Party, Father, Mother, Son and Daughter. The children are afflicted, but the Parents are well. They had made a fire and were cooking and eating the fruit.

We gathered a bag full and then came home. On our way back I stoped and looked at Kahoalii's Cave.[2] I was looking at the Trees that grew around it, Breadfruit, Koa, Ohia, Kukui, Hala, and several other Trees, when my man called my attention to a large flat rock, and pointing said, that that was the place whare Kahoalii would sit and receive the cup of Awa as it was passed to him.

I sat on my Horse looking at the Cave and around me, and all was so still and quiet and nothing to break the monotony save my own voice, I left and began to climb the banks. When I reached the top, I turned and looked at the place I had just left. I could have sat there and [listened] to Ghost stories to perfection, as the place was quite appropriate for such a tale. As my Eyes wandered along the coast, I saw the Schooner *Kinau* going your way, so raising my Hat I waved it to the little Schooner that bore me safely here, then turning to Oahu as I returned Home I sang "Sweet Home."

3 P.M.—The *Warwick* is off the Landing but I think that the Captain is afraid to land, as the landing is rough.

8 P.M.—The Schooner have sent the Mail ashore and sent word to the Luna Ragsdale that she will lay off and on until tomorrow and if the Breakers have subsided, she will land her Cargo, so I will send my man down in the morning. I have had the Rheumatism all this Week. It left me when we were at Kauai, but it has returned.

I send you my first flowers. Not the last Rose of Summer but the first Rose of my Winter here. Their are Eleven Buds in all on the Bush, but these are the ones most likely to blossom first.

My Creeper looks quite healthy and also all the rest of the plants. The manure in the Holes are not yet decayed enough to put the Trees in, so I must wait a bit yet. We have flying showers almost every day, but not enough to wet the ground.

Napela and I took a walk this morning up the Pali. It put me in mind of our Tour to Kilohana.[3]

Fanny says in her letter to me that the King is still unwell and can only drive out. I hope he will recover soon and also to hear of you as Successor to the Throne.

Napela gives his Aloha to you. . . .

Ever Yours
KEKUAOKALANI

1. The poi shortage worsened through November and December; see Letters 60, 61, 62.

2. Kahōāli'i was a historic conqueror of Molokai who became a deified hero or human god; Peter and Emma included him among their sacred ancestors. Emma's descent from Kahōāli'i is celebrated in one of her surviving name chants:

> A name chant for Kaleleonālani,
> sacred grandchild of Kamehameha,
> Keli'imaika'i's descendant,
> of the rank who bow down in full obeisance to none, . . .
> Kahōāli'i shall now reveal
> the kapu of Kaliko'okalani

3. In the spring of 1871, Queen Emma, accompanied by a large retinue of attendants and retainers, among them Peter Kaeo, visited Kauai, including the mountainous region of Kilohana on that island. A chant, "The Upland of Kilohana," ("Ka Uka Kilohana"), commemorates the occasion Peter remembered so well.

Letter 57
Peter to Emma

Honolulu[1] [Molokai]
November 1, 1873

Queen Emma

Thanks, Thanks, Thanks for the Papers and Fruites which you have so kindly sent up. . . .

The news by this *Warwick* here is that this Schooner *Kamoi* went down to Honolulu twice and each time full of Lepers and the Hospital at Kalihi is so full that they were all sent to the Queen's Hospital, and all those that have got the disease and Kamaainas of Honolulu are allowed to go at large and under the treatment of a man by the name of Kaanaana.[2] This rumor I cannot hardly credit, for I am well aware that if such is the case, you would not be so unkind as to deprive me of information.

Kaawa is like a man drowning, grabing at straws. He has told me that he was told in a dream that the red Earth will cure this disease, and have asked me to try it on my Hands. I told him that he had better try it on himself first and if it cured him, that I would willingly consent to his wishes, and if he cured my Hands, that I would recommend him to the Board of Health. He said that I was *Hoopohala*.[3] I informed him that he was correct in his thinking so. I again informed him this disease could not be cured by washing the Skin unless a remedy was taken inwardly in order to clense and purify the Blood, so we dropet the subject.

The new Catholic Church[4] at Kalaupapa was finished yesterday, and all the Catholics have gone down to enter it. All of the Catholics are dressed in White.

I have had pain in my Chest for several days past, and cough, so I have left off takeing Trousseau's medicine and am takeing Kenedy's, my former medicine. It has cured my Cough and also releaved me of some pain in the chest. Kenedy's agree with me better then the Dr Trousseau medicine. It works on my whole system as well as my Bowels.

I am trying Ash water and Salt on my fingers, as prescribed in the *Hawaii Ponoi*, knowing that it would do no harm as long as I do not take any inward medicine save the one I am takeing.

When it rains here now it is cold and damp, and the poor Invalids complain of Cough, Headache, chill, and other disagreeable things.

I must now close with my never ceasing Aloha for Emma and Fanny. I remain

Truely Yours
KEKUAOKALANI

1. Peter's final choice of a name for his Molokai cottage; henceforward in this book the address "Kalaupapa" printed within brackets has been supplied by the editor in order to avoid confusion.

2. Peter's first reference to the Chinese herb doctor, Sing Kee Akana, who put him through a course of treatments in 1874; see Letter 79, note 1.

3. A skeptic; nonbeliever.

4. Before Father Damien arrived on Molokai on May 10, 1873, a small chapel known as St. Philomena's had already been built by Father Bertrand in 1872. Damien mentioned his new chapel in a letter to his brother, Father Pamphile, November 1873: "I have just built another chapel two miles from this [St. Philomena's, at Kalawao], at the other end of the settlement [at Kalaupapa]. The Chapel cost me 1,500 francs without counting my work as carpenter; and I am only 25 francs in debt." (Quoted in Vital Jourdain, *The Heart of Father Damien, 1840–1889*, trans. by Francis Larkin and Charles Davenport [Milwaukee, Wis.: Bruce Publishing Co., 1955], p. 122.)

Letter 58
Peter to Emma

> [Kalaupapa]
> November 4, 1873
> 2 P.M.

Queen Emma

After I had dispached my last to you by the overland mail I rode to the Beach to see the sights. All the Catholics had gone their as their new church was to be opened that day. The fife and drum was playing all sorts of Negro Airs, the Natives were collected in and outside of the enclosure, talking as the Natives do do, while inside a service was being held by Father Damien.

Leaving, I rode by the Beach until I reached my old bathing place. From thence I rode up and into Kauhako. I rode in around it, looking for some more Breadfruit ripe enough to pick, but observing none I returned Home....

On Sunday it was Showery and damp. but in the afternoon it cleared cleared up, and it was so pleasent and enticing that I asked Mrs Napela to take a ride along the Beach before sunset. She consented and so she, Hila, and I rode along the Beach until quite late we returned.

On Monday we three rode early in the morning to Kalawao to the Store, as that was the only time fit for anybody to purchase and pick what they wish. I bought a fiew yards of Twil to make me some frocks—*Palaka*[1]—as those I got from you are old and will not last. Mrs Napela and Hila bought some Holoku and Muumuu, but when we were buying the Natives began to come in and crowd one another to be first at the counter. I resigned my place to them with pleasure, as the Store then although yet early was quite crowded and unhealthy. In all my goings in the open Air or in the Store I always wear my Handkerchief around my neck, and at one end right under my jaw— at the end of the Handkerchief—I have a lump of champfire tied, so that in breathing I always could smell the Campfire. I noticed Trousseau when he was here last use Champfire as Colongue is used. He sprinkles the Campfire on his Person, Dress, and Brest, before mixing with the Natives, but I not knowing how to disolve the Camphire into liquid have to use it as I have above stated, which I think answers for the same purpose.

Mrs Napela and Hila having bought what they wished, we rode Home. We met the Natives comeing up, as they too wanted to get at the Store before it is crowded. Having reached Home, I had my breakfast when my domestics had had theirs. Keleau's Wife and Kamaio came and began to cut the cloth which I had purchased, [using] one of my China Frocks for patern. I laid on the Sofa and read the *Graphic*. As it was showery the greater part of the day, I did not venture out any more. As I write, it is still raining and has been so all the morning.

My old man Maloi came back from the Store just now and informed me that a woman by the name of Wahineiki was at the Store while he was their. [She was] standing at the counter and holding in one hand a quater of a Dollar while in the other she had some Lace, when she was taken with fit and fell to the floor senseless. The Natives lomied her for a long while, and not recovering, Halulu who was standing their remarked while the woman was still senseless, ^ "If she is dead, take the body away quickly and bury it, before it stinks like a turnip." ^

I saw the Woman afterwards on her way Home and I asked her what was the cause of her fainting. She replied that while standing at the Counter in the Store, she observed that everything in the Store was moveing, and from that until the time of her recovery she was perfectly ignorant of what took place. Only one thing she is shure— and that is that she is minus of her Quarter of a Dollar.

This Woman is not a Leper but a Kokua. Her Husband is Sick and a first Cousin to Halulu. . . .

Truely Yours
[KEKUAOKALANI]

1. Peter's twill "frocks" (shirts) of the 1870s were not the same as the familiar Hawaiian "*palaka* shirts" of the twentieth century. The latter, popular today as a recurrent and revived style or fashion, are distinctively recognizable by their woven (not printed) blue-and-white checkered pattern. In fact, the plaidlike pattern has apparently given rise to the relatively recent supposition that the word *palaka*, thought perhaps to be a transliteration of English "block," refers to the blocked blue-and-white squares of the figure, though these are characteristically woven and not printed into the fabric.

Peter's underlining of *palaka* shows that he intended the word to be understood as a transliteration of the English word "frock." He probably also wanted to emphasize the point that he needed some hard-wearing shirts for riding and for work outdoors. It is clear that for Peter and his Hawaiian contemporaries the word "frock" (or *palaka*) primarily suggested a man's loose-fitting shirt, without tails, made of some sturdy material like twill or duck, for wearing comfortably outside the trousers, and especially suitable for work purposes outdoors.

This definition is in total accord with the interesting history of this complex word, as illustrated in the *Oxford English Dictionary*:

> FROCK . . . 3. A loose outer garment worn by peasants and workmen; an overall; more fully *smock-frock*. . . . 1777 Watson *Philip II* (1839) 525. Three officers, disguised like the peasants of that country with long frocks. 1840 Richard Henry Dana *Two Years before the Mast* xxxvi. 136. The duck frocks for tarring down rigging. . . .

I have discussed the substance of this note with Professor Samuel H. Elbert, who has kindly permitted me to quote his conclusion concerning the relation of *palaka* to English "block" and "frock": "In Pukui and Elbert, *palaka* is defined as 'block print cloth: formerly a shirt of this material. (Perhaps *Eng.*, block.)' Kaeo's letter indicates that the word is from English 'frock' rather than from 'block.' Linguistically either interpretation is possible, as English *b* and *p* transliterate as *p* in Hawaiian, and English *l* and *r* transliterate as *l*."

Letter 59
Peter to Emma

[Kalaupapa]
November 8, 1873
7 P.M.

Queen Emma

I was out Sea bathing when the *Warwick* arrived. Although she was sighted this morning, she did not come to Anchor until late this afternoon. I did surmise that little parcle containing $4 was for Haa. . . .

You mentioned in your letter of Hua's being my confidential

[friend] and also Ragsdale. Whoever wrote that wrote a falshood. I have not had anything to do . . . with Hua ever since I had the Griping of which I wrote to you about. I have only seen her once since then, and that was on Monday the 3d. She had been to the Store to purchase some goods with her Draft, and on her way home . . . touched at Mrs Napela's and it was their that I saw her. As for Ragsdale, I have had very little to do [with him]. Ever since he has been Luna he has been buisy, and the weather being disagreeable I have not been out. It was only yesterday that we met at Waikolu. . . .

Poor Kiliwehi is at last out of her misery. I am glad to hear that She sent for the Bishop on her dieing bed.

Napela has told me that Hua has told himself that you are going to Rule over us as Queen, and when Napela asked her when that is going to take place, her reply is, ˄"Look ahead to the future of the king-dom."˄ She also says that the King is not going to live long. She said one day when she was at Napela's, that if you were to get married you would have one more child, and that would be a Girl and your last offspring. I like to listen to all this, however ridiculos. . . .

Truely yours etc.

P. Y. KEKUAOKALANI

Letter 60
Peter to Emma

[Kalaupapa]
December 9, 1873

Queen Emma

I hear that you are still at Kona and in good health, which I am happy to learn.[1] The *Kilauea* arrived here on Sunday with Wilder bringing rice for us, which was not too soon as our Settlement was on the point of Starvation.[2] By the Steamer I received a letter from Aunt with 4 Bags of Kalo[3] and a bag of Salt Beef from Lucy. Please thank Lucy for me if she is with you.

All the Sick are mostly taken down with the Disentary caused by eating Rice and Salmon. I have been liveing on Salt meat, *Pork* and Fish, both of which the Doctor Prohibited me from eating too much, but since fresh meat has been stoped by the Luna Ragsdale, we have contrived to Jog along in this Molokai the best way we can. I have eat

Ilailau[4] although a native Vegatable with my pork. The Ilailau and I being strangers we do not agree. It is a Melencolly sight to see the poor Sick with Sunken Eyes look at you and when asked how they fare reply, ∧ "We're hungry—without even liquid nourishment." ∧

On the 15th of last Month, two men died from Hunger. One Kealohi[5] had been liveing on Rice and Salmon for two Weeks until he could not eat any more of it, as it bound him. However, he had an Injection which releaved him. On the 15 of the Same Mounth the little Sloop which takes up pai arrived late in the afternoon Satuarday. Being quite dark she could not discharge her cargo of Pai. On the following day the Natives asked Ragsdale to have the Pai landed. Being Sunday, Ragsdale refused to do so, although the Natives beged and prayed that they were ∧ "terribly hungry and in want of food," ∧ but of no avail.

On that Sunday afternoon the Wind began to blow Squally, and continued so until Sunset. It then began to rain until dark. On the next morning, just at daybreak, the natives went to the Landing for their Pai. But alas—no Schooner. The Natives were so disapointed that some sat on the rocks and replied, ∧ "We need food." ∧ Others went Home to inform their mates of the sad news.

Ragsdale is actually starving the poor Natives. It is a common expression of his, when a man or Woman go to him for some Poi, to reply, ∧ "You can go die—the rest will live all right." ∧ He has been forcing Rice on the poor and telling them that no more Pai was going to come, so unless the Natives took Rice they will never have any. The Sick hearing this naturally consented. The man Kealohi died on the 23rd and ∧ "a little poi", ∧ were his dieing words. Ragsdale has also forced Salmon on the Natives. When the majority of them have taken Salmon, then Ragsdale will kill a Bullock, and when the Natives come for some meat the Lunas inform them that they had taken their allowance in Salmon, and consiquently cannot take meat.

Ragsdale has showed me a letter from Wilder informing Ragsdale to force unto the Sick as much Rice, Bread, and Salmon as he could, as they are much cheaper then Pai and Beef. This secrete of Ragsdale's I have told Kaawa and Napela, but forbid them to mention my name. Kaawa have writen a letter to Mr Bishop in regard to Ragsdale's keeping 3 Woman, all Kokuas, who goes by the names of Pilas[6] No 1, 2, and 3. These three Woman have their regular allowance of Pai and Beef, and the poor Sick have to suffer.

By the *Kilauea* Ragsdale received a severe letter from Mr Hall informing him of his bad behaviour towards the poor Sick. When Wilder landed, the Natives had collected on the Landing wishing to inform him of Ragsdale's conduct. But Ragsdale got a Horse for Wilder and took him in to the Store at Kalawao, and while at the Store Ragsdale saw that the Natives were gathering outside of the Store, so took Wilder to look at the Water Works.

After the boats had discharged her cargo of Rice, the Steamer began to Blow her Whistle. The Wind blowing from the Westward took the sound of the Whistle way inland. I had just finished a short letter to Aunt informing her of the safe arrival of the Bags of Tarrow, and was begining to write one to you, when Wilder rode down from Kalawao in a great hurry to go on board. I gave my letter to him, saying it was for the Queen's Mother, with my Aloha Nui[7] to her. He then told me that he was going up on the Steamer and would see you. I requested him to give you Aloha nui loa[8] and also to give you a fair discription of me as he saw me. I have not at all altered, only the natives say that I am very stout. My Hands are quite Suple, but as yet they are not Straight. The Sore on my foot is not yet healed but it has got to be very small, and their it remains. I have not time to thank Mr Crabbe for his Papers, so will you thank him for me please. . . .

Your Humble Servant
KEKUAOKALANI

Haa died on the 3d of this Mounth. I have writen to Fanny about it. P. Y. K.

1. King Lunalilo left Honolulu on the *Kilauea* for Kailua, island of Hawaii, Nov. 17, 1873. Took up residence in the royal country house, Hulihe'e Palace, of Princess Ruth Ke'elikōlani, governor of the island and Emma's sister-in-law. The royal party included Queen Emma, the king's father (Kana'ina), Dr. Trousseau, Col. Charles H. Judd, Mr. and Mrs. Horace Crabbe, Eliza Meek, Mrs. John O. Dominis, Mrs. A. S. Cleghorn, Judge and Mrs. John Kapena (Kamakini). Other guests arrived later for the Christmas holidays. The king did not return to Honolulu until Jan. 15, 1874.

2. What Peter called "starvation" was what today would be described as acute malnutrition: a result of the general physical deterioration which accompanies advanced leprosy, especially when combined with faulty diet. Poi was the staple of the traditional Hawaiian diet. It was associated with thoughts of childhood and home. Lack of it brought inevitable psychosomatic consequences apart from nutritional deficiencies.

3. Taro, the widely cultivated tropical plant (*Colocasia esculenta*); here a reference to the starchy, edible rootstock, to be pounded by Peter's servants and made into poi.

4. The word as spelled by Peter is not a common form. Perhaps a reference to some sort of *la'ila'i*, a variety of native sweet potato or its vinelike leaves.

5. The case of Kealohi came to the attention of the Board of Health through the petition, devised by Kaawa and circulated by the ex-constable Kamaka, requesting that Ragsdale be dismissed from the post of assistant supervisor. According to Ragsdale, Rudolph Meyer, chief supervisor, had made an investigation of Kealohi's death and decided that he had died because of his disease, not as a result of starvation: "I wish to say further that Mr. Meyer had already investigated the matter of the two men (Kealohi and another man, who were said to have died from hunger). One Paukulei, the brother of Kealohi, told Mr. Meyer in the presence of Kaawa that he and his brother Kealohi lived in the same house and that Kealohi died from sickness—and not from starvation or want of poi, as they had plenty of rice on hand, and some poi, which he Paukulei had saved for the use of his debilitated brother. Mr. Meyer asked Kaawa what he meant by making out these malicious accusations, and he said that he was told of it by one Kamaka, a man that I had discharged from work for misconduct." (William Ragsdale to C. T. Gulick, Kalauapa, Jan. 16, 1874 [Correspondence, Board of Health, AH].)

6. Vouchers.

7. Great love.

8. Fondest lasting love.

Letter 61
Peter to Emma

[Kalaupapa]
December 11, 1873

Queen Emma

Our Mailman goes over today to Kaunakakai to take Ragsdale's letters, which gives me another chance to write to you. . . .

Yesterday as I was in my House looking through the Windows at my men working on my little Garden, a Woman came into my House which I recognized immediately as Makanui, Hannah Kahai's Sister.[1] She saluted me and after a while I asked her if she wanted to see me. She replied in the negative. Finally it struck me that she was brobably

hungry, so I asked her whether she had got anything to eat. She replied,
ₐ"We haven't any food."ₐ I told her to go and have something
to eat. After she had eaten she came back into the House whare I was
still watching my men work. I asked her how she had been and was in
Health, to which she replied that her Health was good and [she] had
moved from her former place to one just above mine within hailing
distance, the one which Dr Trousseau stoped in when here last with
Wilder. She had not tasted Poi for three Weeks, neither Beef, and that
she had been liveing on Rice and Salmon until she could eat it no
more, but her *Kupuna-wahine*[2] continued to get her a tarrow or two
occationaly, and that she had to eat with great Econemy and reserve
some for the next meal, until [now] she could get no more tarrow.
Pressed by hunger she came to me, which Thank God I had some food
to give her, and I wish I had more to give to the poor Natives who are
actually Starving, and if Pai do not make its appearance, some more
will actually die from want of food.

Makanui complained after She had eaten of Griping. I asked her the
cause, to which she replied that it was caused by going so long without
eating Poi. Poor Woman, I actually pytied her. The greater number of
men who have Horses and those without have been at Waikolu
watching and waiting for the Pai Boat all day Yesterday, and they
have gone up their again, but as yet no Boat. Fortunately for Makanui,
before she went Home my old fisherman Maloi came back with some
fish. I gave her Eight Aholeole[3] together with a Calabash of Poi and
some of my Salt Pork. Since I cannot at present serve my Queen, I can
however do a little help to my Comrads in affliction.

Ragsdale is geting worse and worse, continually swearing at the
Natives, especially at Kaawa for writing to Mr Bishop and informing
him of Ragsdale's behaveiur, keeping three Woman, supplying them
with Pai and Beef, which by right ought to go to the poor Sick. Since
he has been Luna he has made more Enemyes and less friends.
Kamaka, formely a Soldier, is going around to the Sick to sign their
names to a Petition to the Board of Health to have Ragsdale
discharged for misconduct and have me chosen in his place.[4] Kaawa
has asked me whether I wished to be chosen as Luna, and that it was
the wish of the Natives. I informed him that I did not care for it, not
[because] it was a responsible one,[5] but that I if chosen as Luna did not
wish to be under no obligations to anyone save that I performed my
duty as Luna. He informed me that Kamaka's Petition was signed by

over 200 names. I requested Kaawa to thank the Natives for me, but until then I would stand Neutral.

Since the rain has subsided and the wind abated, we have had very good Wether. I have noticed that those that have died here died mostly from Cold, Disentary and Diarhea, and not from the Leper, but perhaps those other diseases have help to shorten their Lives. . . .

Hopeing to hear that His Majesty is improveing in Health and Your Majesty ever in good Health

I remain ever Yours
KEKUAOKALANI

Aloha to Mele and Kalawaianui.[6]

1. A sister-in-law of John Kahai, member of the legislature; see Letter 82, note 3.

2. Grandaunt; female relative of grandparents' generation.

3. The young stage of a fish, the *āhole* (*Kuhlia sandvicensis*), also called "sea pig"; it was found in both fresh and salt water.

4. The Board of Health, after receiving the petition or petitions, requested Ragsdale to comment on the charge that patients were being "starved" and that at least two had died. On Dec. 11, in a letter to E. O. Hall, president of the Board of Health, Ragsdale denied both charges and described the petitions as spite work of J. H. Napela and several of Napela's fellow malcontents, including Peter Kaeo: "I can say however that the allegation made against me in these several petitions are not true, but it is a tissue of falsehood from beginning to end. Kaawa is a boon friend of Napela, our Mormon Elder here at this place, and for this reason he was to have been appointed Sheriff of the place, if Mr. Napela had succeeded in getting Halulu discharged, who was Sheriff when Napela was Luna and who is still Sheriff of the place and a very worthy Officer. . . . Napela is making or trying to make the people believe that they will be ordered to their homes as soon as the Legislature meets and of course the ignorant believes him, and several have become Mormons under this illusion. I verily believe that Kaawa was instigated to do what they have done by Napela—who are holding secret meetings at a place call[ed] Kauhako, a round volcanic hole—and I am told that the signers of the several petitions against me are Mormons, who used to live like Princes when the latter had the key to the supply or food house of this institution. I wish to convince your excellency by my *works* that all the charges made against me by the afore-mentioned parties is based upon *untruths* and *spite*, and is without any foundation whatever in fact. . . . On last Saturday Mr. Kaawa complained of eating too much salt food—I told him that I could not help it. My orders is one week in Salmon and the other Beef, but to keep the peace I bought him a fowl (although he is said to be a moneyed man) and did the same for Mrs. Napela who made the same complaint. . . . I did this however on principle to shew

these parties that I was willing to give them anything that belonged to myself but I could not give them anything that belonged to the Board of Health beyond my orders." (William Ragsdale to E. O. Hall, Kalaupapa, Dec. 11, 1873 [Correspondence, Board of Health, AH].) One month later, Ragsdale named Peter Kaeo along with Napela as his chief enemy: "I have no doubt but that you noticed in all petitions against me Kaawa's name as one of the foremost leaders, Kaawa being the boon friend of Peter Kaeo and J. H. Napela, who are trying to do all they can to make mischief amongst the ignorant portion of the lepers under my charge." (William Ragsdale to C. T. Gulick, Kalaupapa, Jan. 16, 1874; Correspondence, Board of Health, AH.)

5. Peter probably means that he does not wish to avoid responsibility, but only wants to remain his own man.

6. Probably an elder brother of Grace Kamaikui Kahōali'i, Emma's young cousin; Mele was perhaps his wife. For main note on Kalawaianui, see Letter 122, note 1.

Letter 62
Peter to Emma

[Kalaupapa]
December 17, 1873

Queen Emma

Your Majesty cannot form any Idea how ancious I am to hear from you, but I must wait. In Aunty's last letter to me, she inform me of your being detained to stop a while longer by Keelikolani and Trousseau, in order to cheer the King, and [because] without you His Majesty does not Eat.

I also learnd of your going over to Waiaha. Perhaps your Majesty have forgoten that the last time you and I were their together was the morning that we rode to Waiaha and you told me to look into *Halia*[1] and see if you could obtain your wish in regard to Keelikolani's health. But when I read in Fanny's letter and saw that she stated of your going over their, all came to my memory—Your Late Lamented Husband, the Young Prince, the happy days, all, all is past and never to be forgoten by me, as I linger here alone in this Hour of my Exile. But I still Hope for better to come, and with the Allmighty's help I may yet come Home to the Dearest spot on Earth to me and serve you.

Last Monday I rode in to the Store and bought some Castile Soap. While their Williamson the Purveyor of the Hospital asked me to go over with him to look at a man that he has been expecting to die these Five Weeks past. He Williamson has had three Coffins made for him, two of which Williamson has sold, and their is one waiting for him to be put in. I consented and we went in to one of the Wards. Their on a couch lay a figure of what was once a man.

No power of description which I possess can convey any correct Idea of his appearance. Their he lay. His face was one mass of swolen flesh, his body was reduced to a mere Skeleton with no signs of life unless closely watched. When I observed that his covering moved just at his middle, I did [not] neither could I remain in their longer. I asked Williamson how his appetite was before he was so week. He replied that if he did eat he would eat a great deal, but since Poi has been scarce, he has fallen to what I saw their before me.

The long looked for Pai came at last last Satuarday.[2] The majority of the Sick received their Pai with only a fiew exceptions, who was served on last Monday, as another Boat had come with Pai.

Kaawa is going around among the Natives with a petition to the Board of Health to have Ragsdale discharged. This is the same Petition of which I wrote to you about in my last. . . .

5 P.M.—I have just returned from my ride. While out by the Hospital Williamson called me and informed me that the Boy who he and I looked at was just dead, and it was a curiosity to see it. So Ragsdale, Williamson and myself went in the Ward, and their he laid. What was left of him was nothing but skin and bone, although he had a good breakfast, so Williamson say. When I returned from my ride my fisherman had come back with some Kala and Aku.[3]

Hopeing to hear well of your Majestys . . . .

> I remain Ever
> Your Humble
> KEKUAOKALANI

1. Halia was the old name for a "magic" pool at Waiaha, North Kona, island of Hawaii. The incident recalled by Peter suggests that the pool was believed to be inhabited by a water spirit, probably a lizard god, who could fulfill wishes. The word hali'a, meaning a sudden thought or remembrance of someone loved, appears to be related to the pool's restorative power.

2. As early as Nov. 7, 1873, Rudolph Meyer had warned C. T. Gulick, chairman of the Board of Health, that its regulations in the matter of food rations failed to reflect changing conditions of supply and demand: that is, the number of lepers was constantly increasing at Kalaupapa while the amount

of poi contracted by the board for distribution remained stationary. On Jan. 9, 1874, Meyer wrote again to Gulick pointing out that the failure of the *Warwick* to land supplies at Kalaupapa in time to replenish food reserves would mean that "the people will be pilikia [in trouble]." It was not until Feb. 26, 1874, two-and-one-half months after the original notification, that the board finally took action to change its regulations, when Samuel G. Wilder made a formal report at a board meeting. It would appear that Peter Kaeo's complaints helped materially to spur the board into meeting the crisis. Wilder said first that Peter Kaeo's charge that lepers were being starved was without foundation. Then he went on to explain that the present rations to lepers were too small and needed to be increased: ". . . Mr. Wilder reported that he had visited the Leper Asylum on Molokai on the 24th instant and investigated the charge of Peter Young against W. P. Ragsdale, and found that they were entirely false. Mr. Wilder further reported that the Lepers complained that the rations of rice and meat were too small, and that as far as his observation went their complaints were well founded, and he recommended an increase of one pound rice and one pound of meat to the weekly rations, which was acceded to by the Board of Health." (Minutes, Board of Health, Feb. 26, 1874 [AH].)

3. *Kala* is a kind of squirrel fish; *aku* is the bonito or tuna fish.

PART TWO / *Torches in a Cloud*

January 6, 1874–December 29, 1874

Kailua, on the Kona Coast of the island of Hawaii, where King Lunalilo spent the Christmas holidays of 1873, from mid-November to mid-January 1874, served for many years as pleasure ground and rest haven for high chiefs and rulers of the Hawaiian Kingdom. After the last of his conquests, Kamehameha the Great passed many a month on the unstrenuous Kona shore. There about the year 1838 John Adams Kuakini, brother of Queen Ka'ahumanu, built the royal country house called Hulihe'e ("Turn-free," an allusion perhaps to the spot as a peaceful waterside retreat), and there during the 1860s and 1870s the Princess Ruth Ke'elikōlani dispensed to notable visitors traditional Hawaiian hospitality. Sophia Cracroft, touring the Kingdom in April 1861 with Lady Franklin, remembered well Hulihe'e's provincial coral-block "palace" and grounds, where she and her elderly companion had luxuriated amidst unbroken repose: the uncluttered parlors, airy bedrooms, grassy enclosure, and lava sea-wall where a Hawaiian-style belvedere—an open pavilion of plaited palm-fronds—gazed directly upon the soporific wave.

> Of a truth, if we *have* worked hard we are now idle: yet never *idle*—only in perfect rest. We have a great house all to ourselves—every door and window open, scanty furniture (only one bed, a sofa, table and chairs) but the litters still make the best of beds. . . . As I said, we repose—amidst books, writing, watching the surf-riders. . . . In the evening we go out on the litters, as it is not a climate for much walking, though the most delightful when one need make no exertion.[1]

A perfect spot, clearly, for a capacious two-storied cottage or combination health resort and private hotel.

Of the royal party, only Dr. Trousseau and the adjutant general, Charles Judd, lodged in Hulihe'e at night, in rooms adjacent to Lunalilo's. The rest of the entourage, numbering about thirty persons, distributed themselves among nearby grass houses and rented quarters in the Kailua neighborhood, and the king's old father, Kana'ina, was lodged "in a Chinaman's shop" in the village. At dinner in the evening, sometimes as many as sixteen select guests joined the royal table at Hulihe'e. It is pleasant to think of a gay Lunalilo presiding over the festivities of the season, with musical entertainment as a regular feature: ". . . singing to Guitar, mouth consatinas, and accordion. . . . The King is much better already, eats well, and has danced each evening. He is getting better and the Doctor hopes to see him continue to improve."[2]

Unfortunately the improvement was but an illusion; too often one good day was followed by two that were bad. In early January, after an ominous sudden return to Honolulu, Lunalilo's hold on life weakened visibly. "Come . . . as quick as you can, the King is in danger," Emma in Honolulu wrote on January 19 to Lucy Peabody, who was lingering behind in Kona.

> There is a great move to get Kalakaua appointed successor and it is represented that it is the wish of the people but it is not the truth. Only his party thinks so and talk to stir the people up in favour of it. The King is firm to have me appointed. This is a secret, he told me so himself just now, never breathe it to anyone but send word to Kewiki and to Simon for me, to work openly in my favour for they need fear nobody. I shall be chosen. The King says come what may, no one but me shall sit on the throne.[3]

Nor were Emma's hopes to succeed to the crown of the Kamehamehas unfounded. Sources unsympathetic to her aspirations, including the Honolulu newspapers in English, admitted that Lunalilo would probably have chosen Emma as his successor if only he had been able to follow his own desire. It was the king's chief minister, Charles R. Bishop,[4] who drew an observant distinction between Lunalilo's personal wish and his irresolute will. True, Lunalilo wanted Queen Emma as his successor, but he didn't want to make the legal decision. Although Bishop does not precisely say so, perhaps the fact of the matter was that at the age of thirty-nine the boyish king could not bring himself to realize he must soon die.[5]

> Of course we are very anxious that [Lunalilo] should appoint a successor [Bishop wrote to Judge E. H. Allen in late January] so as to avoid the damaging effects, trouble and expense of another election; and though we have used every argument and entreaty we have not succeeded. The public mind seems to be settled upon Kalakaua as the coming man, and as it is very doubtful if a majority of the Nobles would approve of any other, we have tried our best to have the King appoint him. Queen Emma, Ruth Keelikolani and Mrs Bishop have each given him the same advice. Kalakaua has behaved in such a way towards the King as to offend him grievously, and it seems impossible to appoint him—he has indicated a preference for Queen Emma though he has not said he wants to appoint her. He has not *named*

anyone. Some would prefer the young man, brother of Kalakaua, William Pitt Leleiohoku, but there are strong objections both to Emma and to him; and Kalakaua, under the circumstances, will probably be the next King either by appointment or election, and most likely by the latter mode.

I think Kalakaua has been a good deal misrepresented. Should he have the responsibilities of a Sovereign put upon him, I trust that he will be reasonable, impartial and careful. You and I are aware of his weaknesses and faults, but what can we do, except to make the best of our position. There are strong fears that Queen Emma would be partial to a clique. Perhaps they do her injustice. The people would prefer a King to a Queen, and yet a Queen who would be impartial, select the best advisers to be had, and *trust* fully in them, would be better than a stupid and conceited King. The curse of this little community is that there are so many advisers. The influence of elections, flattery and demagogism has been damaging.[6]

King Lunalilo died on February 3, after a succession of profuse lung hemorrhages. The election of David Kalākaua to the vacant throne took place at the courthouse in Honolulu on February 12. Kalākaua won by a substantial legislative victory—thirty-nine ballots in his favor to Emma's six. During the days and nights preceding the election, the queen was deep in session at Rooke House, the home of her childhood, attempting to improvise a winning campaign. She relied much on the services and advice of a native secretary, a learned poet and genealogist named Kepelino,[7] who composed proclamations in the native tongue and acted as royal emissary between the queen and supporters about the town. Kepelino even risked a charge of treason by drafting a petition in the form of a letter to Queen Victoria, praying that six British gunboats be dispatched to Honolulu to aid Queen Emma in her cause.

Meanwhile hordes of native townsfolk crowded into Emma's open yard at Rooke House as their overflow, swelled by straggling late arrivals from outlying Oahu, poured into the neighboring byways and lanes. Within the yard, Hawaiian chanters recited their florid odes, some of them composed especially for the occasion—"The Highest of the Kingdom," "The Blossom of Honolulu"—celebrating Emma's ancestry and international renown.

> Lovely is the Lady Emalani,
> flower of Honolulu town,
> reposing by the quiet garden of Rooke House.

Her fame spans oceans,
far away Britannia breathes of her fragrance.[8]

Emma's landslide defeat at the ballot box was followed by the inglorious Courthouse Riot. A mob of "Queenites," her *kipi* supporters, on hearing the election count, stormed into the courthouse, destroying furniture, books, and valuable public records, as well as manhandling several Hawaiian members of the legislature. There is no clear proof that Emma wilfully plotted such turbulent behavior, but there can be no doubt that she sympathized with the ringleaders of the riot (Peter did so heartily) and by her failure to curb their loyalty gave her followers encouragement and moral aid.

Kepelino's scheme, however it was hatched, that Queen Victoria or the emperor of the French might be persuaded to intervene unilaterally in Hawaiian internal affairs came to nothing. Not a speedy flotilla of British men-of-war but the sight of three "national vessels" already at anchor in the harbor, and the very visible presence ashore of marines and able seamen from the U.S.S. *Portsmouth*, the U.S.S. *Tuscarora*, and even H.B.M.'s *Tenedos*, restored a sense of security to an anxious capital, and to none more so than its foreign residents.

Peter learned of King Lunalilo's death promptly from Queen Emma; he had news again from his cousin on the twelfth and the twenty-first. It was not until two days later, February 23, that he could bring himself to frame an answer, and even then he could hardly complete his last page: "I will rest and finish in the morning, as my eyes pains me, and am still a little weak."

1. Alfons L. Korn, *The Victorian Visitors: An Account of the Hawaiian Kingdom, 1861–1866* (Honolulu: University of Hawaii Press, 1958), pp. 71–72.

2. Emma to Lucy Peabody, Kailua, island of Hawaii, Nov. 22, 1873 (BM).

3. Emma to Lucy Peabody, Honolulu, Jan. 19, 1874 (BM).

4. Charles Reed Bishop (b. Glens Falls, N.Y., 1822; d. Berkeley, Calif., 1915), banker, Hawaiian official, philanthropist; in 1850 married High Chiefess Bernice Pauahi (1831–1884). Arrived in Hawaii 1846, member of mercantile firm Aldrich and Bishop in 1850s; collector of customs 1849–1859. In 1859, he left government service and established, with William A. Aldrich, the first Hawaiian bank. Appointed by Kamehameha IV to House of Nobles 1859, but held no political office until reign of Lunalilo; minister of foreign

affairs and head of cabinet 1873–1874. Advocated negotiation of reciprocity treaty with the United States; in favor of offering to cede Pearl Harbor in return. Like his wife, Bishop supported the native monarchy and held aloof from the annexationist movement: "The Hawaiian Government and people are, at present, opposed to Annexation, whatever you may hear to the contrary. The latter is, with native Hawaiians, considered so 'out of the question' that it is not worth while to discuss it." (Bishop to S. U. F. Odell, Mar. 18, 1873 [Foreign Office Letter Book 52, AH].) Under Kalākaua, Bishop was president of the Board of Education from 1874 to 1891, except for a brief period when Walter Murray Gibson took his place. The banking firm he founded, now the First Hawaiian Bank, has been in continuous operation since 1859. After the death of Pauahi in 1884, Bishop disposed of his financial interests in Hawaii and became a vice-president and director of the Bank of California, in which he had been a stockholder since the early 1880s. For his role in establishing the Kamehameha Schools and Bernice Pauahi Bishop Museum, see Letter 55, note 4; and for a biography, Harold W. Kent, *Charles Reed Bishop: Man of Hawaii* (Palo Alto, Calif.: Pacific Books, 1965).

5. It is tempting to find in Lunalilo—poet, actor, sportsman, lover—shadowy glimpses of certain of the recurrent traits associated with the chieftain-hero of Hawaiian myth and legend: "He is ultra-sensitive; insults or slights which touch him to the quick may provoke him into cruelty—or retreat or even suicide. . . . He is not preoccupied with religion any more than he is with family life, for he alone ordinarily has the privilege of breaking taboos, and he laughs at ghosts. A restless adventurer and romantic, he is a lover of the beauties of nature, of the delights of sex, of the mirth and eroticism of the dance, of the cadence, symbolism, metaphor, word play, and antithesis of chanted poetry. As a hero of narration he is blessed with eternal youth, and if he should die of unrequited love his sister or grandmother revive him and his dramatic life goes on." (Samuel H. Elbert, "The Chief in Hawaiian Mythology," *Journal of American Folklore* 69 [Oct.–Dec. 1956]:318.)

6. C. R. Bishop to E. H. Allen, Honolulu, Jan. 20, 1874 (Elisha H. Allen Papers, Library of Congress; microfilm, Gregg M. Sinclair Library, University of Hawaii, Honolulu).

7. A Hawaiianization of Zephyrin. For main note on Kepelino, see Letter 76, note 3.

8. The chant, headed *"Pua o Honolulu,"* is one of a set composed during the election by one of Emma's supporters; from the same collection of Queen Emma chants cited earlier, preserved at the Bishop Museum.

Letter 63
Emma to Peter

[Kailua, Kona]
[Island of Hawaii]
January 6, 1874

Dearest Coz

To you I take up the pen for my first letter this year and with it indite the heart's earnest wish of the writer 1874 may be a truly happy year in every sence of that expression to you. Come home soon. Do not forget to prepare yourself for the intellectual life [and] struggle at home, when that time comes, for you must now throw off sloth and inactive existance. Albert, you and I are decended from a line of ancestors the men and women of which have acted their parts well and shewn that upward and onward was evidently the motto they acted on as their illustrious deeds tell. They have always kept their stations high as well as renowned, and it becomes us their decendants to do likewise. It is never too late. I do so covet to see you astonishing the foreigners and our countrymen on the return by a complete, improved self, gained through study, aplication, and practice.

[During] these days of your probation there, dear Peter, be ambitious and bold to hold our ancestral renown ever in its place high. Let not inferiors step into our places. Speak and act with weight or authority where you are at present. [Speak] often—either to few or many—[so] that by frequent practice it grows to a habit. [Thus you] perfect yourself to public speaking besides accomplishing one end, which is bringing those people to look to and lean on you as the head mover in all things.

You see an illustration of all this in Taffy. He has stumbled on and on to the shagrin of everybody year after year till actually now he claims the consideration of our entire public. He is of course not good. Still we cannot deny he has made a stir in the world, and this is what I wish you to accomplish also, by constantly speaking to the people at Molokai. Never mind whether or not the delivery is clear or your manner taking at first. They may even come and tell you not to attemp such things again, as in Taffy's case. Still never be discouraged. Have perseverence. Make a name to yourself and consequently add another laurel to the ancestral tree. Help your brother and lastly me.

Leleiohoku, it seems, received the makaainanas on New Year's day,[1] by Keelikolani's desire, as she was herself ill. [They] came with Hookupu for His Majesty, [and he] made them a short address which was well spoken of. He advised them to be united, which is a great thing in any public or private undertaking. He has a book on self-government with him from Mr Jarrett,[2] which he is evidently studying well, and being a cool-headed, cool-mannered young person he I suppose did make a good hit—now at this stage of affairs.

I am anxious we should not be cut off by outsiders. Read the papers well, and mark how Mr Gibson comes out strongly advocating Taffy as our future King.[3] It is just as you wrote me about him. Do you divine Taffy's object in soliciting the Morman party, so as to secure their votes in case of anything happening to His Majesty before a successor is appointed? The King is so dreadfully childish on that subject, lamentably void of any anticipation of trouble or responsibility. Why our very independance as a nation is in eminant peril of anihilation because the Americans are watching us greedily as prey.

Dear Coz, do not miss preying, asking and conversing with Our dear Lord for all things. He will surely look with pleased eyes on those who try, though the effort be awkward. I know you will always remember our King for wisdome and health, long life and conversion to our Church.

Now it really is too bad that I have launched forth into a sermon instead of chatting about ourselves and doings here. Pardon me.

Midnight.—The steamer is not in yet, and I have run up to the dining-room for quiet writing, as the Governess has monopelized our one lamp of the Hale Ololo[4] for her game of Muggins. The King has ordered Mr Crabbe to write and have Wilder send the *Kilauea* here next week instead of to Kauai, in case he grows weaker and no chanse of getting home soon directly. He has been cheerful and merry this evening and eat a good dinner for him. He had a plate of soup, a plate of rice pudding, a bit of Maomao[5] fish, paiai, eggs and milk.

Dr Oliver[6] says the King has consumption, but he has not told anyone that save myself for fear of trouble. He says the lung is like sponge, full of air tubes, and the matter with the King's lungs is there are tubcules or lumps formed on the mouth or opening of several of these air tubes which if they increase in size will often run into one, at the same time eating into the lung and mak[ing] a hole through. He says the King's trouble may heal altogether, but he can never have the sound health of other days. He is a consumptive man and will have to be careful of himself. Sunday the fourth I went into his bedroom and saw him for the first time since the glimpse at Christmas.

Ruth desired me to send her love to you and also, if you can, deliver her remembrance to Poopuu, a woman of Kona nei[7] who lives in Bill Ragsdale's old house—her Kane is one of his Lunas.

So poor old Hueu[8] is dead. Kewiki arrived 2 hours before his death, overland, whilst Lucy and Kamai landed by *Kilauea* half an hour after he breathed his last.

[KALELEONĀLANI]

1. The ceremonial gift-giving (*hoʻokupu*) by the local natives (*makaʻāinana*) took place at Kailua, Kona, where Leleiohoku was a member of the royal party.

2. William Jarrett (1814–1880), secretary of Department of Foreign Affairs since 1844; arrived in Hawaii 1841 on U.S.S. *Vincennes* with U.S. exploring expedition under command of Capt. Charles Wilkes. Since 1872, Leleiohoku had been employed in Mr. Jarrett's department as clerk and copyist, his chief accomplishments up to that time being his musical skill and exquisite penmanship. According to the *Hawaiian Gazette*, Feb. 25, 1874, "While in the Foreign Office he read, under the supervision of Mr. Jarrett, an excellent work on the Science of Government by Holmes...a branch of instruction to which all in government service should pay more attention."

3. A reference to Gibson's article, *Nuhou*, Jan. 6, 1874, on "The Succession." After listing Lunalilo's possible successors, including Kalākaua, Emma, Mrs. Bishop, Ruth Keʻelikōlani, and Leleiohoku, Gibson named "the one of this stock of Chiefs ... as the choice of the whole nation ... is the High Chief David Lonoikamaka Keola Keoua Kalakaua. The high blood, and the experience in public affairs of this gentleman, eminently qualify him to be the successor of the Kamehamehas and King Lunalilo." On Jan. 20, Gibson emphasized that Kalākaua was above all the choice of the native population and that Emma was not: "The political hopes of the native people are now concentrated upon [Kalākaua's] person whereas Her Majesty Queen Emma... who we are sure takes no part in any political intrigue, and whose name is brought forward by a cabal, or ring of foreign interests, does not satisfy the national hope as Successor to King Lunalilo."

4. Literally, "Long House." Emma and the Princess Ruth were staying in this native-style grass house of ceremonial proportions, standing at the Kohala end of the premises, while King Lunalilo and some of his attendants were occupying Huliheʻe. Huliheʻe Palace, at Kailua, Kona, island of Hawaii, was

built 1836–1838 by John Adams Kuakini, brother of Queen Ka'ahumanu and governor of the island of Hawaii until 1844. Ruth had inherited the house as the widow and heir of Kuakini's adopted son. Hulihe'e has been restored in the present century and is a regular point of interest for tourists visiting the Kona Coast.

5. Probably the same as *mamamo, mamo-pohole*, a fish (*Abudefduf abdominalis*) about seven inches long.

6. Dr. Richard Oliver, traveling physician and a member of the Board of Health.

7. Here at Kona.

8. George Hueu Davis (1800–1874), grandfather of Lucy Peabody, Emma's lady-in-waiting. Son of Isaac Davis (?1757–1810), Welsh mate of the American sloop *Fair American*, who was detained on Hawaii by the natives in 1790 and who assisted Kamehameha I in his conquest of the Islands. Kewiki was George Davis' son, George Hueu Davis II (?1825–1896).

Letter 64
Peter to Emma

[Kalaupapa]
January 25, 1874

Queen Emma

As a man goes over the Pali, I avail myself the opportunity to pen you a fiew lines.

I am happy to learn of your Safe arrival at Honolulu in good health, but I am exceedingly Sorry to hear of the King's being so ill. Ragsdale has received a letter from Honolulu, from Someone informing him that the King is not expected to live, but I hope it will not come to that but will hope for the better.

By the arrival of the *Warwick* I received the Foreign and Local Papers with the *Nu Hou*, and about Taffy's being Illustrated by Gibson as a High Chief and the only one fit to rule the Hawaiians, and likewise the Natives' choice.[1] This showes clearly how Taffy is trying to win the favour of the Yanks, but I hope Taffy, Gibson, and all Taffy's backers will be foiled in the purpose which they are pursueing, inasmuch as the majority of the Hawaiian people still love their young King, but for my part, I must wait for the best or worst.

Please do not omit to give me information concerning the King's Health by the first opportunity, as I am very anxious to hear. Fanny stated in her last to me that the King's "Kaikuahines," probably Mrs Bishop and Ruth, do not agree with Taffy.[2]

Aikoe requested me to inform her if Kamakaaiau's Baby was mine or no, and if mine, that I am to let her know and She will Nurse it. I will write to Aikoe informing her that I had never had anything to do with her save conversing.

I am in good Health. Remember me to Aunty.

Ever Your Servant
KEKUAOKALANI

1. A reference to Gibson's article of Jan. 6, 1874; see Letter 63, note 3.

2. Prepositions were easily confused by English-speaking Hawaiians. Perhaps the meaning is that Lunalilo's female cousins ("*Kaikuahine*") did not "agree about" Kalākaua's fitness to rule. Or perhaps they disagreed over genealogy or about whether or not the king would die.

Letter 65
Peter to Emma

[Kalaupapa]
February 11, 1874
Tuesday, 6 A.M.

Queen Emma

The Mail Man goes over today, so I avail the opportunity to pen you a fiew lines.

The time is drawing near for the Election for a new Ruler to our little Kingdom. I have heard numerous remarks passed about the Person being fit to be a King or Queen in our little Community but not enough to satisfy me. I know the numerous odds which are against you, and your Enimies are trying to make Might Right, but the Supreme Being I know will have it that Right is Might, which if so your Majesty [will prove] the only one among the Hawaiians fit to fill the vacancy of the vacant Hawaiian Throne.

Mr and Mrs Napela and I are Praying every morning on your behalf, beseeching our Lord that he may in his infinite Power turn the tide of Election in your favour and be Victorious over your Enemies, and subdue your Enemies which infect the name of Hawaii and speak falsely about our little church.

I am very anxious to hear the result of the Election, come what it may for better or worse, the Lord's will be done, and I'm thinking of Him who died for us miserable sinners, who help the rightious and not the Wicked and who saved Daniel from the Lions—[he] will save you from your Enemies. This and this only is my Consolation.

Tomorrow being the last day, and before the Election, Napela and I are going to *Fast* and pray at some lonely place either on the Plains or in the Woods and ask our Saviour to spare you and assist you in your undertakings. At your Home or elsewhare Night or Day may the Lord be with you. I must now end. Hopeing to hear of your Success, I remain

Ever yours
KEKUAOKALANI

Letter 66
Peter to Emma

[Kalaupapa]
February 23, 1874
8:30 at night

Queen Emma

Yours of the 12th and 21st have duely come to hand,[1] also with the things which you had so kindly sent up to me.

After I had received my letters and Papers and on my way Home, I was attacked with a severe griping in the Stomache, and when I reached my little cottage the pain was so severe that it rendered me incapable of reading my letters and [I] was quite helpless for the greater part of the day. During the afternoon I took two doses of Pain Killer, but that did not releave me of the Pain so I took a dose of Castor Oil and now I am quite well, but a little weak.

Yours of the 21st has greatly releaved me of the Suspense from which I have been labouring under. Although Your Majesty is defeated, everyone knows that it was by unfair means, with the basest of falshoods on the winner's side, and a disgrace to the officials. The riot[2] on the Election day speaks for itself, showing clearly the wish of the people for your Majesty, and with the combined Prayers of Your Majesty's Subjects, Our Lord in Heaven will yet put you on the Throne of Hawaii which really is yours, and your Enemies be subdued. Then, and not till then, will they know that Right is Might.

I am sorry for Hiram and Kapo's leaving you,[3] and I am aware that they on leaveing you left their best wishes towards Your Majesty, and also left the Home that has Sheltered them for Years, and I can say boldly and truely that they not only left a good friend, but a truer Master nor a kinder Sovreign they never can find. I am happy to learn that Mr Pratt is yet on your side, and I hope he will yet be rewarded[4] for his kindness towards your Majesty.

I have not the least doubt that Pilipo's[5] being imprisoned will stir the members of his church up, and their be another riot, worse then the first. Ragsdale has informed me that Dowsett has tried to Bail out Pilipo but the result of it he does not know. I will rest and finish in the Morning, as my eyes pains me, and am still a little weak.

8 A.M. Tuesday, February 24.—I am quite well after a good night's

rest. Today we are expecting Wilder down here, as he was sent for by the Sick to come up and try Ragsdale for selling 210 Pounds of Sugar which was sent up here for the use of the Sick to a Chinaman, Achew.

I send back 9 Bags. Please remember me to Aunt Kekelaokalani. And believe me

Ever Your Humble Servant
KEKUAOKALANI

1. Emma's correspondence with Peter for 1874 has been almost entirely lost or destroyed. By her own wish Peter burned all his letters from Emma up to mid-July 1874; see Letter 84. Possibly Emma, or some interested party, likewise destroyed all drafts or copies of her 1874 correspondence with Peter; she did not, however, entirely dispose of a few miscellaneous rough notes and jottings of scattered dates.

2. For brief earlier comment on the "Election Day Riot," see Introduction to Part 2. Besides destroying furniture, books, and papers, the rioters assaulted various Hawaiian members of the House of Representatives, concentrating their revenge on some of Kalākaua's foremost Hawaiian followers. Kalākaua meanwhile, with the approval of his chief minister, Charles R. Bishop, and John O. Dominis, governor of Oahu, asked the American minister, H. A. Peirce, and the British commissioner, James H. Wodehouse, to land marines from three vessels in the harbor, the U.S.S. *Portsmouth*, U.S.S. *Tuscarora*, and H.B.M.'s *Tenedos*. The arrival of these outside forces prevented further overt rebellion. An important result of the disturbance was its effect on future policy. Foreign residents generally agreed that a system of elective, constitutional monarchy could never survive in Hawaii without adequate power of government to enforce laws. An editorial in the *Pacific Commercial Advertiser*, Apr. 14, 1874, addressed itself to this problem:

> It is true that the community is filled with such rumors as—that the Queen Dowager has encouraged the mob, first to expect another vote, and then to expect aid from England for which she has written to Queen Victoria, and much more of equal absurdity. And however fallacious and childish this kind of talk may appear to us, it is undeniably true that among the weaker-minded and ignorant of the native population, if with no others, it has the effect to create a feeling of uneasiness and apprehension that is to be deprecated. It may be assumed however as very certain that everything said or done in this community,—so far as it pertains to law and order—is well known to the authorities, and further that ample preparation is made against a second outrage.

3. Hiram Kahanawai, Emma's steward, was related to Kalākaua; Kapo'oloku, Emma's lady-in-waiting, was a younger sister of Queen Kapi'olani. It was in keeping with Hawaiian custom for Hiram and Kapo, now that Kalākaua was king, to demonstrate concretely their kinship and loyalty to him by leaving Emma's service and entering his own.

4. Rewarded by being given political appointment, in the event that Emma should become queen.

5. The Rev. George W. Pilipo (1828–1887), Congregational clergyman, legislator, and supporter of Queen Emma, educated at Lahainaluna Seminary. Ordained pastor of church at Kailua, Hawaii, 1864; called to Kaumakapili Church, Honolulu, 1872; served as representative from North Kona, Hawaii, 1872–1886. In February 1874, he was suspected of complicity in organizing the Courthouse Riot, but the legal charge was dropped. The *Hawaiian Gazette*, Apr. 15, noted that at "a regular meeting of the Hawaii Evangelical Association, held yesterday, Mr. George W. Pilipo was unanimously dismissed from the pastorate of Kaumakapili Church in this city." Under Kalākaua, Pilipo's opposition to the policies of Walter Murray Gibson won him approval among those persons who had turned against him earlier for his support of Emma.

Letter 67
Peter to Emma

[Kalaupapa]
March 1, 1874

Queen Emma

Yours of the 23d and 25th have both come to hand, also the 4 Bags of tarrow.

Taffy and his crowd have at last reached the Goal which they have so long been Dreaming for. But how long they will retain it, God only know, for the Allmighty will I am sure listen to the neverseasing Prayers of the numerous Natives who are beseeching him to put on the Hawaiian Throne the true and only rueler.

I see in the Funeral Programe that you come in the third,[1] but let them have their way, for I hope that they will find out before long that the majority will yet rule, and as the old Proverb say, "It is not only Gold that Gliters." I am glad that Kanaina has detained you to remain with him—Poor Man, at last deprived of the only Son and Relation on Earth, but I am sure if he is in nead of a friend he will find one, and a true one in you. Poor old Man, [he] must take it to heart a great deal, and only you to pasafy him.

I am happy to learn that those who were arrested are let out under Bail,[2] and like a true and Loyal subject, though defeated, [will] rally again around their Soverign Master. Our local Papers I am perfectly disgusted with—nothing excepting Taffy, praising him in a way which is known only by *Yanks*.

I have received a letter from Nahaolelua, but I am sorry that I cannot answer it just now as the Mail Man is waiting. Remember me to Aunt Fanny and also to poor Kanaina. Good Bye.

God Bless and Protect you

KEKUAOKALANI

P. S. Please send me some white Envelopes. Their are none here save this kind which I enclose my letter in. P. Y. K.

1. According to the *Pacific Commercial Advertiser*, Feb. 28, 1874, the carriage bearing Queen Dowager Emma and her mother, Hon. Mrs. Naea, appeared immediately after that carrying Princess Ruth Ke'elikōlani, Mrs. Dominis, Mrs. Cleghorn, Mrs. Bishop. In the first carriage rode King Kalākaua, Queen Kapi'olani, Prince Leleiohoku, and the father of Lunalilo, Kana'ina.

2. Up to Feb. 20, seventy-four persons involved in the riot had been arrested, of whom fifty-five were committed for trial at the April term of the supreme court.

Letter 68
Peter to Emma

[Kalaupapa]
March 18, 1874

Dearest of Cousin
Queen Emma

I have received your letter, but I am exceedingly sorry to learn that Dominis has been so bold as to deal so unjust with you, knowing you to be in Pilikia.[1] He has taken advantage of it and is pressing you all he can, but I hope and pray that he will be disapointed in his undertakings. I really cannot see how you can easily get over this affair, unless by a Sacrifice of some of your Property. But the Ever Merciful God will I know Guard and help you through as of Yore and [you will] be Victorious over your Enemies.

I hope and Pray that my next letter from you will be that you are out of Pilikia. Aikoe has writen to me Saying that She is going to pull tarrow for me. I am well in Health. . . .

Ever your Humble Servant
KEKUAOKALANI

P. S. My Papers I have not as yet received but I will ride to the Landing and inquire. P. Y. K.

1. The trouble in this case was financial; see Letter 69, note 1.

Letter 69
Peter to Emma

[Kalaupapa]
April 3, 1874

Queen Emma

Thanks, Thanks, dear Queen for yours of the 28th and 1st of this Month. I am happy to learn that Messrs Pratt and Pfluger have given their Aid on your behalf, which will evidently take J. O. D. by surprise,[1] as well as check him in his evil intentions to injure you. It is but too true as you say, that it will take a long while I am sorry to say.[2] But time at last will set all things even. And I have always, and am still asking the Allmighty in my Prayers to help you, and at the expiration of the time, and before, that you will be Victorious over your Enemies one and all, and be a Mother and Sovereign for the Hawaiian Nation.

In yours of the 1st you mentioned of Hoapili's death.[3] I am not at all surprised, and I think that the Allmighty in his infinite kindness to spare the poor Man from a Murderer's death, as he has sought to take your Life, has removed him from this to another World. Thus before any of David's party have accomplished their evil design, you are still alive, and they to conspire for their own Ruin, they believing in "Anaana."[4] I hope that Hoapili's death will be a warning to them.

I am exceedingly delighted to learn that you have dismissed that little impudent fellow from transacting your affairs.[5] David, Buff,[6] and Koii[7] will I am Sure be baffled in their Plot to Poison you, and if this goes to the People's ears, they will I know rise one and all and with a unanimous cry shout death to the Poiseners, and [stir themselves] up so that the Second Riot will be worst then the first, and David probably fall from the place sooner then he anticipated, which I hope he will.

In regard to the Hulumanus[8] which Buff is drilling, I think that they will be more for ornament then for use, and all their Forming will be of no service, for the Natives are naturally cowards, with the exception perhaps of the Half whites. "And as Man Proposes and God disposes," I do not think that their is much fear from them. At all events, their is no harm in looking out for One's self, and I am sure that their will be no Lack on the part of the kind Natives who are so kind in watching you.

The boy which you mentioned that went to Buff's and saw them drilling, who has a Uncle among them, will be a good Spy, thus giving you warning, so that you may be on your guard for any emergencies. Fail not if you please kind Queen to give my Heart's feeling to kind Mrs Weed who will be another Stumbling Block to David's party. And when I think over these things, I can Immagine how true and kind Our Saviour is to you, in this your hour of Trial. . . .

I hope your visit from Hartwell[9] was of a friendly nature. If so all is well. A kahuna by the name of Kalamaia died last week, and while the worms were crawling out from his right arm and [he] was dying, he said faintly, ‸ "I shall die for I have taken the $50 from Hoapili to *ana ana* Kiliwehi."[10]‸ Hua has said openly that David will perhaps open the comeing Legislature, or may not, and when he is extinct, that his brother will shortly follow. "Come happy hour and Welcome," I say.

Makaula has writen to me saying that you have received a letter from Judge Allen,[11] informing you to wait until he arrives by the Steamer on the 4th, tomorrow Satuarday, and that he will put all to right, and he has got Lunalilo's Will appointing you as his Successor, and that he was sorely grieved at the Representatives' conduct, and approved the People for what they did, and that you had forbiden them from mentioning this to anyone, until the time comes. These rumors I cannot credit . . . unless I hear from you. . . . [I know] that you will not fail to give me [the facts] but I hope it is true and Pray so.

I have received all that you have had sent up here for me, safe, but my Hat was a little injured through the carelessness of the Captain. It was wet and had shrunk so that it is too small.

Ragsdale has received a letter from Wilder informing him that he will be here with the new President of the Board of Health, Widemann,[12] Trousseau, David and Wife and Suite on the 11th, Satuarday. I wonder how we will meet. I am sure that if they come on Shore the only Place fit to enter, without being afraid of catching the disease if Contagious, will be mine, but I am sure that if the greeting between David and myself will be pleasent yet my Heart will I know be burning for Satisfaction, which will with the Allmighty's be given him, if Hua's Prophesy do not hinder us. But if, as Kaawa says that he has got a letter from his Wife saying that he

David is going to liberate us all, I may yet come Home and act as one of the Watchmen over yours and yourself, but since I am confined I must humbelly Bow my Head to the Lot which has befalen me and wait patiently for the comeing Hour, which I know is comeing sooner or later.

Please remember me to kind Mrs Weed and Miss L. Peabody, so dear Queen Good Bye. With the greatest of Faith that I will yet meet you in the Dearest Spot on Earth to me, I remain

Your Majesty's Humble Servant
KEKUAOKALANI

1. According to Emma, John O. Dominis was foiled in his evil purposes when F. S. Pratt and J. W. Pfluger came to her aid, probably by arranging a loan for her.

2. A long while to pay off the loan.

3. The death of William Hoapili Kaauwai (1835–1874) on Mar. 30, 1874, was announced in the *Pacific Commercial Advertiser*, Apr. 4, 1874; see also Letter 72, note 1. He was a relative and supporter of Kalākaua, a former magistrate of Maui, and the first Hawaiian to be ordained as a deacon in the Hawaiian Reformed Catholic church. Hoapili accompanied Queen Emma to England and France as her chaplain (1865–1866), but left her service after becoming involved with a French woman at Hyères. His wife, Kiliwehi (Mary Ann), also of a chiefly family, from whom he was later divorced, accompanied Emma on the same journey as a lady-in-waiting, and remained Emma's friend. There is no record of Hoapili's conducting any clerical duties after his return to Hawaii in 1867. During the last months of the reign of Lunalilo, Hoapili shifted his allegiance to Kalākaua and worked for his kinsman's election. For an account of Hoapili Kaauwai and his wife, see Andrew Forest Muir, "William Hoapili Kaauwai: An Hawaiian in Holy Orders," *Sixty-First Annual Report of the Hawaiian Historical Society* (1952): 5–13.

4. Evil sorcery.

5. The dismissal of John O. Dominis as Emma's business agent.

6. A nickname for Leleiohoku, Kalākaua's younger brother.

7. Koii Unauna (1828–1877), a prominent court genealogist and distant kinsman of Kalākaua; also a practising attorney.

8. Kalākaua's new royal guard; the name "Birdfeather" (*Hulumanu*) had been used by a select guard made up of court favorites of Kamehameha III. Walter Murray Gibson's *Nuhou*, Mar. 3, 1874, announced that Kalākaua's government was taking systematic measures to strengthen the power of the government to preserve law and order. Under the heading "Our Special

Police Force," it was reported that "devoted adherents" of Kalākaua had been organized under the direction of Attorney General Hartwell: "They have only had two short drills under the soldierly direction of Major Moehonua, acting as drill sergeant. . . . When this special corps has its full complement of men . . . it will be able to take care of any future riots in this town."

9. Judge Alfred S. Hartwell, attorney general during the reign of Lunalilo; for main note, see Letter 55, note 3. About 12 o'clock noon on Mar. 29, 1874, Hartwell called on Queen Emma in person to get her signature to a document he had prepared announcing formally her allegiance to Kalākaua and her disapproval of the riotous actions at the courthouse:

> Many entirely false reports have been made concerning the Queen Dowager since the election of King Kalakaua. The Queen Dowager did not at first think it necessary to notice or deny them. But so great are the misrepresentations, that she now takes occasion to say through the newspapers that the reports are utterly false and without foundation which declare that she desires to see ill feeling stirred up against His Majesty the King. It has even been stated that she intends to send to the Queen of England for assistance in placing her on the Throne. It is all so absurd that she would not think it worth noticing if some people did not seek to think that some foundation exists for such reports.
>
> The Queen Dowager is too loyal a subject of King Kalakaua, and too true a friend to Hawaii, to lend any sanction to anything that is opposed to the laws and peace of the Realm, or to allegiance to the King. She does not for one moment countenance the violent acts of the mob at the Court House, nor does she wish her name to be associated with any who wish to violate the law of the land.

There is no record among Emma's papers of her having signed the document just quoted, headed in manuscript "Communication from Her Majesty the Queen." Nevertheless an announcement based on the text of Hartwell's draft was published without significant change in wording in the *Pacific Commercial Advertiser*, Apr. 14, 1874.

10. The kahuna confesses that he himself is a victim of retributive sorcery for having allowed Hoapili Kaauwai to bribe him to work evil magic against Hoapili's former wife, Kiliwehi.

11. Elisha H. Allen, chief justice of the supreme court, who had been sent to Washington, D.C., to negotiate a treaty of reciprocity. The notion that Allen had in his possession a will of Lunalilo naming Emma as his successor was, as Peter suspected, a fabrication.

12. Herman A. Widemann (b. Hanover, Germany, 1823; d. Hawaii, 1899), prominent planter of Kauai, jurist, legislator. Member of House of Representatives at various sessions during 1850s and 1860s; from 1874 through 1880s member of House of Nobles. Kalākaua appointed him minister of interior and president of the Board of Health in 1874. A royalist and Roman Catholic, married to a Hawaiian wife, he served later as minister of interior in Queen Lili'uokalani's first cabinet in 1891. After the revolution of 1893, he acted as Lili'uokalani's agent on a mission to Washington in her interest.

Letter 70
Peter to Emma

[Kalaupapa]
April 10, 1874

Queen Emma

You must Pardon me for my last letter, which ended so abrubtly, but as the Mail Man was in such a hurry to go over, and did not even allow me time for my Dressing, I had writen in the Night with the intention of finishing it in the morning, but could not. However, I will make it up in this.

In my last I omited to inform you about Napela. Before David was Elected, and when you wrote to me informing me of Hoapili's Threats towards your Life, I informed Napela of it. He did not say much, but when we met at his House for Prayer, beseeching the Allmighty to choose you as our Ruler, which we did morning and Evening, to my Surprise Napela in his Prayer asked Our Father in Heaven to shorten Hoapili's life if he had anything to do with David and his Evil designs, and if Hoapili ment to carry out his threats, which I do really believe he would have done but fortunately for the poor Man, he was arrested and now lays low, to appear before his Ruler and maker.

Last Monday Napela and I rode to the Beach for a Ride, and touched at Hua's. After we had conversed on diferent Subjects, Napela asked her her opinion in regard to the new King. Useing her own words, she replied: ˄"What of it? We are safe on earth, on solid ground. Let him look out for himself. The descendant of Keliimaikai still moves and will keep moving until she who holds the *wohi* rank[1] occupies the throne."˄

I then informed her of David, Buff and Koii's seeking to take your Life. She replied again: ˄"This woman has had sorcery practiced against her a long time, but she has not died. Because of her great virtues she will not die, and because of her righteousness God is with her."˄

I then asked her if their were any hopes of your being Our Queen. She replied: ˄"That Kalakaua is now King is the sign of her future reign. I see now again what I saw before the death of Lunalilo when I saw Kalakaua going with torches[2] on each side of him as he went between them. Now the mouth of his calabash is turned down,[3] and the earth is open just as it opened for Lunalilo after his death. Now I see it is Emma who goes before the many torches. Because Kalakaua and these other persons were involved in the death of Lunalilo, they too shall perish."ˌ

She then turned to me and replied, ˌ "Be patient and do not worry about your cousin. God is watching over her and He will set her up on high."ˌ

Her remarks had produced such an effect upon me that when Napela and I returned, I felt so happy that I sang "Sweet Home," "Annie Laura," and several other Songs, heedles of what Napela was saying, until I discovered that we were nearing the Houses at the landing, which arrested me from my Singing fit. When we were on our way Home, my Companion informed me that he believed every word that Hua had spoken, and then remarked, ˌ "Now my children and grandchildren shall live."ˌ

We have not mentioned this to anyone, but Hua has told the Natives at the Beach, and when I recieve any letters from you, on the arrival of the *Warwick* the Natives generally flock to whare I am, and anxiously wait for the ˌ News of the Royal Court ˌ which no one has but me.

In one of my former letters, I informed you of a Rock which fell from the Pali into the Sea. Napela remarked that that Rock was for no one else save the King or a high Chief. Lunalilo died shortly after. In another one of mine of a later date I mentioned that Napela and I saw another Rock fall. Hoapili died shortly after. Last night a Point up on the Mountain back of my place broke from whare it has been and fell, carrying with it all the trees and other bushes that were in its way. The two Rocks that fell have been interpreted. Now who this will be for I cannot say, but if Omens and Signs are to be believed, shurely this Omen, if Omen it is, are for the Seekers of your Life. The Natives are ever anxious to see the David come and set us free, but for my part I hope he is takeing his first King look and last, and then [will] retire from the Stage *Forever*.

Since my last, I have had Egs from my Poultry, and consiquently have had Custard dayly, but Since Mrs Weed "cannot" partake of my Dish, which I would willingly offer, I can think of the Noble Woman and be Silent.

Good Bye. . . .

Ever Your Humble Servant
KEKUAOKALANI

1. Because of her rank, including both priestly and godly lineage, Queen Emma could claim various kapu privileges. She derived the *wohi kapu* from a high chief who was exempted from prostrating before royalty. Her three other sacred kapus were the "burning fire" kapu, permitting the burning of torches in her honor in broad daylight; the *welo kapu*, celebrating her descent from a noble Kauai family named *welo*; the *akua kapu*, or godly kapu, from a high chief related to Kahōāli'i, a deified hero greatly respected by Kamehameha I. Emma's *wohi* rank is mentioned in one of a set of chants composed when she was a candidate for the throne, competing in 1874 against Kalākaua:

> A *wohi* chiefess rising upward
> is she who is highest of all,
> the foremost of eminent persons
> in the Kingdom of Hawaii.

(Translated; from Collection of Queen Emma Chants, BM: "*Nani wale o Emalani. . . .*")

2. An allusion to the sacred "burning fire" kapu, authorizing the burning of torches in daylight. Both Emma and Kalākaua were entitled to this honor. The *Pacific Commercial Advertiser*, Mar. 24, 1874, in an account of "The Royal Progress at Kauai," noted that "the daylight torches, '*kukui o* Iwikauikaua,' recalled the especial prerogative of the Kalakaua family, that whereas other chiefs might have torches borne before them during the night, the blood of Kalakaua claimed the tribute of an unquenched flambeau both night and day."

3. Sign of someone's death.

Letter 71
Peter to Emma

[Kalaupapa]
April 14, 1874

Queen Emma

The expected day of arrival of the *Kilauea* here has come and past, but no man in the Shape of David K.—to my delight, and disapointment to the Natives, who according to Ragsdale's and Kaawa's orders had flocked to the Beach to see him and ask him for their Liberty, as their great point is that this disease is not Contagious.

Mr and Mrs Napela were both dressed, and their House Decorated with *Awapuhi*,[1] etc., as Kuihelani was expected with their Son-in-law, S. Parker.[2] They both asked me when I was going to dress to receive him, D. K., to which I replied that I was clean enough to meet him or any other Man. Lelekahanu was also at the Beach ready to Hula[3] when he D. K. comes ashore. A Schooner was in sight from the Windward, and was coming with a good Breeze. After Noon the Schooner neared enough for us to see that she was bound for the Westward. As that was the day that the *Kilauea* was expected, the Natives did not give up the hopes until quite late in the afternoon. Mr and Mrs Napela had changed their Dress with disgust. I had been up to the River and back, so [I] dressed and took a ride. While the Natives were returning, I asked them in joke if David had said anything about our going Home, to which they replied that he had come and had gone away without saying anything.

I rode by the Beach with my Man to buy Potatoes, as my Poi was out, as the *Warwick* is a Week and a half since she was here last.

10:30 o'clock.—The *Kilauea* is seen and hailed comeing down, also a little Schooner, supposed to be the *Warwick*. So I must bid you Adieu till again. . . .

Ever Your Humble Servant
KEKUAOKALANI

P. S. I think the least I say to the Man the better. So I have altered my mind and will not say anything in regard to our Liberty, for I know he will say that I beged him for my Liberty. P. Y. K.

1. Wild ginger.

2. Samuel Parker (1854–1920), prominent part-Hawaiian rancher and landowner, of Waimea, island of Hawaii; grandson of John Palmer Parker (b. Newton, Mass., 1790; d. Waimea, 1864), agent and purveyor of Kamehameha I, who supplied the king with produce for bartering with foreign vessels. Samuel Parker married the Napelas' daughter, Harriet ("Hattie") Panana, 1871. Appointed by Kalākaua to the House of Nobles in 1886. He became minister of foreign affairs in 1891 under Liliʻuokalani and a central figure in cabinet struggles (1891–1893). In August 1894, Parker was a member of a three-man commission in Washington, D.C., appointed by Liliʻuokalani to further her interests and try to persuade President Cleveland to take steps to restore the monarchy. On Jan. 24, 1895, Parker was one of several royalists who acted as witnesses when Liliʻuokalani, held prisoner by the Provisional Government, signed the instrument of her abdication.

3. To recite chant suitable to the royal visitor and occasion.

Letter 72
Peter to Emma

[Kalaupapa]
April 25, 1874

Queen Emma

Thanks for the information of Yours of the 16th and 18th. I wonder whether this is David's last appearance on the Stage, and then [he will] follow Lilikalani. The Papers also make a great deal of him. I am not at all surprised at the Natives being so Jubilant at the Sudden deaths which are hapening to David's party.[1] [They] are clinging closer to you, which showes evidently that you are their choice. Surely this is God's doings and will, I am shure, one day grant the People their wish. I suspected that David or his Party would report a false report about me, if I did go to the beach, but fortunately all the Foreigners who knew me, knew that I did not go to see the Man, neither did I care. But Cleghorn showed in his Eyes what he did not utter to me then.

I see poor Hulu's name in the Papers as one of those who are convicted.[2] Poor G. Bell. I Hope that he will escape a heavy fine, if not get clear all together. You mentioned of J. Naone. He is one of the Prince of Hawaii's own,[3] and several other young men who I hear are on your Side, which showes clearly, as you say, that God has some object for doing and allowing these things to happen.

I had returned from a mountain ride Yesterday with my men, looking at the Patches of Tarrow which they are to work by Widemann's authority, when Napela sent over for me. I went over and saw Hua, Kaawa, and Mr and Mrs Napela waiting for me. Hua boldly informed me that David might open the Legislature, and if he does, that he will not live long after. [She] wished Kaawa to inform David of it. I rather liked her for speaking so boldly, but [it] made Kaawa Hoka,[4] as he beleaves every word that Hua says—Signs, Omens, and Dreams are the orders of the day here, and all on your behalf.

In the last *Advertiser*, I see that it says that the People's tears rolled down their cheeks.[5] Only two cried, and these two cried with Piolani. But if some of the Party had only remained ashore to hear the Languages used towards David when he left, they would have felt Scared, as several remarked that they were Naaupo[6] for leting David go, since David's Party were only a fiew in number, and could have been easily dispached before any assistance could have come, and that [since] they [the] *Natives* were sent here to die, why not die then—and other words too Vulgar to mention. Ragsdale thought it better to leave them then to interfere, so left.

Before David came here Kaawa had sold his bed and some of his clothes, so shure was he of going home, but now he is crying over the Spilt Milk. I was at the Store Yesterday to buy a Tea Kettle, when I heard that some of the Sick are to be released from here, but Ragsdale is afraid of his being one of the number and is going to write to the Board of Health not to let anyone go. He is afraid of my going Home, and if I set as Nobleman in the Legislature that I will inform the Public how things are carried on here, and approved by the Majority of the Board of Health, which I know is Speculation on Human Being, charged and paid by the Government for the benefit of their own Pockets, thus increasing the expences for this place.

In the Early part of this month, I wrote an article to the *Hawaii Ponoi*, contradicting an article in the *Kuokoa*, but it never came out, so whatever is now printed must pass for true, and the Public at large take it for granted that all is true, and believe it as such. And not for a Moment dream of Men's Cruelty to Human being. And I am aware that until you become our Ruler all will be rong, but I still keep courage, and Pray for the comeing Day, yes Hour. . . .

Ever Yours

KEKUAOKALANI

P. S. The *Warwick* has just arrived and I am going down. I have got a very bad cold and am quite Hoarse. P. Y. K.

---

1. On Apr. 4, 1874, the *Pacific Commercial Advertiser* announced the "Sudden Death" of W. Hoapili Kaauwai, of Wailuku, Maui, who died "of heart disease, in this city Monday last. Mr. Kaauwai had been designated as His Majesty's Chamberlain on Friday last. . . . He had been suffering from a pulmonary complaint for some months." The *Hawaiian Gazette*, Apr. 22, 1874, noted the unexpected deaths of three supporters of Kalākaua: "During the last few weeks, three notable Hawaiians have died, Judge Lilikalani, A. M. Kahalewai, formerly judge of the Maui circuit court, and William Hoapili Kaauwai, formerly of Wailuku, Maui." In a temperance address delivered in 1875 to Hawaiian soldiers, King Kalākaua singled out several of these same recently deceased public figures as examples of the "poisonous

character of alcohol ... and the grievous loss of valuable men, chiefly by drinking poisoned alcohol, such as Kahai, Lilikalani, Hoapili, who went to England, and others." (*Pacific Commercial Advertiser*, Aug. 7, 1875.)

2. The *Hawaiian Gazette*, Apr. 15, 1874, in its account of the trial in the supreme court, noted that Hulu, who pleaded guilty, was sentenced to three years' imprisonment. George Bell was found not guilty and was released without fine, as Peter hoped. The *Pacific Commercial Advertiser*, Apr. 11, 1874, reported that the riot was not the result of any "deep or lasting conviction in the minds of the people but merely the momentary frenzy of a few ignorant thoughtless ones." The same article noted that "unfortunately the real authors of the mischief go unpunished while their poor dupes are made to feel the power of the insulted law."

3. Member of rifle company first formed under patronage of Prince Lot Kamehameha, who succeeded his brother Kamehameha IV as Kamehameha V.

4. Kaawa became worried and anxious.

5. The visit of the royal party to "The Leper Asylum of Molokai" was reported in the *Pacific Commercial Advertiser*, Apr. 18, 1874: "Their Majesties the King and Queen landed at Kalaupapa at half-past 12 o'clock, and were received by the assembled lepers at the beach with hearty cheers. The people then formed in line while the King made them a short but feeling address. While His Majesty was speaking, his afflicted subjects listened with fixed attention, and tears of gratitude rolled down their cheeks at the thoughtful understanding of their King in thus coming and speaking to them, who were, to use their own expression, already in the grave. ... Then after a few words of kindly recognition to personal acquaintances, and a general "aloha oukou" ["aloha to you all"], their Majesties returned to the steamer, painfully affected by the sights of human affliction that they had witnessed."

6. Stupid.

Letter 73
Peter to Emma

[Kalaupapa]
May 29, 1874
8:30 at night

Queen Emma

Thanks, Thanks, for the News of yours of the 24th. By this Mail I received a letter from Nawahi,[1] the Hon. Member from Puna. He Speaks very highly of you and regrets that I am not in my Seat as Nobleman.

I have omitted long enough in not informing you that besides Hua, I have had another Kahuna to work for our interest. This Kahuna's name is Kukeliaiau. This is the Kahuna that Hakaleleponi got to *Kuni* the Person or Persons who Ana Ana'd Kamehameha III,[2] and Paki died shortly afterwards. So he say, when I engaged him to work for us. I have had a little House put up for him, so that I can go to him and consult without being disturbed or mistrusted. As fortune would have it, all what he asked for was got without any expense—Awa growing in the Mountain, Pigs I have, etc., meeting his wish whenever required, my Man Keleau puting so much faith in the Kahuna that all went on well. And now we are only waiting for the result, which the Kahuna Predicts will shortly take place.

A Woman by the name of Haniole also came to me and said that you will be our Queen shortly, and that D. K. and family will all die. Two men also came and told me their Dreams. Hua has boldly and openly informed the Natives that D. K. and his family will all die and let you Reign in Peace, as You are the Makaainana's wish[3] and their Prayer, and that the Allmighty have heard their Prayer and will shortly grant them their wish by puting you on the Throne of Hawaii nei.[4] Hua have also told Kaawa to write to D. K. informing him of what she says.

This Noon as I was laying on my Sofa reading, Napela came in and asked me to go out and see the Mea Hou.[5] I went out and he pointed to the Ring around the Sun—"Luakalai."[6] I told him that that was not anything extriordinary, as I had seen several of the likes around the Moon. He replied that it was often seen around the Moon, but that very fiew have seen it around the Sun. He remarked that that was for the King and him only. Hua when she heard of it remarked that D. K. will not live long [and that] his family will all follow.

Oh! I am so happy to hear that the Haoles are feeling freightened about their Property of being burnt, of selling out, and sending their Wives Home, D. K. showing his cowardly collars, the Foreigners being disgusted with the Man especially Cleghorn's remarks about the Natives' dislike towards D. K.[7] convincing him and others that all what is reported in the Papers [is] entirely false, and his cold reseptions by the People of Koolau—all combined makes me feel quite jolly.

I have received a letter from Aunty informing me that D. K. sent for my Makua Honowai[8] at Waianae to come up and pray me to death but the kind man refused to do so and also would not come up. But Aunty have asked me to write to him to come up to your place, which I have done. Nawahi is well aquainted with the Man. It must have been a false report about Koakanu's[9] and others trying to assist us poor unfortunates for Mr Nawahi do not mention a word about it, but we have received a letter from the Member from South Kona[10] asking us to answer him his three Questions, Viz. 1, Do we get enough or not of food? 2, Is their a Medical man with us to serve out Medicine? and 3, Is the climate favourable to the Sick?

The Natives held a Meeting and answered him, but I wrote to him privately, giveing him a full detail of how the Sick are treated by Ragsdale the Luna and what he does, and approved by Wilder, which I know if the truth is made known, we will be set at Liberty with the exceptions of probably a fiew who are really bad and destitute.

I must close now as my Eyes are weak. . . . God bless you is the never ceasing Prayer of

Your Humble Servant

KEKUAOKALANI

I am liveing on Potatoe which I buy from the Natives [at] $1 a bag as no more Poi has come, and not likely to.

---

1. Joseph K. Nawahi (b. island of Hawaii, 1854; d. San Francisco, 1896), member of House of Representatives 1872–1882, 1890, from Puna (Hilo), Hawaii. A descendant of the family of Kalaniʻōpuʻu, he was a supporter of Emma and Liliʻuokalani and a lifelong royalist. Peter evidently regarded him as one of his staunchest friends in the legislature. After dropping out of office during the 1880s, he reemerged in 1891 as organizer of the National Liberal Party, but opposed Robert Wilcox and certain fellow-members who advocated making Hawaii a "democratic republic" under Hawaiian autonomy. In December 1894, after Liliʻuokalani's fall, Nawahi and John Bush (a National Liberal colleague) were arrested for conspiring against the Republic of Hawaii. At his trial on May 9, 1895, the jury cleared Nawahi of the charge. On Sept. 4, 1896, he died of tuberculosis in San Francisco. His funeral in Hawaii was

noteworthy because of its huge crowds and the prominence of various Hawaiian "patriotic societies" represented, including the Women's Patriotic League. An obituarist in the *Independent*, Sept. 30, 1896, reminded readers that Nawahi's dedication to Hawaiian independence and "to the exclusion of any dominant influence of the whites" represented "a principle existent in the hearts of the Hawaiians and especially of womanhood. The mothers reared us and will protect the autonomy of the country."

2. Hakaleleponi was Queen Kalama, consort of Kamehameha III. There seems to be no other written source for the belief that the High Chief Paki, father of Bernice Pauahi Bishop and a councillor of Kamehameha III, was involved in practices of black magic (*'ana 'ana* sorcery) against the king to cause his death. According to Kukeliaiau, the queen had persuaded him to work retributive magic (*kuni*) against the king's enemies.

3. Choice of the common people.

4. All Hawaii; the united islands.

5. News.

6. A halo around either the sun or the moon.

7. Emma's informants had reported that Cleghorn believed local newspapers were overrating Kalākaua's popularity.

8. An "in-law" relative, here probably a male parent of some former sweetheart or mistress of Peter.

9. P. F. Koakanu, a high chief of Kauai and a member of the House of Representatives, 1868, 1874.

10. Simon Kaloa Kaai (d. 1884), member of House of Representatives, South Kona, island of Hawaii, 1870–1874, and supporter of Kalākaua. Educated in schools of Wailuku, Maui; briefly turnkey of Oahu Jail and deputy sheriff, Kona, during late 1860s. Though Emma hoped that Kaai would be loyal to her side, he became instead a leading figure in Walter Murray Gibson's "Young Hawaiian" party; along with Prince Leleiohoku and John Kapena, he was appointed by Kalākaua to the House of Nobles to strengthen the royal power in the legislature. As minister of finance, 1880, he stated at a public meeting that "the King has the absolute right to make and unmake cabinets, and that no one has the right to object or criticize no matter what he does or how he does it." (Quoted in Kuykendall, *The Hawaiian Kingdom: 1874–1893*, p. 219, who comments: "This statement is of great interest, for it contains the very essence of one side of the constitutional controversy that raged in Hawaii for the next dozen years.") In February 1883, about a year before Kaai's sudden death, he was dismissed from office for "dereliction of duty" (chronic intemperance), and John Kapena was appointed minister of finance in his place. For Kaai's activities in 1875–1876, see Letter 111.

Letter 74
Peter to Emma

[Kalaupapa]
June 3, 1874
2 P.M.

Queen Emma

I am happy to inform you that I am well, with the exception of my Voice, which is yet a little Hoarse. I commenced my usual rides yesterday by first having a Sea Bath. This morning I rode on the Plains for three or Four Hours although the Sun was hot, but the breeze by the Seaside was quite refreshing.

Last week the French Priest asked me to their Corpus Christo Procession,[1] and [to] hold one of the Ribons over the Ark—"Hale Lana,"[2] but I declined, giveing my excuse to him as politely as I could, that I have got a Sore foot, and cannot possibly walk any distance without making it worse. He replied that at Tahiti Queen Pomare's two Sons, Ninito's Husband[3] and a young Nobleman holds the Ribons, and that it was also an honor to do so. I informed him that I regreted very much [but] could not comply with his wish, and that my Church was the Church of England. He looked at me for a while, then replied that formely the English were Catholics, but Henry the 3d or 8th, I forget now, in order to marry a French Woman, had it reformed—thus the present Church of England.

I did not wish to argue with him so remained Silent and let him do the talking. He after talking asked Napela if he Napela could not go. Napela also excused himself by saying that on that day he and Six other Natives were going to Fast, and that he was a Mormon. The Frenchman then turned and had quite a dispute with Napela, and both stuck to the religion which each belonged to, and at the end they were both Victorious, but I favoured the Priest.

Last Week the Natives watched dayly from Wednesday till Friday for the Pai boat to come but no boat and consiquently no Pai, but on Satuarday the Pai boat came but brought only 40 bundles of Pai. Fortunately there were ten Pai for sale, and my Man got at the place whare the Pai is landed just in time to get a couple. The owner of the Pai refused my money, as he had stayed with Albert under Kalama.[4] His name is Kaanau. After Ragsdale had helped himself, and gave some to his Punaheles,[5] [he] had the Pai served to the Sick at a Pound a Person. I would have willingly gave some of mine, but I did not know when I will get any more Pai. Long before the Natives reached their [fill] they had ate their only Pound and could not get any Rice, as it was late in the afternoon.

One of the Sores of my Foot is healed, and another sore is healing nicely. I cannot say much about my Plants, but the Vine grows splendidly—it is now fully 6 foot high. . . . May you enjoy good Health, with the Allmighty's care is the Prayer of

Your Humble Servant
KEKUAOKALANI

1. Father Damien was organizer of the Corpus Christi celebration. Damien's co-worker, Father André Burgerman, wrote a description of this sacred spectacle in which Peter declined to play a part:

> In front, choir boys were swinging censers, preceded by little girls in blue and white who were throwing flowers. Another band closed the procession.
> Without stopping, the band alternated with the choirs, while the faithful were reciting the Rosary. Everyone able to move was there. Even Protestants followed respectfully or uncovered their heads as the Blessed Sacrament passed by.
> The priest walked under the canopy carrying the monstrance. He walked slowly, timing his steps to the cripples who followed painfully. The crowd of lepers sang the Lauda Sion with a burst of gripping enthusiasm. On returning the songs were a little quieter. (Quoted in Vital Jourdain, *The Heart of Father Damien, 1840–1889*, trans. by Francis Larkin and Charles Davenport [Milwaukee: Bruce Publishing Co., 1955], p. 200.)

2. Tabernacle; literally, "floating house."

3. Ninito, Tahitian wife of John Sumner, part-Hawaiian, owner of valuable Honolulu waterfront properties; for her Tahitian connections, see Letter 51, note 14.

4. Albert Kūnuiākea, Peter's half-brother, had been adopted by Kamehameha III, and was loved and indulged as a son by the childless Kalama (Hakaleleponi), Kamehameha III's widow. For a number of years after the king's death, Albert lived in the household of Dowager Queen Kalama, an arrangement that perhaps contributed to some of his youthful delinquencies.

5. Favorites.

Letter 75
Peter to Emma

[Kalaupapa]
June 8, 1874

Queen Emma

I am happy to inform you that my Hoarse is improving, but Slowly.

My "Kukeliaiau" had been wishing to see me Personally for some time back, but I could not go and see him on account of my ill Health. But yesterday being a fine day, I went to See him at the little House which I had put up for our use. —After being asked, and answering several questions, we proceeded to work. He asked me whether I believed in him, which I replied that I did. He then told the Men and Women who were then in the House, those that wished to go out were to go then, and those who wished to remain to remain, as no one were to go out nor in while he was performing. A Woman with a Suckling Babe moved to go out, but I detained her. He then asked me whether it was my wish to detain the Woman. I replied that it was, as it was not right for the Mother to go out in the Wind with the little child. He replied that after he had gone through some movements, he would let me know the reason why I detained the Woman.

When all was ready, he told a man to go and fetch a nice peble. One of my men went and brought a peble. He then laid his Kauila cane[1] on the Mat, and the peble also on the Mat close to his Cane between us, and after mutering something told me to pick which ever I chose of the Cane or Stone promiscuously, and that all was in our favour so far, and this being our last trial informed me that all now rested on my promiscuous pick. I informed him that I was ready, so closing his Eyes he replied, ∧"May the family gods of your ancestors guide your hands. Now choose."∧

I then picked the peble and informed him that I had picked what I prefered. He then asked me what it was. I informed him that it was the peble. He then replied that it was the power, *Mana*, of the other side, *D. K.*, that made him ask those who wished to go out to go, but our Aumakuas[2] were too strong for theirs, *D. K.s*, and that was the reason why I detained the Woman, and the Woman with her Suckling babe was a Omen that when you set on the Throne as our Queen and the time is not far, that your Reign will be a prosperous one, and the People will multiply in numbers.

In regard to my picking the peble in preference to the Kauila, he stated that although the Kauila is a hard Wood it is blown down by a Strong wind, and also cut by an Ax, but the Stone will never rot and will remain for ever, so my promiscuous picking of the peble was a sign that your Reign will be a long one.

He then informed me that in order that I may put more faith in him I am to see a Rainbow for three days. I informed him that I had seen one at Sea this morning (Yesterday), but he replied that I am to see another one this afternoon (Yesterday), tomorrow and Tuesday, which is a Sign that his Prayers have been granted by the "*Po.*"[3] He told me to have patience as the time is drawing nigh every day.

After a while I bade him a Aloha, then rode to the Beach to Hua's, but she was not at Home, so rode on to Kapeau's, Okuu's son, whare Mr and Mrs Napela were waiting for me. They had been to the afternoon Service, "Mormon." After spending an Hour or so we left and rode Home. The Afternoon being nice, I rode in to Kalawao and touched at Ragsdale's. After remaining their for a while I returned and ordered tea. While at my meal my man Keleau pointed out of the Window and said, ^"There is one fine rainbow."^ I looked out and saw one of the Prettiest Rainbows that I ever beheld, and [it] was quite near my Cottage. I remembered then what Kukeliaiau said in the morning. This morning after I woke I saw another Rainbow at Sea, and the Third and last will be tomorrow.

Tuesday, June 9.—This is the Third day that I am to see Rainbows, and almost one of the first things that I saw after I woke was a Rainbow at Sea, and it is now raining. This rain have rained just in time, as my Butt of Water is very near out. . . .

May the kind Providence ever spare and protect you is the Prayer of

KEKUAOKALANI

1. The carved tabu stick or cane used for ceremonial purposes. It derived its Hawaiian name from the wood it was made of and its tree, *Alphitonia ponderosa*, a member of the buckthorn family. Some of the trees on Molokai were believed to be poisonous, and sticks made of this variety were used in early times for sorcery.

2. Ancestral gods.

3. The revelation of the gods, as in omens or dreams.

Letter 76
Peter to Emma

[Kalaupapa]
June 12, 1874

Queen Emma

Thanks, kind Queen, for yours of the 8th which have been duely received. I am glad that Bishop was chocked by Mr Cartwright,[1] and his being called a Swindler in public will I am Sure produce some effect on the Haoles who have always thought Bishop to be an upwright and forward man.

The Shooting affair between the Spy Kauhaka and J. Auld[2] will I know cause a Stir among the Natives, as well as the Foreigners. Why! A Person cannot know whose Company he is in, Friend or Foe, and if he Speaks his own mind he is liable to be Shot. So on that Account all had better go armed, and the first shooter is the best off. I hope that the Natives will take it up and rise in a body and demand Satisfaction of Kaukaha, and if not granted, either to seaze Kaukaha or the D. K.s, and to make short work of them, and having put the proper Person *You* on the Throne, "bust" the Bastards from the Country.

I wonder how Kalahoolewa felt when Kepelino[3] sat in the Same Pew with him. Why! he the Heir Aparrent as he is called—to Sit on one Seat with a Commoner. Men who stoop to you, and would not even dare to stand before you? Why! if the Europeans were to hear of this, they would know immediately that the family to which he come from are not of the Family who ought to be on the Throne. I hope that while Lord Charles Hervey[4] were here, he heard the right side of the Story and knowing it to be true, turn a deaf ear to the numerous false reportes which fills our little community. However, although they are *now* on the Throne, for how long God only knows, they see and know that you assosiate with Peers of other Nations, while they befriend outcasts.

My once Makua-honowai, Keaona, I presume wishes to be made a Special Kahuna by yourself and Aunty, and that was probably the reason why he made the remark of "Your" being Sovreign, and will not recognize him when the time comes. But I hope that Aunty will not make too much of him. And I am sure that if the numerous predictions are to turn out as I hope, that you will not fail to recognize one and all of your Staunch Makaainanas.

Last Wednesday I rode to the beach to see the Akule haul, and while their, She and I (Hua) held a private conversation on the Rocks overlooking the Sea beneath whare the Fishermen were. She informed me that Signs which predicts to death, which she had formely Seen on Several occasions, she has again seen, and also you will be Victorious over all your Enemies. I told her about the Shooting affrey of Kaukaha, and she replied that all who had anything to do with Anaana-ing Lunalilo are all going to die, and when all these D. K.s are removed from this Earth, then you will Reign in Peace.

When the Akule were caught, I bought her 50cts worth—20 fishes —then returned Home as it was late in the day, and [I] just escaped a good Weting.

Their is a rumor sirculated here that the members of the Board of Health have all resigned for fear that they will have to pay the debt from after the 1st of June for the Leper Settlement, if the Appropriation Bill does not pass, as they have asked for $50,000. If this is true, then the Lepers who are able to scale the Pali will leave tomorrow, as we have only, now, about 150 sacks of Rice in the Store House, and Wilder has wrote up to Ragsdale that they will not buy, nor be responsible for anything for the Lepers, unless they be allowed to provide, or an appropriation for the Lepers be passed. I for my part am ready to scale the Pali.

Makaula wrote to me in one of his letters, saying that a Petition had been signed by the Natives and presented to the Legislature for a new Election for Sovreign. Is this the same one? or another one which you refered to in your last, and the one Kepelino is takeing around for Signatures?[5] I am happy to learn that J. O. C.[6] and some other Foreigners are in favour of it, and hope e'er long to hear of their Success. Good Bye.

A Schooner have just arrived and my Man have just come back with your letters. Thanks, Thanks, ever good and kind Queen for this capital News. I really do think that D. K. is about to retire from the Stage, and live an outcast, and Buff to live in the House destined to be his future one—"Kawa."[7] ...

God Bless you [is] the Prayer of

Your Obedient Servant
KEKUAOKALANI

1. Alexander J. Cartwright (b. 1820, New York City; d. Honolulu, 1893), commission merchant and general shipping agent. Became Emma's business agent 1874, taking over management of her affairs from John O. Dominis. Arrived in Hawaii, August 1849; active as general agent of New York Board of Underwriters 1851. There seems to be no other record of his alleged assault upon Charles R. Bishop.

2. D. Kaukaha (d. 1875), member of House of Representatives from Kauai, 1868–1874, a supporter of Kalākaua; one of several legislators injured by Queenites in Courthouse Riot. James Auld, a member of the publishing firm of Auld and Black, was part-owner of the *Hawaiian Gazette*. There seems to be no public record of this reported shooting incident. Perhaps Kaawa was correct in charging that affair was "all a made-up story"; see Letter 77.

3. John P. Zephyrin Kahōāliʻi (?1830–?1878), Hawaiian teacher, historian, poet; acted as Queen Emma's secretary in February 1874, when she opposed Kalākaua in election for kingship. For Kepelino's arrest, trial, and conviction on a charge of treason, see Letter 88, note 6. He was born in Kailua, island of Hawaii, to parents of alii and priestly lineage who became Catholic converts about 1840. He was taught by priests and sent to Honolulu to qualify for a teacher's certificate, but advancement was delayed because there was as yet no Roman Catholic high school. In 1847, he accompanied Father Ernest to Tahiti to assist him at a Catholic mission, but Father Ernest reported to Bishop Maigret that Protestant clergy were intimidating native parents and preventing them from sending their children to the priests' school: "Since then Zephyrin, having nothing to occupy him, has got bored; he has begun to play pranks and as I am afraid that idleness may become a cause of his getting lost in this Babylon of ours, I have resolved to send him back to his parents. I ask you, Bishop, to send him to Hawaii at the first occasion." After returning to Honolulu, Kepelino received further training at the newly established Catholic high school, Ahuimanu; contributed controversial letters to Catholic periodicals; belonged to a small circle of natives who met to discuss Hawaiian history and old native ways. His activities as Emma's secretary are reflected only flickeringly in written records of the period, but it seems probable that he assisted both in matters of genealogy and rhetoric, and composed certain of her proclamations to her native audience. It was believed that a letter he wrote to Queen Victoria "asking for warships to support Emma's claim [was] intercepted by Kalakaua, who was acting postmaster and recognized the writing." Kepelino never married; little is known of his checkered career during the last three years of his life. Knowledge of his background and interests is largely based on the work of Father Reginald Yzendoorn, historian of the Roman Catholic church in Hawaii, who was the chief source of biographical information used by Martha Warren Beckwith in her introductions to two of Kepelino's works: *Kepelino's Traditions of Hawaii* (Bishop Museum Bulletin, No. 95, Honolulu, 1932); and *The Kumulipo, a Hawaiian Creation Chant* (Honolulu: The University Press of Hawaii, 1972).

4. Arrival of Lord Charles Hervey (1808–1894), descendant of earls of Bristol, and David Lee, of England, was noted in *Hawaiian Gazette*, June 10, 1874. He was the Right Reverend Arthur Charles Hervey, D.D., bishop of

Bath and Wells (1869), formerly rector of Ickworth and Horningsheath, Suffolk. Queen Emma had met him during her visit to England in 1865, when she was attending numerous meetings in behalf of the Anglican mission to Hawaii.

5. Probably a reference to the petition which caused Kepelino to be tried and convicted on a charge of treason; see Letter 88, note 6.

6. Joseph Oliver Carter II (b. Honolulu, 1836; d. Honolulu, 1909), accountant, business agent, public official. One of six children of Joseph Oliver Carter, sea-captain from Massachusetts; his younger brother, Henry Alpheus Carter (1837–1891), was one of the commissioners who negotiated the treaty of reciprocity with the United States 1875–1876. In his persistent support of a monarchic system in Hawaii, J. O. Carter II differed from other prominent haoles of similar background (W. R. Castle, the Judd brothers, Henry B. Whitney, etc.) born of Americans settled in Hawaii. After schooling in Boston, he worked briefly as a reporter for the *Pacific Commercial Advertiser* during the 1850s. At public meetings in 1870s, he opposed proposals to introduce contract labor as an economic solution to the population problem. He was among the Americans who argued against the Pearl Harbor project both in speech and writing. Business agent of Queen Lili'uokalani and member of her Privy Council in 1891. In 1893, Carter was one of a small group of haoles who went to the queen after her dethronement and offered to assist her in any protest she wished to make. He was associated with C. Brewer and Co., sugar factors, during the 1880s, but opened his own office as financial agent in 1894, specializing in matters related to land management. He was a trustee for the Bernice Pauahi Bishop Estate, James Campbell Estate, and Kamehameha Schools. In 1898, he went to Washington, D.C., to oppose the annexation of Hawaii.

7. Prison.

Letter 77
Peter to Emma

[Kalaupapa]
June 16, 1874

Queen Emma

I am Sorry to inform you that I have had a little fight with Kaawa. Last Friday evening I knocked him down for striking me with his Kauila cane and the force of my blow made me fall over him. Striking my Head on a Cask of Water which stood at the corner of the Verandah cut it a little, but [it] bled considerable.

Mrs Napela ran out of the House, as it was at their House that this occured, crying. When I turned Kaawa was rising and seeing me

Scratched my face. I knocked him down again, then stepit over him and came Home. His mouth bled so much that the floor was covered with blood, and when Napela came out and asked who the blood was for, I not being their to speak for myself, [Kaawa] reported that the blood was for me.

He has sirculated a story here that he licked me for my being a Kipi, and will probably write down to Honolulu as such. The cause of the fight was my telling Mrs Napela of Bishop's being choked by Mr Cartwright. He replied very strongly saying that it was all Wahahee,[1] and that all my letters from you are all hoopunipuni.[2] I told him that I was speaking to Mrs Napela and not to him, so after a while I told Mrs Napela of the affrey between Kaukaha and J. Auld. Kaawa again said that it was all a made up story. Although I was then ready to strike him, I avoided it by whistling. He then remarked that because D. K. has got to be a King, that the other Party are making [up] storys falsely about D. K. and his Family.

I could not stand it any longer. I rose and said, "If you utter another word I will hurt you." On that he rose and struck me with his cane, and was knocked down by me. He has now a sore Jaw and face and I a cut Forehead. Wen Hua heard of my being ∧ badly beaten by Kaawa ∧ She and two more Women came up to see me. Before she started to come up she said before the Natives, ∧ "I am going to see my fellow sufferer, for he and I are two of the worst rebels Kaawa is always writing about to D. K." ∧

On their arrival I was reading my *Graphic*. She came up and said to me, ∧ "Where is your wound?" ∧ I pointed to my forehead and a scratch on my neck. She looked for a while, then said, ∧ "We have heard that you are badly hurt and cannot walk but instead we find you merely scratched—scratched by a calabash [of sorcery]." ∧

After a while she asked me privately to go over to Napela's, as she had something to tell me. At Noon I went over. Mrs Napela after a while asked Maria and Mahuna, the two Women who came up with Hua, to go and look for her Cats, and [that] left Hua, Napela and myself. Hua then informed Napela and I that D. K.'s ∧ calabash ∧ which she had seen ∧ is turned upside down and the bones ∧ are now scatered and turned to ashes. I asked her what the Signification of that was and she replied: ∧ "They are dead. They appear only in the shape of shadows. You will hear that they are dead. You will recognize a stench arising like the recent stench of the fish at Hilo. If you and I are to be arrested and sent to prison for treason, we will not be there very long before we shall hear that they are dead. Only one way remains to avert this bitterness of blood, prevent this stench of ashes: that is to place Emma on the throne. Therefore be patient for a little while until we hear of their downfall.",ₐ

She informed us that Kaawa had been to her and asked her to ₐ free D. K. from evil influence ₐ and if she consented, that she will be returned to Honolulu. Hua told him that it was too late, that all those who had anything to do with the late Lunalilo's death are going to ₐ die,ₐ saying, ₐ "They will all end up as ashes.",ₐ

She also said to Kaawa, "How can I do anything? Here I am on the Verdge of the Grave. You Kaawa tell D. K. to resign the Throne and give it to its proper owner, Emma, then ₐ it will be better. They will not live. They will die." ₐ This made Kaawa so mad that he has been writing letters to Honolulu, saying that Hua and I are Anaana-ing D. K. and family.

Ragsdale said to the Natives at Kalawao that he has received a letter from D. K. asking him Ragsdale to watch for the Rebels—*Kipis*— here, and that he wanted their (Natives') assistance, and if anyone hears of anyone speak[ing] ill towards D. K., to report to him immediately. Whare Ragsdale can find one that speaks in D. K.'s favour, I can find fifty to back me in your cause.

Good Bye. My Aloha to Hipa and all. May God spare you is the Prayer of

KEKUAOKALANI

9 at night. I have been to Hua's this afternoon, and she informed me to notify you to tell Albert to look out for himself or the D. K.s will have him, so please inform your poor wild Cousin. P. Y. K.

1. Lying.

2. Delusion.

Letter 78
Peter to Emma

[Kalaupapa]
June 20, 1874

Queen Emma

Yours of the 18th have been received, but the one of the 17th I have not yet received. I was taken ill very suddenly on the Evening of last Thursday just as I returned from my afternoon ride—Dizziness and Vomiting and lost of Appetite. I have only had two meals since then, a plate of Soup which I had made Yesterday, and a bowl of Milk and Rice this morning. I laid in bed all day yesterday and would have laid in bed today had not your letter with some others arrived announcing the comeing of the Representatives tomorrow.

I had read my letters when the new Catholic Priest[1] came in to see me. He had looked at my sore foot formely and said that he could cure it. He was waiting for some Alcahol which he had sent for, and [said that] if it came he will mix [it] with some other stuff, and that would be the best medicine for a Sore of long standing like mine. He has cured some Natives here and is waiting for more Alcahol. He has asked me if I could get a bottle of Alcahol up here, [saying] that he would mix me up some stuff to apply to the Sore, which on applying he pronounce to be sure cure, as he has had experience at Tahiti and here. So if you can procure a bottle of Alcahol and will send it up for trial, you will much oblige me. You must excuse me for this short letter, but I feel so curious that I cannot possibly write longer. If I cannot write by tomorrow, Kuihelani will bear to Queen Emma the Aloha of her afflicted Cos,

KEKUAOKALANI

Sunday June 21. 6:30 A.M. — I feel a great deal better after a good night's rest. The *Kilauea* is in sight. The Natives informed me last evening through Napela that they wished me to speak to the Honourable Members on our behalf, and that they would approve to what I said. I will write again after the interview. I have told my Man to take 3 Horses only to the beach, for Hon. Kauai, Nawahi and Poikai,[2] and to give [them] to no one else.

God bless you
KEKUAOKALANI

1. Not Damien; probably Father André Burgerman, who had a special interest in the medical aspects of leprosy.

2. N. Kepoikai, member of House of Representatives from Wailuku, Maui, 1866, 1867, 1870, 1874; also member of the legislature of the Republic of Hawaii, 1898. His later career makes it evident that he was not a supporter of Kalākaua.

Letter 79
Peter to Emma

[Kalaupapa]
June 23, [1874]

Queen Emma

I presume that you have heard all what took place here on Sunday through Hon. Kauai, with the exception of my being examined by the Chinese Doctor and Mr Powell,[1] the coulard Doctor. I regret exceedingly for having not opened and read your letter, which Hon. Kauai gave me in due time, although he asked me to do so quite frequently. But I hope that you are aware of my feelings on seeing so many of my old aquaintances, and on seeing the Hon. Gentleman especially who delivered your kind letter. Knowing that I could answer your letter at some future time, and the Hon. Kauai then in my presence and for only a fiew hours, I did not wish to do anything else but to speak to him only, and bear to you Verbally what little I had to say, which I hope he did.

While we were on our way to the Beach from after seeing Kauhako Crater, I pointed out to him the little Hut[2] which I wrote to you about. The eatables which you sent up I did not get them up to my Cottage until long after they [the Representatives] had left, neither had I anything to give. My Pigs are runing on the Plain at large or I would have given him one or more—Pig, as the case may have been —with the greatest, greatest of pleasure. . . .

When I was examined by the two Doctors they both agreed that they could cure me, saying that I being a strong and hearty man I ought to be cured inside of a Year. The Chinaman told me privately that if he is chosen by the Legislature to tend after the Sick (Lepers) he would send me back to Honolulu and tend to my case seperately. I was striped by both and was examined seperately. Robert Charlton[3] was with me at the time.

After the Hon. Members had left, I rode home and heard that Hua had told Okuu and H. Kahanu that D. K. will not set long on the Throne, and Okuu replied, ‸ "We shall pay the strictest attention to our chiefs. You hold firm on your side and my son will hold firm on his. We shall be under no illusions about the chiefs. The chiefs certainly knew us in the days before their present prosperity. But now that they are rich they take no notice of us.",‸

Hua then replied, ‸ "I know my *Alii* by the signs in the heavens. Here is Emma standing, visible everywhere. I know that Emma will reign, and it will not be long before we all shall see it happen. This woman's goodness of heart has been famous from the time she shared the Throne with her husband the King. She was never haughty nor proud. During their reign no man was debased. But with D. K. all men are thrust down. When these ones laid low rise again the persons who prostrated themselves before D. K. will never be lifted up again.",‸

Some Weeks past we were made known that D. K. had given $243.62½ for us, and that the Luna Ragsdale was to call a meeting and ask the Sick what he shall do with the Money. He Ragsdale had given one Ahaaina[4] before, and those who went complained of not having any Pork, as $20 was spent in bying Pig. So when the Natives heard of Ragsdale's giving another Feast, the Natives came up to me this morning and asked me to assist them, saying whatever I wished them to do, whether a Feast was best or they have Money from the Money which D. K. sent up, [I was to decide]. I informed them that I will ride up to Kalawao and speak with Ragsdale.

So after breakfast I rode up, and within 100 yards of the Hospital premises, Kamaka the Soldier and Kaimimoku came towards me saying that Ragsdale had had the Natives not afflicted stationed behind him armed with Knife and Axes, and some of the Sick stationed on both sides of me, ready at a moment's notice to jump on me. I told Kaimimoku that I did not care for the Men. Kaimimoku replied, "Ragsdale is also armed with a Pistol and a knife." So I said to him, "I am going to see if their is any shooting in him."

As I entered the House, Halulu a Constable moved a bench across the door. I steped over it and stood in front of Ragsdale, telling him what brought me up to him. I stood so near to him that he turned pale. He stood with one hand in his Coat brest, but could not move back as the door behind him was full and could not be passed, [because of] the man he had stationed to guard him in case of immergency. After I had told him what my business was with him, he replied that as the money had not come up I had better write to Mr Wilder. So leaving him I returned. As I got out of the yard, the Natives knowing Ragsdale to be armed, and might use the Weapon, had armed themselves with Stones and Sticks. The Cook House being near, [some] were also ready to set fire to the building, while others pelted Ragsdale and his backers with Stone, thus keeping them in the House, but nothing however hapened.

On Account of the Sunday affair the Store is closed, but I asked the keeper Williamson for some articles which I wished to buy, but the Store was out of [what] I wished. I should like to have a fiew bars of Soap, some Matches and Horse rope.

Good Bye. Kuakanu stole one of my Leis, all the rest I have received. . . . May the kind Providence ever spare you is the never ceasing prayer of

KEKUAOKALANI

Please enclose this and send it to Nawahi. If any letter from here bearing the title of Hon. is seen, knowing it to be for some of the Representatives it is either torn or never sent. P. Y. K.

---

1. When the Select Committee of the legislature visited Kalaupapa June 21–22, Peter was examined by two new physicians, Dr. William P. Powell and Dr. Sing Kee Akana. Powell, an unlicensed Negro physician recently arrived in Hawaii, claimed to have been successful in treatment of leprosy at the Sailor's Home, New York City. Akana was already widely known in the native community. On May 9, 1874, a petition bearing 7,000 signatures was presented in the legislature, praying "that Dr. Sing Kee Akana be permitted to attend the lepers at Molokai." It was understood that Dr. Akana would base his treatments on principles of Chinese herb medicine. The medical knowledge, theoretical and practical, of the "coulard doctor" was an as yet unknown quantity. The pending appropriation bill carried a provision of $6,000 to cover both Powell's and Akana's services. When the Board of Health then set up specific conditions for treatments, Dr. Powell became offended and soon embarked for San Francisco. Dr. Akana conducted a full course of "experiments" extending over months. An official assessment of results was published in the annual *Report of the Board of Health* for 1874. Several members, including Dr. McKibbin and Samuel G. Wilder, had been skeptical from the start about Mr. Powell's training and stability and Dr. Akana's methods and competence. These members were not surprised when the scheme emanating from wide public concern and the well-meaning but uncritical intentions of the legislature proved a failure. For the next several months Peter's letters reflected his fluctuating hopes that one or the other of the two practitioners might cure, or at least arrest, the progress of his disease.

2. The hut of the kahuna Kukeliaiau.

3. One of Peter's good friends and a supporter of Queen Emma; for main note see Introduction to Part 3, note 3.

4. Feast.

Letter 80
Peter to Emma

[Kalaupapa]
June 26, 1874

Queen Emma

As an extra Mail goes over today, I avail myself the opportunity to write to you. On the night of the 23d, the day that Ragsdale was armed for me, a rhumor was sirculated that the Sick at Kalaupapa were going to gather in a body armed and headed by me, were going to Ragsdale's and ask for satisfaction, and if not satisfactory given, that we were going to burn his House together with the Hospital. Ragsdale was in such fear of his Life that he had the Kamaainas collected at his House at Kalawao who watched him all night.

On the evening above mentioned, I rode to the beach and asked Kaimimoku to go to a certain Kanelanahine, a well man, and ask him to come up to my House on the following morning. As I was going to the beach alone, some of the Kamaainas who were on their way up to watch Ragsdale saw me going down, took it for granted that I was going to the beach and [would] then march up. This Story they told to Ragsdale, who immediately sent out Spys to ascertain when and how we were comeing. In the meantime, I told Kaimimoku that I wanted the man to take a note for me to Mr Meyer, the Agent for the Board of Health, inform him of the Day's doings, and how I was asked by the Natives, etc., and its results, thus giveing me a chance to pen you a fiew lines.

The Moon shone bright so I lingered at the beach longer then I intended, as this is the first time that I ever left my Cottage at Night during the time that I first set foot on this Soil. When I returned enjoying the Moonlight and my Dog Spring leading, my mind was carried away and thinking of you and Home and other little incidents, . . . on looking up I [found I] was nearing Home [and] as I entered the yard a Horseman passed me going up, evidently one of the Spys for me. On the following day, I dispatched my letters and also received one from Meyer informing me that he would come down.

Yesterday he came and he, Ragsdale and I talked the Subject over, and Ragsdale said that he was misled by the diferent rhumors, and was glad to appoligize to me. I asked him whether he had any recollection of what he said towards me, and if he was ready to take it all back. He replied that he was carried away at the time by the Spur of the moment, which he was very sorry for. I informed him that for the future he had better not let his judgment be led by his passion. After a fiew more words, we parted. But as soon as I got Home, Kaimimoku and some more of the Sick came to me and said that they were not Satisfied, as I did not speak in public so that all could hear. I told him to wait and see what will next turn up. . . .

12 Noon.—A man have just come from Kalae with the Mail and by the Mail I have received yours of the 16th. I presume this is the only one which you wrote of having sent by the *Nettie*, as I see by this that you mentioned about the Representatives comeing up here. Since the Petition of the Honolulu's have had no effect on the Legislature, [I] hope and pray this one will[1] . . . .

Kaawa's jaw is very sore and the place which is sore is taking effect with his throat, and he is Hanapilo.[2] He Kaawa have been using Bernice Pauahi's name in order to get good Potatoes from the Natives and send it to his Wife, Hamanalau. The Sick are waiting patiently to hear what the result will be of the Representatives reporting to the House what they heard up here. Simon put on a great deal of Airs whilst here but was unnoticed by the Sick, who remarked, ʌ"How conceited that one-handed man is.[3] The younger one has a pleasant face.",ʌ Thisʌ pleasant-facedʌ individual is the Hon. Mr. Nawahi.

Please send me up a fiew note papers when you send me up the Envelopes. Good Bye. God bless you is the prayer of Your Servant,

KEKUAOKALANI

1. The petition urging that Dr. Sing Kee Akana be employed by the legislature to commence a course of treatments for selected lepers.

2. Hoarse.

3. One of Simon Kaai's hands had been amputated after an injury sustained while firing a cannon.

Letter 81
Peter to Emma

[Kalaupapa]
June 29, 1874

Queen Emma

Since my last, our little community is quite Still, but I can see that the Sick are only waiting for a chance to show their anger in deed towards Ragsdale. They have asked me not to interfere. . . .

Mrs Kate Napela had a dream on Satuarday night. She has informed me that this kind of dream is "Kuluma"[1] to her, and that is the third time that She has dreamt that kind of dream. She dreamt that she saw Kahalekula,[2] Hoapili and their Mother laying on one bed, and each had a white gown on, and all three were laying on their back, and a fourth person was also laying on his side, also robed in a white gown. On Mrs Napela's advancing to ascertain who the forth person was, it rose and stared "Hoaa"[3] at her. She was so frightened that she moved back. On her moveing back, the fourth person laid down along side of Hoapili, and all four laid on the same bed and all wore white gowns. On her moveing forward again to see who the person really was, she saw that it was D. K., so she moved back exclaiming,ᴧ "Oh! So Kalakaua is dead,"ᴧ and in her effort to cry she woke.

She has informed me that the first time that [she] dreamt a dream simular to this was when Kahalekula was alive, and not long after Kahalekula died. And while she was at Wailuku, she dreamt of seeing Kiliwehi, Hoapili and Kahalekula all robed in white gown and all were laying on the same bed, and this is the third dream of the same nature.

Last evening, Napela, Kaawa and I were seting on Napela's Verandah. While they were conversing, I was watching the Clouds. Finally I saw the Clouds form into a shape of a man sleeping, so turning to Napela I whispered to him about the Cloud. He looked at it and beckoned me to keep silent, asking me what I was thinking about. I replied that I was thinking of You and Home, as it was the 28th of June, being the day that I left Honolulu for this place.

After I had spent a hour or so I returned. This morning I went to Napela's, and he informed me not to say anything of what we saw in the Clouds, nor about his wife's dream, for if it went to D. K.'s and his Kahunas' ears, that they may *Kala* it,[4] as it can be done. So this is a secrete to us.

Kaawa has been privately to Hua, asking her to get D. K. out of his pilikia, and that he will reward her handsomely, but she has answered him to his face, saying, ∧"You shall not live, nor shall the race live through the *Alii* you so greatly desire, an arrogant Chief who does not show concern for his people. He has but a short time on the Throne, and then Queen Emma shall reign. This is the Chiefess through whom these bones shall live, and the whole race too. The face of Hawaii shall again turn upward, while Kalakaua here is reduced to ashes."∧

The Sick here are going to forward a Petition to the Legislature to allow the coulard Dr Powell to come up and cure us if he can, for whilst he was here, he said that my case could be cured and that he has cured a worse case than mine. For the past three or four days, I have felt week in the Stomach. Poi, I can scarce eat, for it makes me Vomit, so I have been eating Pai up to the moment. In one of my letters lately to you I asked you for a Bottle of Alchohol. I have altered my mind, as one of my Sore foot is well from the Medicine which I got from Dr Trousseau. So I will still use the medicine which I have, although the French Priest has told me that Dr Trousseau's medicine was only fit for new Sores, and that it contained Mercury, which is very bad and will not cure Sores of old standing like mine, and that he has had experiance while at Tahiti when the Natives were effected with the Leper, and he also caught it, but was fortunate enough to get well.

12 Noon, July 30.—I have writen to the Hon. J. Kauai and have also told him Mrs Napela's dream, for Kanepuu[5] might wish to hear it. A Woman, one of my domestics by the name of Kainea, is a Daughter-in-Law to Kanepuu.

After I rested on my litter yesterday I rode in to Waikolu to see the Akule haul. All my Men had gone up in the morning, so at noon I rode in. After I had remained for a while, I returned and rode by the Beach. When I got Home, my Men had come back with the division of which I am entitled for my Net. The number of fish was one Kaau or 40 fish.

Sunday was the day that I left you and dear Home, and today is the day that I first set foot on Kalaupapa (Inoino).[6]

God bless you, and with his help I hope that we may Succeed, is the Prayer of your Servant.

KEKUAOKALANI

1. Customary.

2. Probably D. Kahalekula Kaauwai, a brother of William Hoapili

Kaauwai. D. K. Kaauwai was a member of the House of Representatives in 1854 and 1855.

3. Glared.

4. By using counter-sorcery, free themselves from adverse magic.

5. A Hawaiian of Molokai, an authority on Hawaiian history, and a prolific writer of stories and articles for the native newspapers. He sometimes wrote under the pseudonym "Kaniwelani."

6. Shattered.

Letter 82
Peter to Emma

[Kalaupapa]
July 4, 1874

Queen Emma

Your last have been received. I am sorry to hear that Aunty is not well. Perhaps it is the effects of her old Age, and I hope she will get over it.

D. K. may well tremble in his skin and detain the *Benicia*[1] as long as he can, for his time will come, and that not long from now. His Mamalahoas[2] leaving him will I have no doubt cause a great uneasiness among his family. Kahai[3] I presume has had a hand in with D. K. and he will be called away to answer for what he has done. . . .

The Traitor Simon[4] has at last ventured into your premises, but his Concious forbad him going any further. That was the reaon why he gave that poor excuse. I will wait patiently for the comeing next letter, for I am ever anxious to hear of Mr Hasslocher's[5] advice, and also of Mrs Wodehouse's opinions of recent events,[6] for I am certain that their are something worth hearing in what they say. T. Martin[7] was one who voted against you, and now he has come to ask help from your hands. Why do he not go to D. K.? (Away with him.)

So D. K. is on another Wild Goose chase, "Kahuna Hunting." If he does not look out the Kahunas will Kahuna him. Hon. Kauai have informed me in his letter that a large star was seen in broad daylight.

I am well and the sore on my Poomuku[8] foot is entirely healed. All what you have sent up is received. . . .

May God be with you is the Prayer of

KEKUAOKALANI

1. The U.S.S. *Benicia*, after an absence of about a year, arrived from Panama February 26–27, 1874. Remained in Hawaiian waters until Nov. 17, then sailed for San Francisco with King Kalākaua aboard, accompanied by his official staff. The *Hawaiian Gazette*, Nov. 18, noted that "His Majesty will have the honor of being the first crowned head who has ever visited the United States since the establishment of government."

2. An allusion to the recent deaths of various supporters of Kalākaua (W. Hoapili Kaauwai, Judge Lilikalani, etc.). The term *māmalahoa*, suggesting an elite royal guard, derives from the name of a special company of warriors of Kamehameha I.

3. John Kahai (1830–1874), member of the legislature, 1874. His death of heart disease, according to the *Pacific Commercial Advertiser*, Oct. 31, 1874, was believed by Peter to be a result of anti-Kalākaua sorcery; see Letter 85, note 8.

4. Simon Kaai.

5. Eugene Hasslocher (d. Ashland, Ore. 1895), native of Germany and intimate friend of Queen Emma; language and music teacher in Honolulu during early 1860s, also military instructor in Household Guards 1861, with rank of major under Kamehameha IV. In 1863, he married a part-Hawaiian lady, Mrs. Charlotte Coady (widow of Richard Coady, American sea captain). The Hasslochers were living in Karlsruhe, Baden, Germany, when Queen Emma visited them in 1866. Appointed Hawaiian consul for Grand Duchy of Baden 1866; envoy extraordinary and minister plenipotentiary 1871. In later years a resident of San Francisco. During 1870s Emma corresponded with both Hasslochers (see Hasslocher Collection, AH). Hasslocher appears to have supplied the queen with interesting political advice after the election of Kalākaua, but none of his letters bearing significantly on Emma's political intrigues in 1873–1874 have been preserved in public archives.

6. No letters for this period between Emma and Mrs. Wodehouse (Annette Fanny Massey, m. 1861; d. 1929), youngest daughter of William Massey, of Wooten, Norfolk, and wife of Major James Hay Wodehouse, British commissioner and minister resident in the Hawaiian Islands 1866–1894, are known to exist in public archives. Those that once existed may have been destroyed or remain in private hands. Major Wodehouse (b. 1824; d. Abingdon, England, 1911), descendant of an ancient Norfolk family of knights and baronets, took an Oxford B.A. and saw military service in India before entering the British foreign service. He owed his Sandwich Islands appointment partly to his impeccable background and Foreign Office connections, being a relative of John Wodehouse (1826–1895), who succeeded his grandfather as third Baron Wodehouse in 1846 and was created Earl of Kimberley in 1866.

7. William Thomas Martin (d. ?1886), rancher of Ka'u, island of Hawaii, and supporter of Kalākaua; long-time member of legislature, House of Representatives 1863–1873, House of Nobles 1874–1884. Martin was British-Hawaiian, the son of an English sea captain and the grandson of a

Scottish planter in the West Indies and a Negro slave. Thomas Martin is mentioned in the earliest guidebook to the island of Hawaii: "This village of Waiohinu, the name signifying 'shining water,' is the paradise of Kau, and here the Hon. Thomas Martin, a noble specimen of the half-caste race, dispenses the hospitalities of the place, and exhibits the advanced civilization of Hawaii most worthily." (Henry M. Whitney, *The Hawaiian Guide* [Honolulu: 1875], p. 96.)

8. The lame foot.

Letter 83
Peter to Emma

[Kalaupapa]
July 7, 1874

Queen Emma

I am most anxious to receive your next letter, but I presume that by the time that you have received this of mine, I shall have received yours of which I am so anxiously waiting for. As I was enjoying my usual afternoon ride Yesterday Evening and inhaling the Sea breeze, a large Vessel passed quite near and as I was on a little Hill, I immagined that I could See Men on the Afterdeck and I am quite sure that if anyone looked at the direction whare I was I could be seen, as I was dressed in White Trouses and frock.[1]

As the Vessel sailed on its course to Westward, I followed by land watching as she was plowing the Sea. I could not see Sweet Home, so following the Vessel with my Eyes, I thought of Home and of those so dear to me, and you especially, surrounded by so many Wicked People, till the comeing night made me seek my Cottage on the cliff. So on looking again for the Vessel, I saw it but a Speck on the Ocean, so waving my Hat in the direction whare Oahu is seen, and reciting the words "Adieu, Adieu, my Native Land,"[2] I rode back, as it was then after Sunset. The Evening being nice and cool, I walked my Horse all the way, thinking of you and of Home, meditating on the past and the future, till weary of my immaginations, I would sing, and was only checked by reaching Home.

I presume the Vessel that I saw got to Honolulu by next morning (today). We saw a Comet here for three days, and [until it] disappeared on Sunday night. Although it is Summer yet we have rain, which is very beneficial to the poor Natives who have to walk a

Mile and over to procure freash water. We hear that the Colard Man
Powell is coming up here to treat the Sick, and Ragsdale has hinted to
me that I will not remain here two Months longer, saying that two
Sick persons will be sent to Honolulu for trial, one by Powell and one
by the Chinese doctor.

A woman came up from Honolulu to see her Son who has lately
died, and told the Sick that all the People of Oahu are ready to put
D. K. from the Throne, and [choose] You as their Queen, and are only
watching and waiting for the *Benicia* to leave.

Good Bye. My Aloha to Aunty and Wikani (ma).[3] May God bless
and protect you is the Prayer of

KEKUAOKALANI

1. Not a frock coat. An open-necked shirt or smock, not tucked inside
trousers; equivalent to the modern "aloha shirt."

2. Another echo of Childe Harold's farewell ("Adieu, adieu! my native
shore") from Byron's *Childe Harold's Pilgrimage*, Canto the First.

3. "And all the rest."

Letter 84
Peter to Emma

[Kalaupapa]
July 13, 1874

Queen Emma

I received last Wednesday yours of the 3d, together with yours of
the 21st, 25th and 26th of last Month. Whare they have been all this
while I know not, but since I have received them all is well.

What will be the result of Albert's doings I really cannot make out.
He [is] going with Pinehasa[1] at night and into the Palace, and
assosiating with D. K. privately, and knowing that it is rong to do so
yet he has done so. I should not at all wonder that he will be a Traitor
to us, if he is not allready, and also a Spy. I am sure that if his Forging
case is not settled properly with Watson, he will go over with the
D. K.s in order to escape the Prison. So I think it will be best to keep
a watch on him when he comes to see you, especially at Night.

I am sorry to hear of Kamakaaiau.[2] No wonder as you say that your enemies speak of your assosiating with Prostitutes—but let them say what they will. There is One above all who knows that you are innocent of the false reports, [which are] only a falsehood made by your Enemies who are in such dread for you, and are trembling in their Shoes for fear of the comeing day when they will kneel to you as their Queen and Ruler.

I am happy to learn that Mrs Wodehouse has not turned to the numerous false reports which she has heard, but [holds] still to her firm belief that you are, as you always were, Kind, True, and Humble, and I am sure that she knows these reports to come from your Enemies, in order probably to try if they can to ruin your character and be like theirs.

I have heard from Ragsdale that the Foreign Community at Hilo have disliked D. K. for appointing Kipi[3] as Governor, a man who is greatly disliked by the people of Hilo. Mr Hasslocher's letter and advice is splendid, if it could only be carried out, but as you say who can you trust besides G. B.?[4] I am in great fear that unless something extriordinary takes place, according to predictions, it will be quite a long while before we can Conquer these Enemies of ours. "But God I know in his infinite kindness will not let you remain long, and be abused by these Wicked People, for he is always with the Weak and Humble, and when he has subdued your Enemies for you he will then —as you have been faithful over a fiew things—make you a Ruler over many things—make you our Ruler and Queen as of Yore."

Their is a report rhumored among us here that D. K.'s intention, and asking for a loan of $1,000,000,[5] is to get the Government in Bankrupt so that when it falls over to you, the National debt will be enormous—that [the Nation] will either be Sold or the Yanks have it.

Ragsdale have got a letter from Wilder informing him that One or more of the Lepers here are to be sent to Honolulu for a trial by Powell. [He must be] a person that can obtain what Powell wishes to have procured, and Wilder has mentioned my name to Ragsdale as one who will be sent down. Now for my part I would rather remain here and take the chances, sooner than go and add more trouble to you, for I think that Powell will wish for this and that, and all most likely to be got by money. My remaining here will save expence more then it will by my going down. I am sure that I have been very expensive to you and I hope that you are aware that I should suffer sooner then to give you any Pilikia. (Please let me know your mind on this subject.)

Ragsdale have also offered to bet me that I will not remain two months longer. After I had read your last letters I concluded to burn them, so gathering all your letters I burned them all.

You remarked in your last of Mr Cartwright's leasing all of your Lands. I am very glad to hear that he is receiving something from them, thus helping to pay. Now that showes the diference between the two men, One a Gentleman and the other a Beast.[6]

After I had read Kaawa's letter I sent him a copy of it, and now he has been very civil to me and calls me his Hanai.[7] He is not yet well from the effects of the Blow on his jaw, which is considerably Swolen. The Natives are greatly taking to being bled (oo),[8] and a woman by the name of Luka, a Sister of Kepola, was bled on Satuarday last, and nearly died from the loss of Blood. My health in general is good. A woman by the name of Piko lately came up here to cry over the Grave of her Son, who has lately died. This Piko's husband is stoping with Ruth.[9] . . .

May God's Blessing and Protection be with you is the Prayer of

Your Humble Servant
KEKUAOKALANI

1. William Pinehasa Wood, part-Hawaiian military officer and politician; appointed member of Privy Council by Kalākaua in 1874. His family owned an extensive cattle ranch on Oahu and were connected with the family of Edward Boyd, royal chamberlain, in the meat business. Queen Emma had formed a very poor opinion of Pinehasa Wood even before he became identified politically with the "D. K.s." Writing to Major Hasslocher, Feb. 17, 1873, she deplored several of Lunalilo's early appointments after his accession: "There is very great feeling of insecurity in the Community. Pinehasa Wood, a half-white, once a Member of Parliament for Honolulu at former Legislature, but a low demoralized fellow and a butcher, received a billet of Circuit Judgeship of the Island in place of Judge Kamakau." (Hasslocher Collection, AH.)

2. A reference to her recent misfortune; see Letter 51.

3. Samuel Kipi (d. 1879), governor of Hawaii 1874–1879.

4. Great Britain.

5. A bill introduced by Governor Kipi, under Kalākaua's sponsorship and

with the support of Attorney General R. H. Stanley; first reading in legislature July 25, 1874. The colloquial title ("the million dollar loan bill") came from its first section which, according to the *Hawaiian Gazette*'s critical summary, July 1, 1874, authorized the government to borrow "not over one million dollars, for which Coupon Bonds, Registered Bonds, or *Treasury Notes*, may be issued '*in such portions of each*' as may be deemed advisable, bearing not over six per cent interest and redeemable in ten to twenty years." The most dubious feature of the bill, upon which not even members of Kalākaua's cabinet could agree, was what its opponents called its "obnoxious paper money clause." William L. Green, minister of the interior, on July 27, moved to strike the clause authorizing the treasury notes: "Nobody would take these notes without interest to keep, they could only be taken to pass again to someone else." As result of Green's opposition, the paper money clause was omitted and instead an amendment was inserted requiring all transactions under the bill to be based on coin. In final form the much amended bill was approved Aug. 1, 1874, by a vote of 26 to 14. Among those who opposed the measure and voted for indefinite postponement were Emma's most consistent supporters, Representative Nawahi, Pilipo, and Kauai. Among those in favor, in addition to such regular "D. K.s" as John O. Dominis, A. S. Cleghorn, W. L. Moehonua, S. K. Kaai, and Samuel P. Parker, were several of Emma's close friends, notably Governor Paul Nahaolelua and Huaka Kuihelani.

6. John O. Dominis, her former business agent.

7. Foster relation. Why Peter made a copy of Kaawa's letter is not clear, unless Kaawa was too crippled in the hands to do so.

8. Peter provides the Hawaiian word for "blood."

9. This sentence and the one immediately preceding have been transferred from an earlier paragraph.

Letter 85
Peter to Emma

[Kalaupapa]
July 16, 1874

Queen Emma

Thanks for yours of the 7, 8 and 11, which I received yesterday. I will answer yours according to their dates. Oh, if I only knew that the Vessel which I saw was the "Queen Emma" I would have sang "Maikai Waipio, he alo lua na Pali"[1] with uncovered head, but I sang the *Dearest Spot* in its place. . . .

Is Kapiolani so scared of her life that she runs away when a trifling alarm is given? How funny—the Queen as they term her, running for her life. The next time she runs, she will run into a *hole* that will never allow her to return. . . .

I have received a letter from Nahaolelua and I am greatly surprised that he does not mention anything about you, but says, ∧"The King is well, as are all of the royal family,"∧ informing me of D. K.'s health, as though I care a straw about him or his family. What a blockhead Kilinohe[2] was, for he will never have another chance to tell D. K. his mind, if he had any such intention, but I presume that the fool was really scared.

I have read Powell's letter to Mr Green,[3] and I think it is a very nice one. He ought to be allowed to try, for I think that if I had a fair trial I would have been cured, and their are others here besides me. I hope that your next in regard to F. Brown will not be so bad, as I am afraid it will [be], especially by the tone of your letter. Ever since you asked me to Pray for fear of the intended Loan, I have never ceased to do so, but in regard to fasting I think that I am fasting now, as my Poi is out, and what Poi I get now I buy but very dear. So I have to be very economical with what little Money I have left, as the Government Pai are taken to pieces, weighed, and then served by men who are bad with the disease. It is awful, *hoopailua*,[4] and Mr and Mrs Napela have remarked at my eating so little, yet keep so stout.

Now the *Camelion* have come,[5] the Yanks will not have much to say. And I hope and earnestly Pray that the Admiral will turn a deaf ear to the falsehood which I have no doubt will be told him by your Enemies. As you stated about the Natives' rhumer, I have it by Makaula's letter. He said that when the officer [from the *Camelion*] jumped on the Dock, the Haoles saluted him, but he did not notice them but kept right on up town.

Perhaps D. K. availed himself of the cheap Liquor at Mr Jagger's marrage, and so got tight, and not satisfied with that but he must need go and gamble and loose $400,[6] and the next thing which he will loose will be his *Head*.

Since the *Camelion* has come, Rycroft[7] will have a splendid chance to speak to the officers and inform them of what was done to him by D. K.'s soldiers and the cowardly D. K.

Kahai I hope is reaping the Seed of what he helped to plant, and D. K. riding about while he lays on his death bed.[8] Kamaipuupaa's and others' predictions I hope will not fail. Hua is always telling me that D. K.'s and family's time is short, and she says that when you set on the Throne that she will go Home and not wait for the Board of Health, and she is sure that the time [is] drawing nearer. I wished it were in olden times, as Ruth wishes. I being a desendant of *Puhi Ahi*[9] will gratify others by Puh-ing her—and see how she likes it. And I should like to hear them offer to sell our Country—why they would not last a day. I hope what Waahia[10] did say was in your favour, for I like to hear reports in your favour. I am happy to hear of Mr. C.[11] making your lands pay, for every little helps.

Kapo kneeling to her Sister—well, let her kneel, she will be kneeling yet with tears in her Eyes by her Sister's deathbed. It not only sound strange to me, but I cannot bring it to word—the Crown Prince Master Ke Koi[12]—how funny. Well—let it pass, as they all will.

I am sure that there are among the foreigners *English* who will tell the true story to the *Camelion* people, and when the truth is made known they will also turn their noses up too, like the foreign Kamaainas. . . .

My Prayer for you always.

KEKUAOKALANI

1. A "traveling" mele (chant) in a traditional style celebrating certain localities famous for scenic beauty on the islands of Hawaii and Maui. A portion of the song was set to vocal music by Princess Likelike (Mrs. A. S. Cleghorn) and published in *Johnny Noble's Royal Collection of Hawaiian Songs* (Honolulu: 1929).

2. Unidentified.

3. William L. Green, minister of the interior, read Powell's letter aloud before the Legislative Assembly, July 7, 1874, frequently interrupting himself to make his own sardonic comments. After full discussion, the House referred the report back to a special committee on the Kalaupapa hospital and settlement, with a recommendation that it confer with the Board of Health with respect to Mr. Powell's offer.

4. Nauseating stuff.

5. H.B.M.'s steam corvette *Camelion*, Commander A. J. Kennedy, thirty days from Callao, arrived at Honolulu July 12. The visit seems to have passed in routine manner, despite Peter's expectations. King Kalākaua visited the vessel at noon Aug. 5; on Aug. 20, the *Camelion* sailed for Tahiti, after thirty-nine days in port.

6. In a "Memo for Molokai," July 13, 1874, Emma noted that Kalākaua had gone to a hotel "attended by his Butcher Aid de Camp Boyd and J Cummings...and plaid a game of Poker with the Proprietor Emerson, the Ethiopian serenader, and one or two other low associates—treated them at bar, and got beaten $400."

7. Robert Rycroft (b. Leeds, England, 1843; d. Honolulu, 1909); originally a plumber; in later life, general merchant and planter. During 1870s, he operated an ice factory (the first to use the "new ammonia process") and soda works. His "Fountain Restaurant" and soft-drink parlor, sometimes referred to as a "temperance saloon," was situated opportunely at the foot of Fort Street, on the "esplanade"—i.e., directly on the waterfront. His British background and business location would have given him easy access to officers and men of the *Camelion*. A member of the Hawaiian Reformed Catholic church. Nothing is known of his troubles with Kalākaua.

8. Emma had suggested that Kahai was a victim of sorcery: "Kahai is growing worse. He has vomited blood and is swollen at stomach which is one of the signs." ["Memo for Molokai," July 13, 1874.]

9. Literally, "burning fire." An allusion to a kapu right by which the possessor could command that someone be burned to death. The reference here in connection with the Princess Ruth ("Puh-ing her") probably reflects Peter's displeasure at Keʻelikōlani's support of Kalākaua. The scornful allusion below to Prince Leleiohoku, Ruth's adopted son, further suggests that Emma had reported to Peter some incident disparaging to both Ruth and Kalākaua's heir-apparent.

10. A female kahuna, wife of Kamaipelekane; for main note, see Letter 103, note 4.

11. A. J. Cartwright, Emma's business agent.

12. Literally, "the young red snapper"; another nickname for Prince Leleiohoku. *Koʻi* is a name for the young stage of *ʻulaʻula*, red snappers. The name of the fish is a reduplicating form of *ʻula*, meaning red, scarlet, or brown, as in the skin of a dark Hawaiian. The satiric nickname apparently plays on the idea of Leleiohoku's immaturity and on his dark skin, presumably similar to that of Kalākaua.

Letter 86
Peter to Emma

[Kalaupapa]
August 3, 1874

Queen Emma

Thanks for yours of the 19th, 21st, and 27th. Mrs Napela and I had been to the afternoon Service at Kalaupapa and had returned, and as the Sun had not then Set I took a ride in to Kalawao and back. My Man informed me that a mail had come although it was Sunday. I was so delighted that I dismounted and rushed in the House to read my letters, and with the greatest of anxiety while reading for fear of meeting with what I do not wish to hear nor learn in regard to any Pilikia which may befall you. But the kind God is still protecting you.

While I was at the beach yesterday, before I received yours, I had heard from Ragsdale that a man had come up from Honolulu and reported that he had heard that the Natives intended to kill all of the Representatives who voted for the *Loan*.[1] As we all do not believe what he Ragsdale say, I only listened without believing, but he told me that he has received letters stating that the Majority of the Hawaiians there are all drunk from D. K. down, treating and drinking at the Bar like any comon man. Whare he got his information from I do not know.

I wonder whether Mr Rhodes's call on you is really as he say a friendly call or no. However you know best, but I should think if his call was really a friendly one he should trust you, and tell the names of those you asked [about]. I am quite sorry that the intended *Plan* did not succeed, and I hope that it will not rest long ere another and more successful one will be made.[2] I really believe this to be true, or faithful Mrs. W.[3] would not use the names of which she mentioned to you.

I hope J. O. D. is quite satisfied with what he saw in the Pantry.[4] I hope that he has found out that in saving the Wolf, he has lost the Sheep—*Akola*.[5] I can well understand how you must have felt after a Sleepless night, [having] to meet the Hookupu on the following day, and a Reception in the afternoon. And I most sincerely hope and Pray that it is for the best. I am really glad that Boyd[6] spoke so abrubtly to Captain Kennedy, which I hope will confirm Captain Kennedy of the company which D. K. assosiates [with]. As Captain Kennedy said, D. K. is not, nor ever will be, known in England or anywhares else, save perhaps at *Africa*.[7] I am really tickled to hear that the Natives gave Reath to the Russians, and above all their Hookupu, thus showing their love for you, and all those who visit you.

You do not mention of Kalahoolewa's visit to you, as you said that he said to Kapiolani that he went to see you.

August 4th.—I am in for it now. My Domestics (Kamaainas) have been grumbling at my hoounauna-ing[8] them too much. Now everyone know that they do very little but eat a great deal, and still they are not satisfied. . . .

I see in the Papers that the Board of Health intends to take measure to send away all those who are not Sick, and leave us to our fate. I am thinking of geting me some more domestics, but these are to be from the Sick who are not bad, especially the hands. I thought of Kaimimoku, who is not very bad, especially the hand. He has got a Mistress, and I presume that if he does come with me he will wish his Woman to come also. There are several young Men who I can get to come with me, but they are so poor for want of clothing, and as I have very little money left, that I cannot spare any. I will have to for the future hire a Woman to wash my clothes, and a Woman to make my bed and sweep the House and dress me. This woman I thought of [is] Maria Unauna. She is very clean, but [in] want of Eyebrows. I will have to commence anew, and in order to do that I will ask you for $20 or more, as you may think proper. . . .

9:30 at Night.—I have just returned from Napela's. I always call their before I return to while away the weary hours.

After I had writen the last page of No. 2, I went and choped wood, as my Native had not returned, and the first thing that I did while choping wood was to hurt my finger. Mrs Napela saw me choping wood so came over and asked me if my domestics had not returned. I replied that they had not, but I could see them making a fire for something. After I had the wood choped, the two Woman came up [to] the Cook House whare I was. I told one of them to strike a match and light the wood, while I went out to catch a fowl. I caught one and killed it and was waiting for the water to boil, when I asked the woman that use to tend on me, "Whare is Keleau?" She said, "He is cooking *Pu*."[9] After all was ready and the fowl cut up and put in the Pot, and as it was showery, I availed myself and had a shower bath. My hands were black with the stuff of the Pot and also smelt strong of Smoke.

After a while the Man came back. I asked him if he thought that I could live without eating. He said that he was cooking for the sick man. I was so mad that I could have choked him, but I kept quiet. After a while he asked me whether they were all to be sent away by the Aupuni.[10] I said that if Ragsdale said so, it must be true. He then said, ∧ "I feel sorry for you." ∧

I [walked] away. The two Woman returned and I waited for tea, which was ready by Sunset. After tea I made sure by lighting my lamp of [having] a light by my return.

I will wait for your aproval of my taking Maria Unauna for a Woman to dress me and look after my House, or not. What you say to me is *Law*. . . .

God bless you is the never ceasing Prayer of

KEKUAOKALANI

1. Peter reports nothing further about this astonishing rumor. A total of twenty-four members of the legislature, including twenty-one Hawaiians or part-Hawaiians, voted in favor of the loan bill.

2. Perhaps a reference to the "treasonable" petition drafted by Kepelino, which led to his arrest; see Letter 88, note 6.

3. Mrs. Weed. She perhaps furnished a list of prospective signers of the petition.

4. Emma's supporters had provided an impressive tribute (*ho'okupu*) in honor of herself and her British and Russian guests, at the reception mentioned below. Hence, Peter's point that John O. Dominis, her former agent, should be chagrined at this evidence of prosperity. Local newspapers in English did not report this social event at Rooke House July 16. 1874. Those honored included Commander A. J. Kennedy, H.B.M.'s *Camelion*, together with fellow officers; Capt. P. Tyrtoff, Imperial Russian Navy, in command of corvette *Haydamack*, along with sundry lieutenants, the engineers, doctor, and several midshipmen; H.B.M.'s commissioner and consul general, Major James Hay Wodehouse; and J. W. Pfluger, commission merchant and Russian vice-consul at Honolulu (see "Visitors' Book, Rooke House," BM.) The *Camelion* and *Haydamack* arrived almost simultaneously on July 12. The *Pacific Commercial Advertiser*, July 18, described the Russian ship as a "modern built, clipper looking vessel of 250 horsepower, with an armament of 7 guns, carrying 170 seamen."

5. The expression (also spelled '*aikola*) involves a double meaning, here referring to a sheep and also serving to express scorn—"Bah."

6. Edward H. ("Ned") Boyd (1834–1875), part-Hawaiian son of Robert

Boyd, carpenter in employ of Kamehameha I and later sheriff of Oahu under Kamehameha III. Edward H. Boyd served briefly as royal chamberlain under Kalākaua 1874–1875; member of House of Representatives 1864–1870; major on staff of Governor Dominis 1873. The Boyd family owned an extensive cattle ranch at Waimanalo, Oahu; in early 1870s Edward H. Boyd operated a "Family Market" on Hotel Street; also an *awa* store on King Street.

7. An allusion to Kalākaua's alleged Negro paternity.

8. Bossing; putting to work.

9. Variety of sweet potato.

10. Government.

Letter 87
Peter to Emma

[Kalaupapa]
August 7, 1874

Queen Emma

Yours of August 1 have been received, and I am exceedingly delighted to learn of the kind reception with which your Subjects [welcomed] the Russians. No wonder that D. K. would not speak to W. Pfluger,[1] the fellow D. K. knowing that it was the love which the Natives bear towards you that they gave with open Heart their *Little* to those who appretiated your kind Company, notwithstanding the false reports[2] about you, which I hope that they now have found to be a base Lie.

Mr Sheldon[3] is well aware that all what the Natives are doing is far from Treason, and why should he go to Mr Pratt in such a insinuating way? He Sheldon being a Kamaaina [should know,] as Mr Pratt say, [that] in Kamehameha V's time it was neither thought or spoken of as treasonable, and because the Natives do not like D. K. that this should be called Treasonable [is absurd]. "It is folly to be wise, Whare ignorance is bliss."

Mr Cleghorn got rather a blunt answer from Pamalo and I hope that it learned him a lesson, and not again face those who are afraid to tell a lie and ashamed to speak behind a person's back, and telling him Cleghorn that it is not only him Pamalo but the whole Community who dislike D. K. If he cannot find better company than a butcher,[4] he had better put his head in a bag and go to Hamohamo whare he comes from.

I am glad to learn that McGrew has fallen out of Royal favour. He having been so long and intimate with them, what he does say about them will produce a strong effect among the Foreigners. I have not the least doubt that the officer sirculated McGrew's remark among his shipmates and friends. That was probably the way Meyer got it, and went and Hookolokolo-ed[5] McGrew only to meet a true and bold confession. [This] I presume agravated Meyer so [much] that he asked McGrew for his Bill. In order to agravate Meyer more, McGrew put in that Hope it would be paid soon. All these [doings] are really Jolly. And if I am to hear of such News as these all the time, I think it will cure me of my disease, for I feel very near so.

I did always think all along that Hiram was for you, and think so now, for I knew that he disliked D. K. and hates him for Kapo, and now D. K. has it all his own way as a *Thing*.[6] What must Hiram do but watch for the Hour?

Since my last, my Ohuas have returned after a long coaxing, but I hear that they intend to leave as soon as I speak harsh to them. Since they returned, the Man only cooks and I go after my Water at the Butts to wash my face. I have been looking for a sick person that is not bad in the face and hands, but it is like looking for a pin in a Hay stack.

My Aloha to all. A Schooner is in sight. Good Bye.

KEKUAOKALANI

1. At the social occasion honoring the Russians, King Kalākaua ignored the presence of J. W. Pfluger, even though the latter was the Russian vice-consul.

2. The "false reports" about Emma perhaps furnish substance of a "Memo to Molokai, July 14 [1874]." Mrs. Weed had chatted with Frank Brown, nephew of Godfrey Rhodes, planter and importer of wine-and-spirits. Mrs. Weed reported gossip to Emma who relayed it to Peter:

> F. Judd's lie as to my urging him [Lunalilo] for senate [and] to appoint me successor/ my runing after Lunalilo to Kona & sticking round him for sake of it / my want of modesty in going without him asking me [to go] / Lunalilo, K IV & K V, K III all bad men / I was made to lomi Lunalilo's foot while Eliza lived like his Queen therefore he was bad / Lydia [Mrs. John Dominis] had done more for the Hawaiians than I / Kapiolani was a pure woman & no man was shot on her account / I was not pure

Hawaiian [but] was Dr Rooke's daughter [and] therefore not fit [to rule] / people all over Islands are in favour of DK & against me / Nawahi and Kauai afraid to go home for fear of being mobed by the natives of their districts . . . / I ought to go and call on Piolani / KV was avaricious and bad [and] had $80,000 or $100,000 debt / Lunalilo also was bad & kept a mistress / Queen Emma was poor [and] had no lands & owed him large sums of money. . . . / F. Brown cooled down & agreed to Mrs Weed that there was no chief whose birth, morals, character was as good as mine & high / you will imagine the height of excitement they both were in. . . .

3. Henry L. Sheldon (b. Rhode Island, 1824; d. Honolulu, 1883); writer and newspaper editor, translator and interpreter of Hawaiian; arrived in Hawaii 1846. At various times also land agent, California gold miner, judge, notary public, labor contract agent, member of House of Representatives 1852, 1855, 1858–1859. According to Peter, Sheldon considered it to be treasonable arrogance for a high chief other than a reigning monarch to permit subjects of the king to present him with tribute (ho'okupu). The dangerous impropriety of the custom—an "ancient ceremony of land tribute and acknowledgment of sovereignty"—was noticed in Nuhou, Mar. 24, 1874, not long after the Courthouse Riot: "A divided power is dangerous to the peace of a country. . . . A formal presentation of tribute or hookupu by hundreds of persons going in procession, as recently unto Her Majesty, is an acknowledgment of subject fealty that should not be overlooked by Ministers, who are in duty bound, pledged to support the honor, dignity, and the sovereign authority of the lawful Ruler of the Realm."

4. Kalākaua's "butcher" friend, Ned Boyd; see Letter 86, note 6. Peter's jibe plays on Boyd's "low" occupation, as an animal was sometimes slaughtered when the head was enclosed in a sack.

5. Quizzed.

6. It is possible that Hiram disliked Kalākaua and remained devoted to Emma, or at least tried to keep on good terms with her while hoping to profit from Kalākaua's rise to power. There is no doubt that Kapo received royal favors from Kalākaua and fully shared in his ambitions. She was known for her fiery temper and in many ways was a far more dominating personality than the gentle Kapi'olani.

Letter 88
Peter to Emma

[Kalaupapa]
August 8, 1874
5:45 morning

Queen Emma

Yours of the 6th instant have duely come, together with the Papers and 8 bags of Tarrow. The Schooner arrived last Evening and sails as soon as she discharges, which will be this morning.

Can't their be a leader found to head our men? It is indeed too bad, but I hope that their anxiety will not remain long, and again hope to hear by your next of their progress in some way. I am glad to learn that the Police are with you. That man Kamoana ought to have been arrested,[1] and inquired what he was doing their.

When the Schooner arrived, and after I had received my letters at the beach, I rode away from the crowd to read it, and after reading returned to see that my tarrow was put on the cart. The Natives gathered around my Horse and asked me the *Mea Hou*,[2] [and] whether the English Admiral had done anything in assisting you to the Throne, and when another riot is going to take place, as they wish to make a disturbance here and regain their freedom, and several other questions. I informed them that the greater part of my letter was personal affair, but that the Doctors Powell and Akana are greatly objected [to] by the Foreign Doctors, and unless they show their Diploma that they will not allow Powell and Akana to treat any Sick, here or elsewhare.

Instead of speaking ill of the Foreigners, the [Natives] mentioned D. K.'s name with ∧ expressions of scorn: "This is a most despicable chief. He has no thought for the common people, it would be better if he were dead,"∧ etc. You can use your own judgement in regard to your letters. If indeed their is pilikia in the way, then keep the secrete, for I would do without it sooner then any of your letters be found. But I think that for the fiew weeks to come their will be no fear, as the *Warwick* will come here direct, conveying the sick from their to here. As Ragsdale say, Wilder is going up by the *Kilauea* to collect the Sick of the diferent Islands, and then have them all sent up here.

I thought of making a disturbance here, and by so doing, will probably bring the troops up here, as it was with Kaona,[3] thus taking some of D. K.'s strength away, that your Men may have a better chance of seizing the fellow D. K. and party. But I see he is going to run away up to Hawaii. Their might be more meaning in what the Policeman said in regard to the danger drawing near. And the Natives who are watching also—a Luna ought to be appointed for every Watch. That Policeman's prediction might turn out true yet, as Hua's is also. She still says openly that you will sit on the Throne, and that she will go Home without waiting for the Board of Health, although she has been laughed at for her predictions, yet she still stick to what she has always said, and furthermore tells the Natives that she has got all the Natives marked out who do not believe in what she says, and [that] when you set on the Throne they will remain here.

Kuihelani have sent up here to Napela the Laws which they have passed in regard to the Lepers, and also for Powell and Akana to treat, and he has also informed them that 10 are to be sent from here [to] their for trial, and I am among [the] 10. So here we are in the midst of all these numerous reports. D. K.'s party was indeed very strong in regard to the Loan Bill. Although three of the leading Men of the Country fought against it, yet with all their exersions, they have failed to carry their point.[4] Surely if anybody ought to be hung, all those who voted in favour of it ought to be, together with the proposer. As Gibson has praised D. K. so much, he will probably get into office,[5] and he together with Harris will make away easy enough with the Loan money.

The Captain and crew of the *Warwick* had nothing to say or any Mea Hou, so I think it is only me who know of anything important. I see that [the] Hon. Kauai has really fought against the Bill and not succeeding, is now trying to save the people by telling them what to say and do. Kauai acted very kind both to the people and our poor Country. I would like to say something about myself, but it sounds so much like bragadocio that I will not. D. K. must indeed be frightened going up to Manoa personally and telling his Men to be ready, and also to come into town—the bastard coward.

I most sincerely hope that Kepelino will escape all harm and be Victorious in every way.[6] I think the sooner an outbreak takes place the better, as it will end all anxiety on both sides, and probably I will hear of D. K.'s defeat, and he and his held a prisoner in the hands of those who he has been wishing to imprison. Pfluger said that Kalahoolewa and Hiram never said a word while at his Party.[7] Probably Hiram was afraid of betraying himself.

I return 12 Bags. Since my last of Yesterday the 7 [of August], a report has been sirculated that I am to return soon for trial, and my domestics are feeling very sorry of their behaviour towards me lately, and has told some of the Natives who stop with Napela that they did so because I took the Poi in my own House to give to them, instead of having their own way as heretofore, eating at any time of the day and night which I do care very much about. But giveing to their Daughter to take away, I do not allow, nor will. So when a barrel is filled, the rest is made into Pai, and while the pounding is going on, I watch them, which they do not like, and since they have no Poi, I've got them.

My time is up. My Aloha to all, God Bless you. Hoping to hear that my beloved Cousin is Sovreign and Queen of the Hawaiian Islands and in our Heavenly Father's Protection, I remain

Your Majesty's Obedient Servant

KEKUAOKALANI

1. Throughout 1874, after Kalākaua's victory, Emma feared for her personal safety. She was informed by Attorney General Hartwell, Apr. 20, 1874, that he had "asked Mr. Parke to see that a proper guard is placed to prevent any anxiety on your part owing to what are undoubtedly idle rumors. . . . Of course the assemblage of thirty or forty men in your yard at night will occasion suspicion which must be avoided by all means. It is my duty to inform you that the public mind must not be excited by such measures, and that it is the Marshal's duty to prevent crowds from assembling who may be suspected of exciting riot and sedition. It will also be his duty and pleasure to see that all suitable precaution is taken to relieve you from anxiety." The *Pacific Commercial Advertiser*, Apr. 25, printed an item headed "Unnecessarily Scared," noting that a certain D. Kanuha, a partisan of Queen Emma up to the time of the Riot, but who tried to keep order among the crowd, had been seized by Emma's personal guards, hauled into the police court, and fined $10 for possessing a pistol "for personal defence."

2. News.

3. A religious leader named J. Kaona, head of a short-lived messianic sect in South Kona, island of Hawaii; he was educated at Lahainaluna Seminary. In October 1868, he and his followers took possession of a church building and, armed with lassos, clubs, and stones, refused to vacate it when ordered to do so by Deputy Sheriff Richard P. Neville. Neville died as the result of a fractured skull received in a skirmish. When Kaona threated to kill all persons who would not join his church, help was called from Honolulu. In all, sixty-six men and twelve women were committed for trial, of whom all but eight were discharged. Kaona was sentenced to ten years' imprisonment. There is no record of what became of him. Ralph S. Kuykendall has pointed out that some of the circumstances of the rebellion "suggest a doubt as to the culpability

of the Kaonites for the violence that occurred." (*The Hawaiian Kingdom: 1854–1874*, p. 106.)

4. Representatives Nawahi, Pilipo, and Kauai were leading supporters of Queen Emma who opposed the loan bill to the end.

5. Gibson was appointed by Kalākaua to the Privy Council Sept. 1, 1880; the Board of Health Sept. 2, 1880; the House of Nobles 1882–1884, 1886. Between 1880 and 1886, he also served, sometimes simultaneously, as commissioner of Crown Lands, attorney general, minister of interior, premier, secretary of war and navy.

6. On Aug. 7 and 8, Kepelino and four other natives were arrested on a charge of treason, for having written and circulated for signatures a petition requesting the French commissioner at Honolulu to cause a French man-of-war to come to the Islands to remove Kalākaua from the throne and turn over the Kingdom to Emma Kaleleonālani. At a preliminary hearing on Aug. 15, the four natives were discharged, but Kepelino was committed for trial at a later date. At trial before the supreme court on Oct. 6, he was defended by Kauai, district judge from Waimea, Kauai, and J. Porter Green, prominent Honolulu attorney and member of a missionary family. The jury was reminded of facts brought out at an earlier examination: the memorial never reached the French official to whom it was addressed; nearly all the "several hundred" names appended had been written by two men and not by the purported signers; only about a dozen persons had ever seen the offending document. The attorney general, William R. Castle, argued that "the conception and execution of the document were folly in the extreme" and could be considered a treasonable act under terms of the Hawaiian Penal Code. The petition had urged that the election of Kalākaua be "set aside and revoked" on a variety of grounds, including the unsubstantiated assertion that Lunalilo had left an unsigned will naming Emma as his successor; that Kalākaua came to the throne by "rebelling against the Queen"; that undue pressures had been exerted upon legislators to cause them to vote for Kalākaua; that in an unofficial poll taken on Feb. 11, 1874, Emma had received 3,091 ballots; that "this *false king* is doing that which will destroy our independence and cause great disturbance in the future. For this false king (D. Kalakaua) is very desirous of mortgaging the government to some foreign government for a million dollars. . . ." Finally, the petition declared Emma to be the rightful sovereign on both genealogical and moral gounds, as one who was "amiable and good, and suited to the people." The finding of the jury, reached in about twenty minutes, was a unanimous verdict of guilty. Though section 1 of chapter 6 of the Penal Code prescribed the death penalty for treason, the presiding judge pointed out that "the King, by and with the advice of His Privy Council, has the power, under the Constitution, to grant reprieves and pardons, after convictions, for all offenses, except in cases of impeachment." For an account of Kepelino's sentence on Oct. 12, see Letter 98, note 3.

7. Probably a party given by J. William Pfluger, acting Russian vice-consul, for Capt. Tyrtoff and other guests from the *Haydamack*.

Letter 89
Peter to Emma

[Kalaupapa]
August 17, 1874

Queen Emma

Yours of the 14th instant came to hand yesterday by the *Warwick*.
I was dressing for the Afternoon Service to go with Mrs Napela, when
Ragsdale and Crowningburg[1] came up, and my little Cottage
standing right on the road, they both came in, and in order to prevent
them from coming into the House, I went out and met them at the
Gate. Crowningburg gave me his hand and we shook hands, thus
disobeying your kind request. I would not have shook hands with him
had I known any way to prevent it. While he was holding his hand
out to me, I was fumbling at my Shirt so that he may return his hand,
thus allowing me a chance to speak instead of shaking hands, but no,
his hand was held out till shook by me. And Oh, you cannot form any
idea how sorry I felt in thus disobeying you, and still feel it as I write.

In the Evening Mrs Napela and Maria came over to my place and
sat in the Moonlight conversing, when Ragsdale and Crowningburg
rode past from the beach. They were both drunk. Ragsdale
dismounted and from outside of the fence spoke to us, but I told him
that they best go Home and sleep their drunk off. They left.

After I had read the contents of your letter, Napela being related to
poor Hiram, I informed him of Hiram's sudden death, relating to him
[the facts], as you informed me. He replied immediately that poor
Hiram met his death by *foul* means—*Poison*. His Wife regarded him
for saying so, but he said strongly that Hiram was Poisoned and I
think so too. I hope that Hartwell and Jones will get Kaai and others
clear,[2] and I am quite sure that they will as their will be no Crown
evidence. I am quite sure that the *Lie* is laid onto poor Hiram, because
as you say "dead men tell no tales." But if Hiram did really meet his
sad fate by foul means (?) then let that party make ready to meet
theirs. Time will set all things even. . . .

Satuarday before last the 8th, while I was at Napela's in the Evening
chating and passing the evening, Ragsdale came up from Kaawa's to
invite us to Kaawa's wedding, which took place that night, and after
he was asked several questions by Napela, he Ragsdale said to us that
he is not Superstitious, but he had seen something in the Clouds that

he wished to tell us. On the Evening of Friday the 7th he saw a figure of a Man in the clouds in a standing position, and the Head bowed as though in repentence for some act, and was then being tried, and a large black cloud was in front of him, and he said that that Cloud ment something, and asked us to see by our letters if anything unlikely was to be heard on that day Friday the 7th or on the following day, the day for the Prorogation of Legislature. Now Hiram must have died at the time that he saw the figure in the Cloud.

Okuu came up by the *Warwick* and has been drunk with Ragsdale and Crowningburg. Ragsdale and Okuu are still drinking, a good example for the Sick set by the Luna.

I have received the 4 bags of Tarrow and the writing [paper] and Local Papers and Ink.

My Aloha to Aunty and all. How is Wikani? You do not mention about her. May the ever kind Providence keep you in his kind care is the Prayer of

KEKUAOKALANI

1. William Charles Crowningburg (d. ?1876), also called Ke'eaumoku IV, named after Ke'eaumoku I, most noted among the five warrior chiefs who supported Kamehameha I in his conquest of the island of Hawaii. He was of mixed Hawaiian and German (or German-American) ancestry, descended on his mother's side from Kala'imamahū, son of a half-brother of Kamehameha I. His mother, Auhea Kekauluohi II, was a niece and namesake of Kekauluohi, mother of William Charles Lunalilo; his father, an early Maui settler of obscure background, was William Isaac Jesse Crowningburg (1819–?1856). It is the maternal connection that undoubtedly accounts for the role of Ke'eaumoku IV as kinsman-aide in the household of King Lunalilo at the time of the barracks mutiny in 1873. He was an elder brother of Emma's young protégée, Lydia Keomailani Crowningburg (1859–1887), later Mrs. Wray Taylor, who in 1873–1874 was being educated in England at Ascot Priory, at Emma's expense, by the Devonport Sisters, an order of Anglican nuns. For further details, sometimes confusing, concerning various Ke'eaumoku-Crowningburg descendants and their intermarriages and family ramifications with other alii and kamaaina families, see miscellaneous newspaper writings by Samuel Crowningburg Amalu (b. 1919), especially *Honolulu Advertiser*, June 21, 22, 1956, but these should be compared with later articles and, if possible, sometimes verified.

2. No criminal charges were ever brought against anyone for being implicated in the death of Hiram Kahanawai.

Letter 90
Peter to Emma

[Kalaupapa]
August 21, 1874

Queen Emma

Yours of the 3d was received last Wednesday. Whare it had been all this time I do not know, but I presume it is through the negligence of the Post Master at Kaunakakai. You mention of Tarrow's keeping if put in Water. I have found it out also by my last 4 bags, which I had put in a Box from Sunday Noon till Tuesday morning, and when cooked [it] was, as you say, good as ever. . . .

On the following day, Okuu came up from the beach and called on me. We had a long chat on various subjects. He informed me that the Natives are strong as ever for you and he is certain that another outbreak will take place ere long. He brought up old affairs of Kapaakea's[1] not having anything to eat when Kapaakea stoped at Hamohamo, but use to send to him for eatables—Keohokalole likewise, and D. K. and Sister. All what he gave to these parties he gave with open Heart, and he have always thought that they will help him in some way. When D. K. axidently got to be a King, he having treated them kindly, was sure to meet with what he asked for. He went and asked him, D. K., to allow him to come and //[2] remain here with his children, and the answer that he got was, No, he could not allow it, as the Foreigners would not like it, and he owed the Foreigners for the Kingship. [Okuu] also informed me that Ruth and Bernice are both stoping at Waikiki. Ruth told Mrs Okuu to tell Okuu that Ruth wanted Okuu to look out for the Land and also to be her Fisherman, as he was for Kamehameha V. But he told his Wife that Ruth did not treat him as a Alii ought to treat her Subjects, and he has made up his mind not to serve any more Alii save Queen Emma—then, pointing to me, saying, ∧"Your cousin,"∧ and he said he knows for certain that should you assend the Throne, ∧"The Hawaiian people will live."∧ It was towards Sunset when he left and the day was quite showery.

On the following day I woke to find myself suffering with pain in my leg—"Anakoi"[3]—as the Natives call it. This Pain in the Leg is accompanied with a severe chill which makes me shake all over. I have had it so often that I know that as soon as it goes away a sore on my foot will break out again, as one of my foot has been well for the past two Months. I suffered so much from chill that day that I did not leave my bed till Evening, when I woke to find the Woman who I had engaged to wash my clothes waiting on the Verandah. I woke quite weak, as I had had nothing to eat all day. The chill was so severe that it took my appetite away. . . . Mrs Napela was very kind to me. She brought me a cup of Coffee during the time that I was shivering, which did me a great deal of good.

On the following day, Friday, yesterday in the morning, I took a dose of Salts to help the Pills work which I had taken on Thursday night. Feeling relieved of the Pain and chill, and as the *Warwick* was expected back from Wailuku, I sat down in the afternoon to write, only to be disturbed by Crowningburg, and that was the reason why I ended so abrubt on Friday, marked with //. Although I have no more pain and chill, I am still a little Weak and do not feel quite right yet.

By the overland mail of Wednesday last, Mr and Mrs Napela received a letter from Kuihelani informing them that they, Kuihelani, Nahaolelua, and Simon, had been to D. K.'s and asked him D. K. to sign an Act which they had with [them which] the Legislature had passed and was awaiting his Signature. Both Nahaolelua and Simon, says Kuihelani, pleaded quite strongly on our behalf to allow Powell to try and cure us if possible, at a place set aside by our Relatives, according to the Act with its Restrictions, or if not [thus], at Kalihi, and if not their, to allow Powell to come up here and try some of the Sick here. Kuihelani told D. K. that Powell was willing to come up here and try a fiew cases, providing that the Government through the Board of Health would provide him with Boarding and Lodging while here, as says Kuihelani. Powell said, "Since they will not allow me to try any cases here, let me go up to Molokai, and I will convince them that I can cure the Leper, but the Board of Health must provide my Staying their. Since I have cured the Leper at New York, I can cure the Leper here," but says Kuihelani, "they have only had a promise, and here the Legislature is over and that promise [is] not fulfilled."

I must now end, as the Schooner is near the Port and I must take my letter down for delivery to the Captain. . . . May God bless you is the Prayer of

Your Obedient Servant
KEKUAOKALANI

Satuarday 22.—As I was writing this letter Yesterday, I was interupted by the appearance of William Crowningburg at my door, and as I could not help it, I asked him in. This is the first time that I had a good opportunity to look fairly at him and to ask him about this disease. He showed me his Skin and other parts, and I must really confess that he is better than two Thirds of the Lepers here. He is not disfigured about the face, which is a little swolen, but half of each Eye brow is gone. Both of his Hands are perfectly well and no Sores, which is one of the things which Dr. Trousseau told me always to look first before I shake anyone by the Hand. He has a sore on the Instep of his foot, which he said he got by being drunk with Ragsdale on the day of his arrival. I do not write in his favour in order to win your approval and assosiate with him, but I let you know of this so that you may know that he is not so bad as he was probably pictured to you. And if you had seen him, then you can judge for yourself how bad the majority must be, when I say that he is better in appearance then Two Thirds of the Lepers here. After he had stoped a while, he went Home into Kalawao, and as I did not feel incline to renew the writing I rested till this Morning.

[P. Y. K.]

1. Kapaʻakea and Keohokālole were father and mother of Kalākaua, Like-like (Mrs. A. S. Cleghorn), and Lydia (Liliʻu) Kamakaʻeha (Mrs. John O. Dominis). Okuu claimed that there never was enough to eat at Kalākaua's house in Waikiki, Hamohamo.

2. At this point Peter was interrupted by the arrival of Crowningburg. What immediately follows was the interpolated material under the date of July 22, which for convenience I have printed under its proper date heading at the end of letter.

3. Inflammatory swelling, sometimes of lymph gland.

Letter 91
Peter to Emma

[Kalaupapa]
August 28, 1874

Queen Emma

Yours of the 25th was received Yesterday, together with the Papers, the 4 bags of Tarrow, 7 Water Mellons and the Bunch of Bananas. Their is nothing so relishing to us, and so cooling as a good Mellon. When mine landed I could have sold them easily for 25 cts and 37½ cts a piece, and the Natives who had collected at the Beach look with their Eyes saying, "I wish I had one of those Mellons."

Napela and I went to a little Lanai and their we had a really good *Tuck* out. . . .

A rhumor here is Sirculated by Maria Unauna that D. K. is going up to Hawaii with Kaina, as he Kaina is good at *Anaana*, and as D. K. wishes to make away with all his Enemies, he is hoopunaheliing[1] Kaina. For my part, I really do believe that the Man is frightened out of his wits and is after any one who is reported to be good at Anaana, like a dyeing man grasping at Straws.

I am happy to learn that your Staunch Subjects are still true to you, of both Sexes and Ages. A man was here this morning in my House, and after he had looked at Your Husband's Picture which hangs in my House, he remarked that Liholiho was a Alii Maikai,[2] and I asked him, how about D. K.? He replied, saying, ‸ "A bad man who will come to a bad end. . . .", ‸ He further said that here in Molokai among the Lepers are some who have prayed D. K. to death, and are only waiting for him to step out. . . . And, says he, ‸ "When Emma becomes queen, then we shall all be restored and flourish.", ‸

You remarked of Bill Kaauwa's trying to get the Boy Palale to go and stop with D. K. in order to get a clue on you. The Brute is so scared of himself that he is trying all sorts of foul means to injure you. And after he shall have acquired all that he wishes, he will be the very first to tumble in, and followed by all his Family. I can well picture to myself how Kapo feels—the Queen's "Sister." It is well that she is riding [high] while she is about it, for when the smash does take place it will be a smasher.

Yesterday Hua received a letter from Honolulu and her Husband

showed me the hand writing outside, which look[ed] very much
like Kalahoolewa's hand writing. After I have delivered this to the
Captain of the Schooner *Waikolu* I will ride to Hua's and learn the
contents of the letter, and let you know by next.

Good Bye. My Aloha to all. My love and Prayer ever for you.

KEKUAOKALANI

1. From *ho'opunahele*, to treat as a favorite; in other words, Kalākaua is
cultivating Kaina.

2. Good chief.

Letter 92
Peter to Emma

[Kalaupapa]
August 31, 1874

Queen Emma

After I had delivered my last by the *Piolani* instead of the Portugese
Schooner, I rode down to Hua's, but found the letter to be from
another sorce. On the following day, Satuarday, Ragsdale received a
letter from Buff. On Sunday, Yesterday, Ragsdale stopet at my place
on his way from the Beach and told me that N. Boyd was a
Superstitious man. On my inquiring why, he replied that N. B. and
D. K. went over to Koolau and tried to buy a man and woman's life
for $50 to injure others, and not succeeding is probably the reason
why D. K. have gone up to Hawaii. I remarked that D. K. was
making a flying trip, and he replied that D. K. will be absent about
three Weeks. I asked him who he got his information from and he
replied from Buff.

When Mr Meyer was down here last Satuarday, he informed me
that he had heard a report that D. K. will touch here again, on his way
down, but he Meyer will not say that the report is true.

On last evening, as I was at Napela's, and after all was quiet and
dark, Mrs Napela told her Husband to tell me the ^"depressing
news,"^ as she says. Napela went out to ascertain that all was quiet
and nobody around. He requested me not to let anyone know of
what he was about to tell me, as it ^ will get me into serious trouble.^

... I replied that I would keep it to myself, and he told me [that]
Ragsdale had been to Kaawa's and told him Kaawa that *you* are going
to be arrested. Kaawa asked him the reason and Ragsdale replied for
Treason. He Kaawa then asked him how he came to get the
information, and Ragsdale told him that he read it in the News Paper.

Kaawa told this to Napela on their way from the Beach Yesterday
afternoon, and I was told so last eve. (Napela have always told me to
tell such News as the above in the night, as it would produce no effect
on the Party intended, especially on us, but if on other parties, to tell
in daytime, as it was always costumary so to do, from our Ancestors,
and that was the reason why he did not tell me when first I went their
in the Evening.)

I had read my Papers also, but could not find anything in it in
regard to your arrest, but saw one in reference to Zepherin, or as the
Paper says, Kahoalii. I am going up to Ragsdale now and see if I can
get any more out of him, as I think that he got this story from Buff's
letter.

Sept. 1st. Tuesday. 2 P.M. I did not learn anything from Ragsdale
yesterday. I have just returned from Napela's and have just learned
from a Man, Pupule by name, who has told us that he is a Kahuna,
that he is trying for Ragsdale to keep D. K. on [the] Throne, but he
has told Ragsdale that D. K. is King but "Lewa".[1] I will use his own
lingo.

I asked him first whare he came from. He replied that he is one of
Kekuaokalani's own Servants,[2] and that Kekuaokalani and desandants
are the only ones ‸ "capable of punishing Kalakaua." ‸ [3]

He said: ‸ "The land, once under firm control, has fallen into the
hands of D. K. Now it is swaying, its foundation shaken. The King
has no control over its center, only Queen Emma keeps it steady." ‸

Then turning to Napela he said: "If you were to look at the Two
Stars close together in the West after dark, you will see that one is
stationary and one is moving all the time, sometimes on the side of
the one stationary, sometimes above, and the moveing one is brighter
then the stationary one. The moveing one is D. K. ‸ The star moves
according to the motion of the person possessing the star. The steady
fixed star is Emma's. So is her power to govern fixed and firm." ‸

I then asked him if any obstacle was in your way. He said: ‸ "It is
evident that troubling forces have been working against Emma, but

their designs will not be fulfilled. Native Hawaiians and white foreigners alike approve of Emma and everywhere pray for her welfare. God will watch over the righteous one and turn away from the wrongdoer. Hence this coffin you have beheld moving in the clouds—it will descend to earth, there be lowered into the grave. . . . Emma's star will not change. She is the one who will reign, as we shall hear. Events are moving now in favor of the chiefess of *wohi* rank, the descendant of Keliimaikai. Her enemies will be destroyed both high and low when their head, the King, is extinguished.",

This evening Napela and I am going to look and watch these two Stars. Their are names which he named but I cannot call them to memory.

My domestics are still with me [except for] the Woman, and are still acting very unkind. I saddle my own Horse, as they generally leave after breakfast, and do not return till quite late. I have hired a Washerwoman, and if I can get one [want to] hire a Horse boy. . . .

God Bless you is the Prayer of

KEKUAOKALANI

1. Insecure.

2. The word carries the idea of Hawaiian *ʻōhua*, the traditional term for attendants to a chief, particularly privileged retainers who were often blood relatives and who could not be dismissed. Notice that the kahuna Pupule, Kekuaokalani's "desendant" (like Peter), though privately a supporter of Emma, has nevertheless been helping Ragsdale "to keep D. K. on the throne."

3. For "to *Poalo* his Eyes," referring to an eye gouge for punishing criminals by torture.

Letter 93
Peter to Emma

[Kalaupapa]
September 3, 1874
3 P.M.

Queen Emma

... I was writing this morning when Kamaio came in. She
informed me that she requested to come and see me personally and to
ascertain the state of my Health, etc., and to report it to you and
Aunty when she returns. I informed her that my Health was good, but
as for my features she is to judge for herself and to report as such. ...

The more that I read and hear of Mrs Weed, the more I like the
Noble Woman. While others have left you by false pretences, she is
ever true and faithful to the *Chief* she loves, and I am sure that she will
be well rewarded ere long, as that strong presentiment ... is still
speaking within me, saying—"Patience."

In mine of the 1st I mentioned that Napela and I were going to
watch for the Stars which the Kahuna Pupule told us [about]. That
night was so stormy that I did not watch for the Stars, but the next
day Napela informed me that [he] saw the Stars and that was all. ...

I believe your presumption to be true. Pauahi did really assist the
D. K.s, thinking that by so doing her Husband will maintain the
Ministry, but she was mistaken. Her name together with Ruth's are
hardly mentioned while the Papers speak of the D. K.s as Prince and
Princess. And while one of the natives call them alii, Hundreds of
natives are calling you by the name of Moi Wahine,[1] and are not
satisfied with that, but must wear ribons on their Hats with your name
on it, and in presence of D. K. at that.

These Predictions and Dreams, etc., will yet prove true, and all
what they say of making away with the Islands prove false. Their
concious will surely disaprove of their doings and worry them to
Sickness, and then the Lunalilo affair[2] will frighten them so that they
will all pass away like a bad dream and leave the Hawaiians to be
Ruled by a Person Worthy of the Position and loved and liked by her
Subjects—You. ...

May our kind Providence keep you ... is the Prayer of your
Humble Servant.

KEKUAOKALANI

1. Queen.

2. An allusion perhaps to the notion that Kalākaua and his supporters had practiced evil sorcery against Lunalilo.

Letter 94
Peter to Emma

[Kalaupapa]
September 9, 1874

Queen Emma

I presume that Mrs Drew has informed you of my Health and appearance. When she left Mrs Napela and I at the foot of the Pali, I did wish to ask her what state of affairs were going on concerning you and the D. K.s, [but] for fear of commiting myself I kept silent and waited for her to speak first on the Subject, but she did not. I omited in my last to inform you that Mrs Napela have received a letter from Mrs Everett, saying that Mrs Cleghorn was going to give a party at Iao Valley previous to D. K.'s arrival from Hana. Mrs Napela says that it is for Kahuna purpose. . . .

September 8th.—I was riding yesterday afternoon and called at Ragsdale's. After a while he remarked that he wished to write to you. I did not wish to prevent him from so doing, as he has lately received a letter from Buff, and this might give you a insight to something worth knowing. He also remarked that if D. K. ever goes abroad he will die abroad, and that you have got plenty of Friends. All the time that he was speaking I did not say a word, but merely replied, "If you wish to write to the Queen, why not write?" I think that he has some object in view.

I cannot understand his reasons for wishing to write to you. But he has always said openly that if he were at Honolulu he would turn the Tide in your favour. I think this is all a Plan to get me to say something, but I will not give him a chance.

My Domestics are yet with me and I hear that they are going to put up a House of their own. I am well. Good Bye. My Aloha to All and My Prayers always for you.

KEKUAOKALANI

Letter 95
Peter to Emma

[Kalaupapa]
September 16, 1874

Queen Emma

Yours of the 3d instant was received by the overland Mail of last
Wednesday, and yours of the 11th came by the *Warwick* on last
Monday. She did not touch at Kalaupapa, but drifted during the
night to the Eastward and anchored at Waikolu. My men had all gone
to the Beach when my letter came, so I rode in and well I did, for
when I got their, all my things were scatered about on the Beach. If
you did not send me a list I never should have found them. I had to
overhaul others' things in order to find mine.

Mrs Drew sent her Mother up 10 Mellons and out of 10 she got 5.
The bundle which came in my Box I gave to her Woman, who had
come to my place hunting for Kalua's things from Napela's. I had
quite a Feast by myself that afternoon. I got some Sausages from
Kahea, Salt Pork and Beef from Mrs Napela, and my Luau, Limu and
Palu[1] all together was really a Feast—Mellon as Desert, which comes
in nicely for our hot days here.

I am very much afraid of the Algiroba slips which you sent up will
all die. Our Water is so scarce that we have got to keep what little we
have to drink and the Water that I wash my face [in] is the only Water
that they get, which I water every morning.

In my last I mentioned of what I should like to have, but I omited
to mention the Stockings. I should like to have some thin ones. I have
two long Wollen ones, and [these] are yet good. These are the ones
which you gave me, some of your Husband's Upper clothes. I have
enough for the present.... I have Aunty's shawl which will do in
place of a Pea Jacket—Oh, a Comforter I should like to have. I believe
that is all I would require. If I have forgoten any, I will write by my
next....

I have frequently spoken to the Natives in regard to Hua's
Predictions as to your ascending the Throne, informing them that
should you be our Ruler, you are to abide and not to go or act
against the Constitution. I also told them that I was one of the Law
makers, and that this Law was made in order to check the Progress of
this horrible disease, and should Queen Emma allow all of us to

return to our Homes, thus allowing this disease to spread, Why, it would be the ruination of the Hawaiian Nation and perhaps the whole World.

It would immediately stop our Commerce, no Foreign Vessels will touch our Ports for fear of this disease. All the Foreign Powers who we are in Treaty with will not Sanction this Act of Queen Emma's, and what would be the Consiquence—why, we lay ourselves liable to be seized at any moment, for favouring a fiew hundreds—Queen Emma will be the cause of the death of Thousands. I for my part would be willing to remain here, for says I [by] remaining here I have saved some 10's, and *oukou*[2] some Hundreds, who would be sure to catch it should we be allowed to return. We ought to be satisfied to remain here by knowing that the Person, *Mea*,[3] on the Throne using your name is a good Queen, and a Mother to her Subjects. I am sure that if anything is wanted to make us happy and comfortable (?) in this our Isolated state, that Queen Emma will not fail to give her aid through her Board of Health. But I again went on, If their are some here among us that the Doctor with the Board of Health thinks is not a Leper, and not a dangerous case, then I am sure that if the Board of Health will let that or those persons go Home, the Queen would really feel happy to allow them. And again, If their are some persons who can afford, or their Relatives, for them to put a House for that Sick at some place away from the well people, and be under Rules and restrictions of the Board of Health, that the Queen would also allow that, for she will allow anything Human and Sencible. She not only feel sorry for me alone, but for all those who were torn away from their Friends and Relations.[4]

Their are some who take it in that light and have approved of what I say, but some are hard Headed and are only waiting for Hua's Predictions— ʌ"If we sit by quietly until all of this family are dead and until the pulse of the Life of the Land rises again, then when the Grandchild of the High Chief sits on the Throne all will be well in the Kingdom. When that rightful and honorable Chief has attained the sovereign power, then there will be no rebellion. The People and the Government will endure."ʌ

Mr Wilder came over Yesterday and slept at Ragsdale's last night, [where he] was Serenaded by the Lepers, and this morning he went by Sea on a Boat to Wailua, a place which is way to the Eastward of the Island.

I presume that the not growing of the Algeroba on the Plain is that the Cattle eat it up, but as soon as the rainy Season sets in I will first plant in my yard, then strew the rest of the Seeds on the Plain in among the rock whare the cattle cannot get at them. I have received all what you sent up, with the exception of one Bag of Kalo. In your list it was 5, but I received only 4. The Captain was with me when I was on the beach looking for my things. . . . May God Protect you is the never ceasing Prayer of

KEKUAOKALANI

P. S. I think that by next month I will be compelled to send for more then the usual amount of Tarrow, so as to have it made into Poi for the Comeing Winter.

3 P.M.—I have just received yours of the 14th through Napela,[5] and still hope for the best. P. Y. K.

1. Young taro tops, edible seaweed, and a relish of fish parts.

2. You (together).

3. Peter's translation. The term *mea* as used here seems to imply the special personal status of one who possesses something; compare *mea'aina*, "possessor of land."

4. In native speech, leprosy was sometimes called *ma'i-ho'oka'awale* (disease of exile), also *ma'i-ho'oka'awale 'ohana* (the disease that tears families apart).

5. Letter perhaps was sent "through Napela" to prevent interception.

Letter 96
Peter to Emma

[Kalaupapa]
September 22, 1874

Queen Emma

Yours of the 19th was duely received Yesterday by the *Warwick*. She only landed the 3 bundles of Pork and 2 bags of tarrow at Kalaupapa, and as the Sea was so rough she had to sail up to Waikolu, whare I also rode in and received the remainder of the things. . . .

The Chinese Doctor and I have had a talk, and he has informed me that Kanaina has requested him to Act on me. How true this is I do not know. I have learned from some of the Sick here who he has treated while at Honolulu that they were forbiden to eat Beef and several other things, and are only allowed to eat Fish that have large Scales, like the Uhu. Chicken is also prohibited but Duck is allowed. Now if I am to be treated by this Man, I do not know whare I am to get all these. I have not yet spoken with him of his tending on me, but I have heard that Ragsdale and I are to be treated by him, but outside of the number which the Board of Health allowes him, as he is only allowed by the Board of Health to tend on not more then Five, and those who he is to tend not included in the Five are to pay him seperate from the Government's [share]. However, before I allow him to tend on me, I will first ask him what I am to eat, and everything pertaining to his restrictions. And If I see fit, I will allow him to treat me, otherwise I will not allow him to treat me. I am told by those who have seen his Medicine boxes open that some of the Boxes contain the shell of Turtle, Mamo flower[1] dried, Pride of India leaf dried, and several other things in the shape of Bark and Leaves. He told me on last Satuarday that he would call on me on Monday Yesterday, but as the Schooner had come I was too buisy and could not see him. I expect him today. About Twenty or more Sick goes by this *Warwick* to Honolulu for Reexamination by the Board of Health. I think this is to prevent Dr Akana from Practicing on those who are not bad. He complains of the shortness of the time allowed him, which is Six Months and no more.

Mrs Napela have given one of her nephews a Native name, and named [him] after your Reath—Leimokihana[2]—and he is quite proud of the name, so he writes his Aunt, saying it is a prety name, Signing his name "George Kaleimokihana Richardson." I am going in to Kalawao and will finish this when I return, as the Chinaman has not come.

3 P.M.—I have just returned from Kalawao but did not see the Chinaman. [I] learnt from W. Crowningburg that he intends to tend on me and that I am not one of the Five, but [he] will tend to my case seperately and [I will] pay him myself. In regard to paying myself I think it is fair, but before I consent to it I will have an understanding— that is, that I will pay him provided that he cures me and that cure [is] approved by the Members of the Board of Health and the Doctor. So on this I cannot say any more, but will by my next.

I hope that some of the Foreign Kamaainas have learnt to look on the D. K.s as a lot of bad People, and especially J. O. D.[3] [for] insulting a young man, Mr Walker,[4] who I have no doubt will talk of this Dominis as a rude, ungentlemanly Man, both in his manners and speech, and let the rest look on him as such.

Wednesday, 23d, 3 P.M.—I have just learned from Mrs Napela that Ragsdale was their and informed her that he Ragsdale and Buff are holding communications in regard to the Throne, and that he *Bill* has writen to Buff that in order for D. K. to Rule the Nation firmly, D. K. ought to make friends with Queen Emma, and his brother marry you. But, says Ragsdale to her, "If I can only hear what Peter says in regard to the Matter, then I can settle it for them. But Peter will not tell me anything about it. Perhaps he has told you, Mrs Napela, something about it." She replied that all Peter's letters are kept away and [neither] "I nor my husband know nothing of his secretes," so Ragsdale left her. If I hear anything more I will inform you. The Schooner is in Port and I must ride down to deliver my letters. . . .

God Bless you
KEKUAOKALANI

I return 12 bags.

1. Probably false saffron or safflower (*Carthamus tinctorious*), a branching annual from Asia, with yellow flowers resembling certain feathers of the now extinct Hawaiian honey-creeper, also called *mamo*.

2. Lei made of small anise-scented fruits of a native tree (*Pelea anisata*) found only on Kauai; such leis represent Kauai in the leis of the various islands.

3. John O. Dominis.

4. Probably Thomas Rain Walker (d. 1908, England), member of the British firm of T. H. Davies and R. C. Janion, shipping agents and commission merchants; arrived in Hawaii, December 1868.

Letter 97
Peter to Emma

[Kalaupapa]
September 29, 1874

Queen Emma

Yours of the 25th was received yesterday by the *Warwick*, together with the Bag containing the Limu, 4 Watter Mellons, 4 Cocanuts, 1 Aku, and 22 Oranges (some of them were mashed) and 7 bags of Tarrow—not 8 as in the list, so their must be a mistake somewhares.

I am exceedingly sorry to learn that Nawahi is arrested,[1] and hope that his Constituants will stand firm for him and release him from Custody. Kawainui I am sure is acting a Spy and is trying to get Pilipo into a snare, but I hope that Pilipo will see it and be on his guard. J. Opunui[2] is indeed very kind to give you this bit of information, however true it may be. It is however important.

In regard to geting you to consent to young Kekoi's hand,[3] I am not in the least allarmed about you, and they will find out that the Woman who they wish to entrap in their evil designs will be ever ready to meet them—yes, and be more of a Match for them. I am aware that they are Scared of you and are trying to the best of their knowledge to ruin you in some way. But kind Providence will guard you, as He has through your travels over Sea and Land, while you were far away from Home and Kindred, and no hand to protect you save him who Rules all, as the race is not always for the Swift, nor the battle for the strong.

Ragsdale is working on a Wharf, so I cannot learn any more from him yet. But I have asked Mrs Napela who is on our side to ask his opinion when he calls again on her, and [to find out about] their correspondence with Buff.[4] Ragsdale has said aloud in the Store that the only way for D. K. to maintain the Throne is to get his Brother to marry you, and when that is done then all will be safe. He has also hinted to me that if he could only see some of your letters to me then he would know how to write to you, but I took the hint and replied that just as soon as I read your letters, and having no place to put them, I always burn them.[5] So if their is anything which I wish to refer I write to you for it.

A man by the name of Liloa came up by the Schooner and said that all of the Natives are strong for you, and they dislike D. K. for not approving what the Legislature had passed. All this this man said they heard from Mikalemi.

The Chinaman have not tended on me yet. I Presume that he is waiting for me to ask him, but I am going to wait till the rest are cured. I am well. My foot is very annoying. Instead of healing altogether, little sores break out in its place. My Aloha to all.

God Bless you

KEKUAOKALANI

1. I can find no record of Nawahi's arrest at this date. However, it is likely that he had several brushes with police authority during his long political career, though he was never convicted on a criminal charge. In 1894, along with two other native Hawaiians, he was accused of attempting to "maliciously and unlawfully combine, confederate, agree and mutually undertake and concert together to levy war against and oppose by force the authority of the Republic of Hawaii." At his trial on May 9, 1895, the charge against Joseph Nawahi was dismissed.

2. Probably J. W. Opunui, member of a well-known Oahu family with interests in land and fishing rights. During the 1880s, Opunui and David Malo II served as commissioners of private ways and water rights for Ewa and Waianae, an area becoming exceedingly valuable for sugar purposes.

3. A reference to the rumored match with Leleiohoku.

4. Leleiohoku.

5. For earlier mention of the destruction of letters, see Letter 84.

Letter 98
Peter to Emma

[Kalaupapa]
October 19, 1874

Queen Emma

Since my last, Kaimimoku have come and is now with me with his Woman, a Boy and a Girl. The two latter are in their faces better then Kaimimoku and Woman, but Kaimimoku's whole body are free from Sores. My Domestics now number Seven.

On the Evening of last Monday the 12th just after Sunset, Napela sent word for me to look at the Clouds. I went over to his place, but he had gone with another Mormon, Puhi by name, to their Evening devotions on the Plain. As I sat on his Verandah waiting for his return, I saw at the West a Cloud like the figure of a enormous Squid, with the arms branching up and out. I had seen the clouds in the same shape heretofore, but this one exelled all those that I had seen. The coulor was dark ash. I asked Mrs Napela what the Sign of that Cloud ment, and she observed that she did not know, but remarked that when her Husband went out and saw the Cloud he asked her to send word to me, for me to look at the Cloud. Napela had informed me on a previous occasion that he had seen the Clouds form in the shape that I saw it then, and that it was a death sign to whoever was seting on Throne.

After a while, Napela and Puhi returned, and they asked me if I saw the Cloud, as it was then dark. I replied that I did. Napela then observed that when they went out, they first saw it at the East, and after they had arrived [at] the place whare they had intended to go, and on being seated, and facing to the West, they both saw another Cloud in the same shape, with its arms also spread and meeting the other one's arms overhead. After they had compared the two, both in size and coulor, and had come to the Conclusion that they were of the same size and coulor, and therefore must be of the same meaning, Puhi remarked, ∧"Both of these cloud formations were similar to those in Keakua's dream."∧

In the early part of this year, a man by the name of Keakua now residing at the Beach dreamt that he saw D. K. standing in the East and holding a Black Kahili, with his face to the West whare his Brother was standing also holding a Black Kahili. And you was standing in the Center holding a White Kahili, and the natives were shouting. He then saw D. K. break his Kahili and throw it on the ground, so he Keakua looked at Kalahoolewa and saw that his Kahili was broken, but you still stood holding yours, and your Kahili seemed to grow, and the natives were flocking towards you, and he in his effort to run to whare you were, woke.

Napela again remarked that the Cloud that we saw ment death. Puhi then replied that last year, in the Month of July, he and Napela saw a Cloud very simular to this, and that Napela informed him, Puhi, that that was the sign of the death of a King. Puhi, not knowing the truth of what Napela said, did not then believe it, but when Lunalilo died in the following year, he Puhi told Napela that his Predictions had [turned out to be] true.

On the following day Tuesday, he Napela went to Kaawa's and told him to write to D. K. and inform him not to go abroad as he D. K. is going to die. Napela also told Kaawa that the Sign that he Napela had seen is a Sign that predicts death to the person on Throne, and that nothing will prevent it. He had noticed it on former occasions, and it was always followed by the death of a King. I rebuked Napela for warning Kaawa of it, but he replied and asked me not to Fret myself about it, that he as a Christian do not wish to see D. K. die, but as this sign was *Kuluma* Accustome[1] to him, that he has nothing more to do but to wait and hear of D. K.'s death—then Pray for the poor fellow's Soul. As Napela says, ∧"His death was inevitable."∧

After I was made acquainted with the Sign of the Cloud and its particulars, I was overjoyed with it, thus giveing me freash hopes for the long looked for day. I have asked Napela if their is any remedy for it, and he has said that he has not heard of any, as he first saw it before Kamehameha III died and has seen it Three times since, just before the death of his Three Successors.[2]

In one of my last letters, I wrote to you to send me up the Cloth with the Stripe on the Side. I have found that to be the best to wear, it is both warm and strong. I am transplanting my Monkey Pods and have put up boards to break the force of the Wind. My Algiroba I have planted in a Box, and will transplant them out in my yard as soon as they make their appearance. As the Rain is seting in I will go with Kaimimoku out in the Plain and plant the Algiroba seeds. Oh! the Algiroba slips have all died.

The Wether now is quite damp, passing Showers are quite frequent. The wind which have been for the past days quite moderate are begining to blow strong again, making it quite cold.

Good Bye. Ragsdale told me that Kepelino is to be hung on the first Monday of March.[3] My Aloha to all.

God Bless you
KEKUAOKALANI

1. Peter's translation.

2. Kamehameha IV (1836–1863); Kamehameha V (1830–1872); King Lunalilo (1833–1874).

3. Kepelino's death sentence for treason was delivered before the Supreme Court Monday morning, Oct. 12, by Mr. Justice C. C. Harris. Attorney

General William R. Castle having moved for sentence, Judge Harris read to the prisoner section 1 of chapter 6 of the Penal Code, under which Kepelino had been pronounced guilty on Oct. 6: "Treason is hereby defined to be any plotting or attempt to dethrone or destroy the King, or levying of war against the King's Government, or adhering to the enemies thereof, giving them aid or comfort, the same being done by a person owing allegiance to the King-dom." When asked by Harris whether there was any reason why a sentence of death should not be declared, Kepelino said: "His Majesty has no more loyal subject than I; I would be willing to risk my life for him. On the 12th of February I was requested to use my influence towards quelling the riot, and I did so. I was asked to try and get Queen Emma to come down and quell the riot and I did request her to come." J. Porter Green, defense counsel, read a statement in behalf of Kepelino, requesting that the court recommend him to the king's mercy: first, because he had been led on by others to draft the offending memorial; second, because Emma's friends had urged that since Kalākaua had called in foreign troops to quell the riot, it was proper for Queen Emma to appeal to a foreign power for protection and aid; third, because Kepelino had been "laboring under the mistake that any petition which is for general circulation cannot be considered treasonable, as we Hawaiians always considered secrecy as one of the essentials of a crime of treason." After further consideration of extenuating circumstances, Judge Harris reviewed Kepelino's actions but denied his innocence: "You declare that you endeavoured to quell the riot of February last. Your memorial would indicate the contrary, for therein you say: '*We* shed the blood of the Representatives, and destroyed the property of the Government.' . . . You say you was [sic] led into your course by advice. This is a too frequent excuse by Hawaiians." Judge Harris finally said he would submit Kepelino's request for mercy to His Majesty: "It is not for me to say what may be the result." Peter was in error about the date set for Kepelino's execution. According to the *Pacific Commercial Advertiser*, the sentence ordered that John P. Zephyrin Kahōaliʻi be placed in Oahu Prison and kept there until the first Friday in March 1875, when "on that day, between the hours of 9 and 12 o'clock in the forenoon, you be taken to the place of execution and then and there be hung by the neck until you are dead." Although the sentence was later commuted, Kepelino was not freed until Sept. 24, 1876, after Kalākaua, acting on advice of the Privy Council, granted "a full and final pardon [of Kepelino] for the remainder of his term of imprisonment, and the officer having the said Kahoalii Zepherino in charge is commanded to allow him to go free." (Privy Council Records, 1875–1876, vol. 12, pp. 117, 119, 133, 135; vol. 13, p. 75; Interior Department, Book 13, p. 460; Oahu Prison Daily Journal, Sept. 24, 1876 [AH].)

Letter 99
Peter to Emma

[Kalaupapa]
October 26, 1874

Queen Emma

Yours of the 18th instant was received last Evening per *Warwick*. Kaimimoku and I rode to the Beach as soon as she came to anchor. The Paper Box I have received with its contents. Although the Box got wet on landing, the articles in it are all safe. . . .

I pitty Kepelino for having undergone such hardships.[1] But in all I like it, thus showing the D. K.s how firm the Natives still are for you. I am exceedingly delighted to learn of Nawahi's success at Hawaii, and am quite certain that Kauai will no doubt receive a warm reception from his Constituants on his arrival at Waimea.[2] Poor Kanoa now is made a Plaything for them,[3] and I hope that the poor fellow is aware of it. I can well fancy how the Palace premices now looks, as D. K. has had all the buildings moved away.[4] His time will I have no doubt come when he himself will be also removed.

I have not yet found nor read Albert's letter in the Paper. What will ever become of the Boy? If he does not alter his course of Life and come back with you, he will surely get in Prison.

In regard to the $30 to the Chinaman,[5] the sum being what he asked me for to buy Medicine with, I do not wish to pay him. Last week as I was at the Store, the Natives brought in for us to look what the Chinaman had had Boiled in a Pot and gave for his Patients to drink as Medicines, was Centipede, a black Skin from a Snake or Eel, Cocaroach, and other nasty things. He also has a stuff (which he Akana has boiled for them) to Bathe themselves. These are our native Kikania.[6] Now if these are the medecins which he thinks will Cure the Leper all right, but for my part I put very little faith in him. Ragsdale as one of his Patients told me that he does not feel the slightest change, but he takes the Medicine according to his humor, and not by directions.

In regard to your letters for the future, if with Napela's address it will be safe, and again if addressed to Kaimimoku it will also be safe, but I think that the latter name will be better, as he is with me, and when a Mail arrives either by overland or Water I will send him for letters, if I am not ready to go. . . .

We have had rain ever since last Week, making the Air quite damp, and is still raining. The Vessel leaves so I must bid you a long *Aloha*. With all my best wishes for your Prosperity.

KEKUAOKALANI

1. After Peter's letter to Emma of Oct. 19, Letter 98, Emma had written to him about the sentencing of Kepelino on Oct. 12.

2. According to Emma, Nawahi's anti-Kalākaua record in the legislature, particularly his opposition to the loan bill, found favor with his constituents. Probably Kauai's home support would demonstrate similar approval.

3. Paul Kanoa, long-time governor of Kauai, was granted a settlement of $2,400 in the appropriation bill, which provided similar benefits for several other officials recently retired from their posts. Peter wondered whether Kanoa saw the political implications of such special favors.

4. The former "old" palace, dating back to the 1840s, had been razed and the grounds were being renovated in preparation for building Iolani Palace, completed in 1879; see Letter 110, note 1.

5. Dr. Akana.

6. *Kīkānia* is a name for various native weeds. It is possible that Peter was thinking of *Kīkānia pipili*, Spanish clover (*Desmodium uncinatum*), a South American perennial with coarse round leaves and burrs surrounding seed vessels, which figures in Hawaiian herb medicine. When mixed with other herbs, the dried leaves were sometimes used in a wash for treating "scrofulous sores, boils and ulcers." (*Hawaiian Herbs of Medicinal Value*, trans. by Aikaku Akana, comp. by D. M. Kaaiakamanu and J. K. Akana [Honolulu: Territorial Board of Health, 1922], p. 51.)

Letter 100
Peter to Emma

[Kalaupapa]
November 3, 1874

Queen Emma

Yours of the 26 instant came to hand last Wednesday through Napela. The clothes, especially the under Shirt, came just in time. Last week on Satuarday the clouds began to gather and threaten us with Rain, the Thunder rolled. On Sunday morning it began to rain quite strong and continued so all day. I kept in doors as the air and ground were damp. The Wind began to Blow very strong. On the following day I woke to find it still raining, and the Wind though less boisterous still muttered fiercely as it passed along. Of course we all kept indoors waiting for it to clear up. After tea we were startled by the Wind which had struck our House. The Rain had abated. This morning the Rain and Wind had both subsided, but the clouds are still threatening us with more Rain.

On Friday of last Week Kaimimoku and I rode on the Plain and strewed Algiroba seeds and we are going out again as soon as the Weather allows us, but I am afraid of the Rats as the Plain are full with them. . . .

I wonder what Koii's intention was for Hookolokoloing[1] Kamai. I am quite sure that they cannot make anything from her. I should not at the least wonder that Kapo has told them some of her Stories which she has invented,[2] little dreaming that it was comeing to this. I have not yet found Albert's letter[3] as you said it to be in the Paper. The Local papers do not say much of D. K.'s brother, perhaps he has received the same reseption as D. K. did.[4]

I do not get any more *Graphic* nor the *Illustrated London News*. Have you stoped taking them? I wish you would send up the Silk Coat that I sent down, if you do not choose to keep it for a Patern.[5]

Good Bye. My Aloha to all. With God's Blessing on you

I remain
KEKUAOKALANI

1. Questioning or grilling. Since Koii Unauna was a genealogist, the purpose of his questioning Emma's protégée, Kamaikui, may have been to find out what Kamai was being taught about Emma's ancestry and on dynastic matters generally.

2. An allusion to Kapoʻoloku's genealogical lore or to her first-hand knowledge of Emma's conduct and character—perhaps to both. As Princess Poʻomaikelani, Kapo later became director of Kalākaua's genealogical society, Hale Nauwa.

3. Albert Kūnuiākea's letter was probably a message from him to Emma's supporters introduced as extenuating evidence in Kepelino's trial for treason, reported in the *Pacific Commercial Advertiser*, Oct. 17: "To you, the friends who keep the peace. Salutations: 1. In order to facilitate and secure your guardianship, and keeping of order, I ask you to be pleased not to oppose the government, the peace and the laws of the land. 2. And as I cannot personally be present to guard my cousin the Queen, I do hereby appoint John P. Z. Kahoalii as my deputy. The verbal directions, or rules that he may make, shall be binding. 3. And I shall be gratified if my cousin the Queen confirms this. Done by my hand this 6th day of May, 1874. [S/] Albert Kunuiakea." The newspaper version of the letter is a translation.

4. On Aug. 24, 1874, Kalākaua and a small party left Honolulu to visit places on Hawaii and Maui at which he had failed to stop during his earlier progress in April. The *Pacific Commercial Advertiser*, Sept. 12, announced the king's return to Honolulu on Sept. 9, but gave perhaps fewer details than was customary about his excursion, except to say that he had received everywhere "a loyal and hearty reception." In the same issue it was noted that Leleiohoku, "the heir apparent, in a quiet way, and accompanied by a few friends," was making a ten-day tour of Oahu: "Although until quite recently unaccustomed to speaking in public, the Prince already possesses an easy flow of words, and a self-possession and grace of manner that indicate the born orator." On Sept. 9, the *Pacific Commercial Advertiser* published a belated "Diary of a Trip to Hawaii and Maui," written by a Judge Wright of Iowa, who had accompanied King Kalākaua on his royal progress. According to this witness, "Everywhere the King was well and gladly received, and nowhere did we see signs of disloyalty or trouble. What little dissatisfaction we found was caused by the tone and teachings of the *Kuokoa* newspaper, and was easily explained away." Emma's statement that Kalākaua's reception had been notably unsuccessful must have been based on private sources of information or perhaps on accounts in *Kuokoa*. As for Leleiohoku's personal attractiveness and skill with language, there is much evidence indicating that praise of his talents was justified.

5. The sentence has been transposed from an earlier part of the letter.

Letter 101
Peter to Emma

[Kalaupapa]
November 5, 1874

Queen Emma

Yours of the 27th is received. As the *Warwick* rounded the Point I rode to the Beach, although it was after Sunset. I had received Makaula's of the 29th informing me of the Tarrow and Rice being left behind, so I did not expect any, which I regret exceedingly as I am entirely out of Poi, and have to make the best from the Board of Health's Sour Pai and my Potatoes.

Since my last, I have hired a Man to watch my Tarrow and also to cook and pound it, as Kaimimoku is not well enough. I am sorry to say that my domestics are all on the Leper list, but not very bad. So I have hired the well man Pukooku who once cooked for me, but since my Kamaaina domestics left me, he also left according to their coaxing. I have bought a Pile of Wood for $4 and [I pay] the Man and Washerwoman $5 between them. The well people will not do any work [at] less then $5 per month, or .50 cts for a job which is for only a fiew hours a day, so I cannot buy any fish or extra eatables for fear of runing short.

I am exceedingly grieved at this scandleous report's geting to your ears. It was also reported here that Maria Unauna is my Mistress, but Mrs Napela put in a word for me saying that she only makes my bed (which she does) but sleeps with us, Mr and Mrs Napela. So that stoped that. I only hope that whoever sirculated this Scandle will make his fortune.

By the overland Mail of yesterday, Mrs Napela received a letter from Kuihelani informing her of his meeting with D. K., of which you wrote to me about. I will use his own words:

ₐI am very busy at the present time. When I was about to sail to Honolulu, I was detained by D. K. He showed me a genealogical record written by Koii,[1] which he told me to read and approve if I found it accurate. When I read it I decided it was full of mistakes and told D. K. so, pointing out that Koii elevated only those he wished to and lowered those he despised. D. K. asked me for Kaoo's[2] book of genealogies, and I told him that I still have it and will give it to no one. Upon my death the book will be inherited by my daughter, Mrs Samuel Parker. D. K. asked me to let him copy the genealogies of living members of royalty from the highest to the lowest. I reminded him of Unauna's slanderous remarks when Emma married Liholiho, claiming that she had no royal blood. When Kaoo heard of it he was infuriated and said that there was no high chief living who could deny the rank of Keliimaikai's descendant. Indeed Emma had every right to be the wife of the King. Furthermore, said Kaoo, if Unauna made such remarks about Emma, evil would befall Unauna and his children and so it is that now they have neither position nor importance. I am beginning to copy from Kaoo's book the genealogies of the chiefs, and after completing them I will take or send them to D. K.ₐ

Kuihelani does not state of his interview with Nahaolelua on the following day. I must sincerely hope that the following will be satisfactory to you. If their are more to [be] learnt in regard to what you requested me [to] learn,[3] I will wait until the time comes.

There is a Report here about Wilder. When Wilder was here last he was escorted by a Native boy. That boy has writen to his friend here, Kapeau, Okuu's Son, saying that Wilder has gone to the Coast to purchase a new Steamer for the Government. [This] is the report known but the truth is that Wilder has got the Leper, and previous to his comeing up here Wilder had lost the feeling of one Arm, and in order to avoid being known as a Leper, he has gone to Frisco. Manuia, Kaawa's brother, writes the same to his Brother. The Captain of *Warwick* says that it is known at Honolulu that Wilder is a Leper and that Dr Trousseau has pronounced him as such. So if this report is true, surely you must have heard about it.

If you can spare me some money from my Allowance please send me up some. My Aloha to all. My never ceasing Prayer for you and hoping you [are] well.

KEKUAOKALANI

9 P.M.—It is blowing Blue Guns.

1. Koii Unauna, the supporter of Kalākaua and genealogist mentioned in Letter 69, note 7. For his part in the genealogical disputes of the 1870s, see Letter 105, note 6.

2. The genealogist Kaoo, authority for Emma's descent (and Peter's) from Keli'imaika'i, was perhaps a noted medical kahuna of Oahu during the early 1800s; for his activities, see *Fragments of Hawaiian History as Recalled by John Papa Ii*, trans. by Mary Kawena Pukui, ed. by Dorothy B. Barrère (Honolulu: Bishop Museum Press, 1963), p. 48. The Bishop Museum Library contains at least two manuscript genealogies, in nineteenth-century ledger books with early pencil notations in the flyleaves, indicating that the genealogies were the work of Koii Unauna and of Kaoo. One of these ledgers seems to have been deposited in the museum by a member of the Parker family of the island of Hawaii, and a relative of Mrs. Samuel Parker, adopted daughter of Huaka Kuihelani. The relationship of the Bishop Museum manuscripts to Koii's "record" and Kaoo's "book" mentioned by Peter Kaeo is uncertain.

3. Emma was generally interested in reports by or about persons who had had recent conversations with Kalākaua, particularly on genealogical matters.

Letter 102
Peter to Emma

[Kalaupapa]
November 11, 1874

Queen Emma

. . . In regard to my geting a Well person to be with me on here, I can do so. I could have done so heretofore, but I was afraid of not having cash enough, but since you feel uneasy about it, I will procure one for the amount of which you mention—$5—but I will wait for your approval. . . .

It is too true, as you say, that I have been tempted to go with Women, but I can boldly say that I have not allowed my passion to be ruled by the Temptation.

I really believe that If I had any medecine which would help me in any way, that I stand a very good show of being healed, but as it is I have only to take the chances. Although without any medecine, I am well and have not at all changed both in health and appearance.

It has been so stormy these past fiew days that I could not go on the Plain and plant more Algerobas, but will do so the first chance. I was not aware that you are taking only but one copy of the Foreign Papers, so if you choose you can retain them and send me only the Local. By so doing I will not deprive you of the Foreign news, and can learn some of the Local. I presume since Buff is the Minister of Interior he will make a trip around the Islands.

I must now end as it is late in the Evening. The Captain of the *Warwick* says that he will make his usual trips here. . . .

God Bless you is the Prayer of your Servant

KEKUAOKALANI

Letter 103
Peter to Emma

[Kalaupapa]
November 17, 1874

Queen Emma

I presume that the Captain of the Schooner *Luka*, Kaai, have told you of his calling on me. I requested him to inform you of my Health as being well, and likewise of my features. He informed me that he is called as one of the *Kipis* but, says he, ˄ "I am moving with the times.", ˄ He also remarked that the D. K.s are not noticed by the People.

Yesterday afternoon, the day being nice and warm, I rode in to Kalawao and saw the Natives enjoying themselves at Horse racing. I stood for a while with Father Damien, who was looking for a Policeman, as a man had died in the morning and was to be buried that afternoon, but the Horses were comeing and going at such a rate, and so numerous past the Catholic Church that it was not safe to take the Corpse across the road. I left him and rode on, and on returning I saw that Damien was having the Corpse burried.

When I reached Home, Mrs Napela was at my House with another Woman, Luika by name, Wife to Moluhi of Waimea and Kaikuahine[1] of Waiahole, the old man who told you that I got drunk on my arrival. Lucy I presume know this Woman. This Luika is a Kaikuahine to Kamaipelekane[2] and have held correspondence with Kamaipelekane ever since she has been here. She informed me that she is a Kahu[3] of ours, and came to inform me of a letter which she had lately received from Kamaipelekane informing her of what had hapened and also of Waahia's[4] Predictions. He says:

˄ Here is news. A while ago, D. K. sent for me to come and see him. This was before his departure for Hawaii. D. K. asked me and my wife, Waahia, to help him. I gave my consent. I then

reported to Waahia, and this is what she told D. K.: that he must
sail to the east and on his return keep quiet, and that she would
take care of the rest. But if he sailed to Hawaii another time he
would be ignored by the people. Another thing he must do is to
release persons in trouble with the law. He agreed and promised
that he would release all troubled ones on the first day of October
—a promise he failed to keep. Furthermore, he went to Hawaii
once again and was snubbed by the people of Hilo and
Makawao: Waahia's warning was therefore right. Waahia waited
until the first day of November arrived, and still D. K. had not
kept his promise. Therefore, I, Kamaipelekane, told my wife
that D. K. is now departing for America and still has not granted
your request. Why don't we support the Queen? Waahia replied,
"She was the woman I foretold would become the occupant of
the Throne, but then we gave our support to D. K. Let him go
to a foreign land and let him thence return in a coffin. I have
already said that the Throne belongs to the English lady, who
will possess it until her own body is loaded with years. The
people will again live and the face of the land will turn upward
to the sun. This is the *Alii* who once ate a portion[5] of my food.
(If this *hakina* be true, you must know something about it.)
She does not despise me. The D. K.s still trample upon everyone
and everything. They will yet lose their power and perish.

When Kalahoolewa returned from his trip around Oahu,
Kaleikuaiwa asked, "How was your trip?" He replied,
"Discouraging. The people are still rebellious and very angry.
They all but manhandled us." Kalekuaiwa said, "That is because
of your brother's indifference and his failure to play his proper
role. It has been prophesied that death awaits you all. Therefore
now is the time to take thought. As your brother is leaving for
America before the affairs of the Kingdom are settled, you will
live but to see strange things come to pass. ⌄

After Luika had left, I studied at what this Hakina could be, but up
to the present moment I am just as Wise as ever I was. The above is
what took place between D. K., Kamaipelekane and his wife, Waahia
the Prophetess, a fiew Months ago, and what Kamaipelekane heard in
regard to Kalahoolewa's tour around Oahu.

Yesterday and today have been very calm and hot, with hardly a breath of Air, but the Sea is quite Boisterous. The man who I have promised to engage is Pukooku, a Nephew of Kalanikahua's.

I am well and hope to hear that all at Home are also well.... God Bless you is the Fervent Prayer of

KEKUAOKALANI

November 18. 8 A.M.—The *Warwick* has just past as the Wind is so boisterous that she cannot touch—and [a] heavy Swell.

1. Sister or female cousin.

2. Probably E. P. Kamaipelekane, member of the House of Representatives during numerous sessions, 1850–1859.

3. Honored attendant.

4. The kahuna Waahia, wife of Kamaipelekane, was well known in the community as a healer and prophetess. The *Pacific Commercial Advertiser*, Oct. 12, 1872, reported that Waahia had been summoned before a police court for practicing her profession without a license:

> Gone to Jail.—Several months ago, a noted native woman doctress, named Waahia, was fined one hundred dollars in the Police Court of this city, for the offense of practicing medicine without a license. The patient in that particular case had died under the hands of the doctress, and it was believed that death had been hastened by her treatment. She appealed to the Circuit Judge, W. P. Kamakau, and the decision of the Police Magistrate was confirmed. She appealed to a jury, and at the July term of the Supreme Court, a verdict was rendered against her. Through counsel, she then took exceptions to the rulings of the presiding judge, with a view to obtaining a new trial. On Monday last the exceptions were argued before the full bench and were overruled. Now Mrs. Waahia is a bit of a prophetess and seer as well as a doctress—in fact, she is what the American Indian would call a "big medicine woman." She prophesied that if she were sent to prison, the walls thereto would fall apart, and she went there on Tuesday last, in confident expectation of the coming catastrophe, which for some unaccountable reason has been so far delayed. But she has many dupes among the natives who are seriously looking for something to happen in her behalf.

5. *Hakina*: portion or fragment. The next sentence in English in parenthesis is Peter's interpolation. He playfully uses the phrase "this *hakina*" as a way of saying this "bit" of information.

Letter 104
Peter to Emma

[Kalaupapa]
November 22, 1874

Queen Emma

After I had delivered my letter of the 17th to the Mail Man on Wednesday last, I rode in to Kalawao to See if the *Warwick* had touched at Waikolu, but to my disgust I learned that her course had been Averted by the Strong Wind which was blowing then Fearfully. I asked of the Kamaainas whare she would most likely go to for Shelter and was informed that Halawa was the only Haven for a Vessel to put in to, especially if it Blew a Kona.[1]

While I was at the Store the Wind was blowing so strong that it lifted the Boards from the ground and tossed it about, then threw it to some distance from whare it formely laid. I also learned that 4 or 5 Families had been made Houseless during the Night and had moved into the School House. The Wind, which blew through the Valley in Puffs, though brief in duration, was frightful. After a Puff a Lull would set in, and during the interval which lasted for some time, the Natives would avail themselves of the chance and would go in to the House and take out what they could carry to some place of Security.

I for one took advantage of the Lull and mounting John Puni I rode Home, but I was overtook on the way. It blew so strong that I had to rein in my Horse to a walk, and sometimes the Horse would stand while I held my Hat with one Hand, the Reins with the other, and press the Sides of my Horse with both Legs in order to retain my Seat. When a Lull would set in I would raise myself from my stooping Posture and start my Horse at a Brisk pace. Thick folds of heavy black clouds were blown over the Pali to the North at a Terrible rate. It blew all that day and night.

On Thursday the Wether was as boisterous as the preceding day. The Beach was one white foam. Heavy Billows came rolling in and breaking on the Beach sounded like the roaring Thunder. In the afternoon the Rain fell in Torrents. I looked through the Window and watched my poor Plants at the Mercy of the Wind being tossed about. In the Evening, the Wind which had been blowing from off the Land Northward, blew from the West. It blew so strong that it shook my House so that I could not rest easy till very late, for fear of a Mishap.

On Friday, after a restless night, I woke to find the Wether worst then the two past days. It was still raining and everything both out and indoors was damp. The Breakers were so high and large that it hid— or I should say drownded—the Buoy which is easily seen from my Cottage. The whole Coast as far as the Eye could scan was one White Line of boisterous Surge. At Noon the rain ceased, exposing to view the Cascades on the side of the Pali, which looked very pretty. The old dried-up River was now full of Water, and as though anxious to take its part in the Storm was roaring on its winding way to Seaward, and carrying before it all that may happen to fall in its way.

Later in the day the Wind moderated a little, so I went to look at my Plants. Although they underwent a good deal of shaking, they were not injured. In the night the Moon shone out brightly. I sat up till near 9 and was preparing to retire when I was startled by the Wind's striking my House—and actually shook it. That was enough, for it banished all thought of Sleep from me. I watched with the greatest of fear, not knowing what may betide my Cottage. This blew stronger then it had. It muttered fiercely as it passed, Whistled through the Blinds, and at times it would howl so, shaking the House, that at one time I thought it would tumble down. It blew steadily so all night, thus keeping me awake for the greater part of the night, waiting with the greatest of Solicitude for the comeing Morn, which came at last with the Welcome Sun.

The wind had abated a little which made us hope that Satuarday would be a fine day and allow the *Warwick* to come. But alas, our hopes were in vain. Although the Sun shone, the Wether was still boisterous. In the afternoon I rode in to Kalawao to see for myself the distruction which the wind had made. Twenty-two Houses were blown down flat to the ground, and 50 more were so damaged that nothing was left but the frame. Tall Papaia trees were without leaves and some were broken in two, and the Stumps left. Whole groves of newly planted Bananas were blown down, Acres of "Koli"[2] which the Natives had allowed to grow to break the force of the Wind, and also for *Aho*[3] for Houses, were all destroyed. Puhala trees were pulled up and thrown to some distance. In fact, everything that the Natives had planted were more or less damaged and bore a Grave aspect. Homes which once held a Family of 5 or 6 Tenants were now chackes. A large House in the Hospital Premises is given to those who are in need of House, but that is full and if this Wether does not let up they will have to go into the Church.

Today, Sunday, the Wind have died off to nearly a Calm, but the
Sun have not shone, the clouds are still hanging overhead, indicating
that the Storm is not yet over. I am sure that this distruction will cost
the Government at the very least calculation $3,000 if not more. It is
now near Sunset. All is calm save the low murmur of the distant
Waves. Good Bye. My Aloha to all. God Bless you is the Prayer of
your Servant

KEKUAOKALANI

1. Name of a leeward wind.

2. Probably *koli'i*, a native lobelia shrub (*Trematolobelia macrostachys*),
which grows to six feet with lateral branches and makes an effective wind-
break.

3. The *koli'i* was also used as a thatch for lashing together rafter and roof,
especially for fastening in place a horizontal purlin rafter (*'aho*) as a support.

Letter 105
Peter to Emma

[Kalaupapa]
December 1, 1874

Queen Emma
   On Friday last I rode to Hua's and informed her of your interview
with D. K. After I had told her the particulars, she looked at me for a
while [and] then remarked:

   ˄ No living person has had hula all night long¹—that is for the
   dead—dancing of that kind is for mourning. If D. K. knows
   that he is going to die, and if that is the reason for the hula
   dancing, then it is good. Certainly he is well supplied with
   Kahunas, who know what is proper and correct. Why otherwise
   did the Kahunas permit the hula dancing? It looks therefore to
   me as if all this is a fulfillment and a consequence of Kalakaua's
   own deeds. Those very words are true, but nevertheless his deeds
   are revealed through them, just as if he had said: "It is better for
   me to speak first to the person whom I have treated badly. Then
   I shall be better prepared to die." The white garments worn by
   D. K. before he boarded the ship are a garb that releases him

from the influence of the evil he has committed. Uli[2] who looks
on the right side and Uli who looks on the wrong side is the god
concerned in this matter. If D. K. was involved deeply in
mischievous sorcery practiced upon Lunalilo, then it is the power
of the prayers of the Kahunas that is taking D. K. away to die in
a foreign land, where no crowd of people will be at hand to
observe his death. For Uli will look on the side that is right and
not on the side that is wrong. Uli had nothing to do with Buff's
intention to bring about the death of Emma. Earlier, when Buff
was seriously ill, I treated him until he recovered, but before I
did so I asked him, "Have you the Kalaipahoa?"[3] He remained
silent a long time and finally answered yes. I asked him again,
"Whom did you get it from?" He answered, "From Kalaualu it
went to Kaunaohua and from Kaunaohua to me." I said, "You
are not suffering from anyone but yourself. You have sent the
Kalaipahoa to destroy others, but you did wrong, and therefore
it has returned to you and is destroying you." He promised and I
treated and cured him. If something now has been sent to Emma
from Buff, that will be the Kalaipahoa. But Uli knows that
Emma is a righteous woman. Therefore she will not die. Those
who think evil are the ones who shall die, but Emma will prosper
and be at the head of the Government. ∧

After our conversation I rode Home. In the Afternoon, Jim, the
Man who shot at Dr Trousseau, came to see me. All my Men were
pounding Pai, so I was left alone. I asked him if he had any Mea Hou,
and he replied that he had, and that it was for my Ear alone. I
informed him that I was alone and that I was ready to here what he
had to say, so he began as follows:

∧I have a little news from Kealiikanakaole. ∧ (This Kealiikanakaole
is a kahu[4] of Mrs Bishop's. Aikoe knows him.) ∧ He came to see
me and I (Jim) asked him, "Perhaps you have some news?"
Kealiikanakaole said, "Yes, I have a bit of news, here it is. I was
with Pauahi in Haleakala[5] when Bishop entered and sat by the table.
He held his head in his hands. Pauahi asked, 'Are you ill?' Bishop
looked at us with saddened eyes and said, 'Yes, I am ill over you.'
He wondered why the people wanted Emma as Queen, and when
Haoles asked them, 'Why did you want Queen Emma?' the people
answered, 'Emma is the right person for the Throne. Emma, Pauahi
and Ruth belong to Kamehameha I.' Haoles asked again, 'How?'

The people said, 'Pauahi and Ruth belong to Keliimaikai, Kamehameha's own brother.[6] Emma, Pauahi and Ruth are of one blood.' Bishop said also to Pauahi, 'I thought that D. K. was the close relative of Kamehameha I, and that this woman whom we ill-treat is quite distantly related. In any event Emma is related to you two and to Kalakaua and others very distantly. Now why did you mistreat your cousin? The people informed us that Keaweaheulu was merely a chief under Kamehameha. Yet you choose the one beneath you and put him over you, while you two who are superior—own descendants of Kamehameha I—have lowered yourselves beneath the descendants of Keaweaheulu. I am greatly ashamed. On this account I want to speak to D. K. about the way he goes to the hotel to gamble and to waste the money of the Kingdom. Kamehameha IV and Kamehameha V were not wealthy kings, but certainly they never used government money for gambling. D. K. has never had any money of his own. When I talked to him, he said that I had no business to speak to him in this fashion, for he was King. I said to D. K., "Don't think that you are King because of your rank. You are King because of my influence and my money—the money I helped you with." This is what I fear,' said Mr. Bishop. 'D. K. is getting ready to go to America, and if I am not mistaken perhaps in two or three months another and even greater riot will occur. The Natives assisted by some white men will enter the Palace and place Emma on the Throne as ruler of Hawaii Nei. When that time comes who will restore to me the money I spent in helping D. K.? It was you, Pauahi, who told me to help Kalakaua, and now this is the result—my getting into this trouble. Is it because Ruth adopted Kalahoolewa that the two of you should behave this way? Why did you not tell me before, Pauahi, that you are related to Emma? Then the Courthouse would not have been broken into and there would have been no riot. Indeed it is very plain that Emma will be the future ruler. The Haoles know that D. K. is not fit to be King. Perhaps sometime a man-of-war will not be here to interfere. It will not bring help because the ruler at that time will be the ruler the people choose. Yes, it is very plain that Emma will be the future sovereign. But I do not care. If another riot occurs I shall return to my native land, America, and take my wife along.' Then Pauahi put on her shoes and went up to Ruth's." I, Jim, inquired: "What of the future?" Kealiikanakaole answered, "Not certain. The lips of the people speak only of Emma, and it seems the time is ripe for rebellion. If there is a riot the people will unanimously turn to Emma, and this will be a greater riot than the one before. The Haole Bishop is worried, stays in Haleakala, muttering to himself, looking very pale. The people have been warned not to guard Emma, but secretly they are keeping watch over her.",∧

The above is what Kealiikanakaole heard Bishop say to his wife in Haleakala, and he was present. Jim also says the Kealiikanakaole told him that when Mrs Bishop left her Husband she went to Ruth's and Censured her for all this. Mrs Bishop said to Ruth, ∧ "I shall weep over you if Emma becomes ruler. Woe betide you for you have no people in your support. You and I have treated Emma badly. My husband will take me away and you and I will be separated. Alas for you when I am gone.",∧

Now this Coroborates with what you informed [me of] some time ago, if you recollect, when Pauahi said [to Ruth] at Waikiki, ∧ "Had we aided Emma then, by now my husband would be premier. I stood by you and we have fallen badly. Not so badly for you, Ruth, as it is for me.",∧

The man Pukooku which I wrote to you about as my Cook is now Cooking for me. He commenced this morning. The wether is very cold and the days cloudy. We have frequent showers. Although the Wind has abated, yet the Sea is still boisterous, thus depriving us of freash Fish. I am as ever quite well. . . .

May God Protect and assist you to your Throne is the Prayer of

KEKUAOKALANI

1. Hua's point seems to be that proper nocturnal ("all night") hulas should never be performed to honor the living but solely to celebrate the dead. The implication is that since Kalākaua's dances went on until morning, he must have realized he was as good as dead already.

2. Chief deity of sorcery; a judicial goddess, said to have come from Kahiki, who decided issues of right and wrong in the affairs of the alii. According to Samuel M. Kamakau, the old Hawaiians believed that Uli was the presiding deity for the different branches of "the *kahuna ʻana ʻana* [who prayed people into illness or death]; for the *kahuna ʻana ʻana kuni* [who divined the source of death from *ʻana ʻana* and retaliated in kind]; for the *kahuna kuni ola* [who also divined the source of the *ʻana ʻana* illness and who saved and avenged the victim]; and for the *kahuna ʻana ʻana kalahala* [who freed one from his 'sins of commission and ommission' that had been the cause of being a victim of

'ana 'ana]." (Ka Po'e Kahiko: The People of Old, trans. by Mary Kawena Pukui, ed. by Dorothy B. Barrère, Bishop Museum Publication 51 [Honolulu: Bishop Museum Press, 1964], p. 119.)

3. An allusion to certain woods, some of them supposedly death-dealing, and to the tree-forms of several gods, two of them male (Kāne-i-kaulana-'ula and Kahuila-o-ka-lani) and one female (Kapo) associated with these woods in black magic. The woods employed were *kauila*, *hioi*, and *'ohe*, but only fragments of the wood at Mauna-loa, Molokai, were considered to be poisonous. Kamakau described *kālaipāhoa* in his account of "The Sorcery Gods of Molokai": "The trees themselves would have been harmless if they had not been combined with something else [spirits] that caused death, or if they had not been worshiped (*ho'omana'ia*). . . . It was only after they had acquired mana, and their mana was known, that they were worshiped. The basis of their mana was in their power to kill. If anyone were fed a small fragment of their trunks (*kino*), even the smallest bit, or if it was rubbed against his skin, or if it had been beseeched for his destruction (*kalo ho'ola'a 'ia*), the person would die." (*Ka Po'e Kahiko: The People of Old*, p. 128.) The *Pacific Commercial Advertiser*, Sept. 18, 1875, noted that *kālaipāhoa* had figured in a recent trial for manslaughter: "From Hilo we learn that two native *kahunas* (doctors) were committed by the Police Magistrate of Hilo on the 8th inst. for trial at the next term of the Circuit Court, for causing the death of a native named Wailee. They commenced to doctor him on the 28th of July, and he died on Aug. 2d. The medecines they gave him were *kalaipahoa* (said to be a virulent poison), *Ahakea* (a species of wood) and *Koali* (the convolvulus)."

4. Personal attendant and steward.

5. "House of the Sun"; name of the Bishop house and grounds, in the vicinity of the present (1975) Bishop Trust Company Building at King and Bishop streets, Honolulu. The name was associated with the great mountain and crater on the island of Maui, Hale-a-ka-lā, where according to legend the trickster-god Maui lassoed the sun to lengthen the day.

6. The reported conversation between Charles R. Bishop and Bernice Pauahi reached Queen Emma at third hand. Assuming that some such conversation was overheard by Kealiikanakaole, correctly reported to Jim Kamai, who in turn repeated truly what he had heard to Peter, it is still difficult to follow the thread of Peter's final written account. For one thing, it is unlikely from the start that Bishop, clear-headed banker and member of the House of Nobles, who arrived in Hawaii in 1846, who knew personally each of the Hawaiian monarchs, and who took a special interest in the succession crisis of 1872–1873 at the time of the death of Kamehameha V, would have failed to acquire over the years a fairly accurate notion of his wife's dynastic ties and her genealogical connections with Queen Emma, the Princess Ruth, and the family of Kalākaua. For example, Bishop would surely have known that Bernice Pauahi, Emma Kaleleonālani, and Ruth Ke'elikōlani were "of one blood," in the sense that all three were descended from the same set of eighteenth-century high chiefs, Heulu and Keawe-a-Heulu, ancestors

of Kamehameha I. (For their various pedigrees and forebears in common, see genealogical tables and comment in Abraham Fornander, *An Account of the Polynesian Race*, 3 vols. [Trubner and Co.: London, 1878, 1880, 1883], especially vol. 1; W. D. Alexander, *A Brief History of the Hawaiian People* [American Book Co.: New York, 1891, 1899], Appendices; *Liliuokalani, Hawaii's Story by Hawaii's Queen* [Charles E. Tuttle and Co.: Rutland, Vt., and Tokyo, 1964], Appendices; Milton Rubincam, "America's Only Royal Family: Genealogy of the Former Hawaiian Ruling House," *National Genealogical Society Quarterly* 50 [1962]: 79–91.) One of the most puzzling features in Peter's version of the domestic dialogue of Mr. and Mrs. Bishop is his assertion that "Pauahi and Ruth belong to Keliimaikai, Kamehameha's own brother." If Peter meant simply to convey the idea that Pauahi and Ruth were great-grand-nieces of Keli'imaika'i there would be no problem. Both were related to Keli'imaika'i by being great-grandchildren of Kamehameha I through the same high chiefess, Kanekapolei. Emma's relationship to Kamehameha I was less direct, since she could claim descent only from his half-brother, Keli'imaika'i. However, Peter was no doubt familiar with the claims of rival genealogists, notably Kalākaua's kahuna supporter Unauna, denying that Emma was a descendant of Keli'imaika'i. The stalemated argument over Emma's claim of descent from Keli'imaika'i is implied in an earlier letter, Letter 101, where Kuihelani is quoted as referring to "Unauna's slanderous remarks when Emma married Liholiho, claiming that she was not of royal blood." In 1856, at the time of her marriage to Kamehameha IV, certain court genealogists, including Unauna, held that Emma's (and Peter's) grandmother, Kaoana'eha, was a daughter not of Keli'imaika'i but of Kalaipaihala, a half-brother of Kalani'ōpu'u, uncle of Kamehameha I. During the genealogical skirmishes of the 1870s, Samuel M. Kamakau, historian and Queenite, defended Emma's claim, while Koii Unauna, John Kamakini, and various informants of Abraham Fornander, erudite judge and ethnologist of Swedish origin, insisted on the descent from Kalaipaihala. The fact that Peter's extant letters nowhere specifically mention the notion that Emma was a descendant of Kalaipaihala does not mean that Peter had never heard of this well-aired charge. Indeed, it may have figured more clearly and prominently in some of the lost or destroyed letters of 1875 and 1876. It is probable, however, that at least before 1874 Peter's knowledge of his own and Emma's ancestry was more spotty, or occasionally confused, than it was exhaustive. An intensified interest in genealogical history among some leading Hawaiian families, an earnest but by no means rigorously systematic concern encouraged greatly by King Kalākaua for his own dynastic purposes, dated from 1886. In that year, Kalākaua officially established a kind of genealogical society, a "secret order," with himself as president, known as the *Hale Nauwa* (or *Naua*), inaugurated according to *The Hawaiian-English Dictionary* for "the study of the ancient Hawaiian religion and manner of living." The name of the society referred to "a place where genealogy was scanned to see whether applicants were related to the high chief and therefore eligible to become members of the royal household." For contemporary reaction to this institutional innovation, from a haole and American point of view, see Ralph S. Kuykendall, *The Hawaiian Kingdom, 1874–1893*, p. 345fn.

Letter 106
Peter to Emma

[Kalaupapa]
December 8, 1874

Queen Emma

I hope that you have received mine of the 1st of this Month. I feel quite uneasy about it. If you have received it, please let me know. Since my last we have had rain dayly, in fact a little too much. Although the Weather in some measure has abated, yet the Sea is still boisterous and unsafe for anything to venture out. . . .

The Sore on One of my Foot has broken out again, so now I am confined to the House, but since I have applied the Poultice which Dr Trousseau gave me, it is looking quite healthy, and I hope that I will be able to leave the House by the End or begining of the next Month. Buff is reported to be comeing up here sometime this month.

I wish you would send me up a Bottle of Syrup. I dreamt last night that I was picking one of my front Tooth, and in so doing it came out in Pieces, and the last piece hung to a piece of Flesh, so I bit it and spat it out. I told Napela of it and he interprets it as a bad Omen, saying that as it came out in pieces it must be a Relative of mine, but a distant one. *We* are in Blood connected with the D. K.s by our Grand Parents,[1] and it probably might be them. If you recollect, I had a dream simular to this some Years ago, and told you and Aunty of it. Some time after, we heard of poor Kalalahi's[2] death. He was connected to me through you, so if D. K. is connected to me through somebody, then All Right—let this Dream then be for him. The news of Kalalahi's death came across the Sea, and probably D. K.'s might be the Same.

I am well with the exception of Foot. My Aloha to all. . . .

KEKUAOKALANI

1. Various degrees of great-grandparents would be closer to the facts.

2. Unidentified.

Letter 107
Peter to Emma

[Kalaupapa]
December 9, 1874

Queen Emma

Thanks, Thanks, for yours of the 3d, 6th, and 7th, which came by the *Warwick* this morning. In regard to the Tarrow, if the Vessel sails direct for here, it is best to have it cooked here, but if she sails for another Port previous to her touching here, then it will be best to have it cooked their.

The Americans must have been dreadfully scared of you and your English Sympathies, as they term it. Why, they show clearly now that they care only for their Idol the Almighty "Dollar."

The man who I have hired for Cook is also my Waiter at Table. He is not a Leper or I would not have him. A Man by the name of Kamakini has come up by the Schooner, and he told Napela that while he was at Honolulu he lived in the same House with one of D. K.'s Kahunas, a Woman, and this Kahuna told them that D. K. asked them whether he will return safe, and they all told him, D. K.: ^"If you persist in being so stubborn and going on the journey, you will return in a box like that first earlier king of yours who died on a journey"^ (Kamehameha II).[1]

I am happy to learn that you have received mine of the 1st, for I was quite uneasy about it. I have received the $25.00 and also the Poi. ...

Good Bye. Hoping for the best, and with God's help and Protection.

I remain your Servant
KEKUAOKALANI

P. S. Their is no Limu.

1. The first Hawaiian king who died on a journey overseas was Liholiho, Kamehameha II (1799–1824), eldest son of Kamehameha I by Keōpūolani. Both he and his wife, Queen Kamāmalu, who was also his half-sister, died of measles while in London, on a mission to achieve a formal alliance with Great Britain.

Letter 108
Peter to Emma

[Kalaupapa]
December 16, 1874

Queen Emma

Yours of the 12th have duely come to hand. Thanks, Thanks, for Wreaths which you have sent up. You say that the White Wreath put in seperately is the one which is your own making.[1] Now which one is that? The White one came in a Paper bundle with a Pink one, and another White one was in the Box with the Hat and coat. The Yellow one was in the Hat. The one which you made yourself, I will wear on my Hat myself. I am wearing the White one that came in the Box and I hope that it is the one which you made.

As my foot has healed faster then I thought it would, I have left the Poultice and am applying a black Stuff which Dr Trousseau also gave me, so when the *Warwick* arrived, I rode to the Beach. When the Captain came ashore we all noticed his Wreath around his Hat and wondered what Flower it was. My Boy Luther came up to me and gave me a Paper bundle, saying it was a Lei. When Kaimimoku came to me with my letter and [I] saw that it mentioned about the Wreath, I rode Home, and having put the White one on my Hat, I again rode to the Beach to show my Wreath.

When I got to the Beach, my Wreath attracted the Natives' attention, and Napela asked me about it. I informed him of the particulars, and gave the name as "Queen Emma." After I saw that my Tarrow was on the Cart, I rode Home. As soon as I reached Home, I opened the Box which my Boy took up and found that it contained two more Queen Emmas. So I had to refer to the letter in order to make sure that the one which I will wear will be the one which you made. So I am wearing them alternately until I learn which one is the one you made.

My little Black Hat with the Yellow Queen Emma looked really pretty. I am quite delighted with it, but unfortunately under the Sircumstances. Yesterday I rode in to the Store and bought some Horse Rope, Yest Powder[2] and Sugar, and while thair, the Natives looked at my White Queen Emma which I wore on my Hat and wondered what kind of Flower it could be and asked me about it. I told them again, giveing the name of it as Queen Emma. Ragsdale has [along with] several others asked me for a Wreath, and I have given them my promise to send to Honolulu for more, so if you will send me up some more of your *Name*, I can give it to some of my friends. You can't send me up too many, the more the better, for I wish to give some to the Sick who I know are bragadocious, so will help in obtaining my wish, which is in spreading the name of the Queen Emma Lei. Says the Captain of the *Warwick* at the Beach: ‸"Because the whites like Queen Emma so much, and so do the Hawaiians, therefore they wear them on their hats and call them Queen Emma's Lei."‸

Now since I am the first one that is wearing it, it has attracted the attention of the Natives so much that I will not at all be surprised to here that the Natives will send for it to come by the next Vessel. However, if any should come it is allready known as the Q. E. L.

The four English pieces cannot pass here for more then $4.75, but I have sent one up to Mr Meyer and hope that he will value it as you say [at] $4.90. As I deal with the Natives, [I know] it is very provoking to make them understand.

I have had the Picket Fence taken down at the back of my House and have used the Pickets to shelter my Plants from the Wind. I have had a Stone Wall put up, making my yard 25 ft. wider. On the comeing New Year I am going up to Kalawao and dig up young Puhala Trees, and on the following day, January 2d, Your Birthday, if nothing should Happen I will plant them with my own Hands back of my Cottage, both for Ornament and for Use.

I wish you would take the *Chimney Corner* for me for the comeing Year—it is $5 a Year as Advertised by Mr Whitney in his Paper. After the *Warwick* had left I found my Limu. Please send me up some Clothes Line.

December 17.—Mr Meyer has come down and takes my letter over by the *Nellie Morris*, as the *Warwick* is at the Windward. Mr Meyer has informed me that the English Sovreign is valued as you say [at] $4.90. I knew that you were in the right as to its Value, but as the Store and the Natives put it to $4.75, I have done as I have, in order to show the Natives of their error.

The Wether is still boisterous and damp. I am well. . . .

For your Success is the Prayer of

Your Humble Servant
KEKUAOKALANI

1. The seasonable leis were made of paper. Their sudden vogue was noted in the *Hawaiian Gazette*, Dec. 16, 1874: "Fashion.—A new *lei* composed of paper stars, and worn on the hat, is now the rage with Hawaiians, male and female, in Honolulu, to the disadvantage, no doubt, of the flower-lei business. For several days past, various papers have been much sought after. It is probable that the occurrence of the recent transit of Venus suggested the style of this new wreath." The connection with the planet is speculative. A natural flower lei also associated with Queen Emma was the *pīkake* lei. Star-shaped flowers of paper may have been intended to imitate the smallish blossoms of *pīkake-hōkū*, or star jasmine (*Jasminum pubescens*), a shrubby vine from India, still very popular in Hawaii.

2. Baking powder.

Letter 109
Peter to Emma

[Kalaupapa]
December 29, 1874

Queen Emma

I copy this from mine of the 23d, which I sent by Kaunakakai last Wednesday, with order to my Man who took it over to give it to the Captain of *Warwick*, or return it, as the *Warwick* then was at Kaunakakai and reported to be on her way here. My Man reports having seen the Schooner but not the Captain, until [the moment the *Warwick*] left for Honolulu. So [my man] returned the letter.

Dr Akana has succeeded in making a "Queen Emma," but unfortunately the right kind of Paper is inprocurable. Dr Akana gave me a black stuff to put on my foot which he says is better then the stuff which Dr Trousseau gave me. He pronounces this stuff of his to be the best for sores of long standing like mine. Trousseau's he says is very healing, but the sore will break out again, as the matter which ought all to be drawn out is not thoroughally drawn by Dr Trousseau's. Since I have applied Dr Akana's Stuff I have found it to be very drawing, drawing the matter more then the Stuff which Dr Trousseau gave me. Consiquently I have quite a faith in it, for I am sure that if the matter is thoroughally drawn the sore will heal of itself. I intend to buy some from Dr Akana, as what little he gave me is nearly used up.

On last Satuarday the 19th, at Evening, as I was watching the *Nellie Morris* leave, leaving her Captain behind as the Sea is still boisterous, I happen to look up to the Clouds and saw that a black cloud had formed itself into the form of a Coffin. In the evening I went over to Napela's and informed him of it. He observed that he had also observed it. On the following Monday, the 21st, as the afternoon was mild and pleasant, Mrs Napela and I rode to the Beach and called at Hua's. After we had conversed on various subjects, Hua looked up to me, as I was still on my Horse, and remarked, ^ "How are you?" ^ I replied that I was well, but that my Foot was sore, and that necessitated my being unable to dismount. Her Eyes were still on me and again [she] replied:^ "Look to our welfare, think upon it. Here is the land, here are the people. The fulfillment of the prophecy which I had spoken about to you two[1] is now drawing near. This is the time for you to think about it, while it is yet in the future. There is no time to lose. The others are beginning to fall away. Remain quiet, take no part in pleasures, do no wrong deed, but act with forethought. Care for your people as your cousin did." ^

After she had spoken, I informed her of what I had seen in the Clouds on Satuarday Evening. She replied that that was shown in order to confirm me of what she had predicted heretofore. When we were leaving, she bade me "Hoomanao,"[2] to which I replied, "Ae." After I reached home I could not help thinking of what she told me— her looks and the manner she spoke, slow and clear, and so sidate that I could not help ponder over it long after I had retired for the night.

Napela has asked me to write to you. And I have also asked him to refrain from so doing, until a proper time, especially if he wished to advise you, giveing him to know that if you were in nead of advise, you know whare to look for it. This, together with what I have learned from you, gives me a freash inspiration and hope that our Prayers may be realized. . . .

May God spare and protect you is the constant Prayer of

KEKUAOKALANI

1. Peter and Mrs. Napela.

2. To remember and continue to pray.

PART THREE / *The Release*

January 6, 1875–May 10, 1876

R eaders in the habit of scanning Honolulu obituaries learned of the death of Peter Kaeo from the *Hawaiian Gazette* for December 1, 1880: "The Hon. P. Y. Kaeo died at his residence on Emma Street on Friday night [November 26, 1880]. The funeral took place on Sunday and was largely attended by the retainers and friends of the family. The hearse was surrounded by *kahili*-bearers as becomes the dignity of a chief." A belated and even more curtailed item in the *Pacific Commercial Advertiser*, December 4, simply noted that Peter was buried with "appropriate honors" among his famous forebears at the Royal Mausoleum in Nuuanu Valley.

None of the several notices in local newspapers reminded readers of Peter's sequestered years at Kalaupapa. No announcement was ever published, of course, of the action of the Hawaiian Board of Health when, on June 27, 1876, having determined that "the Hon. P. Y. Kaeo . . . was actually better than when sent away," the Board then unanimously resolved to allow Peter to return to Honolulu, under certain specified conditions: "as for instance, that he should remain under the surveillance of the Board, that he refrain from mingling in public life, and should the disease eventually develop, that he will submit to their decision and subscribe to their regulations."[1]

The detailed causes of this almost miraculous denouement in the story of Peter Kaeo are dim. Official records bearing on Peter's case are sketchy and few, making it difficult to determine what deliberations may have led Mr. Wilder to sustain the very generalized medical findings of Dr. McKibbin, or persuaded the rest of the Board to resolve that "the Report of Dr. McKibbin be adopted and the recommendation as to conditions be carried out." But the lack of documents based on substantial medical evidence is only one layer in a thick fabric of official mysteries. It is quite possible that Peter's case had revealed an unaccountable remission in the progress of his disease. Yet as recently as November of 1875, only six months before his discharge, Peter had made an appeal to the board "to have one of his old servants sent up to him, as he was failing rapidly"—presumably because of his worsening leprosy—and the plea had been promptly granted.[2]

Less of a puzzle than the medical proof behind the shifting appearances is the question whether or not Peter Kaeo's return to Honolulu was a result of behind-the-scenes political influence: the status of Kekuaokalani as a third- or fourth-string member of the dwindling Kamehameha dynastic line. Though the medical facts might have justified the decision of the board to restore Peter to freedom, it is hard not to conclude that the intrigues that preceded his release were politically instigated and do not solely belong to the history of public health in Hawaii. Because of a paucity of documentation, there is much about Peter's life as a whole, before, during, and after his stay on Molokai, that can never be known.

Admittedly, Peter Kaeo and Queen Emma were exceptional individuals. Peter never forgot that he was first of all an alii. He was Kekuaokalani, not a commoner, and not one of those other Hawaiians whom he himself perceived as simply "the natives." His years at Kalaupapa, so deeply and dramatically complicated by his cousin's ambition to achieve the Kamehameha throne, form no more than a single episode in the century-long struggle of his people to create a nation and establish a polyglot, racially mixed community upon pacified but still disintegrating tribal foundations, and "be ambitious to hold our ancestral renown high." Nevertheless, despite limitations and biases, the day-to-day lives of Peter and Emma as described in their own words can perhaps serve as a partial, fragmentary expression of certain Hawaiian attitudes and values, whether conscious or unconscious: especially of the more piercing emotions that sustained some of those values, not only into the last quarter of the nineteenth century, but also very evidently beyond.

Our sole source of direct knowledge concerning the personal Anglican-Polynesian-Hawaiian-American world of Peter and Emma during his last months on Molokai (from January 1875 to May 1876) is a series of thirteen nonconsecutive miscellaneous letters. Only four from Peter to Emma are here published, and these tell us little of his situation that is new. Obviously, during these years many other letters must have been destroyed, or hidden away, or perhaps irretrievably mislaid. Fortunately, nine letters in Emma's hand, though written at scattered dates, provide biographical information and historical clues of interest. Among other matters, one of these letters reveals that in December of 1875 Emma was herself absorbed, as she had apparently never been before, in kahuna prophecies concerning the fate of the Kalākaua regime and the future of the Kingdom. In fact, on at least one occasion, with the collaboration of the Reverend G. W. Pilipo, Emma took part in a religious sacrament in which vestiges of old native practice appear to have been commingled in a curious marriage of Christian and Polynesian ritual.

A strain of "nativism"[3] obtruding in Emma's surviving correspondence, a readiness to draw upon the Hawaiian past for occult understanding and mana, should not be taken as a sign that Emma's essential Christian faith had wavered: only that the ways of Divine Providence, according to the highest authorities, are, as Emma well knew, exceedingly mysterious. Nor is there proof that her behavior, in the exercise of the very little effective political power that she possessed, had reverted far in the direction of old Hawaiian custom and belief. On the contrary, at the same time she was receiving prophecies from kahuna sources (sometimes messages relaying their reports at second hand), Queen Emma was becoming more and more involved in practical politics, even in the routines of campaigning at the local district level. She busied herself trying to get her friends and well-wishers elected to office; she was spasmodically realistic and resourceful. She took pride in the thought that certain of her supporters in the House of Representatives were well-versed in the laws of the Kingdom, and she was deeply pleased when she detected in them signs of skill and cunning in the procedures of parliamentary bodies.

Unfortunately, because of the loss of important letters (drafts as well as originals) on which to base conclusions, it is difficult to describe, let alone try to appraise, the queen's conduct during this period. Less given to bursts of vituperation than her ordinarily mild cousin, she nevertheless reveals here and there a touch of malice, even of venom. It is as if the polar strands of her character, the teachings of her Anglican faith and her mid-Victorian and womanly devotion to duty and civic good works, had become confusedly entangled with her yearning as an alii to wield political power: to win the Kamehameha throne and play her rightful part, as she saw it, on the ancestral stage. In any event, while poor Kepelino languished in prison, the queen's suppressed but restless conspiratorial impulses continued uneasily to cast about for satisfaction. With the encouragement and secret counsel of a quixotically chivalrous Englishman, Edward Preston, one of the more talented attorneys of the time, Emma conceived of an audacious plan for Peter's rescue. She would arrange to have Peter smuggled back to Oahu. A canoe manned by two accomplices, Bob Charlton[4] and Peter's old crony Jack Smith, was to cross the Molokai channel after sunset, meet Peter quietly on the beach opposite his cottage, and then, after taking him aboard, strike out across the channel and land him preferably before daybreak at some secluded spot on Oahu's stony windward shore. Precisely when or how the plan was hatched is not at all clear; possibly certain missing letters may have concerned the circumstances of its gestation. According to Emma, citing Preston as her legal authority, Peter needed only to appear boldly in Honolulu among his own people to be safe for the rest of his days. Nobody would dare lay a hand on the returned Kekuaokalani: not because he was to be shunned as a leper and an escapee from the settlement but, as Preston put it, "once you landed here everyone would be in defense of your rights and this would bring things to a climax. He said a stir is now wanted to check the present unscrupulous management of the Government."[5]

A silent journey over dark water: a rendezvous on a deserted beach: a rebel chieftain circumventing the wiles of an upstart Crown: the plot was worthy of that favorite of Peter, the author of *Waverley* and *Rob Roy*. That it was never carried out was neither Peter's fault nor Emma's. Bob Charlton had talked too much. He had been "so indiscreet as to tell many people of the object of his trip, and everyone had it on the tip of their tongues. . . . Of course this rheumor reached the Palace, and that was where I feared for you in case the powers-that-be would overleap the mark and take the law into their own hands."[6]

Perhaps what most bothered Emma was the possibility that Kalākaua, discovering what was afoot, might have Peter clapped into jail like Kepelino and tried on some trumped-up charge of treason, for which the penalty (though it had never been exacted) was death. Despite all dangers, Emma did not abandon the escape plan entirely. If Bob and Jack could not be counted on, at least one other loyal Queenite was ready: Kalawaianui (another quasi-cousin of chiefly ancestry of Peter and Emma) who in addition to the requisite daring and seamanship possessed the desirable good sense. It was Kalawaianui, a quiet worker, who first brought to Emma the news that Plan Number 1 had proved a fiasco: "When Kalawaianui walked into my mauka bedroom silently I could not guess what the issue had been. [I] left him to break the subject, and then felt both relieved and disappointed."[7] However, there was still a hope. Kalawaianui, who was already in league with Peter, even in direct communication with him, offered to stage the rescue operation by himself, without amateur help from outside.

Why the revised scheme was never attempted, or whatever may have caused it to misfire, is not clear. The last surviving letter of the correspondence is that of Emma to Peter, May 10, 1876, in which Kalawaianui first appears along with Emma in the role of arch-conspirator. Between this date and that of Peter's release from Molokai, June 27, 1876, occurred a lapse of approximately seven weeks. Fortunately, from other sources besides the letters, including official records of the Board of Health and items in local newspapers, it is possible by a bit of guesswork to form a flickering picture of Peter's vexatious situation during the last months— the most obscure period truly—of his three Molokai years.

Indeed, it would seem that his status as Kekuaokalani and as a member of the Hawaiian House of Nobles now, at last, began to bring tangible reward. We know from Emma's correspondence of 1876 that various members of the House of Representatives were more or less on her side. If not identifiable as out-and-out Queenites, they were at least anti-D. K.; a few extreme renegades may even have hoped to turn Hawaii into an independent native republic. One or two allusions to this dissident group suggest that several of its weightier members, such as Pilipo and Nawahi, were pulling wires to get Peter discharged so that he could return to Honolulu and swell the ranks of Kalākaua's opposition. Peter himself in late March 1876 mentioned a certain inmate newly arrived at the settlement who reported to him another "rumor at Honolulu that I am to be sent for to take my seat in the Legislature as of yore."[8] Emma replied that she too had heard of such an interesting proposition, but was by no means convinced as yet that anything substantial would come of it:

> So you have heard of the rheumor of your coming to your seat at the Legislature. There is a report of such [a] thing, but because I have not yet found it tenible I have not told you of it, but should I know it as a fact then will write.[9]

Up to May 10 at least, the possibility of Peter's discharge, if it existed, did so in only an early and still amorphous stage. That there was a sound basis for such a rumor is strongly hinted, however, in a newspaper article describing the visit to Kalaupapa of the special "Committee of Thirteen," composed of leading members of the legislature who had been officially charged with the task of investigating "the present condition of the lepers."

Upon landing at Kalaupapa on Saturday, June 20, the blue-ribbon committee was welcomed immediately by "Governor" Ragsdale, who escorted the visitors to Kalawao, "stopping, however, on the way," according to this eye-witness, "to call on Mr. Peter Young Kaeo, who is styled by local courtesy ke aliʻi, the chief. . . . Mr. Kaeo appears about the same as when he went to Molokai to take up his abode, his malady having made no material progress."[10] The Committee of Thirteen then proceeded to the first business on its agenda, comfortably out of doors in the open air (a desirable hygienic precaution) on the *mānienie* lawn in front of Bill Ragsdale's cottage. Before the assembled lepers, Pilipo, serving as chairman, launched the meeting by asking inmates to voice their needs and complaints. How did they like the climate of the peninsula? Was it true that Kalaupapa weather was usually either too hot or too cold? What about food and diet? And apart from ounces and pounds, was the quality up to standard?

After the ventilation of these and other problems and grievances, Pilipo invited all those present who considered themselves to be free of disease to step forward. Because of their obvious condition, a number of the overeager and most appalling of these volunteers had to be rejected on the spot. The Committee of Thirteen then recommended that those remaining, between thirty and forty, should be examined at once by the Board of Health members on hand, assisted by a visiting medical expert from outside the Islands, Dr. Woods, of the U.S.S. *Lackawanna*. On the basis of this cursory, impromptu inspection, only two cases were declared to be doubtful and these were immediately authorized to return to Honolulu. Peter, however, was not included in the lucky pair.

His own clearance for leaving the settlement was granted a little later on the same day. As they were making their way on foot or horseback down the road leading from Kalawao to the landing, the Committee of Thirteen had paused again at Peter's cottage to share in his customary hospitality. Without seeking special medical advice, and acting quite independently of the Board of Health, the committee simply announced to Peter that he was "not a leper," at least not in their present view, and that he could accompany them back to Honolulu on the return trip of the *Kilauea*: "He hastily picked up some of his effects and went down to the beach, there only to be informed by Mr. Wilder that he could not leave except by permission of the Board of Health."

None of the official records illuminate the reasons, medical, political, or whatever, that might have induced the Committee of Thirteen while at Peter's cottage to authorize his immediate discharge. It can be assumed, however, that the committee's abrupt action on Molokai must have had a direct connection with the subsequent formal decision of the Board of Health at its next meeting in Honolulu several days later. In any event, while it was Mr. Wilder who first prevented Peter from embarking for home on the *Kilauea* on the evening of June 20, it was also Mr. Wilder who on June 27 supported the recommendation of Dr. McKibbin that Peter be granted his release and, under proper restrictions, be allowed to take up residence in the capital.[11] In all probability, Peter Kaeo quietly returned from Kalaupapa to Honolulu about June 29–July 1, 1876, if not an image of perfect health, at least as a man who had succeeded, more or less bravely, in surviving a grievous ordeal. Nothing is known of Peter's reception in Honolulu nor of his welcome at Rooke House by Emma, Aunt Fanny, Lucy Peabody, Mrs. Weed, Wikani, and faithful Kahele and Aikoe.

After his release from Molokai, Peter Kaeo quickly fades from view.[12] However, newspaper accounts of the Legislative Assembly of 1878, as well as official records of the sessions, chronicle the fact that the Hon. Peter Y. Kaeo reoccupied his old seat in the House of Nobles, attended almost every one of the meetings, spoke from the floor very seldom, and cast his vote loyally on the side of Kalākaua's opposition. He was especially strong for all measures that would curb what he, along with many other citizens of the day, both native and haole, believed to be the dangerous extravagance of Kalākaua's government. Peter's sole original contribution to the session of 1878 was a motion that a group photograph be made of members of the two legislative chambers. Unfortunately this progressive proposal, an innovation at the time, was roundly defeated by Peter's more economy-minded peers.

Peter's death in 1880, only three months after the death of Fanny Kekelaokalani, cast for a time a shadow upon Emma's later life. What may have been her last allusion to her cousin appears in a New Year's letter she wrote to her old teacher, Mrs. Sarah Rhodes von Pfister, with whom as a child she used to read in the Book of Common Prayer.

> Thanks so much for your kind letter of October received when I was again entered into mourning for my dear Cousin Peter Kekuaokalani. I ought to have answered it before this but really have not had the courage to speak or write of the sorrowful events which have come to me. Not quite three months had passed after my dear Mother was so suddenly taken from me, when the Cousin who had always been as a brother to me also passed, after only five days illness, to the unseen world which now holds all that is dearest. The loneliness of those left behind came over me once more as I seemed to feel well nigh overcome. [The] near presence of child and husband float near to comfort me. I went off to Kauai shortly with my sister-in-law who has been very kind throughout, for a two weeks rest, returning for the Christmas season.[13]

1. Minutes, Board of Health, AH.

2. Peter Y. Kaeo to S. G. Wilder, Molokai, Nov. 16, 1875 (Correspondence, Board of Health, AH).

3. I use the term "nativism" with reservations, because such religious and political movements may include dynamic and creative elements as well as regressive ones. See "Tribal Religious Movements, New," in *Encyclopedia Britannica* (1974), vol. 18, p. 98.

4. Another of Peter Kaeo's obscure "half-caste" English-Hawaiian friends, also a loyal supporter of Queen Emma. Robert Charlton, whose name appears very rarely in written or printed records of the period, was almost certainly a descendant, most probably a son, of Captain Richard Charlton (d. England, 1852), first British consul assigned to the Sandwich Islands. During Charlton's twenty years in his post, he was frequently embroiled in a variety of legal, financial, and personal disputes with the missionary community, especially with certain privy councillors presumed to reflect missionary influence. Modern historians of Hawaii describe Charlton and his opposite number, the American commissioner, John C. Jones, also a "trading consul," as leaders of an "anti-missionary party," together with the High Chief Boki. By 1836, Charlton's high-handed acts had become so offensive to many natives that Kamehameha III wrote a letter to King William IV requesting Charlton's dismissal. The king charged that Charlton treated certain Hawaiian chiefs like criminals, threatened to chop off heads, and spoke of calling in a British man-of-war to bombard the native population. Furthermore, Charlton had violated common rules of decency: "This too is one great thing of his, although he may perhaps be married to his wife according to the laws of Great Britain, his child by a Hawaiian mother is living with us here in these Islands, and he gives full support to such shameful things." (Kamehameha III to King William IV, Honolulu, Nov. 16, 1836 [Foreign Office and Executive (trans. 1836), AH].) In 1843, Charlton was finally replaced as British consul in Hawaii by General William Miller, hero of the Peruvian war of liberation and a man of integrity. If Peter's Queenite friend, the *hapa-haole* Bob Charlton, was Captain Richard Charlton's son, as seems entirely likely, he would have been at least thirty-eight in 1873, a few years older than Peter, but a man of roughly the same generation. Bob Charlton's occupation is not made clear in the correspondence. His presence on Molokai during several official visits to the island, as well as his role as purveyor of political news and gossip, suggests that he may have been a minor functionary of government, perhaps in the Interior Department.

5. See Letter 122.

6. Ibid.

7. Ibid.

8. Letter 120.

9. Letter 121.

10. *Pacific Commercial Advertiser*, June 28, 1876.

11. Two days later, after having been promptly notified of the action of June 27, Peter wrote to Mr. Wilder stating that he was "willing to go down and pass a reexamination, as well as treatment by the medical expert of the Board of Health. In abiding by the conditions . . . , I hope that your Honorable Body will not deprive me of the exercise which I am habituated to, for my health." (Peter Y. Kekuaokalani to S. G. Wilder, June 29, 1876 [Correspondence, Board of Health, AH].)

12. That Peter's presence in Honolulu was noted and disapproved is indicated by a letter to the editor in the *Pacific Commercial Advertiser*, May 4, 1878, headed, "The National Health" and signed "Righteous Indignation": "The number of lepers, in and about Honolulu, is simply appalling; and the total indifference of authorities is an outrage. We know of several well authenticated cases, and complaint of them has been made to the Board of Health, but that august body returns answer that they know all about these cases, but it is not policy to notice them. Cool, is it not?"

13. Emma to Mrs. von Pfister, Honolulu, Jan. 17, 1881 (AH).

Letter 110
Peter to Emma

[Kalaupapa]
March 23, 1875

Queen Emma

Excuse me please for ending so abrubtly in mine of last Evening, but I could not help it. When my Kalo came up in the Ox Cart, about a third was Stolen. I was riding on the Plain when the *Warwick* came in Sight and to her moorings at Sunset. I had ridden to the beach, and when the first Boat came with 4 Sick and the Mail, it was quite dark. As soon as I got my letters and Papers, I rode Home thinking that the Schooner would not leave till the Morning, and [I] was just getting my tea when Ragsdale spoke from the road, saying that she was to leave right away, or as soon as he would send his letters off. So I read yours and answered it in the abrubt way which I did. By your discription, the old Palace grounds is one large open Space.[1] Does D. K. think of improving it? Or what?

I presume that the D. K.s are very anxious to make friends, and as you say, no sooner had you returned D. K.'s call then Mrs D. K. must return yours—"Bah." The ignorant Woman who does not know when and how to make a call—trying to Hookohu.[2] However, she was Hookohu'd. They all Seem to be quite eager to have your Company in their Parties, which is positive that they do not wish to loose what they think they have allready gained. . . .

What ever will become of Albert? He will certainly be in Jail if he keeps on at this rate. If he can only be punished in some way—but not [in] this Jail.

I was reading over Dr Kenedy's [list] and find that he has a good remedy for Cough, named the Prairie Weed. If you can get me a Bottle please do so. I am quite well but I have a strong Cough which comes on just after I retire for the night, and sometimes a little blood. The only Swelling left on my face is over my right Eye, on the fleshy part just below the Eyebrow and above the lid. Since the good Wether has set in, I feel quite well and have resumed my dayly rides on the Plain and Beach.

We hear here that the Sick are so numerous about the town of Honolulu that the Board of Health does not know what to do with them, as the Board of Health does not know how the Government can maintain them all. They have been anticipating on more deaths here, and have the Vacancy filled with more, but the deaths here lately have been fiew. This Story comes from Ragsdale, who asserts that all his Mea Hou are from Headquaters (Wilder). . . .

Ever for you is the Constant Prayer of

KEKUAOKALANI

1. In 1874, the legislature had appropriated $16,000 to improve the royal enclosure, merely preparatory to building a new official palace. A. S. Cleghorn was put in charge of the project, the final result of which was the present 'Iolani Palace, now (1975) in the process of repair and historic restoration. In February 1875, after the return of Kalākaua from the United States, he was quite surprised to find that the modest old royal residence of the last Kamehamehas, a kind of one-story bungalow with a lookout cupola, had been so promptly torn down, leaving nothing but the cellar and foundations.

2. To make patronizing advances.

Letter 111
Emma to Peter

Remember me at your prayers always and at Christmas, as I will of you.

Honolulu
December 16, 1875
7 o'clock morning

Ever dear Coz

Your letter of the 9th has just arrived. I am delighted to hear your eyes are so much better and trust the troublesome itch [and] sores have left you. I confess I do not feel very comfortable at the thought of Nakilau's preparing your poi after constantly handling his dreadfully lepered son. Now his fishing is not so bad, as he is in a measure washed and purified by the salt-water exertions. Punini did tell me here that Koloa is lazy.

December 17

Again the cookhouse is at a standstill till next week, from a dispute between the carpenters as to what timber is necessary to complete the house, making it large enough for storage and cooking. . . .

Prey send the pattern shoe I returned to you lately, and I will buy

the like of it which I mentioned. The Kumau[1] which goes up today—
its name is Makahuna[2] and belonged to our grandmother Kaoanaeha
—is an heirloom so therefore is valuable. Tell your servants to be
careful with it. This Kumau is your own, for it came with the lot of
things from the Maunakea Street yard where you lived. . . .

Your brother has returned today noon from Lahaina and I shall try
to see him soon concerning his property. He has brought down as
friend the worthless husband of the late old Kaunahi, whose name is
Keawe.

Kalani[3] was arrested last week for various causes kept seacret, but
the austensible reason given is debt and selling a revolver belonging
to Moses Kipi (son of Governor Kipi) which was lent Kalani, and
which said fellow sold to a white man (or rather pawned it to a
grog-shop keeper) for payment of glass of spirits. Some story leaks
out that D. K. gave him the pistol to shoot some particular person.
Kalani says this of course alarms the natives [because they] think it is
me. Isaac Davis tried to conceal the story and back D. K. as clear of
suspicion to do me harm or of any evil intent. He (D. K.) went up
to Kahoolawe by Steamer and will return in her on Sunday morning.
Kahunas ordered him to do so, as a kala for Lunalilo's removal to his
new tomb.[4] Kamakini[5] has invited Kia to accompany D. K. to said
Island, which he has consented to do. Piolani grumbles very much and
says if they had left the Government or Throne to the Queen—
because she virtually has it now and besides it is properly and really
hers—then her kino[6] would now be resting in peace. But now, says
she, I am constantly in trouble and heartache.

Ruth went herself after [?her] servant woman Paalua several times
to go and live with her, but she has refused. She (Paalua) came to tell
me the other day the Kahuna (the man's name is Kaiu) who predicted
long ago from Waianae, ˄ "Rising—vanishing—rising—and entirely
vanishing,"[7]˄ has been to her and said I must ˄ remain steadfast in
prayer ˄ in January, for in February next a soverign will be crowned—
either Albert or myself. All the D. K.s are going to die. Predictions
are again rife as to my accession, four having been told me without
each knowing of the other's previous informant.

I will give the old woman at Kona's first. Reverend Pilipo is here
and gives it to me. He says also that Simon Kaai is a strong D. K. He
speaks strongly and openly at public meetings and other assemblages
of people for D. K. and condemns Pilipo as traitor and stirrer up of

trouble and discontent in the Government and country. Simon supports the Reciprocity Treaty and loan of million $ through thick and thin, whereas Pilipo opposes it to the tooth and nail. The entire North Kona are unanimous to elect Pilipo for the coming Legislature, and Honolulu is quite as determined to vote for him! He has concluded to enter for Honolulu so as to be readily and strongly supported as well as pushed on by his constituents at his back.

Pilipo and Kamakau have both written for newspaper articles against the Treaty and loan and other important matters. But Kawainui[8] is intimidated and refuses to print them for fear of D. K.'s party. The public feeling is now determined (natives) to vote for one ticket: Pilipo, Kamakau, Mahelona—there is one name wanting, [as] they do not know as yet who to choose. Ewa returns a man named Mahi who was arrested at the late Royal election for advocating my cause. Nawahi is a brick and predicts openly that only those who are known to Sympathize with Queen Emma, who is for Independance of Kingdome, can hope to be elected for the next Legislature.

Keolaloa[9] is ordered to go to Molokai in 3 weeks, also Aipalena—both lepers. But Mrs Weed tells me that they all (the Sumners) intend to move to Tahiti when Ninito goes home. They have given the management of their property to Mr Cartwright, and so Dowsett is very anoyed about it and has influenced Wilder to order William Sumner's removal to Molokai soon[er] than was intended. . . .

Oh! I must go back to the old woman's predictions. She gave Pilipo and I the request of fasting Monday, Wednesday, and today (Friday) of this week, which we have done strictly, nothing but water passing my lips, and she was to do the same together with a nephew at Kona. We were all to pray that God would please place me on the Hawaiian Throne, and on coming Monday at noon, December 20th, we should have a little feast. A young lamb should be eaten [with] it at noon, and three drops of its heart's blood with three drops of its gaul should be mixed in a glass of brandy, which I am to drink before eating at noon, representing the heart's blood of natives and the ˄gall to represent the passage of time and the movement of events[10]˄ should be turned towards me. . . . On that day the heavens will be cloudless and some wonderful sign appear . . . and something will happen within ten days after our feast (which will happen on the 20th). She says that the tree with all its roots, branches, etc., will be cut off, meaning the D. K. [party] will all die off.

Another man at Palama predicts and sent [me] one of [the] political prisoners to tell me the time is very near for my accession on Throne, and he advises me to travel in January [and] that all the D. K.s are going to die—every one of them. Another Kahuna whom Nahinu of Napoopoo, Kona, Hawaii, has great faith in told Hoapili and Nahinu, the late Representative of that District, not to have anything to do with the D. K.s or accept favour from them, for they all are going to die soon and Queen Emma will reign supreme, living to a good old age over these Islands.

So these are some of the new predictions. A number of murders have happened which you will hear from others.

With all my love
KALELEONALANI

1. Wooden bowl or calabash.

2. "Beloved-hidden-face."

3. Unidentified; but the name is possibly a short form referring to a member of the Lilikalani family of Kauai, prominent supporters of Kalākaua. The elder Kipi was appointed governor of the island of Hawaii (1874–1879) by Kalākaua, in place of Princess Ruth Keʻelikōlani, who had resigned.

4. *Kala* here means to free from evil influence. The body of King Lunalilo had recently been removed from the Royal Mausoleum to where it prominently rests today, in its own private chapel in the yard of Kawaiahao Church. Kalākaua was obliged to go on a journey in order to free (*kala*) himself from this setback by rival kahunas.

5. John Kapena.

6. Spirit; especially in the sense of the spirit of a living person.

7. "... *keea aela, ke nalo wale iho la, ke eeala & ke nalo wele loa akula*. ..." The prediction probably refers to Emma's becoming queen upon marriage ("rising"); the death of Kamehameha IV and the end of his reign ("vanishing"); Emma's eventual accession to the throne ("rising"); her death and possibly the end of the monarchy ("entirely vanishing").

8. Joseph U. Kawainui (?1841–1895), newspaper editor on staff of *Kuokoa* during 1870s; also legislator and public official under Kalākaua and Republic of Hawaii. Member of Privy Council 1874; House of Representatives 1887; Council of State, Hawaiian Republic, 1895. Educated at Royal School, Honolulu; took up newspaper work under H. M. Whitney on *Kuokoa* 1870; established and operated his own newspaper, *Ka Hawaii Pae Aina*, 1878–1892. Held no appointment under Liliʻuokalani. In the 1890s, he became a leader in

the Liberal Party, a native group which advocated that Hawaii become a republic.

9. William Sumner II, also known as Keolaloa, son of Capt. William Sumner, early English settler; see Letter 49, note 2.

10. "... *au o ka mana wa me ka na me*...." The original of the translated clause contains an example of punning word-magic. The word *au*, meaning gall or bile, is homonymous with a word meaning the passing of time, or a movement or succession of temporal events. Hence Emma's drinking of the gall mixed with blood would seem to be a form of celebrating her identification with her people and of prefiguring or symbolizing at the same time her accession as queen.

Letter 112
Emma to Peter

Honolulu
January 22, [1876]

Ever dear Coz

I write to put down all I can say of knicknacs because my letter today was so dreadfully hurried and short, from intruders. ...

D. K. is raising Kapo to great honours. She is lady-in-waiting to Piolani now and was in attendance on her Christmas day when Mrs Cleghorn's baby[1] was christened in church, and consequently sat in my pew together with Fred Beckley's (Chamberlain) wife and Langhorn's daughter. Of course you have read the accounts of that baptism and the reception and breakfast at Ihikapukalani,[2] on the week after. Piolani gave a public reception at Ihikapukalani to the ladies of town.

5 o'clock evening

I see there is just time to send even this begining of a letter. ...
Mr and Mrs Markham (formerly shipping master) had a row over a looking-glass which he wished to move down to his office at armory, to be in use for D. K. when he went into that office to change his dress, which he often did to drill and parade his volenteer troops. She objected to it and broke the mirror in pieces, and he sent her to Station House today, but Smithies bailed her out.

In haste yours
KALELEONALANI

January 25, 1876

The boy loitered so long on the way down that this letter missed the *Warwick*.

There has been numerous addresses from candidates to the lower house of Parliament, given at nearly all the valleys from Moanalua to Maunalua.[3] David Malo[4] comes out strong in charging and abusing the powers-that-be of unfair management of the Government. He spoke at Market the other day favouring a new election of a Soverign and a Republican form of Government. I am very sorry to hear that sentiment inculcated into the Hawaiian mind. It will make us like shiftless France in time, if such is the case. He is so plausible that I fear he may get in. A great many people at Manoa where he lives firmly believes he is honestly of this [our] country's side, because Malo has been decieved and disappointed both as to promises of Government appointments by D. K. But the majority of Natives mistrust him as using abusive language for a cover to get in the Legislative body of '76, and then come out strongly in favour of all D. K. measures.

Robert Charlton has been helping Kamakau, and therefore D. K. sent for him into Palace to ask him not to help our cause, but to help his boy Lilikalani through. Bob told him the boy was a very unsatisfactory thing to risk one's welfare onto his shoulders [and] to bear and fight for. Besides he was going to Lahaina with Preston.[5] D. K. persuaded him to stay and told him to go to Preston and say, "You are to stop here, giving *my* name," said he. But he did not wish to stop for all the D. K.s, so he has gone to Maui with Preston. Preston wants to get in so as to confound the Attorney General, William Castle,[6] a mear boy.

[KALELEONĀLANI]

---

1. Princess Victoria Kawekiu Ka'iulani Lunalilo, usually called Ka'iulani (b. Honolulu, 1875; d. Honolulu, 1899); only child of Princess Miriam Likelike and Archibald S. Cleghorn; niece of King Kalākaua and Lili'uokalani (Mrs. John O. Dominis). Ka'iulani's mother died in 1887 and three years later, at age fifteen, she was sent to England for her education (1890–1897); Queen Lili'uokalani proclaimed her heir apparent on Mar. 9, 1891. At her christening on Christmas Day, 1875, she was given the name "Lunalilo" at the request of the late king's father, Kana'ina, in order to suggest her eligibility for the throne. The *Hawaiian Gazette*, Dec. 20, 1875, reminded readers that "This is the first birth that has occurred in the present royal family since the accession." The reference later to "Langhorn" (?Cleghorn) may be an

example of Emma's word-play and a sly allusion to a daughter of Cleghorn by some other woman than Miriam Likelike.

2. House built by Kamehameha IV for Queen Emma near the site of the present (1975) Archives of Hawaii. Ihikapukalani was occupied by Kalākaua and Kapiʻolani from time to time during the period between the razing of the old palace and the construction of ʻIolani Palace.

3. The expression dates back to 1859 when the ancient Kona District of Oahu was officially renamed the Honolulu District, with boundaries reaching "from Maunalua to Moanalua inclusive, and the islands not included in any other district, to be styled Honolulu District." (*The Sites of Oahu*, comp. by Elspeth P. Sterling and Catherine C. Summers [Honolulu: Bishop Museum, 1962], vol. 1, book vi, p. 1.)

4. David Malo, nephew of the Hawaiian historian; for main note, see Letter 51, note 11.

5. Edward Preston (b. London, 1831; d. Honolulu, 1890), a close personal friend and adviser of Queen Emma; attorney, legislator, jurist. At first an open critic of Kalākaua's policies, he later held important offices under the regime, especially after passage of the Reciprocity Treaty and with the growing prosperity of the sugar industry. Emigrated from England to Australia and New Zealand 1852; practiced law at Christchurch. Arrived in Hawaii 1870; addmitted to bar 1871. Member of commission to codify and revise criminal laws of Kingdom 1874, 1880. Member of House of Representatives from Maui 1876; served briefly as Attorney General (1878); also commissioner of Crown Lands and member of Board of Health. Member of House of Nobles 1880, 1882; member of Kalākaua's Privy Council 1883. Appointed associate justice of supreme court 1885; served until his death in 1890.

6. William Richards Castle (b. Honolulu, 1849; d. Honolulu, 1935), attorney, legislator, financier; attorney general under Kalākaua Feb. to Nov. 1876. Son of Samuel Northrup Castle and Mary Tenney Castle, members of Eighth Company of American Congregational missionaries (arrived 1837). Educated at Oahu College (Punahou School); Oberlin College; Harvard College; Columbia University (L.L.B., 1873). According to his lengthy obituary, *Star Bulletin*, June 6, 1935, he "returned to Honolulu at the behest of King Kalakaua to accept the position of attorney general." Member of House of Representatives 1878, 1886, 1887, 1888. In later 1880s, he was prominent in the affairs of the Independent Party, along with such anti-D.K. stalwarts as Pilipo and Nawahi. Member of the Hawaiian League 1887, almost entirely a *haole* (but not yet annexationist) organization, favoring "Constitutional, representative Government, in fact as in form, in the Hawaiian Islands." Member of the inner council of the Committee of Safety whose representatives persuaded U. S. Minister Stevens in 1893 to provide "protection or assistance" by landing troops "to prevent the destruction of American life and property." One of the commissioners sent to Washington, D. C., Jan.–Feb., 1893, to seek annexation.

Letter 113
Emma to Peter

Representatives of 1876   Honolulu
Henry Waterhouse[1]   February 4, 1876
Kalaukoa[2]
S. M. Kamakau[3]
Ed Lilikalani[4]

Ever dear Coz

Your letter of January 28th was received on the 2nd, election day. Two of our members have been elected for Honolulu, that is, S. M. Kamakau and Kalaukoa, and Henry Waterhouse had the highest number of votes. I do not know for a certainty what his political platform is, but am told he is vehemantly against the treaty and loan (that is, I mean his father J. T. Waterhouse is) as injurious to their trade as retail merchants. Being importers of English goods they trade at a disadvantage and loss, whilst the Americans profit by the treaty.

The Government Treasury is low down in its finances. Some say there is no money at all, and lately J. T. Waterhouse demanded the payment of his hotel bonds[5] from the Government, because there is such mistrust of present management. The bondholders of Hawaiian Hotel bonds have never received any account of the management of said fund, and not getting a very satisfactory explanation as to the receipts and investments of said fund, Waterhouse sold his interests to other parties, thereby forcing the Government to pay over his dues. [This] at the present junction of affairs pushes the Government in a sore fix. Therefore Henry Waterhouse goes in as an anti-Treaty-and-Loan man (he is the long-necked son—natives call him ai oeoe).[6] We may count him on our side as opposing the Treaty and Loan.

Kalaukoa is a young man of the labouring class who earns his living down in the town on the streets—such as boatboy, dreyman, cartboy, etc., etc., but he was one of the speakers who cheered and encouraged the crowd to back me on the Royal election in 1874 at Court House yard. He is the most popular candidate, together with Waterhouse, but as to stability and information the town look to S. M. Kamakau. They look to him for the offensive and defensive arguments on the people's—which means the country's—side.

Lilikalani is D. K.'s own mouthpiece in the Legislature—a fufu.[7] He choaks with fright at addressing a crowd, but D. K. [being]

confident in his own past awkwardnesses and ultimate success, to the very pinnicle of honor and grandure through perseverance and ambition, intends to push this young fellow through. He eventually no doubt *will* succeed in making a man of him, because practice is the only way to make perfect anything, and a begining has to be made.

So you see that D. K. has developed a great many points of character all through keeping on to speak at meetings, etc., and moving in company till now he actually leads. To be sure, he is not all we want, still he has made his name by his own determined effort. So therefore we must do likewise. The D. K.s have been frightened of their lives for two weeks past, and summoned all the military of town into Palace to guard him. Everyone has been armed [with] firearms of all sorts, constantly loaded. He [hired] the troops so as to secure their votes for his ticket, which was Lilikalani, Charles Judd, Kahanu the shipping agent, and Kakina. Those were the last names settled by them, but [thereupon] they were all rejected by [the] people, [though] Lilikalani got in by tremendously heavy bribes of cash and suit of clothes—had wollen shirts, white trowsers and cap, free lunch and tea at Honuakaha, etc. Mahelona has got in at Ewa and Koii lost place there. Several hundred dollars were spent there and barrels of salmon, rum, etc., were spent there and [at] Waianae. Naukana[8] has got in at Waialua again. J. Naili[9] is returned for Koolau Loa, and Palenapa[10] got Koolau Poko. Naili they say is on our side. We hear this morning that Nakaleka[11] has the most votes at Lanai. I wonder if Kaina[12] has lost his votes at Molokai. . . .

The town has kept in a state of frightful anxiety amongst the whites as to an uprising amongst the Natives upon D. K., he himself circulating the report and strengthening it by keeping all the troops on guard upon himself and family. The haoles are awfully disgusted about him. He wants to throw a suspicion upon me and the people as conspiring to overturn the D. K.'s off throne. Gibson has come out with an article upon same tone. D. K. went off to the English man-of-war the afternoon before election and asked the Captain to send off his men armed on shore, whenever they should see or hear from him of that event, [and] to shoot the natives for rising against him. Ninito told me this. She heard [it] from Ruth direct, who tried to persuade him to go into Palace as the only safe place that night, and to await the election day with fear and trembling, as war was to be opened that day.

Now all this was a great scare and fright on D. K.'s part, and he ingeniously plans to bring about a row so as to seize and kill me and then secure a peaceful reign. He thought too that by so doing the people will be intimidated and thus secure the election of his candidates to Parliament. But the foreigners are so thorougherly frightened at that threat of Natives [as] in 1874 to burn the town, that they and Gibson (as strong as any) at last prevaled upon D. K. not to make any shew of military overawing the people at their election—else they will rise and destroy all lives and property, and kill him as well. So he consented and there was no trouble whatever. Everyone was allowed to vote as they pleased. Restraint being removed, they all voted against the D. K. ticket, save the troops, who could not well elect other than Lilikalani, as they were overlooked and kept under guard.

The beauty of the whole thing is that the people never planed to attack or shed blood that day. The excitement only came from the D. K.s, because they wished to bring things to a climax and so secure their Throne—which they quite forgot to do by [the failure to publish] the amendment of article 22 of the Constitution.[13]

Mr C. C. Harris,[14] F. Judd, D. K. and family, is very troubled over the entrance of Kamakau, Mahelona, Pilipo, Nawahi, Kauai. Preston opposes the Loan and he is thought to succeed at Lahaina as Representative there.

Your $20 is in charge of mate Kamakakoko's hands.[15] Paneku's duaghter, Kahoiwai, has got another boy—born here night before election. Your brother has sold all his furnature in the valley for $80 to Kaiaiki, steward of the *Murray*. Ninito and husband goes to Tahiti on Monday, and Keolaloa has made over all his property to his brother John Sumner. I think both he and Aipalena will shortly go up to Kalawao. Cartwright has got the management of their property.

With love and haste
KALELEONALANI

1. Henry Waterhouse (b. Tasmania, 1845; d. Honolulu, 1904), commission merchant, sugar factor, legislator; son of John Thomas Waterhouse (b. England, 1816; d. Honolulu, 1885), leading Honolulu merchant and naturalized American citizen who arrived in Hawaii 1850. Henry Waterhouse held political office under the monarchy, Provisional Government, and Republic of Hawaii: as member of House of Representatives, Oahu, 1876; House of Nobles 1887–1888; Advisory Council of Provisional Government 1893; Hawaiian Senate, Third District, 1895–1898. Whatever their sympathies may have been in the 1870s for the royalist cause, both Waterhouses eventually became supporters of the annexation movement.

2. A. P. Kalaukoa, member of House of Representatives, Oahu, 1876, 1887, 1888.

3. Samuel Manaiakalani Kamakau (b. Mokuleia, Oahu, 1815; d. Honolulu, 1876), Hawaiian historian, writer, legislator. Royalist and supporter of the Kamehameha Dynasty, Kamakau was first elected to the House of Representatives 1851; served in most sessions until his death in office 1876. Educated at Lahainaluna Seminary, Maui, 1833–1837; later teaching assistant. Member of group (1841–1847) organized to obtain data and preserve knowledge of history of the Hawaiian people; Kamehameha III, president; Sheldon Dibble, secretary; Samuel M. Kamakau, treasurer. Served as chief assistant to Rev. Sheldon Dibble in his compilation of materials used in *A History of the Sandwich Islands* (Lahaina, Maui: Lahainaluna Seminary, 1843). During the 1870s and 1880s, Kamakau worked as an informant with Abraham Fornander on the *History of the Polynesian Race*, 3 vols. (London: 1878–1885). Kamakau was a voluminous writer for the native newspapers, not only on historical matters but also on local issues and Hawaiian politics. Selections from his historical writings have been translated and published in two recent volumes: *Ruling Chiefs of Hawaii*, trans. and ed. by Mary Kawena Pukui, Martha W. Beckwith, Dorothy B. Barrère (Honolulu: Kamehameha Schools Press, 1961); *Ka Poʻe Kahiko: The People of Old*, trans. by Mary Kawena Pukui, ed. by Dorothy B. Barrère (Honolulu: Bishop Museum Press, 1964).

4. Edward K. Lilikalani (?1849–1917), legislator and supporter of Kalākaua; son of Judge G. W. Lilikalani, district magistrate for many years at Koloa, Kauai. Educated at Oahu College (Punahou School) 1873–1876; entered immediately on political career. Member of House of Representatives for numerous sessions 1876–1886; Privy Council member 1883; 1st lieutenant in Kalākaua's military guard; an active member of Kalākaua's Board of Genealogy; colonel on staff of Liliʻuokalani 1892. Member of Territorial House of Representatives 1905; unsuccessful candidate for Senate on Republican ticket 1914.

5. The government-subsidized Hawaiian Hotel, built in 1871 at a cost of about $150,000, opened its forty-two sleeping rooms, verandahs, and gardens to guests in 1872. Established with legislative support as a "joint expenditure of the citizens and the Government," the hotel's primary purpose was to stimulate tourism and help bolster up the Hawaiian economy. John Thomas Waterhouse, merchant and father of Henry Waterhouse, was one of the prominent critics of the government's management of the hotel's shaky finances. Waterhouse felt that the government had not lived up to the terms of its agreement with bondholders: "Our money was lent in good faith," he charged at a meeting of anxious bondholders, Feb. 27, 1876, "... and this attempt to withhold nearly $\frac{2}{3}$ of the profits now in hand, declaring only a 3 and $\frac{1}{2}$ per cent dividend, covering upward of four years when they have ten per cent in hand, is a breach of faith with us, and a stepping stone to repudiation." A compromise was eventually worked out with the minister of finance.

6. Literally, "long neck."

7. A lightweight or "softie."

8. S. N. Naukana, member of House of Representatives 1860, 1870, 1874, 1876.

9. J. L. Naili, member of House of Representatives 1870, 1876.

10. George Barenaba ("Palenapa"), member of House of Representatives 1856, 1860, 1862, 1876.

11. J. Nakaleka, legislator from Molokai, first elected to House of Representatives 1876; served in numerous sessions under Kalākaua and briefly under Liliʻuokalani. Returned to serve three more sessions in House of Representatives 1904, 1907, 1909, after Hawaii became a United States Territory.

12. L. Kaina, member of House of Representatives 1876.

13. At the legislative session of 1874, several proposed amendments to the constitution concerned the succession of the Crown, as regulated by article 22 of the Constitution of 1864. One proposal (which never reached a vote) would have confirmed the succession in the Kamehameha line, though "its passage would involve extraordinary absurdities," according to the *Pacific Commercial Advertiser*, May 9, 1874, "confirming the Crown as it does in an extinct line. The better way, and the one we presume will be followed, will be the substitution of a new Article confirming the crown to the present reigning family." On May 20, an amendment to article 22 was passed which confirmed "the Crown to [King Kalākaua], and failing his heirs, then to Prince Leleiohoku." But the same amendment also attempted to determine the "remote succession," noted the *Pacific Commercial Advertiser*, May 22, and "apparently anticipating things unnecessarily, desires to fix the succession irrevocably in two other branches of the Royal Family. While by no means objecting to the personages indicated for the remote succession, we fail to appreciate the policy attempted to be pursued." The proposed amendment to article 22 was eventually defeated through a parliamentary ruse, noted by the *Pacific Commercial Advertiser*, Jan. 15, 1876: "Constitutional Amendments.— Through the failure to publish the amendments to the Constitution three months prior to the election for representatives, as provided by article 80, those amendments (proposed at the last session) must be deemed to have become void." Emma apparently considered the defeat of the amendment in its final form a satisfactory rebuke to the D. K.s.

14. Charles Coffin Harris (b. Portsmouth, N. H., 1822; d. Honolulu, 1881); attorney, cabinet minister, judge. Leading member of government of Kalākaua in which he served as chief justice and chancellor; presided over Kepelino's trial for treason. Member of House of Representatives during 1850s; attorney general 1862–1865; member of Privy Council 1863–1874; House of Nobles 1864–1872; minister of finance under Kamehameha V 1865–1869; minister of foreign affairs 1869–1872; 1st associate justice of supreme court 1874–1877; chief justice and chancellor 1877–1881.

15. Probably mate of one of the interisland vessels.

Letter 114
Emma to Peter

Honolulu
February 11, 1876

Ever dear Coz

In a hurry as usual I am today, from Ninito's departure to Tahiti, so cannot send some things I wanted to.

Ere this you will have heard of Reverend Pilipo's success as the Representative for North Kona—South Kona has to have a fresh election because the votes are tied between Simon Kaai and Kamauoha.[1] The former is supposed to be on our side, but [it] is not certain. Moanauli tells me that Pilipo is likely to be arrested for debt,[2] because the debt was due last month and not a cent has he paid of it. Moanauli is extremely anxious to get him clear, so as he may sit in the coming Legislature. This debt (if I have not already told you before) is a sum of $1,000 he borrowed 3 years ago which with interest now amounts to $1,200, and Kauai borrowed from same fund $200, and he also has not paid his. So the Government is working on the Kaumakapili Trustees to imprison him for debt.

The news of the week has been the non-election of Waimea, Kauai.[3] Kuapuu, Isack, and the circut judge Miohi arrived on the 7th from Kauai. They would not disclose to the anxious people who had flocked to the wharf to know who had been elected Representatives. They said all they know is that Judge Waua has been returned for Hanalei. However, they went straight up to the Palace and told D. K. their false statements—that because Kauai had used a threat, they the judges of election were aprehensive of a great and dreadful row. [Therefore they] took the first ship for Honolulu, [thus] closing the election, which never happened at all. They three were the inspectors of the election box. They reported here that Kauai had said he would break the ballot box if Kuapuu ma[4] would not give back to the people their tax paper entitling them to vote, and there would be haunaele.[5]

But today I received a letter from Kauai, and he says that D. K. had written to Kuapuu ma to do all they can to prevent Kauai from being returned for that part, and to get Isack Hart in, because (says D. K.) Kauai wants to dethrone him—which is just the words Simon Kaai used about Pilipo to natives. Two or three days before election Kauai asked Kuapuu ma to return the tax papers to the several owners. They said no, and more—that no native shall be allowed to put in their vote unless they hold the tax paper in their hands at the time, which they shall never give them if they should vote for Kauai. Whereupon Kauai replied, "Very well, if you persist in doing things wrong and unlawfully, then I will take the ballot box in my hand," whereupon these inspectors of election took fright and sailed for Honolulu for fear of bloodshed. You will see some mention in today's papers—. . . .

A Japanese man-of-war[6] has just come in, and your papers consequently are not sewed together. . . .

Albert has now sold some stones of the wall round his yard without my consent, and so I am going to sell them all—over his sale—in order to secure the money. He is trying to give me as great a trouble as he could possibly do.

Last Friday the 4th, D. K. and wife went to bid goodbye to Ninito, and the subject of Reciprocity Treaty and Loan of a Million was touched upon. He said the natives were stupid, so therefore opposed them, but they could not affect either [measure] because they are passed and must go into effect. Then after that he goes to U. S. A., to the Centennial in July, and on to all the Governments of Europe.[7] Then [he will] go through the Red Sea on to India and return by way of Tahiti. Now just see what he plans to spend the Government money for—only for his personal gratification and vanity.

When Preston went up to Lahaina, Bob Charlton went with him, and at the last moment again another effort was made by D. K. to bribe him with $300 not to go with Preston but remain and push Lilikalani through. Bob would not back out but went to Maui. D. K. was on wharf at the time but gave him a very cool parting salutation.

When they got to Lahaina Mr Fornander[8] cautioned Preston as to Kamakini's doublefacedness. However, they breakfasted with Governor Makini and at table Emma his wife observed to Bob that through the native newspapers they had read of his exertions to get S. M. Kamakau into Parliament [in] 1876, and how Bob had opposed Lilikalani, Kiha, and others. Her husband the Governor remarked also, "Yes, the King is very angry with you for it, too. He does not like such behaviour on your part."

It seems also that D. K. and the ministers wished Preston to run for Lahaina, but at the last moment they sent up word not to help Preston through at all. So consequently Kamakini the Governor and the Sugar interests worked against him. But Bob was roused and he exerted himself on behalf of his haku haole[9] Preston and won the day, in spite of Governor Kamakini's cheat and fraud [in the matter] of Government permit to voters. He gave people two and three tax receipts, so one man votes 3 times, which Bob detected many times on Election day. Bob ridiculed Joseph Kawainui's brother's speech and brought down tremendous cheerings for himself.

There was a fire in Ihikapukalani on election day. A soldier laid his cigar down on a matrass in drawing-room and burnt a matrass up, nearly burning the house down, but [it was] put out in time. Last night the cookhouse at barracks took fire and the fire engines put it out. Only one soldier was at the gate and could not call any help, so fired off his musket to give the alarm, and thereby neighbourhood and Palace came to his help.

Joseph Kawainui and Lalauli is entirely out of D. K.'s good graces, and they hate him now. They oppose the Treaty and Loan—that is one reason why.

In haste
KALELEONALANI

1. K. Kamauoha eventually won the contest; member of House of Representatives, 1876, 1878. After his defeat, Simon Kaai was appointed to the House of Nobles.

2. Probably a reference to a promissory note and mortgage in the amount of $1,000 held by Abigail K. Drew, dated May 8 and May 28, 1875, and not "three years ago," as Emma believed. She was perhaps confusing the date of mortgage of 1875 held by Mrs. Drew with an earlier promissory note and mortgage held by James I. Dowsett. Pilipo's indebtedness to Mrs. Drew lasted several years and was not settled until September 1880, when some of Pilipo's South Kona property was sold at public auction.

3. Honolulu newspaper editors and their readers had difficulty reconstructing the disorderly election episode at Waimea, island of Kauai. There was general agreement on two points: first, the legal requirement that voters must show their tax receipts should be abolished; second, the election inspectors at Waimea, Judge Miohi, Kuapuu, and Isaac Hart, had conspired to rig the election in favor of one of themselves, and against Kauai, the anti-D. K. candidate. *Hawaiian Gazette*, Feb. 9, 1876, stated that the "facts were simply these: J. Kauai, the opposition candidate, who had the support of the influential foreigners, and would have been elected by a large majority, made a threat a short time previous to election day that if the voters were not allowed to deposit their ballots without producing tax receipts, he would seize the ballot box. This of course was foolish and unjustifiable, but it did not by any means warrant the Inspectors in their subsequent conduct. The Inspectors sent for the Sheriff of the Island, Mr. Wilcox, who went to Mr. Kauai and requested him to recall the threat, but he persisted in it. The Sheriff, however, told the Inspectors to open the polls, assuring them that he was prepared to preserve

the peace.... Inspectors instead put up notice postponing the election. The truth of the matter was they saw that Mr. Kauai was sure of an election, and they determined to prevent this by any means in their power.... They thought their hostility to an anti-government candidate would be endorsed by the powers that be, but they were mistaken. They were severely reproved in a letter from Moehonua, Minister of the Interior."

4. Kuapuu and his followers.

5. Riot.

6. Pressing social obligations, entailed by the arrival on Feb. 11 of H.I.J. Majesty's steam corvette *Tsukuba*, had prevented Emma and her household from completing her regular task of sewing together Peter's newspapers. A vessel of 1,003 tons, the *Tsukuba*, Capt. T. Y. Ito, carried 25 officers, 36 cadets, 16 marines, and 229 seamen, accompanied by three instructors in English, J. W. Austin, E. Yeo, and W. Woodward. An item on "The Mikado's Marine," *Hawaiian Gazette*, Feb. 16, echoing an article in the *San Francisco Chronicle*, noted that the earliest Japanese man-of-war to visit Honolulu and Californian seaports had been much jeered at, but "not so the *Tsukuba Ken*, a fine example of the progress of the Japanese nation."

> In 1860, the *Kandinmarrah*, the first naval vessel of Japan that had ever been permitted to cross the ocean, and about the first craft of the modern Japanese navy, anchored in this harbor [San Francisco]. She was not a formidable ship, and the old tars of European and American navies found much in her appearance and the conduct of her officers and crew to criticise and laugh at. The second visitor comes after an interval of fifteen years, and affords an opportunity of studying the remarkable progress that wonderful nation has made during this short interval in adapting herself to the requirements of western civilization.

7. Kalākaua's tour of the globe did not materialize until 1881.

8. Abraham Fornander (b. Island of Oland, Sweden, 1812; d. Hawaii, 1887), newspaper editor and jurist; linguist, ethnologist, and pioneer expert on Polynesian race, Hawaiian language, and unwritten literature. Arrived first in Hawaii 1838; left on whaling cruise and returned 1842. Associated with Dr. T. C. B. Rooke in a coffee plantation at Koloa, Kauai; worked as surveyor; in California during gold rush of 1849. Married a Hawaiian chiefess, Pinao Alanakapu of Molokai. Editor of *Polynesian*, official newspaper of the Hawaiian government 1860–1864. Member of Privy Council 1864; appointed judge of circuit court, island of Maui, 1864. Appointed inspector of schools by Kamehameha V, 1865; reappointed circuit judge of Maui 1871. In 1878 published first volume of his compendious researches on Polynesian peoples, with special relation to language and literature of Hawaiians, *An Account of the Polynesian Race*, 3 vols. (London: 1878–1885).

9. His white lord and master.

Letter 115
Emma to Peter

Honolulu
February 23,1876

Ever dear Coz

Yours of the 13th arrived yesterday but being one of my busy days [I] had to attend my class of English teaching for native women,[1] and intruders, callers, etc., kept happening in all day.

Your horse again fails its appointment. It seems my man has sent it to Koolau, but by next *Warwick* you shall not fail to see it. The pig which you say Kamaka pointed out as belonging to you from *Warwick*, is true, but I quite forgot to note it on list. The onions in bag is from Joe Keaoa. He bought it of a Chinaman who had them ready to set out in a new onion patch, so they are the sort the Chinamen use for replanting.

I am rejoiced to think the white people are growing disgusted with D. K., as they discover D. K.'s shortcomings. They knew them well enough before but was carried away by D. K., Dominis, Buff, and Cleghorn's and Gibson's representations to the contrary. Serves them well right. We have been made to suffer for their greed and covetous desires of our Islands. So Mr Meyer also is disgusted with D. K. and finds his headstrong, worthless, spendthrift habits out at last.

D. K.'s debt must be somewhere near a $100,000. He is counting upon the Reciprocity Treaty and Loan to wipe out his debts and pave his way on to the satisfying of his every extravigence of shew and revenge against the natives.

You astonish me sometimes with the amount of news that reaches you, and then we get back from you [hearing it] for the first time, such as Mrs Bishop's letter to Kanakaole. Now I believe every word of it is true, [just] as you have written, because she has said so here, before they left for America,[2] and all you say corresponds. They are her sentiments entirely, and what he says of his election—D. K.'s efforts to urge him—is also quite true. I believe I have written of them before to you.

The Mea Hou that the natives gave you of my receiving a letter from Queen Victoria by hand of Hon. Capt. Hare[3] to release the Lepers and [hold] a new election of Soverign is all false—no truth whatever in it, but what Leilii says is quite true.

Leleiohoku wrote a letter to Moanauli on the day he left for Hawaii trying to frighten him from giving Reverend Pilipo a helping hand. He said that it was out of aloha for him lest some evil befall him that he (this Moo[4]) writes. . . . Moanauli consulted Mr Preston about how to reply and whether Pilipo can be arrested for debt and he says no.

In haste [with] love
KALELEONALANI

1. The classes were organized by the Ladies' Guild of St. Andrew's Cathedral. Emma's earlier letter mentioning the classes is missing, but a memorandum among her miscellaneous notes supplies a few details: "We have a women's English class and men's also at our priest's house. The two numbers 100 now. [Kalehua's] wife says Dr. Trousseau's mistress who is in one of the classes told them that the Doctor praises the effort very much on our part, says the foreigners all like it, but he heard D. K.'s party looks with suspicion on the thing as an act of Treason on my part to get the people to stir up a rebellion. Ridiculous people they are. Why they owe their seat to my pacific attempts upon the people. One word from me will pau [finish off] our independence." The implication is that Emma believed that if she had wished to do so, she could have brought about the annexation of Hawaii by appeal to a foreign power, England.

2. The Bishops left Hawaii for San Francisco May 29, 1875. After a leisurely European tour and visits in eastern parts of the United States, they returned to Hawaii late in 1876. During their absence, Mrs. Bishop apparently corresponded on political matters with her retainer Kealiikanakaole, who then relayed news of the Bishops to his Molokai friends; see Letter 105, note 4, for earlier mention of Kealiikanakaole.

3. H.B.M.'s gunboat *Myrmidon*, the Hon. Richard Hare (1836–1903), commander, arrived at Honolulu Nov. 28, 1875, after a voyage of thirty-one days from Esquimault, Vancouver Island. Capt. (later Rear Admiral) Hare was the second son of an Irish peer, William, second Earl of Listowel (1801–1871). The *Myrmidon* was a steam vessel of 877 tons, 200 horsepower, carrying 4 guns.

4. "Lizard" or "lizard god." Another satiric nickname for Prince Leleiohoku. The word also conveys the idea of succession as in a genealogical line. Emma's scornful references to Leleiohoku reveal her knowledge that the young and gifted Leleiohoku was a serious obstacle to her ambition to reach the throne. The prince's early death in 1877 may well have revived Emma's hopes, as is implied in an interesting comment of British Commissioner Wodehouse: "It is useless to disguise the fact that the death of the Prince is a most serious blow to the new Dynasty, and although it was immediately followed by the Proclamation as Successor to the King, should he die without issue, of his Sister the Princess Lydia who is married to an American but is childless, few believe, that in such event, she would be allowed to ascend the

vacant Throne without a struggle, the result of which might, and in the absence of Foreign intervention, probably would end in the elevation of Her Majesty the Queen Dowager Emma, if she wished it, to the Throne of Hawaii. . . . Queen Emma is much, and deservedly, beloved by the mass of the Hawaiian people, and they consider that she has an undoubted right to succeed the present Sovereign." (Wodehouse to Derby, no. 5, confidential, April 26, 1877, Public Record Office [London], Foreign Office 58/155; quoted in Kuykendall, *The Hawaiian Kingdom: 1874–1893*, pp. 196–197.)

Letter 116
Emma to Peter

Honolulu
March 6, 1876

Ever dear Coz

Your letter of the 28 February has arrived together with one signed by Enoki and Reverend Kaholokahiki.[1] Prey tell them that I have had no time for answering their letter from pressure of appointments and illness since its arrival, but will do so by [the] next schooner.

There are no ripe string beans yet in the market fit to plant, but I send some for your table cooking. I send also a silverplated candlestick and will have the glass stand fitted with a tin socket if it can be made, and [will] send [when I get] another chanse. I regrett Aikoe was so stupid as to let your box go unmarked. It is always the case, unless I see to every article myself things always go wrong.

Alex left no written Will. I suppose I must have signed a paper of release of dower—else the Government could not have given me an annuity—but I do not recollect, for I was then utterly unbusinesslike, and besides had no thought of any one thing in this world save the memory and lifeless form of my very dear husband, the man to whom unto God I had plighted my oath of fidelity until death us do part. In my dreams last night Alex came to me but looking so ill and poorly. He was very gentle and tender and oh it was [as] if of yore. Alas, I woke to loose his presence.

Oh! God's ways are mysterious and I must bear his decree. We must praise him though blindly for all he does is good in his Will.

Before Lunalilo died, Mr Crabbe shewed me the account book of Crown lands in Dominis's hands, making out the receipts to be only $17,000 annually, but since D. K. has come on Throne, Dominis and Stanley have raised the rentals and it is nearly half as much again. . . .

Your brother was taken to Station house on Ash Wednesday the 1st of this month for fighting (whilst under the influence of liquer) in the streets at Paalua's house. They let him off however with a warning not to make a row. Next day I went to see him and he was all smiles. He had however said that he had vowed never to see or know me again, but I took him by surprise and he could not help himself. . . .

I am having my portrait painted by a young Dane[2] who has been here about six months, and did Mrs Pratt's for her, whereupon the D. K.s hearing of it would not have theirs done "after the commonality," as they said. So Mr Pratt urged me more strongly than ever to have mine taken, which was begun on your birthday. It rained and thundered dreadfully, but the artist commenced and went on for two hours at the sketch. His studio is on our front verandah, before the drawing room windows. The space is narrow and throws me quite close upon the painter's easel. This portrait painting is going to take two months painting. He says that now he will not paint the D. K.s if they should ask even for it, because they have been ugley to him about it heretofore. It takes two to four sitting every day. . . .

A petition[3] has been signed by many influential haoles of town, pressing D. K. to retrench, but it is so covered over with the plausible subject that Repopulation is the salvation of Hawaii nei, and if D. K. does not stir himself to get people from India, then the decrease of Hawaiians will go on so fast that the European powers will abandon their recognition of our Independance. It is all gotten up by Gibson as a pressure upon D. K. He got our Bishop[4] to sign it and to urge me to sign it, [but] I refused point blanc, telling him it was a very impudent impertinant document, and were I in D. K.'s place, I would have every signer of the document notified to leave the Kingdome at a certain time soon.

It seems they took the paper which was presented by a committee to D. K., and he laid it before the privy Council. Mr C. C. Harris and F. Judd opposed it strongly. Finally it was referred to the ministers to reply, but Harris drew up the thing, which was telling the signers that they must mind their own business, and that their proposal shall not be acted on. Now the reason why Harris has opposed it so strongly is that (one at least of his reasons) if D. K. should listen to it, then Gibson will grow in power here and he will fall under Gibson's directions. The other [reason] is that the objects are really good ones, but improperly presented, and if this should be carried into effect, then the people will be strengthened by new infusion of fresh blood and we increase and multiply, which is contrary to what the Americans wish. Their great joy will be to see us all die out, and the country get into debt irrevocably. . . .

I must close. The ship goes now. Here is a messenger for my letter. ∧ Ever lasting love—∧

KALELEONALANI

1. S. N. Kaholokahiki, Protestant clergyman at Kalaupapa during mid-1870s. The letter perhaps referred to conditions at the settlement. In 1874, Kaholokahiki had written letters to the Board of Health and also to Kalākaua urging that Dr. Akana be permitted to treat patients.

2. Eiler Jorgensen (or Jurgensen), "a Norwegian gentleman now in the city," according to the *Pacific Commercial Advertiser*, Sept. 25, 1875, "whose specialty is, we learn, portrait painting. We hope he may find sufficient encouragement to take up residence here." One of Jorgensen's paintings, a landscape of Wailua Falls, Kauai, exhibited in the window of Henry M. Whitney's bookstore next to the office of the *Advertiser*, was singled out for praise: "Nothing can be truer to nature than the foliage, and especially the pandanus tree. Also the shading of the water." I have been unable to find any trace of Emma's portrait, which of course may never have been completed.

3. The "Memorial" on the population problem was published in a special "Hawaiian Gazette Supplement," Mar. 8, 1876; see Letter 119, note 2.

4. Bishop Alfred Willis.

Letter 117
Peter to Emma

[Kalaupapa]
March 14, 1876

Queen Emma

I avail myself in pening these lines, while fresh in my memory.
Last week, on the Satuarday, I droped into Ragsdale's where I met
Mr Meyer who had come down. They . . . must have conversed on an
article in one of the Local papers, for after Mr Meyer had saluted me,
he remarked emphaticly that the King had no business to make
promises if he could not fulfil them. . . .

If D. K. was a man of ability, he would manifest it by having men
in the Ministry who were able to meet any immergency, and not
such men as Walker. Walker has been Bankrupt twice. Now if he is
not capable of carrying on his own affairs without being bankrupt,
surely he is not able to be a Minister.

Here is another instance of the D. K.'s incapability. He has allowed
himself to be led by Judge Allen [and by] Carter and has allowed the
Reciprocity Treaty to pass. The Treaty is worded so that the articles
specified in the Treaty and imported here from the U.S. enter here
free of duty. And our Sugar, our only Staple is exported through the
Custom house also free of duty. Now whare is our reveniew? The
Yanks now [realize] that they have a soft headed man to deal with,
as they are postponing this Treaty as long as they can, instead of
killing it or passing it and be done.

Kamehameha V knew all about this, so restrained, and would not
allow it, though [it was] beged of him. I would not in the least be
surprised, went on Mr Meyer, to hear of an European power lending
her aid to us, as the Yanks are so greedy. They know our weakness
and are acting really mean. They wish to win us, and having
accomplished it, they will have the Center of the Pacific Ocean.
Kamehameha V was not a man to be trifled with, and the Yanks
knew it, but this one—"Humph."

From this we conversed on European powers and finally settled on
Germany. The ability of the Emperor, his Ministers, and the Crown
Prince was manifested in this late war.

The Crown Prince is a plain person and assosiates with men and
not Loafers, as the King and Princes which we have here now. Mr

Meyer then burst out laughing, saying, repopulate the country, drink
Gin, and plant the empty bottles. He then looked at me still laughing
and said, "Oh, it is really rich. A King having a garden laid out to
plant empty Gin bottles." . . .

The puu puu[1] are breaking out on diferent parts of my body in
little pimples, so I am obliged to use more of the Salt rheum ointment
now then I have heretofore, So please send me up some more. I have
found it to be a splendid remedy for any skin disease. I am also nearly
out of Carbolic Soap, and should wish for some more.

Though we have had, and still have, plenty of rain, and the land
looks green, yet none of my algeroba that Punini planted have made
their appearance. All of my Monkey Pods are more or less destroyed
by the strong wind which we have had. We have showers daily and
wind from the South and West, which makes it both damp and
Sultry. Punini is still swolen about the face and complains of pain on
diferent parts of her body. She is being treated by a native Kahuna,
who predicts that you ere long will set on the Throne of Hawaii Nei.

Sunday 19. Yesterday P.M. I rode to the beach and sent Koloa to
buy fish from the canoes that were returning. He returned without
any—saying that the natives would not sell their fish, but distributed
them among themselves, so I had to go without any. . . .

Poor Enoch is quite weak, and I think that if he has not got it
allready, he will have the Dropsy. No nourishing food is one cause,
as the Sick has been fed on [salt] Salmon for these two months past. I
gave him some freash meat or fish whenever I have any. The Dropsy
in several cases have proved fatal, especially to a person who is
afflicted with this terrible disease the Leperesy.

[P. Y. K.]

1. Eruptions.

Letter 118
Emma to Peter

Honolulu
March 18, 1876

Ever dear Coz

The *Warwick* has been detained from bad weather and contrary winds three days. A case of measels has broken out with one of the passengers of the last steamer from San Francisco, and that patient is the portrait painter's bride,[1] poor man and poor she, only a week here. Both have been sent to the Quarranteen establishment at Kaholaloa. I am sending her some custard now.

We wish very much to get Pauahi married to Aikoe if possible, but prey do not mention it because it has not come to anything yet.

I am in a great way to get Albert married.[2] That is a very important question, because we must have children, and there are only two girls I can think who are anyway suited as to their rank by birth for his bride. They are Keeaumoku's sister, Keomailani,[3] at present in England at school and the other is Owana,[4] Mrs Pratt's niece, who is Kailipalaki's daughter. The only objections I have to these girls are their numerous low relations. Fancy all the Crowningburgs attached to us and the Throne.

Ninito is very anxious to make a match of one of her nieces[5] with Albert. One sister of the young lady is married to the heir of the Tahitian throne, Pomare's son Aliiauwe,[6] another[7] to the American Consul at Tahiti, Mr Atwater, and one is Mrs Brander.[8] One of these three girls must do finally. . . .

Do not distress yourself about those unkind reports of Albert and Hipa's being lepers. There is no truth whatever in it. The D. K.s are cerculating it so as to get [the notion] fixed as a fact and anoy us by having the public Board of Health's attention called to it, and then they must examine them.

Poor William Sumner has been notified to prepare for going up to Kalawao. This is a fact as his daughter told Lucy so, and I suppose Miss Spencer goes up soon. Prey do not handle a leper. Be as cautious as possible about yourself.

With all my heart's love I remain

Your own Coz
KALELEONALANI

P. S. Do try and translate a little this Lent. Tomorrow will be the 3rd Sunday in Lent.

1. Mrs. Rebecca Rogers, of San Francisco, on landing at Honolulu from the *Mikado*, Mar. 9, 1876, was married on the same day to Eiler Andreas Christopher Jurgensen [sic], of Copenhagen, Denmark. The wedding was at the residence of Dr. F. W. Hutchison, the Rev. H. H. Parker officiating. On Mar. 16, Mrs. Jurgensen gave evidence of the early symptoms of measles and was removed to the Quarantine Hospital on the reef in Honolulu Harbor. Previously two other passengers of the *Mikado* who had proved to have measles at the time of landing had been placed in quarantine.

2. In 1878, Albert married Mary Poli, widow of the Rev. Z. Poli, Congregational clergyman. They had no children.

3. Sister of William Charles Crowningburg (Keʻeaumoku). Sent to England in 1867 to be educated at Ascot Priory by Anglican nuns; returned to Hawaii 1880. Married Wray Taylor (1854–1910), American-born organist at St. Andrew's Cathedral; for her Crowningburg and Hawaiian connections, see Letter 89, note 1.

4. Theresa Owana Kaohelelani (1860–1944), a descendant of Keoua, father of Kamehameha I, and a granddaughter of the High Chief Gideon Laanui; also a granddaughter of Jean Dassent Lafayette Rives, court favorite of Kamehameha II. After a first marriage which ended in divorce, she married Robert William Wilcox (1855–1903), leader of the "Wilcox insurrection" (1889) under Kalākaua, and later Hawaii's first delegate to Congress (1901–1903).

5. Ninito's nieces were the five daughters of Alexandre Salmon (1820–1866), English Jew and member of a banking family, and Ariitaimai (1821–1897), the adoptive sister of Queen Pomare IV (1812–1877). According to Tahitian genealogical tradition, Ariitaimai was a descendant, through forty-four generations, of the ancient source-gods and the first Tahitian ruler: "... *authentique rejeton de nos dieux créateurs et le premier souverain de Tahiti.*" (Ernest Salmon, *Alexandre Salmon . . . et sa femme Ariitaimai . . .* [Paris: Musée de l'Homme, 1964], p. 29.)

6. Marau (1860–1934), wife of Aliiauwe, later Pomare V (d. 1891).

7. Moetia (1848–1935), wife of Dorence Atwater (1845–1911).

8. Titaua (1842–1898), whose first husband was John Brander (1814–1877), Scottish trader who made his fortune in pearl fishing.

Letter 119
Peter to Emma

[Kalaupapa]
[March] 20, [1876]
Monday[1]
12 noon

It has [rained] and is still raining from this morning up to the time I write. A Sail is in Sight, but as their is no wind She will not be in if [she is] the *Warwick* till late.

I was reading the two local papers with the memorial[2] and its reply, which is rather good. And when I came to whare it speaks of the "Enlightened Kamehameha IV" in one place, and the "Illustrious Queen Emma" in another, I could see that some of the Whites who had an aversion to the Enlightened Kamehameha IV have relented, probably against their wish, but could not help it, for if any King of Hawaii nei ever tried to repopulate his Country, that King was your Enlightened and Illustrious Husband. I am sure that D. K. do not like it, but your two Illustrious names are writen upon the Sand of time, and never to be obliterated so long as Hawaii nei is a Nation.

3 P.M.—Koloa have just returned with yours of the 16th. After having read it, and being alone, I [?wrapped] the grass in parcels, and having done so I put the pieces or parcels over my two doors and windows.[3] My things I have not all received, but the Schooner sails right away in haste.

KEKUAOKALANI

1. First page of letter missing.

2. On Feb. 29, 1876, a "Memorial" on the population question was presented to Kalākaua by a committee chosen from among its signers. The highly rhetorical document pointed out the crucial relationship between the size of the native population and Hawaii's security as an independent nation. If foreign states sometimes regarded the Kingdom as a mere "chieftaincy" when there were several hundred thousand natives, how will the powers regard the Hawaiian monarchy when the native population has dwindled to a few thousand? The memorial paid tribute to the historically important, but far less than adequate, pioneer efforts of Kamehameha IV to come to grips with the population problem: "And some of us can recall the words of preceding Hawaiian kings, deploring the loss of their people and praying for measures of repopulation, and especially may we repeat at this time the words of the enlightened and patriotic Kamehameha IV, addressed to his Legislature,

when he said: 'A subject of deeper importance than I have just mentioned is that of the decrease of our population. It is a subject in comparison with which all others sink into insignificance; for our first and great duty is self-preservation. Our acts are in vain unless we can stay the wasting hand that is destroying our people. I feel a heavy and a special responsibility in which you all must share.'. . ." After recalling the failure of past legislatures to take adequate action, the Kalākaua memorial made a plea for importing immigrants from "the human hive of Asia," in particular from Southeast Asia. The ideas and style of Walter Murray Gibson, one of the leading signers of the memorial, are evident in its content and language: "It is for you, O Chief [Kalākaua], chosen to be the sovereign and the leader of this feeble, yet most interesting nation:—it is for you, indeed, to be its political savior and its father. You are the only hope of Polynesia. . . . Upon you devolves this great mission, not only of the recuperation of your people, but the successful illustration of a tropical civilization; therefore every device and measure of Your Majesty's Government should be directed towards the acquisition of people, and the preservation of the life of the Hawaiian State." The memorial was published as part of the special "Hawaiian Gazette Supplement," Mar. 8, 1876.

3. The purpose of Peter's bundles is not clear. Perhaps the reference is simply to the Hawaiian use of scented grass to sweeten parts of a house; for example, lemon grass (*Cymbopogon citratus*) was sometimes placed under floor mats; also lemon verbena, "*wāpine*" (*Lippia citriodora*).

Letter 120
Peter to Emma

[Kalaupapa]
March 21, 1876
6:45 A.M.

Queen Emma

Pardon me for ending so abrubtly in mine of Yesterday. Koloa on returning from the beach reported that the Schooner was to leave immediately, so ending my letter, I had taken to the Vessel. At Sunset Ragsdale came up saying that She was to leave tomorrow at 9 A.M.

Jim Kamai[1] last Year came to me and asked the loan of $3—saying that he wished it to pay for a coffin for Kaikuaana[2] of his who was not expected to live. I informed him that I was willing to help the Sick so far as my means would allow. Last month he came and informed me that he had writen to his Wife to pay over the three dollars to you, and he wished to know if you had received the money or not. I replied that I had not received a letter to that effect and did not wish the money back, as it helped the poi pilikia.

By this *Warwick* Miss Spencer came up and Kamoikehuehue's Makuahonoawai.[3] The latter name reports a rumour at Honolulu that I am to be sent for to take my seat in the Legislature comeing as of yore.[4]

If their is a piece remaining of the Stuff which my Shirt was made from, which came up the trip before this, I should like to have it to be made for a Color. The print of the Shirt was like the Ace of dimonds.

All that you sent up is received, and today when I am alone I will chew and rub the Cocanut[5] as requested. I have not time to read the Paper just now, but will do so during the day.

I must end and send this by Koloa, who is taking the bags to the Schooner. Good Bye. My Prayers as ever for your welfare.

KEKUAOKALANI

1. Kimo (Jim) Kamai, leper who shot at Dr. Trousseau in 1863, but who evaded all authorities until November 1874; see Letter 49, note 2.

2. Sometimes spelled *kaikuʻana*. Older sibling or cousin of same sex; sibling or cousin of same sex but of senior line, either older or younger.

3. The unnamed arrival was an "in-law" (*makuahūnōwai*) relative of J. Komoikehuehu, member of the House of Representatives 1870–1874.

4. Though without traceable foundation, the hazy report nevertheless reflected Peter Kaeo's solid support by certain legislators. The *Hawaiian Gazette*, May 31, 1876, noted that at the meeting of May 30 Representative Pilipo had introduced a motion that William Ragsdale and the Hon. Peter Y. Kaeo "be brought before this Assembly, the one to present the complaints of the lepers, the other to answer for his administration."

5. Why Peter should chew cocoanut and rub himself—or the cocoanut?—is not clear. *Niu (Cocos nucifera)*, sometimes the fibers of the green husk and sometimes the young meat, grated or roasted, was commonly used in old Hawaiian medicine, especially in compounds. Conditions so treated ranged from "suppression of urine" to "thrush" (sore mouth) in infants and children. A modern compendium of traditional remedies in native folk medicine states that the "young meal of the cocoanut is good for the brain. It is applied as a rub." (*Hawaiian Herbs of Medicinal Value*, comp. by D. M. Kaaikamanu, trans. by Akaiko Akana [Honolulu: Territorial Board of Health, 1922], p. 73. See also, for a more authoritative account, E. S. Craighill Handy, Mary Kawena Pukui, Katherine Livermore, *Outline of Hawaiian Physical Therapeutics*, Bishop Museum Bulletin 126 [Honolulu: 1934], p. 22.)

Letter 121
Emma to Peter

[Honolulu]
[March ?, 1876][1]

... This is abominable stuff to write upon,[2] but I never found out we were out of paper till this moment, so I must use up this sort of paper to you.

Isaac Davis tells me just now that D. K. has got leprosy, and indeed that has been mooted this week. The people from Palace have said so, but I never believed it. But Mr Pratt saw him at the Emma Square yesterday together with his wife in the carriage. It was the German Emperor's 78th birthday and his subjects here kept it in that way and asked the public generally to go there. Mr Pratt remarked that D. K. looked for all the world as if he had got the leprosy. His face was swollen in red blotches. Isaac says that he has had it before this and that Koii has been doctoring him and [he] got well of it, but now it has come out more than formerly. Isaac says that he sleeps continually now, almost like Kamehameha V.

Prey do not speak of this till others hear of it for it may be laid to uncharitableness on your part, and I want our side to be above smallness of character, such as vulgar joviality over an enemy's fall. Keep it to yourself till we hear further.

Kewiki George Davis this moment says there is a petition going the rounds in native opposing the foreign memorials, and approving Mr Green's views,[3] saying all those active signers or framers of petition such as Gibson, etc., etc., have done nothing for this country although they say so, which is a falshood. Bob Charlton's name is first on the list. There are several names to it. It seems that it was drawn up by Bob himself with [the help of] Kalaaukane.[4]

I am so vexed about your horse. My man John somehow managed either to send the horse to Koolau at the time of *Warwick*'s arrival, or he [still] has it here. It is so poor he says that he [ought] to send it back. Well then—he is ordered again to get it [sent] up immediately, poor or not. He promises but it never comes. Then [he says] a paniolo[5] has to be hired by him, and so on, till even now. I am so very angry but do not know how to manage it. He has promised to have it up tomorrow, thinking that would be the time the *Warwick* would be here, but she has come back sooner than we looked for.

So you have heard of the rheumor of your coming to your seat at this Legislature. There is a report of such [a] thing, but because I have not yet found it tenible I have not told you of it, but should I know it as a fact then will write.

They say it will be very hot this month. Look out for the eclipse of Sun Saturday morning. It will be total so they say from 7 to 10. . . .

John Dominis, wife, and about 20 people—haoles—have gone round this Island. Their servants were all in red shirts.

Again I am in a hurry as the ship goes now. The Canoe is on board of *Warwick.*

Yours with all my heart's love—Coz—

KALELEONALANI

1. Heading and date have been supplied, as first part of letter is missing. A notation on back in Emma's hand reads: "1876/ returned April 2nd by hand of Napela."

2. Her decorated German stationery, with humorous borders showing grotesque figures in color—knights, clowns, fat friars, beer drinkers, etc.

3. The special "Hawaiian Gazette Supplement" on the population problem, Mar. 8, 1876, also printed an announcement of "The Ministerial Policy," signed by William L. Green, minister of foreign affairs, and J. S. Walker, minister of finance, Mar. 3, 1876. The official statement was severely critical of the Memorialists' conclusions on the population question. While the manifesto referred slightingly to the Chinese laborers already introduced into Hawaii, the ministers in their reply singled out the Chinese community for special praise: "The progeny also of these two races [Hawaiian and Chinese] seems so far to confirm your view that the mingling of Hawaiian and Asiatic blood may prove a success, so far at least as the Chinese are concerned." After stating categorically that "the Malay Archipelago cannot be looked to as a source of population for Hawaii," the ministerial reply also charged that the views of Kamehameha IV on population were being disingenuously distorted by persons intent on supplying immigrant labor to build up their own commercial interests. Kamehameha IV's hopes for his people were based on his belief that their greatest primary need was for proper medical care and more and better education. The late king had never recommended the importation of foreign labor: "We and you, gentlemen, are told that Asia will furnish 'consanguineous affinities' which shall effect the recuperation of the Hawaiian race. God grant that it may prove so, but He alone knows what races outside the Polynesian have the affinity to the Hawaiian that may be necessary for this purpose." William L. Green expanded his personal views opposing immigrant labor in a special "Circular," *Hawaiian Gazette,* Mar. 15, 1876, addressed to Godfrey Rhodes, the Hon. A. S. Cleghorn, Walter Murray Gibson, and "the other gentlemen who signed the Address to His Majesty dated 22 February." Green specifically rejected the proposal

that the legislature should appropriate funds for importation of foreigners as a labor force. A more sound course, he recommended, would be to trust to a reciprocity treaty to build up the nation: "If the treaty we are expecting and which will benefit most of us so materially goes into effect, population *must* come. It will come to us as it has come to every country on the face of the earth, in the natural course of human events, and if these events are unfavorable, it will be all but impossible to oppose them."

4. Unidentified; possibly G. B. Kalaaukane, member of House of Representatives 1855.

5. Rider; cowboy.

Letter 122
Emma to Peter

Honolulu
May 10, 1876

Ever dear Coz

Your letter of the 30th April arrived by schooner *Warwick* last week. I confess that I was dreadfully anxious about you after Robert Charlton's departure for Molokai, for the reason that he had been so indiscreet as to tell many people of the object of his trip, Kalaaukane and your brother being one of them, who instantly circulated the tale, and everyone had it on the tip of their tongues.

Bob had first of all arranged (so I am told) with Jack Smith to go up together after you, but afterwards changed that plan because Jack Smith was not discreet enough. Of course this rheumor reached the Palace, and there was where I feared for you in case the powers-that-be should overstep the mark and take the law into their own hands. But yet Mr Preston said throughout, that once you landed here everyone would be in defence of your rights and probably that would bring things to a climax. He said a stir is wanted now to check the present unscrupulous management of Government.

So that when Kalawaianui[1] walked into my mauka bedroom silently I could not guess what the issue had been. [I] left him to break the subject, and then felt both relieved and disappointed. He told me all, as you had written, and says he now knows the coast of that part of Molokai and can very well land at night, walk up to your house and come down together with you and pull off to ship. His destination is Punaluu, Koolau, and [he] says he can well stand off and on at Kalaupapa for you, but I must write more about this when I hear more.

In order to carry on the pretense that I knew nothing of the plans for your rescue (should you have come), I sent as usual every article of food save the sheep or pig. I did not care who gets them in case you did come down, and wrote a non-committal letter which I was not afraid to have read by Ragsdale or others, in case you had left. So that is the reason it was so void of news, and I am so thankful I did send them, as matters have turned out—else you would have gone without anything. Your white shirts are all finished, shall I send them up or no?

Your brother has applied three times to the Court (C. C. Harris) for my dismissal as guardian.[2] I had for two months made him live on the $30—food, clothing, and squander money [included] in it all—[but] he could not endure it, so complained of me finally. I gave up trying to save his money for house, because he got so dreadfully abusive of me—it was worry for no use, because he was determined to go against me in everything. The last thing he did was to go to Cartwright and ask him to take his property in hand, as he cannot stand my treatment of him and property. Yesterday a woman came over to tell us that Albert had sold a bed, table and chest of draws belonging to his Nuuanu house, to her husband for $15. They are at Koolau now.

Good news—[the] Reciprocity Treaty has failed.[3] It was indefinatly postponed. People here are all down in the mouth, but still hope it will be raised by 2-thirds of the House and passed. But I think and hope it will never come up again. Our party in Parliament is the wisest and has the law at their fingers' ends, disconserting the Nobles. But in spite of it they gain because they have 2/3 of the whole House. Simon and Kamakini are the only workers and speakers on the Nobles' part to oppose our party. The hall is full, crowded with natives all day, listening to the debates and cheering our side but calling against those who speak against our speakers. We can never gain any point because the opposition is always 2/3 of the house and we are only 1/3.

The $1 million Loan has fallen through.[4] Our side asked to debate upon it, and next day Mr Green himself spoke against it, saying no one can get money—they are not trusted, and so nearly all voted against it, Simon among the rest. Although in the last Parliament he stuck to it (and Treaty) strongly, now he himself votes it out. Our party is trying to gain their point. D. K. has a bill to make all the fishing rights free to all [but] now everyone is against the bill and I hope it will fall through.

I send you the only pair of green spectacles to be had in town—there are no goggles anywhere. Napela is at Hipa's but I do not choose to see or shake hands with him. He goes up to Molokai per *Warwick* today, so I hear. Mikona's son Peter who is living with me here, and who married Paneku's daughter, lost his baby yesterday—they woke up and found it quite dead. It is only three months old. It was buried yesterday in Nuuanu.

I did not go to the Opening of Legislature. You will see all the news. Do read the newspapers on all subjects—in fact read all there is in it. There is one [proposal] which I had planned long ago—for a long road to the sea from town, round Diamond Head and in over the Telegraph Station, [to] join Beretania Street—naming the new road Kamehameha IV.[5]

I have only just heard of your order for comb [and] scrubbing brush for your horse. It is too late for this ship.

May God place us on Throne.

Aloha a nui

KALELEONALANI

1. Probably an elder brother of Emma's protégée, Grace Kamaikui Kahōāli'i; he was the son of Kalawaianui and grandson of Kahōāli'i, brother of Kaoana'eha, Emma's and Peter's grandmother.

2. In January 1876, Queen Emma, as one of Albert's nearest surviving relatives, had petitioned the court that some suitable person be appointed his guardian "as he is a spendthrift." A witness, Palua, testifying on Albert's behalf, swore that he was a reformed character: "He does not drink as he used to do. He has no occupation at present. He reads sometimes. He does not have hulas now." Though several other witnesses testified that Albert had "changed from what he was," Emma was appointed Kūnuiākea's guardian and continued as such until 1880, when, at the age of twenty-nine, he was at last released from wardship.

3. Emma's rejoicing was premature. The "Treaty Act" was revived later in the session and finally on June 23 was approved by a vote of 26 to 16. Among those who opposed the bill were Henry Waterhouse and A. P. Kalaukoa, representing Honolulu.

4. The *Pacific Commercial Advertiser*, June 10, 1876, noted that "The Million Loan Act, which has been fruitless of results, has at last been repealed." The bill to repeal the measure was introduced by Edward Preston May 5 and passed June 7.

5. Under heading of "Our Public Avenues," the *Hawaiian Gazette*, May 10, 1876, proposed as a "desirable improvement" of the primitive local road system the development of a more direct overland route to Leahi and the Diamond Head region: "an extension of King street past McCully's [property] in a straight line about one mile on to the stone church at Moiliili. ... After reaching the above church, let the road diverge to the proposed public park and race track at Diamond Head, returning over the Waikiki road for the present, but ultimately by a road to be constructed along the seashore to Fisherman's Point." Emma did not mention to Peter the *Gazette's* further timely proposal that the new highway, leading to the present-day region of Kapiolani Park, should be officially named "Kalakaua Avenue."

Epilogue

The last four years of Queen Emma's life, after the deaths of Fanny and Peter, seem to have slipped away without notable event. Though she was never to become reconciled to Kalākaua's rule, Emma allowed herself now and then, if not always graciously, to play a subdued role in some of the official entertainment at the court of King Kalākaua and Queen Kapiʻolani. On one occasion Kalākaua himself, although he had not been formally invited, appeared unexpectedly at one of Emma's own lively evening parties. In 1882, writing to a Honolulu friend, Emma casually mentioned "my dance at Waikiki," where "to our surprise, the King was announced, but I was very glad as I had a message to deliver to him from Queen Victoria [who wished] to be remembered by him; he was rather a little merry with wine . . . kept quiet on the verandah."[1]

Emma's diary of 1881, an intermittently revealing but very haphazard record, shows that she continued to serve as an irresistible attraction to prophets and prophetesses, the native kahunas, still purveying their dark warnings about the affairs of the chiefs (mostly disastrous) and, explicitly or in more symbolic form, the political prospects of the Hawaiian Kingdom. There is no impressive evidence that Queen Emma gave credence to these visions and revelations—revisions rather, inasmuch as Kalākaua continued to rule over Hawaii for a total reign of seventeen years. By the 1880s, Queen Emma was no longer interested in the kahuna folk. She deplored their ignorance. She saw them now as "pitiable."

> . . . At 4 o'clock two men came to tell me of a dream which one of them drempt concerning me. He has been accustomed to dream of similar dreams and certain results have usually followed, generally pertaining to the former Kings. They began narrating part of dream, then left part of it to finish tomorrow. The commencement was a fishing seine made up of three size mesh nets, *Makahi, Malua,* and *Makolu.* These form the bag of net or *Mole.* The other or second net was made up of *Malua, Makolu, Makahi,* which likewise formed an *Eke* or *Mole* of it. These nets were let into the sea and a dreamer saw and heard Ruth Keelikolani say, "Oh, the fish is caught and that little

woman is caught in it." She called to Kapo (Pooloku), "Oh, you pull the net quick so as to secure that little woman" (*kapi wahine*) which was myself. Dreamer saw me and lo! I was covered all over with hair save the middle of my body [which was] quite sound. He says had I been covered over with hair it is certain speedy death, but not entirely covered gives me a chanse of seeking life from amongst skilled Kahunas, but it must be done soon or I die. Dreamer has drempt similar one[s] before—Uncle John's, all Kings, my Mother's recent death. He says he has always spoken of it beforehand—what silly falsehood to play on people. They think to frighten me. Their ignorance is pitiable. Tomorrow they will want money.[2]

Queen Emma rarely mentioned, in writing at least, her own private dreams. Her visionary moments, if that is the right term for them, were generally waking experiences of her first-hand observation and her serviceable (but not always accurate) memory, supplemented by an eager, even exploratory, imagination. Over the years she had developed a capacity for applying her intelligence, totally engaged, to the printed word, and had often encouraged Peter to do the same: "Reading aloud is more improving than you think," she reminded Peter on July 29, 1873. "Interesting subjects or passages I read slowly, and sometimes almost act them [out]." Along with her reading and her writing, she learned to live more and more in the present while, simultaneously, both recent and remote past seemed to merge or disappear into one. As a bride, and even in her thirties as an early widow, she had enjoyed prolonging an evening's pleasure as late as possible, and the next day she had loved to stay long in bed. Now, in vigorous young middle age, she became an early riser: "I could not sleep late, woke at 4 o'clock and wakened the whole household by chanting the sentence in morning prayer, 'I will arise and go to my Father,' 'Love not,' 'I would the Pope's gay life were mine.'" At all times she turned to the words of her Bible, as on a certain morning in her forty-fourth year when she spent much time "hunting out the historys of Penitents mentioned in 'Litany of Penitents' [in] my '*Vade Mecum*,' reading King David's humble confession, also of Solomon's grand history. The reading of these historical events was exceedingly interesting, and really they seemed like new readings to me."[3]

So the queen wrote after waking well before sunrise on the morning of January 31, 1881, the anniversary of "Poor King Lunalilo's birthday."

By her death on April 25, 1885, from heart disease, when only forty-nine, Queen Emma escaped that sequence of irruptive changes, and the political climax, that ended in the revolution, the establishment of the American-dominated Provisional Government and Republic of Hawaii, and the later annexation of Hawaii in 1898 as an overseas island possession of the United States. Unlike the very private services for Peter, her own on May 17, 1885, and the several observances that preceded the funeral proper, matched in interest and scale the celebrations for her husband, King Alexander Liholiho, Kamehameha IV, in 1863. For three weeks, almost from the moment of her death until her entombment in the Royal Mausoleum, the queen was surrounded by the panoply and pomp of a Hawaiian funeral-of-state.[4]

The earliest of the public rites in her honor was an Episcopal memorial service held at St. Andrew's Cathedral, on Sunday, April 26, while the queen's body lay on view at Rooke House nearby. The Reverend George Walker took for his text Ephesians III: 15, "The whole family in heaven and earth," developing the thought that "Angels, living saints, and dead, but one Communion make," and that the dead belong to us no less than do the living.

> They are ours, in a sense, more than they were before. They were misrepresented and misunderstood, but now they have passed to another condition of the undivided family, their characters have put off that which in them was ordinary and commonplace. They stand now in their glory, their brightness, their honor and dignity.[5]

Mr. Walker struck a note of pastoral elegy as he touched upon the historic significance of the occasion, for the nation now as a whole mourned the loss of the queen as the end of an epoch, "closing the line of a royal dynasty of Kings and Queens of an ancient race, once populous as the leaves of the green slopes of the mountains in multitude, now as the grain falling behind the path of the reapers, or the gleaning of grapes when the harvest is done."[6] Even in her mortal state, Kaleleonālani had beheld in spirit "the vision of the King in His beauty, and therefore her life was noble, feminine, inartificial and real."[7]

1. Emma to Mrs. Flora Jones, Honolulu, Oct. 31, 1882, AH.

2. Diary of Queen Emma, 1881, Feb. 7, 1881 entry, BM.

3. Ibid., Jan. 31, 1881 entry.

4. The most complete account of the various services is *Funeral Obsequies*

of the Late Queen Dowager Emma Kaleleonalani. . . . (Honolulu: Hawaiian Gazette Office, 1885.) This is a pamphlet compiled from accounts ("Lying in State," "Memorial Discourses," "Incidents," "The Will," etc., etc.) published in the *Hawaiian Gazette,* April 29, May 6, 13, and 20, 1885.

5. Ibid., p. 11.

6. The dynastic implication of Emma's death was reported by U.S. Minister R. M. Daggett to Secretary of State T. F. Bayard, Honolulu, Apr. 27, 1885, U.S. Department of State no. 233, *Dispatches from U.S. Ministers in Hawaii*: "With the death, a few months since, of Mrs. Bernice Pauahi Bishop, the Kamehameha family, so far recognized, became extinct, and the decease of Queen Emma leaves no one to contest, on the score of lineage, the sovereign right of the existing dynasty, which stands alone, at last, as the sole representative, unless very remotely, of the Hawaiian rulers of the past."

7. *Funeral Obsequies,* p. 13.

Appendix

NOTE ON MANUSCRIPTS AND TRANSCRIPTIONS

Most of the 122 selected letters exchanged between Peter Young Kaeo and Queen Emma published in this volume form a part of the very miscellaneous manuscript letters, diaries, memoranda, papers, and documents that make up the extensive Queen Emma Collection preserved in the Archives of Hawaii, Honolulu. Very little is known about what happened to Queen Emma's private correspondence and family papers at the time of her death in 1885. However, the bulk of these materials now appear to have found their way into the possession of the State Archives.* The materials are divided into three classes.

(1) The "Archives" group: letters, diaries, and documents at the archives in November 1957. The source of these materials is unknown.

(2) The "Flora Jones Collection": letters written by Queen Emma (chiefly during the 1880s) to Mrs. Flora Jones, Honolulu, and bequeathed by her daughter, Miss Maude Jones, former archivist of the Territory of Hawaii, to the archives.

(3) The "Nylen-Altman Collection": letters and documents purchased by the Territory of Hawaii in October 1957 from Mr. Ray Nylen and Mr. Jack Altman, Honolulu.

This last and very substantial portion of the Queen Emma Collection, consisting of rather more than 1,000 items and including the Peter Kaeo-Queen Emma correspondence, dropped out of sight at the time of the queen's death and was wholly forgotten until 1935, when it was discovered by chance in a Honolulu pawnshop.

The discovery of this unsuspected hoard of Hawaiiana was made by Miss Vivienne Mader, a dancer and dance teacher from New York City, during a visit to Hawaii for the purpose of studying the hula. Miss Mader ("Huapala") happened one day to go into the Depot Pawnshop, situated in the River Street section of the old town, while in search of early Hawaiian sheet music and anything else of historic and musical interest. When Miss Mader was shown the Queen Emma materials, including numerous letters written by Emma in England and France in 1865–1866, she instantly realized her good luck. Miss Mader reported her find to Mrs. Mary Kawena Pukui, assistant in Hawaiian culture at the Bishop Museum, who accompanied her back to the pawnshop to examine the materials more thoroughly, especially any manuscripts in Hawaiian.

According to Mr. Ray Nylen, joint-owner of the firm, the store of holograph letters and miscellaneous family papers had come into his hands in 1932, when he had bought them from the heirs of a certain Mrs. Virginia Kalili Makainai, recently deceased, who had been a ward of the Princess Virginia Poʻoloku Poʻomaikelani (1841–1895). Poʻomaikelani, a descendant of ancient kings of Kauai, was a younger sister of Queen Kapiʻolani, the consort of King Kalākaua, and a relative by marriage of Kalākaua's sister, Queen Liliʻuokalani, the last of the native rulers. Exactly how Poʻomaikelani happened to acquire such a large number of Emma's private papers is a puzzle.

It is true that for several years during the late 1860s and early 1870s, Poʻoloku was an honored attendant (*kahu*) of the Dowager Queen Emma and a member of her household. It is also true that in 1874 Poʻoloku married Hiram Kahanawai, a distant relative of Emma and her long-time chief steward. However, after the election of David Kalākaua to the throne, both Poʻoloku and Hiram left the queen's service, became man and wife, and joined the royal entourage of King Kalākaua and Queen Kapiʻolani. Certainly Emma's dislike for Kalākaua, together with her general estrangement from Queen Kapiʻolani and other members of the Kalākaua family, makes it highly improbable that by any wish of Emma herself her papers could have passed into the custody of her former attendant, the recently created princess royal under the new dynasty.

There may be a partial or tentative explanation of the mystery. When Emma died in 1885, her closest male relative and one of her principal heirs was her cousin, Albert Kūnuiākea (1851–1903). Albert was a natural son of Kamehameha III, born to the king by Emma's maternal aunt, Jane Lahilahi Young Kaeo, the mother of Peter Kaeo. Kūnuiākea's boyish scrapes and escapades as a young man ranged from drunken fist-fighting in the streets to forging checks, and he quarreled habitually with Queen Emma. It is not only conceivable but very probable that, soon after Emma's death, Albert may have had opportunity to gather up—to pilfer, in short—some of Queen Emma's private papers.

It is known that Albert brooded over the settlement of Emma's estate. When her will was being probated, Kūnuiākea contested the document, charging that it was not the queen's last will and testament and that she had signed it when of unsound mind. One witness reported that Albert had been seen lurking about his royal cousin's premises, eyeing various of her belongings. If Albert acquired the collection, whether through a legitimate claim or by some more nefarious means, then its existence might easily have come to the attention of the Princess Poʻomaikelani. She had known Albert since his childhood. In general, though he was himself a representative of the Kamehameha family line, Kūnuiākea seems to have been on friendly enough terms with the "D. K.s" and various political supporters of Kalākaua. Furthermore, Poʻomaikelani was publicly recognized as an expert on Hawaiian history and the genealogies of the chiefs. During the 1880s, she served as *Iku Hai* ("speaking officer" or president) of the *Hale Nauwa* ("House of Wisdom"), a kind of genealogical-"anthropological" secret society sponsored by King Kalākaua to investigate and preserve the old Hawaiian way of life. Poʻomaikelani may well have been interested in Emma's private correspondence as a source of revelations concerning Emma's political activities during the 1870s, in particular the dynastic intrigues of the queen during the critical twelve months of King Lunalilo's brief unhappy reign and the very uncertain first years of the reign of King Kalākaua.

An account in a Honolulu newspaper in 1957, describing how Hiram Kahanawai, the husband of Poʻomaikelani (Emma's "faithful family retainer"), carefully preserved the collection down the years, is without foundation. It is fantastic to suppose that Hiram and Poʻoloku could have carried off Emma's voluminous correspondence and family papers when they joined up with Kalākaua and his new regime. Indeed, the collection contains drafts of letters written by Emma together with letters received by her well into the 1880s, years after Hiram's death and at a time when her relations with Poʻomaikelani had become as cool as her dealings with Queen Kapiʻolani. Though it is perhaps impossible to prove conclusively that the manuscripts were ever in her cousin's possession, strong circumstantial evidence points in the direction of Albert Kūnuiākea, Emma's disappointed heir and the aging black sheep of the family.

What is absolutely certain is that after the death of the Princess Poʻomaikelani in 1895, the princess' ward, Virginia Kalili, and finally the ward's heirs, though persons of no prominence and with very little knowledge of things Hawaiian, preserved the mass of letters and documents for more than a quarter of a century, before disposing of them in 1932 in excellent condition to the owner of the Depot Pawnshop in order to pay the cost of Mrs. Makainai's funeral.

I first learned of the existence of "The Pawnshop Papers" in 1956, when the late Clarice B. Taylor, Honolulu newspaper writer and friend to everyone interested in Hawaiiana, mentioned them to me one day in conversation. Through Mrs. Taylor's somewhat vague lead, I was able finally to get in touch with Mr. Ray Nylen, who kindly permitted me to examine the collection (housed not in the pawnshop but in an army footlocker in a Waikiki apartment) and to draw upon it freely for my book on Hawaii during the 1860s, *The Victorian Visitors*. In 1957 and again in 1960 and 1961, I continued my interrupted work on the collection, much aided by the assistance of Mrs. Pukui, who had first studied the Kaeo-Emma correspondence closely in the 1930s, at the time of its discovery by Miss Mader. Indeed, if Mrs. Pukui had never translated the Hawaiian passages in most of the letters, I doubt whether I should ever have ventured upon the job of assembling and editing the present volume. In addition to permitting me to use her translations, Mrs. Pukui on many occasions has supplied me with invaluable, detailed facts about Hawaiian life during Emma's period. I can only hope that this book as a whole reflects in some small degree my profound gratitude to Mrs. Pukui for her kindness and characteristic generosity. In 1957, the collection passed finally into the possession of the Archives of Hawaii, when Governor Samuel Wilder King purchased the manuscripts out of a contingent fund. I am much indebted to Miss Agnes Conrad, state archivist, for having recognized the unique value of the collection and expeditiously arranged for its purchase and transfer to the Archives.

I am also grateful to the late Ralph S. Kuykendall, historian of the Hawaiian Kingdom, who followed my early adventures on the trail of Peter Kaeo with keen interest and encouragement. In 1957, Professor Kuykendall made to me a gift of some notes he had taken on a small portion of the Nylen-Altman materials. These notes were the basis for a number of quotations and footnote references in the second and third volumes of *The Hawaiian Kingdom* (Honolulu, 1953, 1967), cited simply as from "a private collection." Professor Kuykendall's stack of cards carries the notation: "This is a collection privately owned, but was deposited in the Archives for a short time, and I was allowed to read and take notes—1940." A news article by George West, "Story of a Queen's Letters and a Pawnshop," *Star Bulletin*, Oct. 31, 1957, reported that Professor Kuykendall said, "If the entire collection had been available . . .

it would have been more helpful to me than the small part I had access to."

Readers of this book particularly interested in the primary sources and in their possible use for further scholarly and literary purposes will find the following publications rewarding, especially Bushnell's distinguished novel and Daws' important biographical study of Damien: Alfons L. Korn and Mary Kawena Pukui, "News from Molokai: The Letters of Peter Young Kaeo (Kekuaokalani) to Queen Emma, 1873–1876," *Pacific Historical Review*, 32 (February 1963):7–34; O. A. Bushnell, *Molokai* (Honolulu: The University Press of Hawaii, 1975); Alfons L. Korn, "Peter Kaeo's Wreath: A Ballad Performed," *Seventy-Third Annual Report of the Hawaiian Historical Society* (1964), pp. 22–54; Gavan Daws, *Holy Man: Father Damien of Molokai* (New York: Harper and Row, 1973).

EDITING PRINCIPLES

Both Peter Kaeo and Queen Emma were systematic, but also hasty, letter writers. Haste was often a necessity, in order to finish a letter, or perhaps to complete a final draft, in time for a messenger to take it aboard one of the somewhat unpredictable interisland vessels. Peter Kaeo's leprous fingers and hands, to say nothing of his other more transient disabilities, also affected his handwriting variably, and sometimes for the worse. In general, however, his large script in its juvenile copybook hand is at its best easily legible. Furthermore, many of his letters look and read as if they were fair copies, however much he may have sometimes been rushed to complete them. Like Queen Emma, Peter was bilingual; both employed English as their primary language. When Peter chooses to write consecutive sentences in Hawaiian, he is usually recording the remembered pronouncements of a kahuna. Though often stereotyped and ritualized, his scattered single words and short phrases in Hawaiian serve a variety of important expressive purposes and deserve special study.

Unfortunately, Emma's final-draft letters to Peter were for the most part destroyed or lost, so that what has survived of them does so chiefly in the form of quick diarylike memoranda on small scrap sheets, or as preliminary drafts scribbled on both sides and along the margins of a flimsy and transparent grade of stationery. The letters of both correspondents, despite great differences in content and style, have linguistic interest. They illustrate the manner of speaking and writing the English language of two Hawaiians of superior education, members of a bilingual and political elite, fifty years after the arrival in Hawaii of the earliest American missionaries. Their phonetic misspellings, as well as sundry other idiomatic and rhetorical peculiarities, clear vestiges of which survive and sometimes flourish in the spoken English used today by persons of Hawaiian background, are frequently indicative of contemporary pronunciation and the speech patterns in general of English-speaking native Hawaiians of their period.

Thus the editing of the letters has presented both familiar and unfamiliar problems, complicated by the special circumstance that occasionally, particularly in Peter's writing, not only words and short phrases but sometimes sentences and whole paragraphs appear in Hawaiian. Despite obstacles, I have attempted an approximately literal transcription of the English, changing only what I thought might too disastrously impede reading. Though I am by no means satisfied with every result, my specific principles are as follows.

1. The arrangement and punctuation of items contained in letter headings, addresses, and salutations have been regularized.

2. Exact spellings and numerals are retained in the body of the letters, except in a very few instances ("to" for "too," for instance) where I have silently corrected universal inadvertances of no particular interest or made very minor changes to avoid confusion. Incorrect spellings of names of places and persons have been corrected and regularized. I have added capitals when necessary for persons, places, and ships, etc. Most abbreviations, including the ampersand, have been expanded in the body of the letters. To avoid confusion, I have added apostrophes in certain possessives and eliminated their functionless use in various plurals. In printing Peter's letters, I have tried to follow his obsessive use of capitals at the beginning of many words. His practice in this respect seems to have served some private purpose, if only to express a certain spirit of diligence deeply instilled in him by his neat laborious copybook exercises as a little boy in the Chiefs' Children's School. In Emma's more vivacious and slapdash writing, especially when the script makes it uncertain whether she intended a capital or not, I have tended to normalize her usage.

3. Punctuation has been generally retained, especially in the use of the comma for certain rhetorical purposes, but I have also made frequent adjustments where a mark seemed both functionless and seriously detrimental to ready understanding. I have occasionally introduced

dashes and parentheses when these seemed appropriate to the tone as well as the meaning. All sentences begin with a capital and end with a full stop or some other appropriate sign, such as the dash.

4. Very rarely I have altered the arrangement of elements in a sentence where the order was intolerably clumsy or the meaning markedly obscure, sometimes because of the writer's haste. Long continuous passages have been generally lightened by paragraphing. When a blocked series of sentences appeared almost entirely lacking in continuity, I have on several occasions printed a sequence of sentence-length paragraphs, or very rarely regrouped the sentences according to some topical principle.

5. Brackets indicate editorial interpolation.

6. Except for single words (usually nouns) or very short phrases, all original passages in Hawaiian have been translated and are set off by carets.

7. Hawaiian words in the body of the letters are printed as written, without the use of the glottal stop (opening single quotation) or other marks indicative of pronunciation and etymology. Most Hawaiian words as printed in the introductory comment or explanatory notes use the glottal stop and macron (indicating stress) and in general follow the style in Mary Kawena Pukui and Samuel H. Elbert, *Hawaiian Dictionary* (Honolulu: University of Hawaii Press, 1971). Some Hawaiian loan-words, now included in a few standard English dictionaries, such as "alii," are printed without diacritical markings.

8. In Hawaii today, there is a growing movement to encourage the practice of printing diacritical marks as a means of preserving the "correct" pronunciation and of identifying phonetically, in some instances, the semantic reference. I have followed this practice in only a limited way. Thus I print most Hawaiian personal and place names as they would appear today in a Honolulu telephone directory. However, I give the markings for certain names that figure significantly in the genealogical history of the Kamehameha and Kalākaua families—for example, Keliʻimaikaʻi (The-good-chief), Kalākaua (The-day-of-victory), etc. In such names the markings serve as a guide for consulting the dictionary when deciphering the meaning and symbolism of the name. The choice of these selected names has been determined partly by their frequency in several major works on Hawaii and partly by their importance in the context of this particular book.

9. Certain deletions in the body of the letters are indicated by ellipses

(three or four dots), meaning that the original words are illegible, or unduly repetitious, or of slight significance. In no instances have deletions been made to suppress statements of either Peter Kaeo or Queen Emma.

*A number of interesting letters from Queen Emma to Lucy Peabody, one of her ladies-in-waiting, are part of the Peabody-Henriques Collection, Bernice P. Bishop Museum, Honolulu. A collection of nine letters from Peter Kaeo to Queen Emma, written during his stay at Kalaupapa, have been deposited at the Hawaiian Mission Children's Society Library, Honolulu. All nine, dated as follows, have been published in the present volume: July 27, 28, 30, 31, 1873; Aug. 18, 19, 1873; Aug. 20, 21, 23, 1873; Nov. 8, 1873; Aug. 28, 1874; Aug. 30, Sept. 1, 1874; Sept. 3, 1874; Nov. 11, 1874; Mar. 14, 19, 1876.

Indexes

To facilitate reading, four indexes have been provided. The first two are for Persons and Places; the third, to be used especially in combination with Persons, is the topical General Index. In listings for Persons where there are two or more footnotes, main notes are printed in italic type. In addition, a Selected Glossary of Hawaiian words is appended, giving page references to significant usages.

Index of Persons

Achew, 175
Adams, Dr., 82
Ahaula, 136
Ahuihala, Capt., 24
Aikoe, 21, 39, 41n.9, 51, 54, 69, 86, 120, 172,
    177, 264, 305, 310
Aipalena, 289, 296
Akana, Dr. Sing Kee ("Kaanaana"), xxxiii,
    147, 148n.2, 203, 205n.1, 213, 226, 227, 243,
    244, 247, 251, 273
Albert. See Kūnuiākea, Albert
Albert Edward Kauikeaouli, prince of Hawaii,
    xl, 74, 87, 104, 107, 158
Aliiauwe, 310
Allen, Elisha H., 164, 179, 181n.11, 308
Allen, William F., xxxi
Arkady, Father, 110, 113n.7
Atwater, Dorence, 310, 311n.7
Auld, James, 196, 198n.2, 200

Beckley, Mrs. Fred, 291
Beers, Henry A., 22, 23n.2
Bell, George, 186, 188n.2
Bertha, Sister (Elizabeth Bertha Turnbull),
    104, 106n.13, 125, 131
Bishop, Bernice Pauahi, xii, xviii, 37n.1, 85,
    86, 88, 89n.12, 92, 95n.8, 110, 129, 134n.6,
    142, 143, 144n.4, 164, 207, 232, 239, 264–
    266, 267n.6, 303
Bishop, Charles R., xviii, 42, 85, 93, 109,
    134n.6, 142, 143, 153, 164, 165, 166n.4, 172,
    196, 200, 239, 264–266, 267n.6
Blossom, John, 97, 98n.3
Boyd, Edward ("Ned"), 220, 222n.6, 224, 236
Brander, John, 310, 311n.8
Brickwood, Louisa, 132
Brown, Frank, 217

"Buff." See Leleiohoku
Burgerman, André, 192, 202, 209

Carter, Joseph O., 197, 199n.6, 308
Cartwright, Alexander J., 196, 198n.1, 200,
    215, 218, 289, 296, 318
Castle, Samuel N., 59, 62n.23
Castle, William R., 292, 293n.6
Charlton, Robert, 203, 279, 280, 284n.4, 292,
    300, 301, 315, 317, 319
Cleghorn, Archibald S., 58, 61n.20, 64, 93,
    186, 190, 233, 303
Cleghorn, Mrs. A. S. (Miriam Likelike),
    61n.20, 85, 88, 94, 132, 240, 291
Cleveland, President Grover T., 89n.12
Colburn, Mrs., 14, 133
Cook, Capt. James, xxx, 115
Cook, Mr. ("Kuke"), 96n.12
Cooke, Mr. and Mrs. Amos S., xvi
Crabbe, Horace, 33, 34n.6, 91, 92, 95n.1, 102,
    104, 105, 154, 169
Crabbe, Mrs. Horace (Elizabeth Meek,
    "Beke"), 91, 95n.3, 102
Crowningburg, William (Ke'eaumoku IV),
    91, 95n.4, 99, 230, 231n.1, 233, 234, 244,
    310
Crowningburg-Amalu, Samuel ("Samy"),
    231n.1

Damien, Father, xi, xxvi, 24, 25n.1, 30, 56,
    63–64, 141, 149, 192, 258
Davies, Theophilus H., 17n.12, 70n.4, 101n.13
Davis, Isaac, 19n.5, 171n.8
Davis, Isaac George Hueu, II (Kewiki), xxxi,
    xxxii, 111, 112, 113n.11, 164, 170, 171n.8,
    288, 315
Diamond, "Johny," 57, 61n.15

Dole, Sanford Ballard, 101n.15
Dominis, John O., 55, 58, 59n.1, 85, 92, 93,
    98–99, 100, 109, 132, 177, 178, 215, 220,
    245, 303, 305, 316
Dominis, Mrs. John O. (Lili'uokalani), xviii,
    xxii, 41n.7, 49n.3, 58, 85, 86, 88, 89n.12,
    92, 93, 94, 109, 127, 131, 132, 232, 316
Dowsett, James I., Jr., 174, 289
Drew, Mrs., 240, 241
Dudoit, Capt. Charles, 109

Emerson, John S., 59, 70
Emma, Queen: royal ancestry and mixed
    lineage, xi–xii, xiii–xiv, xix, xxxvii, xxxix,
    117, 168, 238, 242, 264–265, 267n.6;
    meaning of name Kaleleonālani, xli; early
    education, xvii–xix; British sympathies and
    distrust of Americans, xl, xli, 26, 57, 59n.10,
    92–93, 109, 136, 304n.1; affectionate
    kinship with Peter, xvi, xix, xxxv–xxxvii;
    marries Alex and becomes queen, xviii,
    xxxvii, xli–xliii, xlivn.13, 305; persistent
    gossip about Kamehameha IV and Queen
    Emma, 224n.2; birth and death of Prince of
    Hawaii, xl, xli–xlii, xliv, 87; her sense of
    divine mystery, xxvi–xxvii, 279, 322;
    instructs Peter about Roman Catholic
    church, 26, 27; encourages Peter to seek
    leadership, 38–39, 117–119, 168–169; warns
    against social drinking, 14, 52, 54; advice on
    household servants, 52; marriage to Lunalilo
    rumored, 42, 48, 49n.1, 52, 54, 85, 86, 245,
    246; low opinion of Hua the prophetess, 56,
    94; forbids all "intercourse with lepers,"
    119; reluctance to seek throne, 85, 86;
    reports discovery of "ana ana bundle" at
    Pawaa turning, 103; reported possible bride
    for Leleiohoku, 137, 245, 246; relations with
    David Kalākaua, xxix, xxxix, 168–169, 263,
    321; and Mrs. Kalākaua (Queen Kapi'olani),
    286, 288; admires Taffy's "great ambition"
    and perseverance, 119; reports Honolulu
    scandals, 132–133; defeat of the "Queenites"
    (1874), 165–166; predictions of her future
    reign, 94, 126, 152, 189–190, 204, 241–242
    (see also General Index: Prophecies; Omens
    and signs); the "Queen Emma lei," 271–272;
    performs kahuna ritual to become queen,
    289–290; engages in practical politics, 279,
    281, 289, 294–296; teaches English class for
    Hawaiian women, 303, 304n.1; plans Peter's
    escape, 279–282, 317–318; her later life,
    283, 321–322; death and funeral, 322–323.
Enoki (Enoch), 305, 309
Everett, Mrs., 240

Fornander, Abraham, 300, 302n.8
Franklin, Lady, xxviii, xxix, xlii, 16n.6, 163

Gibson, Walter Murray, 40n.7, 42n.2,
    101n.13, 134n.3, 169, 227, 295, 296, 303,
    306, 315
Grace. See Kahōāli'i, Grace K.
Green, J. Porter, 43, 44n.1, 57, 58, 61n.16, 104
Green, William L., 217, 315, 316n.3, 318–319
Gulick, Charles, 100, 101n.15

Haa, 151, 154
Haalilio, 80
Hakaleleponi. See Kalama, Queen
Hall, Edwin O., 13, 14n.2, 21, 42, 93, 154
Halulu, 22, 23n.3, 54, 63, 150, 204
Hamanalau, 207
Hanaoile, 14, 15n.2, 69
Haniole, 189
Hare, Capt. Richard, 303, 304n.4
Harris, Charles C., 227, 296, 298n.14, 306, 318
Hart, Isack, 299
Hartwell, Alfred S., 142, 144n.3, 179, 181n.9,
    230
Hasslocher, Eugene, 210, 211n.5, 214
Hervey, Lord Charles, 196, 198n.4
Hila (Mrs. Tallant), 24, 25n.2, 34, 104, 115,
    130, 131, 140, 149, 150
Hinau, 14, 15n.4, 41n.8
Hoapili. See Kaauwai, William H.
Hoapili, J. G., 103, 106n.11
Hoffman, Dr. Edward, 59n.1, 70n.1
Honokaupu, 91
Hua, Paniku, xxii–xxiii, xxv, xxxiii, 45,
    46n.1, 56, 78–79, 79n.3, 94, 126, 151–152,
    179, 182–183, 186, 189, 190, 195, 197, 200–
    201, 204, 208–209, 218, 227, 235, 236, 241,
    242, 263–264, 274
Humphreys, William, 54, 55n.3
Hutchison, Dr. Ferdinand W., 112, 311n.1

Jaczay, Joseph, 98, 99, 100, 101n.5
Jarrett, William, 169, 170n.2
Jasper, Jane ("Loeau"), 38, 39n.1, 43, 44n.2,
    114n.15
"John Puni" (dog), 29, 30n.1, 261
Johnson, President Andrew, xvii
Jones, 230
Jorgensen (?Jurgensen), Eiler, 306, 307n.2, 310
Jorgensen (?Jurgensen), Mrs. Eiler, 310, 311n.1
Judd, Albert Francis ("Frank"), 93, 97n.2, 296,
    306
Judd, Charles, 38, 40n.4, 92, 98, 99, 100, 104,
    110, 163, 295
Judd, Dr. Gerrit P., 40n.4, 51n.3

Ka, William, 85, 86, 89n.7, 127
Ka'ahumanu, Queen, xxii, 45, 46n.2, 163
Kaai, Capt., 258
Kaai, Simon K., 103, 132, 143, 164, 190,
191n.5, 207, 210, 230, 233, 258, 288–289,
299, 318, 319
Kaanau, 193
Kaapuni, 129
Kaauwai, William Hoapili, 44n.1, 112,
114n.14, 120, 132, 136, 138, 170, 179,
180n.3, 182, 183, 187n.1, 209n.2
Kaawa (?"Bill"), xxi, 37, 52, 57, 107, 108,
114–115, 117, 118, 123, 129, 130, 148, 153,
156, 157n.4, 159, 179, 184, 186, 187, 189,
199–200, 201, 207, 208–209, 215, 230, 235,
237, 249, 256
Kaeo, Jane Lahilahi Young (Mrs. Joshua
Kaeo), xiv–xv, 12n.3, 16n.7
Kaeo, Joshua (Ehu), xiv, 11, 12n.3
Kaeo, Kaleikoa, 11, 12n.3
Kaeo, Peter Young: Kekuaokalani's "grandchild," xi, xiii–xiv, 115, 116n.2, 117, 267n.6;
schooling, xvii–xviii; attachment to Emma,
xv–xvi, xxxv–xxxvi; royal aide, xxix,
xxx–xxxii; jealous of David Kalākaua
("Taffy"), xxvii–xxviii; character and self-
image, xxxii–xxxviii; his "civility," xxxiii–
xxxiv; acquires leprosy, 7; arrives at
Kalaupapa, 7–8, 9, 11; leprous symptoms
and general health, xxiii, xxiv, 19, 21, 23,
32, 35, 36, 44, 49, 53, 63, 64, 66, 69–70, 74,
76, 77–79, 79n.5, 80, 83, 94, 148, 152, 153,
154, 166, 174–175, 177, 187, 192, 193, 194,
202, 203, 209, 210, 215, 217, 232, 233, 239,
240, 247, 257, 258, 269, 273, 274, 277, 281–
282, 286, 287, 309; sends greeting to King
Lunalilo, 104; cottage at Kalaupapa
("Honolulu"), 17–18, 32–33, 83, 94, 147,
148n.1; sends Emma sketch map, 84, 88n.1;
Kalaupapa as his "probation" and "school,"
168–169; urged to be studious and read,
38–39; his reading, xvii, xviii, 13, 14, 23,
32–33, 38, 91, 105, 107, 117–118, 131, 150,
154, 169, 176, 177, 200, 212, 221, 226, 231,
235, 237, 239, 253, 257, 272, 286, 308, 314,
319; early dealings with Bill Ragsdale, 7,
32, 34, 38; becomes Ragsdale's rival, xx–
xxii, 157n.4; charges Ragsdale with
"starving natives," 152, 153, 154nn.2, 5;
inspects "curious" dead boy, 159; heated
confrontation with Ragsdale, 204–205;
accepts Ragsdale's apology, 207; friendship
with Jonathan Napela, 18, 47–48, 52;
prayers with the Napelas, 173; his Anglicanism, xxvi; relations with Father Damien,

24, 30, 63–64, 192, 193n.1; lessons in
gardening, 13, 18, 19, 24, 30, 33, 35–36, 52,
65, 69, 73, 81, 82–83, 94, 115, 118, 120, 122,
124, 125, 129, 130, 131, 139, 146, 155, 241,
243, 257, 262, 272, 303, 309; food and diet:
bananas, 235; bread, 10; breadfruit, 145–
146, 149; coconuts, 246; coffee, 233; fowl,
13, 221; luau, 241; limu, 241, 246; mixed
pickles, 131; onions, 10, 303; oranges, 246;
milk, 76, 202; palu, 207, 241; soup, 202;
?sweet potatoes, 10, 33, 207, 255; pumpkins,
10; sausages, 241, 246; string beans, 305;
squash, 10; sugarcane, 131; watermelons, 7
(see also General Index: Food and diet; Taro);
sexual conduct, 88, 108, 172, 255, 257;
reminded to study Hawaiian legends, 46,
56; and genealogical history, 115; meditates
at Kahoāli'i's cave, 146; his new palaka
shirts, 149, 151n.1; troubles with house
servants, 255, 266; knock-down fight with
Kaawa, 199–201; learns of King Lunalilo's
death, 165–174; believes "natives" are
"naturally cowards," 178; words of Emma's
electoral defeat (1874), 166, 173–174;
growth of interest in predictions and magic,
xxi–xxii (see also General Index: Divination
and prophecies; Omens and signs; Sorcery);
first meeting with Hua the prophetess,
45–47; a darker vision, 274; session with
Kukeliaiau, 194–195; considers staging
rebellion at Kalaupapa, 226–227; reports
leprosy no longer considered contagious
disease, 184; prospective patient of Dr.
Akana, 244; his secretive mail, 251; an
arrested case, xii, 282–283; plans for escape,
279–280; rumor of his return to legislature,
314, 316; release by Board of Health, xii,
282–283; resumes seat in House of Nobles
(1878), 283; death and funeral, xii, 277–278,
281
Kahai, Hannah, 114, 155
Kahai, John, 210, 211n.3, 217
Kahalekule. See Kaauwai, William H.
Kahananui, Bennet, 51, 52n.1, 85–86, 88,
89n.8
Kahanawai, Hiram, 14, 15n.3, 21, 23, 43, 58,
74, 86, 100, 104, 110, 111, 120, 174, 224,
227, 230, 231
Kahanu, 295
Kahanu, H., 204
Kahea, 241
Kaheiheimalie, 105, 110, 113n.3
Kahele, 15, 64–65
Kahoāli'i (deified chief), 146, 147n.2
Kahoāli'i, Grace Kamai W., xiv, xv, 11, 12n.5,

14, 38, 39, 42, 170, 253
Kahōali'i, Kalawaianui, 157, 280, 317–318, 319n.1
Kahoe, 127
Kahoiwai, 296
Kaholakahiki, 305
Kahoukua, 137
Kaiaiki, 296
Kaikilani, 56
Kailipalaki, 310
Kaimimoku, 114, 123, 204, 206, 207, 221, 247, 248, 249, 251, 253, 255, 271
Kaina, L., 235, 295, 298n.12
Kainea, 209
Ka'iulani (Cleghorn), Victoria Kawekiu, 291, 292n.1
Kakuhina, 105
Kalaaukane, 315, 317
Kalaho'olewa. *See* Leleiohoku
Kalaipahala, 268n.6
Kalākaua, King David ("Taffy"), xii, xviii, xxii, xxiii, xxiv, xxv, xxvii–xxviii, 26, 39, *40n.7*, 58, 64, 85, 86, 88, 89nn.11 & 12, 97, 99, 100, 103, 104, 105, 109, 111, 112, 114, 115, 116nn.2 & 5, 118–119, 132, 133, 136, 142, 164, 165, 168, 172, 179, 182–183, 184, 185, 186, 188n.5, 189, 190, 194, 197, 200, 201, 204, 208, 210, 217, 220–221, 223, 224, 226, 227, 232, 233, 235, 236, 237, 239, 240, 245, 246–247, 248, 249, 251, 255–256, 258–259, 263–264, 265, 270, 274, 280, 281, 283, 286, 288, 291, 292, 294–295, 296, 300, 301, 303, 306, 308, 309, 312, 315, 319; his noble forebears, 116n.2, 267n.6; as viewed by Emma and Peter, xxii–xxiii, 115, 116n.5; town gossip about his paternity, 97, 98n.3; his interest in genealogy, xxxix, 43n.4, 255–256; appearance and manners in 1860s, xxviii–xxix; his military activities, 39, 72n.1, 93, 136, 178, 180n.8, 99–100, 101n.13, 103; rise to fame, 295; believed to have American backing, 109, 110; wins throne (1874), 165–166; fondness for gambling, 217, 265; rumored to be practicing black magic, 178–182 (*see also* General Index: Sorcery); projected visit to United States and world tour, 265, 300; predictions of his death while abroad, 204, 240, 259, 269, 270 (*see also* Divination and prophecy); relations with Queen Emma in the 1880s, xxxix, 321; his coronation, 43n.4; ominous last years, 41n.7
Kalākaua, Mrs. David. *See* Kapi'olani, Queen
Kalalahi, 269
Kalama, 88
Kalama, Queen (Hakaleleponi), 16n.7, 45,

46n.1, *51n.3*, 102, 189, 193
Kalamaia, 179
Kalani, 288, *290n.3*
Kalanikahua, 260
Kalaualu, 264
Kalaukoa, A.P., 294, 297n.2
Kalauli, 103
Kalawaianui. *See* Kahōali'i, Kalawaianui
Kaleikoa. *See* Kaeo, Kaleikoa
Kaleikuaiwa, 259
Kaliko, 57, 127
Kalua, 241
Kamahalo, Solomon, 59n.9
Kamai, Kimo ("Jim"), 127, 128n.4, 264–266, 313
Kamaio, 76, 108, 150, 239
Kamaipelekane, E. P., 258, 259n.2
Kamaipuupaa, 133, 137, 138n.4, 217–218
Kamaka, xxi, 54, 63, 71, 81, 204, 303
Kamakaaiau, *15n.4*, 41n.8, 70, 132, 137, 172, 213–214
Kamakakoko, 296
Kamakau, Samuel M., 289, 292, 294, 296, 297n.3, 300
Kamakini, 270
Kamakini, John M. *See* Kapena, John M.
Kamakini, Mrs. John M. *See* Kapena, Mrs. John M.
Kamauoha, 299, 301n.1
Kamehameha I, xi, xiv, 9n.1, 51n.3, 145n.4, 163, 242, 264, 265, 277–278, 323
Kamehameha II, Liholiho, xi, *51n.3*, 116n.2, 270
Kamehameha III, Kauikeaouli, xiv, xv, 16n.7, 50, *51n.3*, 78, 79n.7, 189, 249
Kamehameha IV, Alexander Liholiho ("Alex"), xvii, xviii, xxvii, xxviii–xxix, xxxvii, xl, *xlivn.13*, 14, 15n.2, 37n.1, 41n.8, 51n.3, 57, 58, 73, 74, 75, 78, 79n.7, 86, 87, 95n.8, 100, 104, 107, 115, 158, 204, 235, 249, 256, 265, 268n.6, 305, 312n.2, 319, 323
Kamehameha V, Lot, xviii, xxiv, xxvii, xxix, 7, 37n.1, 45, 46n.1, 78, 79n.7, 95n.8, 126, 136, 223, 232, 235, 249, 265, 308, 315
Kamoana, 226
Kamuela, 88
Kana'ina, 38, 39n.3, 86, 93, 103, 111, 163, 176, 177, 243
Kanakaole, 303
Kanelanahine, 206
Kanepuu, 209, 210n.5
Kanoa, Deborah, 57, 59n.9, 133
Kanoa, Paul, 251
Kaoana'eha (Mrs. John Young), xiv, xxxvii, *9n.1*, 116n.2
Kaohelani, Theresa Owana, 310, 311n.4

Kaona, 226, 228n.3
Kaoo, 255, 256n.2
Kapaʻakea, xxix, 40n.7, 98n.3, 117, 120n.2, 232
Kapahu, 91
Kapeau, 140, 195, 256
Kapena, John M., 57, 58, 60n.11, 64, 68–69, 99, 103, 132–133, 288, 300, 301, 318
Kapena, Mrs. John M. (Emma Malo), 132–133, 288, 300, 318
Kapiʻolani, Queen, xxxix, 15n.3, 26, 28n.1, 179, 186–187, 188n.5, 216–217, 218, 221, 235, 286, 288, 291, 300, 315, 321
Kapo. See Poʻomaikelani, Kapoʻoloko
Kapolini, 57
Kapukini, 112
Kauai, J., 202, 203, 209, 210, 227, 251, 296, 299, 300
Kaukaha, 196, 197, 198n.2, 200
Kaunahi, 288
Kaunaohua, 264
Kawainui, Joseph, 246, 289, 290n.8, 300, 301
Kawea, 123
Keakua, 248
Kealiikanakaole, 264–266
Kealohi, 153, 155n.5
Keano, 112, 114n.14, 120
Keaoa, 88
Keaoa, Joe, 14, 16n.6, 33, 34n.7, 111, 303
Keaoua, 196
Keawe, 288
Keawe-a-Heulu, 115, 116n.2, 132, 265
Keawehunahala, 135n.10
Keʻeaumoku IV. See Crowningburg, William
Keʻeaumoku IV. See Crowningburg, William
Keʻelikōlani, Ruth, 37n.1, 89n.11, 93, 94, 95n.8, 99, 110, 126, 127, 129, 131, 136, 137, 142, 143, 158, 163, 164, 169, 170, 172, 215, 218, 232, 239, 264, 265, 266, 283, 288, 295
Kekelaokalani, Fanny Young (Mrs. George Naea) ("Hipa"), xiv, 9n.1, 14, 16n.7, 24, 29, 31, 38, 46, 47n.8, 50, 52n.2, 54, 57, 65, 70, 84, 92, 105, 117, 120, 122, 124, 127, 134, 147, 152, 154, 158, 172, 190, 196, 210, 239, 283, 310, 319, 321, 322
Kekeliaiau, xxxiii, 189, 191n.2, 194–195
Kekina, 295
Kekoa, Niagara, 55, 59n.1, 133
Kekuanaʻoa, Governor, 95n.8
Kekuaokalani. See Kaeo, Peter
Kekuaokalani, Kaouwa, xi, xii, xx, xxi, xxii, xxxvii, 114, 115, 116n.2, 237
Keleau, 76, 108, 123, 150, 189, 195, 221
Keliʻimaikaʻi, xi, xx, 9n.1, 116n.4, 182, 238, 256, 265, 268n.6
Kemoikehuehu, J., 314n.4
Kennedy, Commander A. J., 217, 218n.5,

220–221, 226
Kenway, George, xvii
Keohokālole, xxix, 40n.7, 112, 137, 232
Keolaloa. See Sumner, William
Keomailani. See Kaohelelani, Theresa Owana
Keomailani, Stella (Mrs. Edwin K. Kea), 15n.4, 39, 41n.8, 42, 132
Kepelino (Zephyrin Kahōaliʻi), 165, 196, 197, 198n.3, 222n.2, 227, 229n.6, 237, 249n.3, 250, 251, 280
Kepoikai, N., 202, 203n.2
Kepola, 215
Kewiki. See Davis, Isaac George, II
Kia. See Nahaolelua, Kia
Kiha, 300
Kilinohe, 217
Kiliwehi (Mrs. Mary Ann Kaauwai), 112, 114n.15, 132, 152, 179, 180n.3, 208
Kipi, Moses, 288
Kipi, Samuel, 214, 215n.3, 288
Koakanu, 132
Koakanu, P. F., 190, 190n.9
Koii. See Unauna, Koii
Koleka, 127
Koloa, 287, 309, 312, 313, 314
Konia, 89n.12
Kuakanu, 205
Kuakini, John Adams, 163
Kuapuu, 299
Kuhina, 50, 51n.1
Kuihelani, Huaka, 111, 113n.12, 184, 202, 227, 233, 255–256
Kukeliaiau, xxxiii, 189, 191n.2, 194–195
Kumaka, 112
Kūnuiākea, Albert, xv, 14, 16n.7, 43, 50, 51n.3, 53, 65, 104, 168, 193, 201, 213, 251, 253, 286, 288, 296, 300, 306, 310, 311n.2, 317, 318, 319n.2
Kupihea, 22, 23n.4

Laanui, 55, 75, 91
Lalauli, 301
Lanaila, 120, 127
Laweoki, 75
Leilii, 303
Leleiohoku ("Buff," Kalahoʻolewa, "Kekoi," "Moo"), xxxix, 40n.7, 85, 89nn.11 & 12, 93, 99, 100, 103, 116n.5, 136, 137, 165, 169, 178, 179, 182, 196, 197, 218, 221, 227, 236, 237, 240, 245, 246, 248, 253, 257, 259, 264, 265, 303, 304n.4
Lelekahanu, 24, 29, 184
Lewi, 104
Lilikalani, Edward K., 292, 294, 295, 296, 297n.4, 300
Lilikalani, Judge, G. W., 186

Lili'uokalani, Queen. See Dominis, Mrs. John O.
Liloa, 246
Luika, 258, 259
Lunalilo, King William Charles, 7, 16n.10, 39, 40n.7, 45, 68–69, 72, 78, 84–86, 88, 91–92, 93, 94, 97, 98, 99, 100, 102, 103, 104, 105, 109–110, 111, 120, 126, 127, 131, 134, 142, 143, 154n.1, 158, 163–165, 166, 167n.5, 169–170, 172, 176, 177n.1, 179, 183, 197, 201, 248–249, 288, 322; attitude toward reciprocity, 58, 61n.18, 94, 96n.15; toward ceding Pearl Harbor, 15, 58, 61n.18, 94, 96n.15; no liking for Kalākaua, 86; life with Eliza Meek, 91, 92, 112; the succession crisis (1873–1874), 164–165 (see also General Index: Succession); his damaged lungs, 84–85, 92, 105, 169–170; and addiction to drink, 57, 58, 64, 69, 84–85, 86; as "romantic" chieftain-hero, 167n.5; his death, 164, 165; his remembered anniversary, 322
Luther, 271

McGrew, Dr. John S., 109, 112, 113n.2, 224
McKibbin, Dr. Robert, Jr. (Pamalo), 14, 15 n.5, 51, 84–85, 86, 91, 92, 105, 109, 111, 112, 127, 132, 223, 277
Mackintosh, Rev. Alexander, 92, 95n.5
Mahelona, S. W., 289, 295, 296
Mahi, 289
Mahiole, Kawika, 91
Mahiole, Victoria, 91
Mahoe, 104
Mahuna, 140, 200
Maigret, Bishop Louis Désiré, 27, 29n.7
Maikai, Abigail (Mrs. Samuel), 86
Makalena, J. W., 93, 95n.10, 120
Makanahoa, 50
Makanui, 114, 116n.1, 155, 156
Makaula, 179, 197, 217, 255
Makue, 88
Malo, David, II, 133, 135n.12, 292
Maloi, 123, 150, 156
Mamaina, 75n.4
Manuia, 52, 54, 256
Marau, 310
Maria, 200
Markham, Mr. and Mrs. W. A., 291
Martin, William Thomas, 210, 211n.7
Meek, Eliza, 91, 92, 95n.1, 105, 110, 112, 120
Mele, 157
Meyer, Rudolph, 36, 37n.1, 48, 76, 82, 85, 139, 206, 207, 224, 236, 272, 303, 308, 309
Mikalemi, 247
Mikauahoa, 86

Mikona, 319
Miohi, Judge, 299
Moanauli, 92, 95n.6, 103, 299, 304
Moehonua, William L., 46n.1, 58, 85, 89n.9, 93, 101n.12, 133
Moetia, 310
Moluhi, 258

Naaoa, 133
Naea, George, xivn.9
Nahalau, 14, 15n.2, 33
Nahaolelua, Kia, 57, 59n.8, 288
Nahaolelua, Paul, 49n.1, 50, 51n.2, 53, 57, 66, 69, 72, 85, 93, 110, 131, 132, 133, 176, 217, 233, 256
Nahinu, 290
Naili, J. L., 295, 298n.9
Nakaleka, J., 295, 298n.11
Nakilau, 287
Namahana, 112
Naone, J., 186
Napaepae, 12, 24, 88, 108
Napela, Jonathan, xx, 14, 16n.8, 18, 20, 22, 23, 24, 33, 34, 35, 36, 42, 44, 45, 47, 48, 52, 53, 54, 55n.6, 57, 64, 65, 66, 67, 71, 72, 74, 76, 77–79, 80, 81, 82, 107, 112, 114, 115, 122, 123, 126, 129, 130, 131, 139, 140n.1, 141, 146, 152, 153, 157n.4, 173, 182–183, 184, 185, 186, 189, 192, 195, 199, 200, 202, 208, 217, 221, 227, 228, 230, 233, 235, 236–237, 239, 243, 247, 248, 249, 251, 253, 255, 270, 271, 274, 319
Napela, Mrs. Jonathan (Kiti Richardson), 16n.8, 20, 34, 47, 74, 77, 113n.12, 117, 124, 126, 139, 149, 150, 152, 173, 184, 185, 186, 195, 199, 200, 208, 217, 220, 221, 230, 233, 236–237, 240, 244, 245, 246, 248, 255, 258, 274
Napepe'e. See Ward, Curtis P.
Napoleon III, Emperor, xvii
Naukana, 295, 298n.8
Nawahi, Joseph, 189, 190n.1, 202, 205, 207, 246, 251, 281, 289, 296
Niagara. See Kekoa, Niagara
Ninito (Mrs. John Sumner), 127n.2, 134, 135n.15, 192, 289, 295, 296, 299, 300, 310
Nohea, Miss, 14
Nordhoff, Charles, 48n.3, 57, 59n.10, 63, 94
Nordhoff, Mrs. Charles, 88, 94

Okuu, 140, 195, 204, 231, 232, 256
Okuu, Mrs., 232
Oliver, Dr., 169
Olohana. See Young, John
Opunui, J. W., 246, 247n.2
Owana. See Keohelani, Theresa Owana

Paalua, 288, 306
Paki, Abner, 89n.12, 189
Palale, 235
Palenapa (Barenaba), 295, 298n.10
Panee, 58
Paneku, 296, 319
Parke, William C., *42n.1*, 103, 128n.4
Parker, Rev. Henry H., 57, 58, 60n.12
Parker, Samuel, 184, 185n.2
Parker, Mrs. Samuel, 256
Pauahi, 310
Peabody, Lucy, 18, 19n.5, 21, 38, 55, 70, 91,
    109, 133, 152, 170, 258, 310
Peirce, Henry A., 26, *28n.5*, 90n.14, 98n.3,
    101n.13, 128n.3
Pennock, Adm. Arthur M., 90n.14, 136,
    137n.1
Pfluger, Mrs. William, 127
Pfluger, William, 127, 178, 222n.4, 223, 227
Piikoi, Lydia. *See* Wond, Lydia Piikoi
Piko, 215
Pilipo, Rev. George W., 103, 174, 176n.5,
    246, 278, 281, 282, 288–289, 296, 299, 304
Pinehasa. *See* Wood, Pinehasa
Poikai. *See* Kepoikai
Polapola. *See* Wilson, Charles B.
Pomare, Queen, 134, 135n.16, 192, 310
Po'omaikelani, Kapo'oloko, 15n.3, 26, 42,
    43n.4, 57, 70, 174, 218, 224, 235, 253, 291,
    322
Poopuu, 170
Powell, Dr. William P., 203, 205n.1, 209, 213,
    214–215, 217, 226, 227, 233
Pratt, Franklyn S., 88, 90n.19, 92, 174, 178,
    223, 306, 315
Pratt, Mrs. Franklyn S. (Kekaaniau), 88,
    90n.19, 92, 306, 310
Prendergast, Col. Henry, 85, 88n.4
Preston, Edward, 279, 280, 292, 293n.5, 296,
    300, 304, 317
Puhi, 247, 248
Pukooku, 255, 260, 266
Puni, John, 29, 30n.1
Punini, 287, 309
Pupule, 237, 239

Ragsdale, William P., xx, xxi, 7, 14, *16n.9*,
    20, 22, 24, 32, 33, 34, 36, 38, 42, 54, 55nn.5
    & 6, 66–67, 73, 82, 87, 124, 125, 129, 130,
    131, 139, 140n.1, 141, 146, 152, 153, 154,
    155, 156, 157n.4, 159, 170, 172, 174, 175,
    179, 184, 187, 190, 193, 195, 197, 201,
    204–205, 206, 207, 208, 213, 214, 215, 220,
    221, 222, 226, 230, 231, 234, 236, 237, 240,
    242, 244, 245, 246, 249, 251, 271, 281, 286,
    287, 308, 313, 318

Reeves, John, 88, 90n.19
Rhodes, Godfrey, 59, 62n.24, 220
Richardson, George K., 244
Rives, Jean, 90n.19
Rooke, Dr. T. C. B., xiv, xv, xviii, xl
Rose, S. B., 21, 22n.2, 139, 140, 141
Rycroft, Robert, 217, 219n.7

Selfe, Robert, 86, 90n.18
Sellon, Rev. Mother Priscilla Lydia, 41n.8
Severance, Luther, 33, 35n.9
Sheldon, Henry L., 223, 225n.3
Smith, Jack, 39, 41n.10, 54, 131, 279, 280, 317
Smith, Sheriff, 37
Smithies, John S., 61n.19, 291
Smithies, Miss, 58, 61n.19
Smithies, Mrs. John S., 58, 61n.19
Spencer, Miss, 310, 314
Spreckles, Claus, 40n.7
"Spring" (dog), 206
Stanley, R. H., 305
Steinberger, Col. A. B., 26, 28n.4
Stevens, John L., 89n.12
Stirling, Robert, 93, 96n.11, 143
Sumner, Capt. William, 127n.2
Sumner, John K. (Keolaloa), *127n.2*, 135n.15,
    289, 296
Sumner, William, 127n.2, 289, 296, 310

Titaua, 310
Trousseau, Dr. George, xxxiii, 21, *22n.3*, 24,
    25, 35n.9, 37, 48, 49, 53, 54, 58, 66, 69,
    84–85, 92, 100, 104, 109, 111, 124, 127, 142,
    143, 152, 158, 163, 164, 179, 209, 234, 244,
    256, 264, 271, 273
Tyrtoff, Capt., 112

Unauna, Koii, 178, *180n.7*, 182, 253, 255–256,
    268n.6, 315
Unauna, Maria, 221, 222, 230, 235, 255
Upa, 7

Victoria, Queen, xvii, xli, 165, 166, 303
von Pfister, Mrs. Sarah Rhodes, xviii–xix, 283

Waahia, 218, 219n.10, 258–259, *260n.4*
Wahineiki, 150
Waiaha, 91, 95n.2
Waiahole, 14, 22, 55, 57, 258
"Waialua." *See* Davies, Theophilus H.
Waihoekaea, 88
Walker, Rev. George, 323
Walker, Thomas R., 245n.4, 308
Ward, Curtis P., 85, 133, 135n.13
Waterhouse, Henry, 294, 296n.1
Waua, Judge, 299

Weed, Mrs. Frederick, 93, 96n.12, 103, 126, 179, 183, 220, 239, 289
West, Capt., 132
Whitney, Henry M., xxxviii, 43, 44n.1, 142, 144n.2, 272
Widemann, Herman, 179, 181n.12, 186
Wikani, 44, 45n.1, 57, 70, 85, 111, 231
Wilder, Samuel G., 9n.10, 21, 33, 36, 37, 42, 48, 49, 54, 58, 63–64, 66, 67, 84, 92, 107, 122, 125, 152, 153, 154, 169, 175, 179, 190, 197, 205, 214, 226, 242, 256, 277, 282–283, 287, 289
William I, Kaiser, 308, 315
William II, Kaiser, 308
Williamson, William, 124, 158–159, 205
Willis, Bishop Alfred, 120, 121n.7, 152, 306

Wilson, Charles B. (Polapola), 93, 96n.13, 103
Wilson, John B., 96n.13
Wodehouse, James Hay, 211n.6
Wodehouse, Mrs. James Hay (Annette Massey), 210, 211n.6, 214
Wond, Mrs. William (Lydia Piikoi), 132–133, 135n.9
Wood, J. H., 137
Wood, Pinehasa, 213, 215n.1
Woods, Dr., 282
Wyllie, Robert Crichton, xxviii, xlii, 51n.3

Young, John (Olohana), xiv, xxx, xxxi, xl, 9n.1
Young, John (Keoni Ana), xiv, xv, 322

Index of Places

Beretania Street (Honolulu), 319
Bernice Pauahi Bishop Museum, 145n.4

Chiefs' Children's School, xvii, xxvii

Diamond Head (Oahu), 132, 319

Emma Square, Queen (Honolulu), 38, 40n.5, 315

Fort Street (Honolulu), 85, 133

Halawa (Molokai), 107, 261
"Haleakala" (house, Honolulu), 264, 266, 267n.5
Hale Ololo (house, Kailua, Hawaii), 169, 170n.4
Halia pool (Hawaii), 158, 159n.1
Hamohamo (house, Waikiki), 88, 91n.21, 224, 232
Hana (Maui), 240
Hanalei (Kauai), 299
Hanauma Bay (Oahu), xvi, 31n.1, 34, 69
Hawaii (island of), 227, 236, 259
Hawaiian Hotel (Honolulu), 94, 294, 297n.5
Hilo (Hawaii), 200, 214, 259
Hilo Bay, 26
"Honolulu" (cottage, Kalaupapa), 68n.1, 147, 148n.1
Honuakaha (Oahu), 295
Hulihee (house, Kailua, Hawaii), 163, 170n.4

Iao Valley (Maui), 240

Kahoali'i's cave (Kalaupapa), xxxiii, 146, 147n.2

Kaholaloa reef (Honolulu), 310
Kahoolawe (island of), 288
Kailua (Hawaii), 163, 168
Kalae (Molokai), 70, 207
Kalaieha (Hawaii), 118, 121n.5
Kalakaua Avenue (Honolulu), 319, 320n.5
Kalaupapa (peninsula and settlement, Molokai), xix, xx, 76, 80, 123, 206, 220, 246, 318
Kalawao (valley and settlement, Kalaupapa), 7, 17, 18, 21, 32, 42, 65, 66, 71, 73, 76, 80, 82, 195, 206, 220, 234, 244, 258, 261, 262, 272, 296, 310
Kalawao Hospital (Kalaupapa), 18, 34, 48, 54, 66, 72, 79, 80, 124, 130, 141, 204, 206
Kalihi Hospital (Honolulu), 7, 8n.1, 114, 128n.4, 147, 233
Kalihi Valley (Oahu), 36
Kauai (island of), xi, xxx, 146, 299
Kauhako Hill (Kalaupapa), xxxiii, 7, 17, 18n.1, 32, 145–146, 149, 203
Kaumakapili Church (Honolulu), 44n.1, 103, 106n.10, 176n.5
Kaunakakai (Molokai), 36, 37, 44, 109, 125, 155, 232, 273
Kawa (prison, Oahu), 99, 101n.11
Kawaiahao Church (Honolulu), 57, 60n.13, 64
Kawaihoa (Oahu), 97n.1
"Kekuaokalani's Avenue" (Kalaupapa), 69, 72, 126
Kewalo (Oahu), 109, 113n.1
Kiilae (Hawaii), 111
Kilauea Crater (Hawaii), xxx, 115
Kilohana (Kauai), 146, 147n.3
Kinau Hale (house, Honolulu), 86, 90n.17
Koko Head (Oahu), 97n.1

Koolau (Oahu), 190, 236, 295, 303, 315, 318
Kona (Hawaii), 73, 103, 118, 121n.4, 126, 152, 164, 170, 261, 288, 289, 290, 299
Kua Makela. *See* Kaumakapili Church
Kulaokahua (Honolulu), 126, 127n.1

Lahaina (Maui), xi, 125, 288, 292, 296, 300–301
Lanai (island of), 295

Makapuu Point (Oahu), 8, 9, 82, 97
Makawao (Maui), 259
Malayan Kingdom, 131, 134n.3
Manoa (Oahu), 227, 292
Maui (island of), 300
Mauna Ewa (Oahu), 127
Mauna Kea (Hawaii), xvi, xvii, 118, 121n.6
Maunakea Street (Honolulu), 132, 288
Maunalua (Oahu), 292
Moanalua (Oahu), 292
Molokai (island of), xi, xvi, xx, 7, 31, 35, 56, 84, 87, 117–118, 295, 317, 319

Napoopoo (Hawaii), 290
Nuuanu Valley (Oahu), xxviii, xxx, 36, 85, 128n.4, 318, 319

Oahu (island of), xvi, xx, 8, 9, 36, 44, 48, 82, 97, 213, 259
Old Palace (Honolulu), 86, 251, 286, 287n.1

Palama (Honolulu), 290
Pali (Kalaupapa), 18, 19n.2, 32, 35, 63, 67–68, 146, 172, 240, 262
Pawaa (Honolulu), 103
Pearl Harbor (Oahu), xiii, 15, 17n.11, 26, 33, 65n.2, 94, 101n.13, 142
Pelekunu (Molokai), 54, 107
Pohukaina (house, Honolulu), 86, 90n.16
Polihale (house, Honolulu), 52, 52n.2
Puna (Hawaii), 189
Punaluu (Oahu), 318
Punchbowl (Honolulu), 18, 19n.3, 51, 86, 88

Puukailio (Kolekole Pass, Oahu), 118, 121n.3
Puuloa. *See* Pearl Harbor

Queen's Hospital (Honolulu), xl, 33, 35n.8, 120, 132, 134n.4, 147
Queen Street (Honolulu), 57, 66

Rooke House (Honolulu), 75n.1, 76, 120, 165, 323
Rosebank (house, Honolulu), xxviii, xl, xlii
Royal Mausoleum (Nuuanu Valley, Honolulu), xlii, 14, 15n.1, 16n.6, 22, 34n.7, 277, 323
St. Andrew's Cathedral (Honolulu), xl, 323
St. Andrew's Priory (Honolulu), xl, 41n.8
St. Bartholomew's Hospital (London), xl
St. Philomena's Church (Kalaupapa), 24, 130, 148, 149, 258
Schoolhouse (Kalaupapa), 261
Store, Settlement (Kalawao), 21, 49, 139, 141, 149–150, 154, 205, 271
Sumner's Reef (Honolulu), 127n.2

Tahiti, 135n.15, 137, 192, 296, 299, 300, 310

Waiaha (Hawaii), 158
Waialua (Oahu), 85, 88, 295
Waianae (Oahu), 127, 190, 288, 295
Waiau pond (Hawaii), xvii
Waihanau (stream and valley, Kalaupapa), 115, 122
Waihee (Maui), 44n.1
Waikiki (Oahu), 15, 38, 58, 69, 84, 88, 91n.21, 109, 127, 142, 232, 266
Waikolu (Kalaupapa), 18, 29, 32, 34, 48, 54, 63, 73, 82, 122, 123, 130, 139, 152, 156, 209, 241, 243, 261
Wailau (Molokai), 71, 107
Wailua (Molokai), 242
Wailuku (Maui), 44n.1, 132, 208, 233
Waimea (Hawaii), xvi
Waimea (Kauai), 251, 299

General Index

Animals and pets, 11, 12, 13, 18, 19, 21, 24, 25, 28, 29, 30, 33, 37, 67–68, 76, 79n.2, 115, 122, 129, 131, 139, 189, 200, 203, 206, 221, 238, 243, 253, 261, 303, 315, 319
Annexation, xiii, 15, 17n.12, 38, 42, 48, 49n.3, 57, 58, 60n.10, 64, 65n.2, 73, 86, 89n.12, 94, 110, 126, 137, 169, 308, 323
Apostles' Creed, 87

Band, Royal Hawaiian, 38, 40n.5, 99, 105

Barracks Mutiny. *See* Revolt of Household Troops
Baths and bathing, 11, 18, 24, 29, 31, 34, 42, 46, 63, 69, 70, 73, 80, 82, 108, 109, 127, 130, 133, 151, 192, 221, 224, 241
Beef. *See* Food and diet
Bible, 118, 120, 178, 322, 323; quoted, 27, 54, 87, 104
Bible Corps ("Bible Core"), 99, 101n.9
Blood-letting, 215

Board of Commissioners for Foreign Missions, xxi

Board of Health, Hawaiian, xii, xx, xxi, 7, 8n.11, 11, 14n.2, 21, 24, 33, 36, 37, 54, 73, 76, 82, 107, 124, 139, 140n.1, 141, 148, 179, 187, 197, 221, 227, 233, 242, 277, 282, 285n.12, 286, 310

"Burning fire" kapu (rite), 182, 184n.2, 218, 219n.9

Cabinet ministers, 15, 42n.2, 45, 86, 92, 99, 136, 306, 308

Camphor, 23, 28, 39, 150

Cave, lepers in, 80

Cession of territory, 15, 26, 39, 57, 60n.10, 65n.2, 73, 138n.2, 142. See also Places: Pearl Harbor

Chants, 165–166, 167n.8, 182, 184n.1, 185n.3

Churches. See Episcopal Church; Missionaries, American Protestant; Mormon Church; Roman Catholic Church

Church of England. See Episcopal Church

Clothing and dress, 9, 21, 23, 28, 32, 34, 36, 45, 52, 81, 110, 123–124, 125, 131, 139–140, 149, 150, 179, 212, 221, 241, 253, 271, 287–288, 314, 318

"Committee of Thirteen" (legislative body), 281–282

Communion, Holy, xlii, 87, 323

Constitution, Hawaiian, 241, 296

Cooking facilities, 11, 24, 33, 36, 108, 221, 224, 266, 287, 305

Courthouse Riot, 166, 174, 175n.2, 176, 177n.2, 178, 181n.9, 294. See also Persons: Kepelino

Crown lands, 305

Death(s) and dying, xxxviii–xxxix, 20, 22, 24, 27, 29, 31, 33, 36, 37, 48, 54, 64, 66, 67, 76, 86, 91, 93, 97, 109, 111, 114n.15, 127, 129–130, 132, 134n.6, 150, 152, 153, 157, 159, 164, 165, 178, 179, 182, 183, 200–201, 208, 213, 215, 216–217, 218, 241–242, 258–259, 263–264, 277, 283, 289, 290, 306, 309, 312n.2, 313, 319. See also Population, Hawaiian

Divination and prophecies, xxii, xxiii–xxv, 45, 47–48, 78, 94, 126, 152, 179, 182–183, 186, 189–190, 194–195, 196, 197, 200–201, 204, 208, 209, 214, 218, 227, 231, 232, 235, 237–238, 239, 241, 242, 248, 249, 258–259, 263–264, 266, 270, 274, 278, 288, 289n.7, 291n.10, 309, 321–322. See also Kahuna(s); Omens and signs

Dreams and visions, xxv, xxxivn.10, 35, 45, 47–48, 57, 148, 186, 189, 195, 208, 239, 248,

269, 305, 321–322. See also Divination and prophecies

Drinking and alcoholism, 14, 17n.10, 22–23, 32, 34n.1, 39, 52, 54, 58, 64, 69, 84, 86, 92, 99, 105, 111, 120, 130, 187n.1, 220, 230, 231, 234, 258, 295, 309

Elections, 126, 164–165, 173, 197, 294–296, 299–304, 304n.3. See also Courthouse Riot; Succession, royal

Episcopal Church, xviii–xix, xxviii, xxxv, xl, xlii, xxxii, 24, 26–27, 30, 31, 56, 64, 79n.7, 86–87, 91, 93, 120, 192

Eucalyptus trees, sanifying effect of, 33, 35n.8

Firewood, 255

Fishes and fishing, 10, 13, 21, 28, 29, 33, 42, 57, 76, 80, 108, 127, 133, 134, 140, 152, 153, 156, 159, 169, 197, 209, 244, 266, 287, 309, 321, 322. See also Food and diet

Food and diet, xx–xxi, 10, 11, 12n.1, 13, 33, 34, 53, 63, 71, 74, 76, 108, 115, 122, 123, 130, 152–154, 156, 193, 197, 202, 204, 233, 241, 243, 244, 255, 271, 309. See also Taro; Persons: Kaeo, Peter Young: food and diet

"French priest," 209. See also Persons: Damien, Father; Burgerman, André

"Frocks, China," 150

Genealogy, xix, xxiii, xxxvii, xliii, 43n.4, 115, 116nn.2 & 6, 117–118, 255–256, 264–266, 267n.6, 269

Germany, 308, 315

Gospel of St. John, 72

Great Britain, 214, 218, 220, 295, 304n.1

Greek Orthodox Church, 56, 110–111

"Haole(s)" (foreigners, white persons), xiv, 178, 190, 196, 238, 264–266, 272, 295–296, 300, 306

Horseracing, 258

Hotel, Hawaiian, 294, 297n.5

House of Nobles. See Legislature, Hawaiian

House of Representatives. See Legislature, Hawaiian

Illness(es) and treatments, 23, 28, 34, 44, 51, 53, 54, 66, 69, 74, 76, 77–79, 79n.6, 84, 85, 91, 92, 105, 107–108, 109, 111, 115, 124, 126, 127, 129, 130, 132, 134, 136, 139, 148, 150, 152, 153, 156, 157, 174, 202, 209, 215, 233, 234, 244, 257, 269, 286, 287, 309, 310, 314, 319. See also Death(s) and dying; Persons: Kaeo, Peter Young: leprous symptoms and general health

Independence, Hawaiian, 38, 51n.3, 54, 59, 169, 289. *See also* Annexation

Kahuna(s) (prophets, sorcerers, "experts"). *See* Divination and prophecy; Persons: Hua, Paniku; Kukeliaiau; Waahia
Kālai-pāhoa (poison god), xxiii, 178, 230, 264, 267n.3
Kalākaua family and dynasty ("DK's"), xiii, xxii, xxiv, xxix, 58, 86, 93, 99, 112, 114n.16, 115, 117, 137, 138n.5, 189, 194, 196, 200, 201, 208–209, 210, 213, 217, 218, 239, 240, 245, 259, 269, 278, 286, 288, 289–290, 291, 296, 303, 306, 310
Kalākaua "party" ("DK's"), 86, 99, 103, 112, 176, 178, 179, 186, 187n.1, 189, 194, 196, 197, 200, 226–227, 245, 251, 258, 288, 289–290, 292, 294, 295, 296, 299, 303, 310, 318–319
Kamehameha Schools, 145n.4
Kaumakapili Church trustees, 299
Kilauea (interisland steamer), 21, 58, 111, 127, 136, 142, 152, 153, 169, 182, 184, 185, 202, 226

Legislature, Hawaiian, 126, 233; House of Nobles, xx, xxiv, xxvii–xxxviii, 281, 283, 318; House of Representatives, 202, 203–204, 207, 233, 279, 283, 292, 294–295, 318, 319
Lei(s), 45, 47nn.3 & 4, 205, 221, 239, 271–272, 273n.1
Lepers of Kalaupapa (general), xii, xix, xx, xxi, xxiv–xxv, 7, 33–34, 35n.9, 78, 79n.7, 123–124, 130, 139, 141, 147, 184–185, 190, 197, 204–205, 221, 226, 241–242, 243n.4, 244, 282, 286–287
Letters, loss of, 175n.1, 215, 246, 279, 325 ff.
"Litany of Penitents," 322
Loan Bill ("million dollar loan"), 214, 215n.5, 217, 220, 227, 289, 294, 300, 301, 303, 318–319, 320n.4
Lono-i-ka-makahiki (legendary hero and god), 46, 47n.7, 56

Meat. *See* Food and diet
Medicine(s): Chinese, 244, 251; patent, 53, 54, 70, 77, 148. *See also* Illness(es) and treatments
Missionaries, American Protestant, xvii, xxi, 20n.1, 57, 58, 64, 70, 71, 79n.7, 93
Monarchy, Hawaiian, xxxix–xl
Mormon Church, 16n.8, 20n.1, 169, 192, 195, 247–248

"Nativism," 279, 284n.3

Omens and signs, 194, 195, 200–201, 208, 210, 231, 237–238, 278, 289–290. *See also* Divination and prophecies
Ox cart(s), 30, 33, 77, 286

"Pai" (*pa'i*). *See* Taro
Papal infallibility, 27, 29n.7
Personal names, their symbolism, xxxvii, 83, 122, 244
Pipe smoking, 52
Poi (*poi*). *See* Taro
Poison and poison god. *See* Kālai-pāhoa
Policemen, 130, 226, 258
Police station (Honolulu), 88
Population question (1860s and 1870s), xxxviii–xxxix, 62nn.23 & 25, 306, 307, 309, 310, 312n.2, 315
Potion, love, 88, 95n.2
Prayers and praying, 70, 72, 87, 97, 119, 169, 173, 174, 176, 178, 182, 189, 195, 205, 209, 210, 213, 215, 217, 218, 222, 231, 233, 236, 238, 239, 240, 243, 256, 258, 260, 263, 264, 266, 272, 274, 287, 288, 289, 314
"Primordial" groups, xxxv–xxxvii
Prison, Kalaupapa, 24, 25n.3
Privy Council, 306
Protestantism. *See* Missionaries, American Protestant

"Queenites," 166, 200, 280, 281, 289, 318. *See also* Courthouse Riot

Rebels, xi–xii. *See also* Glossary; *kipi*
Reciprocity, xiii, 43, 44n.1, 57, 58, 62n.24, 94, 96n.15, 101n.13, 136, 138n.2, 289, 294, 300, 301, 303, 308, 318, 319n.3
Republicanism, 89n.12, 97, 126, 292
Republic of Hawaii, 90n.12
Revolt of Household Troops, 98–102, 103
Riot(s), 265. *See also* Courthouse Riot
Roman Catholic Church, 20n.1, 26–27, 30, 31, 56, 130. *See also* Persons: Damien, Father
Russians, visiting, 110–111, 113nn.7–9, 221, 222n.4, 223

Servants, 12, 13, 19, 24, 29, 36, 52, 74, 76, 108, 123, 140, 150, 155n.3, 189, 221, 224, 233, 238, 239, 240, 241, 247, 255, 266, 270, 271, 277, 287, 305, 313, 314, 315
Ships: *Askold* (Russian battleship), 98, 100n.2; *Benicia* (U.S. battleship); 210, 271n.1, 213; *Camelion* (British steam corvette), 217, 218n.5; *Costa Rica* (ship), 82, 92; *Juanita* (interisland), 109; *Kamoi* (interisland), 132, 147; *Kapiolani* (interisland), 236; *Kekuhai*

(royal canoe), 14, 16n.6; *Kinau* (interisland), 7, 10, 14, 52; *Lackawanna* (U.S. battleship), 282; *Luka* (interisland), 258; *Murray* (interisland), 137, 296; *Nellie Morris* (interisland), 272, 273; *Nettie Merrill* (interisland), 207; *Portsmouth* (U.S. battleship), 86, 88, 90n.14, 92, 127, 128n.3, 166; *Saranac* (U.S. battleship), 90n.14, 128n.3; *Tenedos* (British battleship), 166; *Thaddeus* (brig), xxi; *Tsukuba* (Japanese battleship), 300, 302n.6; *Tuscarora* (U.S. battleship), 166; *Waikolu* (interisland), 236; *Waiola* (interisland), 12, 70. See also *Kilauea* (interisland steamer); *Warwick* (schooner)
Soap, 205
Songs and singing, 31, 32n.2, 48, 49n.2, 80, 82, 83n.4, 146, 183, 212, 216, 218n.1
Sorcery, xxii–xxiii, xxiv–xxv, 103, 105n.5, 106n.16, 178, 179, 182, 189, 194–195, 197, 200, 201, 230, 235, 264. See also Divination and prophecies; Omens and signs
Spirits, ghosts, angels, xxii, xxxiii, 45, 46n.2, 87, 146, 147n.2, 194, 208–209, 283, 288, 290n.6. See also Dreams and visions
Starvation, charges at Kalaupapa, 152–153, 156. See also Food and diet; Taro
Store, Kalawao settlement, 52, 54, 64, 79, 81, 83, 130, 131, 139, 141, 149–150, 152, 154, 187, 205
Succession, royal, xxiii–xxiv, 84, 85, 86, 92–94, 103–104, 105, 109–110, 111, 112, 126, 129, 137, 142–143, 152, 164–165, 170n.3, 173, 179, 200–201, 213, 214, 227, 232, 235, 237, 238, 241, 265, 288, 289–290, 294, 296, 298n.13, 303, 304n.4, 309, 319. See also Divination and prophecies
Sugar industry, 57, 60n.14, 62n.23, 62n.24, 62n.25, 300, 308. See also Reciprocity

Taro: (*kalo*, 11, 12n.2, 13, 19, 29, 51, 54, 77, 82, 107, 108, 114, 152, 154, 155n.3, 156, 177, 186, 226, 231, 232, 235, 246, 255, 270, 271, 286; poi (*poi*), 12n.2, 29, 33, 49, 65, 100, 104, 117, 209, 228, 243, 270, 287; shortages of, xx–xxi, 11, 12n.2, 13, 33, 54, 80, 107, 122, 123, 126, 146, 147n.1, 156, 159n.2, 190, 192, 217, 255, 309, 313; "pai" (*pa'i*), 12n.2, 29, 33, 34, 48, 49, 53, 63, 66, 71, 80, 81, 107, 130, 153, 156, 158, 159, 192–193, 209, 217, 228, 255; shortages of, 63, 64, 65, 123, 146, 153, 156, 192–193
Telegraph Station, 319
Theo H. Davies Co., Ltd., 70n.4
Trees, 13, 18, 33, 35n.8, 80, 81, 94, 145, 146, 243, 262, 272. See also Persons: Kaeo, Peter Young: gardening

Uli (sorcery goddess), 264, 266n.2

"Volunteers" (military unit), 100, 101n.14

"Wailuku party" (Maui), 112, 114n.16. See also Persons: Kalākaua, King David; Kalākaua "party"
Warwick (schooner), 19, 25, 33, 37, 38, 49, 50, 51, 53, 55, 64, 65, 66, 68, 75, 87, 104, 109, 114, 120, 123, 124, 125, 130, 139, 146, 147, 151, 172, 183, 226, 227, 230, 231, 233, 241, 243, 244, 246, 255, 256, 260, 261, 270, 271, 272, 273, 286, 292, 303, 310, 312, 315, 316, 317, 319
Water and water supply (Kalaupapa, Honolulu), 13, 19, 24, 25, 27–28, 51–52, 65, 66–67, 72, 73, 82, 108, 129–130, 131–132, 136–137, 138n.3, 154, 195, 213, 224, 241
"Whites." See "Haole(s)"
Word magic, 291n.10
Wreath(s). See Lei(s)

Selected Glossary

'aha'aina (feast), 88, 90n.20, 204
'aho (rafter), 262, 263n.3
'ahu'ula (cape, ceremonial robe), 110
'ai kapu (rite), xi
akakū (vision, trance), xxvi
akua ("Akua[s]") (god[s]), 18, 19n.4
akule (fish), 197
'alalauā (fish), 57
aloali'i (royal court), xxviii, xxxix, 69, 114, 183
'anā'anā (evil sorcery), xxiii, 103, 105n.5, 178, 179, 182, 189, 197, 200, 201, 235, 264
'ape (plant), 103, 106n.6

'aumākua (family gods), 45, 78, 79n.3, 194, 195n.2
'awa (plant, medicinal drink), 124, 146, 189
'awapuhi (plant), 184

haka (spirit-medium), xxxiii, 46n.2
hanai ("hanai[s]") (foster relation[s]), 117, 120n.1, 215
haole. See General Index: "Haole(s)"
holoku (woman's garment), 81
ho'okupu (rite), 169, 220, 222n.4, 223
ho'oponopono (healing practice, rite), 78, 79n.6
hula (chanting and/or dancing), 22, 23n.6,

184, 263
hulumanu ("Hulumanus") (military body), 178, 180n.8

ilailau (?*la'ila'i*) (kind of sweet potato), 152–153, 155n.4

kāhili (feather standard), 277
kahu ("kahu[s]") (honored attendant[s]), 264
kahuna ("kahuna[s]") (priest, expert, sorcerer), 179, 182, 194–195, 208, 210, 218, 237, 263, 270, 288, 290
kala (rite), 208, 288
kālai-pāhoa (poisonous wood and poison god), xxiii, 264, 266n.3
kalo (taro). *See* General Index: Taro
kama'āina ("kamaaina[s]") (native-born), 9, 10n.3, 11, 12, 18, 19, 36–37, 54, 66, 82, 147, 206, 218, 221, 223, 245, 255, 261,
kapa (tapa), 45
kauila (tree and wood), 194n.1, 199, 200
kawa (prison), 197, 199n.7
kīhei (shawl), 52, 53n.3
kino (spirit), 288, 290n.6
kipi ("kipi[s]") (rebel[s]), 114, 115, 201, 258
koa (tree and wood), 32, 34n.4
kōkua ("kokua[s]") (help, helper[s]), 25, 130, 139, 150, 153
koli'i ("koli") (shrub), 262, 263n.2
kona (storm), 261–263
kōnane (game), 56
kū'auhau (genealogy), 115, 116n.6, 117
Kūkā'ilimoku (war-god), xi
kūmau (bowl, calabash), 288, 290nn.1 & 2
kumini (cummin seed), 103, 106n.7
kuni (retributive sorcery), 189, 201
kupe'e (bracelet, anklet), xvi–xvii

lā'ī (ti leaf), 107, 108n.4
lei (lei[s]), 45, 205, 221, 239, 271–272, 273n.1

lei hulu (feather lei), 45, 47n.4
leimokihana ("Kaleimokihana") (name of wreath and person), 244
lei palaoa (whale tusk lei), 45, 47n.4
limu (food), 270, 272
lomi (massage), 76, 77n.2, 129, 150
luakālai (halo effect or rainbow), 189, 191n.6
luna ("Luna") (supervisor), 22

maka'āinana (common people), 112, 115, 169, 189, 196
makua honowai (in-law relative[s]), 190, 191n.8, 196
māmala hoa ("Mamalahoas") (military body), 210, 211n.2
mana (spiritual power), 194
mea hou (news), 189, 191n.5, 226, 227, 264, 287, 303
moe 'uhane (dream; literally "soul sleep"), xxv
mu'umu'u (woman's garment), 81

'ōhua ("ohuas") (retainer[s], servant[s]), 224, 237, 238n.2

pa'i (food). *See* General Index: Taro
pākū (curtain, screen), 76, 77n.1
palaka (garment), 149, 151n.1
paniolo (cowboy), 315
Papa Ola (Board of Health), 73
pā'ū (garment), 45, 47n.5
pō ("Po") (night, revelation, realm of gods), 195n.3
poi (food). *See* General Index: Taro
pū hala (tree), 81
puhi ahi (to burn, burning fire) (kapu rite), 182, 184n.2, 218, 219n.9
punahele (favorite[s]), 193

'uhane (ghost, dirge, chant of lamentation), xxv